W9-ACH-093

145¢/01

MOUNTAIN SHEEP

WILDLIFE BEHAVIOR AND ECOLOGY
George B. Schaller, Editor

MOUNTAIN SHEEP

A Study in Behavior and Evolution

Valerius Geist

THE UNIVERSITY OF CHICAGO PRESS
Chicago and London

The University of Chicago Press, Chicago, 60637
The University of Chicago Press, Ltd., London
© 1971 by The University of Chicago
All rights reserved. Published 1971
Printed in the United States of America
International Standard Book Number: 0–226–28572–3
Library of Congress Catalog Card Number: 77–149596

QL
737
453
G44

3 3001 00593 8955

To my mother

170950

Contents

Preface

It is a custom sanctioned by time to introduce a study with an account of what it set out to explore and how it achieved its goals. However, the history of this study would demonstrate little beyond the point that the best laid plans of mice and men have often gone astray. I am not convinced that an account of this would improve the book, or the popular conception of a scientist at work. Let me instead place this study into a wider perspective and leave that which must be said about its history to the end.

Despite its title, this is not just a book on mountain sheep. It attempts to deal in part with the evolutionary forces that shaped large Pleistocene mammals, using the mountain sheep as an example. This animal happens to be a particularly durable ice age creature, and its evolution illustrates some of the major problems faced by large ice age mammals. A knowledge of the Pleistocene is not unimportant to us academically or practically. It was an epoch characterized by severe climates, by the development of the tundra ecosystems, by the mixing of faunas when land bridges rose and glacial refugia coalesced, by numerous extinctions, but especially by an unusual evolutionary turmoil among large mammals. It produced in a short time and in great diversity new types of creatures, usually giants of their respective families, whose body sizes appear to oscillate with glaciations and who are cold adapted by virtue of thick haircoats, fat layers, hibernation, or culture, who are slaves to the boom and bust economy of the North that allows them to squander resources in the superabundance of summer, but also makes them survival artists in winter. Man is one of these creatures. In his most recent species form, he appeared first in the middle of the major glaciations together with woolly mammoth, cave bear, and reindeer as part of the cold-adapted fauna, of which he remained a member ever since. Scant attention has been paid to this point or its consequences when explaining the evolution of man.

In ungulates from the periglacial regions, evolution seems to have strongly shaped social behavior, perhaps in an unprecedented manner. In general, ungulates that are considered advanced by taxonomists differ from primitive ones less in morphological features which adapt them to the physical environment (habitat) than in an enlargement or greater differentiation of characters which have social significance (i.e., horns, tusks, antlers, rump patches, coat color and hair patterns, skin glands). For this reason our ungulate classifications tend to be a phylogeny of social evolution. Since ungulates considered advanced are mostly of periglacial origin, evidently life in the sight of glaciers required more than an ability to cope with snow, ice, and cold; it required new ways of dealing with companions. Territories, common in African antelope, are almost unheard of among ice age ruminants. Moreover, no epoch saw the appearance of such gigantic hornlike organs as those gracing many ungulates that arose in the Pleistocene. This book attempts to show how the ecological turmoil of the ice ages was translated into evolutionary turmoil and, in particular, how it shaped social behavior.

Although behaviorists are today beginning to form a picture of the behavioral adaptations of ruminants, we were far from it in 1961 when I began a study of Stone's sheep in the Cassiar Mountains. The available studies of mountain sheep were largely ecological in nature, the behavior was inadequately described, if at all, and there was almost no attempt to answer the questions of what selective forces shaped and maintained these animals. Such questions are, regrettably, not in fashion with most students of ruminants as is amply demonstrated in the technical journals. I went therefore into the field without questions based on past research; these had to be and were formulated during the course of the fieldwork.

Although I can only endorse what Hinde (1966) wrote on methods in behavioral research, there was one concern I was haunted by. How could I, the same person, separate the process of data gathering from any thought I might have about those data? As the lone investigator I had to record observations and simultaneously think about the observed events in order to recognize relationships. This is a very important problem, for if data gathering is not clearly separated out, it can be biased by some subconscious preference. It is hence most important to develop a method of data gathering that reduces subjective evaluation to the absolute minimum. The resulting data should then be a trustworthy record of events, and others using the same method can check on conclusions derived from them. These considerations made me divide behavioral events into small recognizable bits of action, which were recorded sequentially with reference to the animals performing them. This reduces subjective evaluation to whether or not an event had occurred and frees one's thought from any further considerations.

I chose the mountain sheep for study because of the advantages these animals offer. They are out in the open and can be kept under observation a long time. They are gregarious and interact frequently. These two factors alone promised a fruitful investigation. My previous experience in observing moose made me appreciate such advantages. The study itself was conducted as best as circumstances allowed; using every lucky break, I investigated what good fortune allowed me to and stuck to no definite plan. The result is this book, which, of course, does not cover everything about the mountain sheep. I have largely ignored the predators, parasites, and pathogens of sheep because I found little of significance beyond that which is known. Moreover, too little is known about the biology of sheep parasites and pathogens to understand how mountain sheep evolved defenses against them. I have not discussed sheep conservation or management. I made use of the agricultural literature on the physiology of domestic sheep when developing concepts about wild ones. When formulating a comprehensive theory of the evolution of mountain sheep, I had to rely at times on inadequate data or descriptions. Even if this should have led to errors, it does make evident the areas where more exacting research is needed.

I would suggest not reading the book from front to end, but rather reading first chapter 1 and the conclusions in chapter 12, then all of chapters 5 and 11, next the introductions to the remaining chapters, and then whatever the reader fancies. The introductions are summaries of the chapters and have been purged as much as possible of technical language. The conclusions are organized to reflect the evolutionary history of sheep.

I also suggest that the reader view the films which are cited in this book (films E 1333–39). These are available to institutions on loan, or for purchase at cost, from the German Institute of Scientific Films in the Encyclopaedia Cinematographica series. The films can be obtained by writing to the Institut für den Wissenschaftlichen Film, 34 Göttingen, Nonnenstieg 72, Germany (B.R.). In the United States they are available on loan from the Audio-Visual Aids Library at Pennsylvania State University, University Park, Pennsylvania 16802. These films will show better than any verbal description some of the pertinent events in the life of mountain sheep.

Between 1961 and 1966 the study was intended to provide material for a Ph.D. dissertation. This phase was supervised by Dr. Ian McTaggart-Cowan, dean of graduate studies at the University of British Columbia, who not only endured me patiently for over five years, but also remained a source of encouragement, help, and inspiration. The social behavior work became in part my doctoral dissertation in 1966. For a few weeks in late 1966 I returned to the bighorns under contract to the Canadian Wildlife Service. A year's stay as an N.R.C. postdoctoral fellow at the Max-Planck-Institut für Verhaltensphysiologie in 1967, under the directorship of Dr. Konrad Lorenz, made me aware of Dr. Wolfgang Wickler's fascinating work. It influenced my thinking and ultimately this book. While in Germany I spent several weeks at the Institute for Scientific Films in Göttingen, editing my mountain sheep films under the stimulating and knowledgeable direction of Dr. Hasso Kuczka. These weeks were some of the most profitable and exciting of my postdoctoral study. I returned to Canada to take a position with the Environmental Sciences Centre of the University of Calgary. Under the encouragement of Dr. J. B. Cragg, director of the centre, I wrote the book and obtained essential supplemental data. In Calgary I am located only a two-hour drive from the bighorn sheep I studied. The last data to be included in this book were obtained in November and December 1968 along the Kechika River in northern British Columbia. At present my graduate students and I are working hard to make this book obsolete.

In carrying out fieldwork and in completing this study I have been aided by many persons and several organizations to whom I wish to express my sincere thanks. During the first Stone's sheep study my wife and I were frequently and generously assisted by Mr. and Mrs. T. A. Walker. During two winters I remained in radio communication with Mr. and Mrs. W. B. Smith and Mr. and Mrs. M. Hess, then of Northern Mountain Airlines. I was aided by Mr. Herman Peterson of Atlin and Dr. A. M. Pearson (Canadian Wildlife Service), Whitehorse. Permission to work on sheep in the Yukon was obtained with the aid of Mr. Fitzgerald, game commissioner of the Yukon Territory. During my last stay in the Stone's sheep country, I was looked after by Mr. "Shook" Davidson.

In Banff National Park, we were helped by Mr. F. J. Coggins, and Mr. J. Rimmer, park wardens, and by Mr. J. C. Holroyd, then assistant chief warden. I am grateful for the cooperation extended to me by the late Mr. J. E. Stenton, then warden of Bankhead district, and Mr. Norman Tithrington of Banff.

The bighorn study was aided by the friendly cooperation extended to us by the Banff National Park Warden Service and I would like to thank Chief Warden R. T. Hand and Mr. G. H. L. Dempster, then superintendent, for this.

Financial support in the form of scholarships and grants was provided by the National Research Council of Canada and Canadian Industries, Ltd. The Canadian Wildlife Service supported two months of fieldwork in 1966. I am grateful for this and for the assistance of the British Columbia Game Branch.

The thankless task of reading the first and second draft of this book and correcting my often Teutonic English as well as providing constructive criticism was undertaken by Dr. R. G. Petocz of the Environmental Sciences Centre, and Mr. W. D. Wishart of the Alberta Fish and Game Branch. Various chapters of the book were read and criticized by my colleagues Drs. D. R. Klein and R. D. Guthrie of the University of Alaska and Drs. S. Herrero, J. Bovet, and P. K. Anderson, the University of Calgary. I am grateful for the criticisms of my thesis by Drs. W. S. Hoar, H. D. Fisher, D. J. Randall, and D. H. Chitty of the University of British Columbia.

I am grateful for the help provided by the service departments of the University of Calgary, in particular, Mrs. E. L. Wittig for proofreading, Mr. W. E. Matheson who did the maps and most graphs, and Mr. N. W. Crichton for photographic advice. Mrs. V. Preuter typed the manuscript.

Above all I am grateful to my wife, Renate Geist, who patiently shared the joys, but also the sorrows and grief, which my research and academic activities inevitably produced.

1 An Introduction to Mountain Sheep

The history of mountain sheep begins somewhere in the early Pleistocene of Eurasia, but we know little of it. The fossil record is poor,
because not only are the conditions for fossil formation unfavorable in
mountains, but also recurring glaciations have ground over the
terrain inhabited by sheep. When sheep first appear in the Villafranchian, a long period of cool climates and maybe minor glaciations which
preceded the ice ages, they are already ox-size giants such as *Megalovis*
in Europe and Central Asia (Kurten 1968). True sheep (*Ovis*) are found
first in the late Villafranchian of Europe and Asia, and from then on
they appear sporadically in the Pleistocene fossil record (Thenius and
Hofer 1960). Herre and Kesper (1953) concluded that large sheep were
present in Eurasia during early and middle Pleistocene times to be
replaced by small, mouflonlike sheep toward the end of the ice ages.
Such sheep were present also in North Africa in the late Pleistocene
(Kurten 1968), a region where they no longer are found. Sheep remains
in Alaska and the southern United States indicate that sheep reached
North America during the late Pleistocene. Some of the early populations were of sheep a little larger than the Rocky Mountain bighorn
(*O. canadensis canadensis*), the largest race of living bighorn sheep
(Stokes and Condie 1961). In itself the fossil record is not too revealing,
but it does tell us that sheep arose about 2.5 million years ago and that
they were part of the large mammal fauna which flooded into Europe
and central Asia during the Villafranchian, presumably from south of
the Himalayas.

We do not know the immediate ancestor of mountain sheep, but
like other caprids, they appear to be offspring of the Rupicaprini,
the goat-antelopes (Thenius and Hofer 1960). The rupicaprids are
short-horned, light-skulled, generally hairy bovids of small size, whose
most generalized representative is the serow (*Capricornis*) from southeast
Asia; the North American mountain goat (*Oreamnos*) also belongs to
this group. The caprids (sheep and goats) have been linked to the

1

goat-antelopes on the basis of paleontological evidence, a link fully supported by behavioral evidence (see chap. 11). Herre and Röhrs (1955) attempted to derive sheep from sheeplike Miocene bovids, but the fossil evidence is too fragmentary to support or contradict their views; the capridlike skulls of some Miocene and Pliocene bovids may indicate only that they fought similarly to caprids, not that they were their relatives.

The closest relative of sheep are the true goats (*Capra*) as well as the "sheep-goats" (*Ammotragus*) from North Africa. Sheep differ from goats in possessing preorbital and inguinal glands and in lacking an odoriferous tail gland. They have interdigital glands on all four feet whereas true goats either lack these glands or possess them on the front legs only; *Ammotragus* resembles *Capra* rather than *Ovis* in all these characteristics.

Sheep and true goats are examples of a peculiar phenomenon of the Pleistocene. With the beginning of the Villafranchian there appear a large number of ungulates which carry enormous horns, antlers, or tusks. Nothing comparable has been unearthed from previous epochs, except for *Arsinoitherium* from the Oligocene. No earlier species of deer are known whose antlers approach, let alone surpass, in size those carried by the giant deer (*Megaloceros*) or even moose (*Alces*) and caribou (*Rangifer*). Among giraffes, large horns evolved in the Pleistocene sivatheres. Among rhinos the largest-horned representatives were *Elasmotherium* and *Coelodonta* of Pleistocene age. Among elephant and mastodonts the largest tusks were carried by terminal Pleistocene species like the mammoth (*Mammonteus primigenius*), the Auvergne mastodont (*Anancus arvernensis*), or the American mastodont (*Mastodon americanus*). Bovids with giant horns were the long-horned bison (*Bison latifrons*), the water buffalo (*Bubalus*), the various species of extinct giant sheep and goats, and of course our present-day mountain sheep and ibex (*Capra ibex*). The large races of sheep from central Asia may carry horns up to 75 in (190 cm) in length, with a basal circumference of 20 in (50 cm). The dried skull and horns of a Siberian argali ram weighed 49 lb (22.5 kg) (Clark 1964), while Russian workers report that the head and horns of a ram of this race may exceed 30 kg (66 lb) (Heptner et al. 1961). These rams, like our own bighorns, may carry up to 13% of their live weight as skull and horns. The horns alone will weigh as much or more than the whole skeleton, which accounts for about 8% of the live weight of an argali ram. What caused such extravagance to evolve?

For sheep we do have an answer today. The evolution of large horns is closely linked to the invasion of terrain vacated by continental or mountain glaciers and can be attributed to the differences in social selection between expanding, colonizing populations that surge into new living space, and stable, stagnant populations. One attribute of sheep is their ability to live at the edge of glaciers (see fig. 2). Might the rapid and spectacular evolution of large Pleistocene mammals be a function of many glacial advances and rapid meltoffs?

Mountain sheep have been a successful group. During the Pleistocene they spread around the Northern Hemisphere to most mountains of Europe, North Africa, Asia, and North America, and they still have a distribution unequaled by any living bovid. They were and are abundant in Canada and Eurasia and are one of man's first domestic animals if not the first (Radulesco and Samson 1962). They survived into our times despite the presence of man, while many late Pleistocene mammals became extinct (see Martin and Wright 1967). Hence, they satisfy the requirements of success such as a wide geographic distribution, numerical strength, and a long period of existence as a clearly recognizable genus.

Moreover, mountain sheep satisfy the requirements of success in another, less familiar manner. In industry as in evolution, imitation is the ultimate compliment to a successful product. Some evolutionary solutions are successful enough to appear in unrelated or distantly related organisms. The "rhino," for instance, has been one of these successful solutions, for it appeared at least twice among the true rhinos (Thenius and Hofer 1960), and it arose in the brontotheres, the embrithopods, the Toxodonta, the Dinocerata—even in reptiles, for the ceratopsians such as *Triceratops* and *Monoclonius* were "rhinos" of sorts. In a like manner the forms "mouse," "wolf," and "saber-toothed tiger" have evolved in marsupials and placentals, while placental saber-toothed cats have evolved a number of times from the felid stock (Kurten 1968). Similarly the form "mountain sheep" has evolved outside of true sheep, and the blue sheep (*Pseudois*) from Tibet, Bhutan, and western China is one example. Its taxonomic position has been a bone of contention as it resembles sheep in external appearance, but its massive skull reveals it to be a goat (Lydekker 1898); it is now recognized as such (Thenius and Hofer; Haltenorth 1963). The Caucasian tur (*Capra cylindricornis*) is also acquiring sheeplike characteristics, but its goat ancestry is still very evident (see fig. 47). It is likely that many characteristics of mountain sheep appear odd, such as the massive horns of rams, but we must remember that we are dealing with an eminently successful ruminant and that these oddities probably exist for good reasons. One might note in passing that nothing has imitated us so far.

As sheep spread across continents, they evolved a bewildering variety of races. There are giants weighing up to 450 lb (200 kg), such as the Siberian argalis, and there are dwarfs such as the Cyprus urials which barely weigh 80 lb (36 kg). There are pure white Dall's sheep and glossy black Stone's sheep; there are long-haired, heavy-maned urials and short-haired desert bighorns; there are sheep that live in hot deserts, such as Nelson's bighorn, and those that live on mountains far beyond the Arctic Circle and successfully face the long and dark arctic winter, such as the snow sheep from northern Siberia or Dall's sheep from the Brooks Range of Alaska. Although varying greatly in external appearance, color, horn size and form, coat patterns, and climatic adaptations, sheep have remained conservative in food habits, habitat preference, and hence in general body build. There are, however, two kinds of body conformations, one found in the Asiatic sheep and the other in American sheep, inclusive of the snow sheep from Siberia.

Asiatic sheep are rather long legged and light boned with well proportioned but not heavily muscled bodies (fig. 1) compared to the short-legged, broad-chested bighorn sheep with their massive shoulders and haunches (plate 1). American sheep are somewhat ibexlike in their build and are superb jumpers and climbers in cliffs, whereas argalis appear to be poor jumpers (Walther 1961), which in captivity also shun rock piles. American sheep race for rocks when in danger, but argalis evade cliffs when escaping (Heptner et al. 1961). The Asiatic sheep appear to prefer open rolling mountains, foothills, and plateaus, whereas American sheep are never far from precipitous terrain. These differences between Asiatic and American sheep are not surprising for Asiatic sheep are found together with ibex or goats; American sheep evolved in the absence of ibex. Thus it appears that Asiatic sheep faced in the ibex a competitor in precipitous terrain so they specialized to exploit open rolling terrain while the ibex became the rock jumpers. American sheep in the absence of a serious competitor in the rocks have exploited both rolling, gentle terrain as well as steep cliffs and are intermediate between Asiatic sheep and ibex in their habitat adaptations.

These two groups of sheep differ consistently in several other respects as well. The rump patches of American sheep are distinctly set off from the dark fur of the body (see plate 3), whereas Asiatic sheep have a

Fig. 1. A Pamir or Marco Polo ram. Note the long, slender legs, diffuse rump patch, thin tail, and deeply ringed horns typical of Asiatic sheep.

diffuse rump patch (fig. 1). The tails of Asiatic sheep are thin and light, while those of American sheep are broad and of dark color. The pre-orbital glands of Asiatic and American sheep differ in external appearance. In the urials and argalis, it appears to be a horizontal slit giving off a waxy, very volatile secretion (plate 2a). A whirl of long hair grows just anterior to the gland. In American sheep it is a vertically oriented, dark skinfold which protrudes beyond the hair (plate 2b). No fluid or waxy secretion is apparent externally. Asiatic sheep seem to have a higher birth rate than American sheep, but also a shorter life expectancy. The rams grow considerably more horn in their early years of life than do American rams. The European mouflon is in most respects an urial, but it does have a broad tail and a clearly set off rump patch and like American sheep rarely twins. The American sheep are the true mountaineers among sheep and differ consistently from their Asiatic and European cousins, although both have evolved in parallel in many characters, particularly those of the skull and horns (chap. 11). At first glance argalis and bighorn sheep appear similar, particularly the females, but similarity can be due to convergence.

There are from thirty-six to forty races of wild sheep living today. The exact number may be agreed upon once sheep from Central Asia and Siberia are more adequately studied. The taxonomic philosophy of the classifier is also an important factor in segregating subspecies, but there has been little disagreement on this point. It would be going too far to describe the various races. This has been done by Clark (1964) in his charming book, to which I refer the interested reader. These races fall into two broad divisions, the Asiatic and American sheep described above. Each of these divisions is formed by three groups. Thus Haltenorth (1963) divides the Asian (or Eurasian) sheep into mouflons (*musimon* group), urials (*orientalis* group), and large argalis (*ammon* group), while the American sheep can be divided into snow sheep (*nivicola*) thinhorn sheep (*dalli*), and bighorn sheep (*canadensis*). The urials are the most primitive of sheep, while the largest of the argalis and bighorns are the most highly evolved ones.

The scientific classification of these sheep is beset by a most unfortunate and utterly sterile controversy. While nobody disputes the genus *Ovis*, and few quibble about the validity of various races, no agreement is in sight on what to call a species. It so happens that diverse races of sheep readily hybridize if kept long enough in zoological gardens. The known hybrids are viable and produce fertile offspring (Krumbiegel 1954; Young and Manville 1960; Uloth 1966). It cannot be denied that all sheep, irrespective of race, form one potentially interbreeding group. No hybrids are known from the wilds, but this is hardly surprising because all sheep, except maybe the urials and argalis in Laddack, India (Clark 1964), live allopatrically. The interfertility of sheep is used as an argument for extremely close relationships among races, but one can also argue that lack of reproductive isolation implies only that sheep of diverse races never met and evolved reproductive barriers. Some goats have done this. Thus *Capra aegagrus* and *C. cylindricornis* live sympatrically in the Caucasian Mountains and do not hybridize, nor is there any evidence of hybridization between *C. falconeri* and *C. sibirica* where they occur sympatrically in Afghanistan and northern India (Heptner et al. 1961; Haltenorth 1961). However, when *C. cylindricornis* was introduced to an area containing a native *C. aegagrus* population, they hybridized readily. Here no reproductive barrier had evolved yet (Heptner et al. 1961). Similarly, the fact that domestic goats and *Ammotragus*, the sheep-goat from Northern Africa, can be hybridized (Petzsch 1957) does not necessarily imply that *Ammotragus* is closer related to *Capra* than to *Ovis*. Attempts to hybridize *Ammotragus* with *Ovis* have failed (Gray 1954). However, there is every reason to believe that *Ovis* and *Ammotragus* evolved reproductive barriers, since *Ovis* was present in North Africa during late Pleistocene times (Kurten 1968). It is also noteworthy that *Capra* does not hybridize readily with *Ammotragus*, and such hybrids are a rarity. *Capra* is found in North Africa, but not sympatric with *Ammotragus*.

I agree therefore with the critique of Heptner et al. that zoo hybridization should be sparingly used as a criteria of classification (also Simpson 1961) and that lumping races to uphold some lofty species concept may be scholarly but not very practical. The crux of the controversy has been whether or not to recognize the natural groupings of sheep as outlined above in formal taxonomy. Should all sheep be regarded as one species? Should there be two species? Should there be more?

There are three opinions: older taxonomists recognized the natural groupings of sheep and gave species rank to many races (Lydekker 1913); some recent authors recognize only one species, *musimon* (Haltenorth 1963; Uloth 1966). Russian workers following Zalkin's lead divided sheep into two species, the Eurasian sheep (*ammon*) and the American sheep (*canadensis*) (Heptner et al. 1961), a division also used by Thenius and Hofer (1960). American type sheep were classified into three species by Cowan (1940), a division confirmed by Cherniavski (1962*a*) and accepted in North America in general. Here the sterile controversy stands. Whatever lead one chooses to follow, one is certain to be damned by the majority of taxonomists. Where does this leave the user? He might as well take an independent course. When experts quibble, far be it from him to take sides!

Of the three opinions I like that of Heptner et al. best; Eurasian and American sheep represent very real divisions. For American sheep a separate subgenus, *Pachyceros*, has been suggested (Gromova 1936, in Cherniavski 1962*a*). Taxonomy, however, has not only an aesthetic value, but also a practical one; the user of a classification wants to put quick unambiguous identification marks on evolutionary groups. It is here that a one-species or two-species classification becomes impractical. Thus Eurasian sheep contain three perfectly good evolutionary groups, the mouflons, the urials, and argalis. Although urials and argalis are linked by intermediaries, they nevertheless represent sheep of different adaptive syndromes. Similarly, although snow sheep and thinhorn sheep have many similarities, they are far removed from each other and represent different evolutionary groups. For the sake of utility, and only utility, in order to talk meaningfully about thirty-six to forty races of sheep, I shall term these evolutionary groups species. Even Haltenorth (1963) and Heptner et al. had to devise taxonomically unsanctioned "groups," corresponding to the species as used in this book, to keep order among so many races. One must not forget that the species is an abstraction and should not confuse it or the name with reality. For American sheep I shall follow Cowan's (1940) classification. One can recognize six species of sheep:

> *Ovis musimon* (mouflons). Originally confined to Corsica and Sardinia in recent times, now widely introduced on the mainland of Europe (Türck and Schmincke 1965). Two races according to Haltenorth (1963).
>
> *O. orientalis* (urials). The primitive sheep from Cyprus, Asia Minor, Persia, Pakistan, Afghanistan, northern India, and the southern U.S.S.R. Haltenorth (1963) gives thirteen races.
>
> *O. ammon* (argalis). The giant sheep from the Karatau, Pamir, Tien Shan, Himalayas, Altai Mountains, and the Gobi Desert in Mongolia and China. Nine races if *severtzovi* is included and the Mongolian argalis are lumped into *darwini*.
>
> *O. nivicola* (snow sheep). American sheep from Siberia. Three races according to Heptner et al. (1961). Similar to our thinhorn sheep.
>
> *O. dalli* (thinhorn sheep). American sheep from Alaska, the Yukon and Northwest Territories, and northern British Columbia. Three races according to Cowan (1940).
>
> *O. canadensis* (bighorn sheep). American sheep whose center of evolution lay in the mountains of the western U.S.A. They occur south from the Peace River in Canada to northern Mexico and east to the Badlands of the Dakotas. Eight races if one counts the extinct Audubon's bighorn (Cowan 1940; Bradley and Baker 1967).

This book is concerned with mountain sheep of the last two species, and I shall give a thumbnail sketch of them as abstracted from Cowan. The northern thinhorn sheep are formed from three races or subspecies: *O. dalli dalli*, the common Dall's sheep; *O. dalli kenaiensis*, the white Kenai Peninsula Dall's sheep, differing mainly in cranial features from the common Dall's sheep; and *O. dalli stonei*, the black thinhorn sheep or Stone's sheep from northern British Columbia and the Yukon

Territory. The thinhorn sheep are remarkable among the other races in their color and in that, like snow sheep, they penetrate far beyond the Arctic Circle. Whereas *dalli* and *kenaiensis* are pure white and carry amber-colored horns, *stonei* varies from silver gray through glossy black in color and looks—with its white rump patch, belly, leg trimmings, gray head and neck, and black body—like a Dall's sheep in evening dress. It is a most attractive animal (see plate 6).

The bighorn sheep are formed from seven living races plus the extinct badland or Audubon's bighorn (*auduboni*): *O. canadensis canadensis*, the Rocky Mountain bighorn; *O. canadensis californiana*, the Lava bed or California bighorn; and five races collectively called desert bighorns: *O. c. nelsoni*, *O. c. mexicana*, *O. c. texiana*, *O. c. cremnobates*, and *O. c. weemsi*. Of these, *canadensis* is the largest, the most northern in range, and the most abundant. Large rams may occasionally exceed 300 lb live weight and hence are among the largest sheep in the world. The smallest, most primitive, and *dalli*-like in cranial and horn characteristics is *nelsoni* (plate 3). It also has the distinction of living in the hottest region of North America, in Death Valley, California. The southernmost bighorn is *weemsi*, which lives in the sight of tropical palms in Lower California. Desert bighorns are smaller in size than other bighorns, but they have longer ears and longer tooth rows. The horns of bighorn sheep are more massive and less gracefully wound than those of thinhorns and commonly have broken or "broomed" tips (see plate 1).

Of the ten races of American sheep listed, I studied three, *stonei*, *dalli*, and *canadensis*; a more detailed description of these animals and their populations follows in the next chapter. So far sheep have been illustrated as extremely diverse, large-horned, successful glacier followers with narrow food habits and landscape preference but great adaptability to climatic conditions. In general, they are not found in areas with high precipitation, be it rain or snowfall, and are therefore confined to dry mountains. There are exceptions to this such as the Stone's sheep which I studied in the Cassiar Mountains. This picture of sheep is incomplete even as a sketch, for to understand their success in the past and the lack thereof in modern times, their essential habitat and social adaptations as well as their reproductive characteristics must be taken into account.

The past success of mountain sheep may be due in no small part to their unique, effective digestive system which allows them to exploit a hard, abrasive, dry forage of poor quality. The sheep, being a ruminant, cultivates bacteria and protozoa in a specialized chamber of its digestive tract, the rumen, to break down the plant cellulose. It cannot digest its own food, only the breakdown products of fermentation liberated by the symbiotic microorganisms in the rumen. The whole digestive system and process, even the basic metabolic machinery of ruminants, differs greatly from man's.

Plant matter is picked up, shredded, and ground by the sheep's teeth to a fine consistency (rumination), mixed with water, salts, buffer, and some urea (saliva), and then dumped into a fermentation vat (the rumen). Here it is broken down by microorganisms under anaerobic conditions (fermentation). The microorganisms fulfill two functions. First they digest cellulose to volatile fatty acids (acetic, proprionic, and butyric acid) and plant protein to amino acids. These products of the digestion pass directly from the rumen into the bloodstream. Second, microorganisms serve the ruminant as a nutritious, valuable food. They pass with undigested plant matter into the true stomach (absomasum) where they are digested by the ruminant's own enzymes and provide high grade proteins, fats, and vitamins.

The process does not rest here, for after the nutrients are absorbed in the small intestines the undigested plant matter is dumped into a second fermentation vat, the caecum, and microorganisms go to work once more. What remains thereafter is concentrated and pelleted in the large intestines and passed out. About 90% of the cellulose digested disappears in the rumen. If we take a look at all organic matter digested, 69% disappears in the rumen, 20% in the small intestines, and 11% in the remainder of the gut (Bruce et al. 1966).

Whereas we primarily use glucose in our energy metabolism, ruminants fuel their metabolic machinery with volatile fatty acids. They also pass some of their urea into the rumen with their saliva instead of dumping it all out in the urine as we do. The urea helps to culture the microorganisms. Since the microflora is digested and serves as food, adult ruminants face no vitamin B deficiencies as these vitamins are synthesized by the bacterial flora. The hard fat or tallow characteristic of sheep is also produced by the rumen. Unlike pigs, which grow hard fat if fed on a diet rich in carbohydrates, but a soft, sometimes fluid fat if fed on a diet rich in polyunsaturated fats, ruminants deposit hard fat regardless of the diet eaten. In ruminants, polyunsaturated fats are hydrogenated in the rumen, pass as saturated fats into the bloodstream, and are laid down as tallow in adipose tissue. If the forage eaten by a ruminant is not adequate in plant protein to support the bacterial cultures, these die out, the rumen content ceases to ferment, and the ruminant starves to death on a full stomach. Winter-killed deer, for instance, show every sign of starvation, yet have rumens stuffed with forage.

This "fermentation vat" digestive system needs a mill to grind the plant matter to a fine consistency so that bacteria can work on a large surface area. The mechanism of "milling" is rumination or chewing the cud. A bolus of food is pressed from the rumen into the mouth and is reground between the grinding teeth, the molars and premolars. One can see the travel of such boli to and from the rumen on the neck of mountain sheep as moving bulges or knots. Rumination appears to be an effective solution for grinding up plants; it has appeared not only in the true ruminants (deer, cattle, giraffes, tragulids), but also in camels, the *Hyrax*, and even kangaroos (Hendrichs 1963). It is not the only solution though, as demonstrated by horses, which also feed on grasses but do not ruminate and have only one fermentation vat, the caecum. They also grind the food to a fine consistency, but they must do it in one milling rather than repeated ones. This is apparently achieved with a formidable battery of large grinding teeth. X-rays show that a horse head is mostly taken up by these long, broad, hypsodont teeth.

Mountain sheep are some of the most specialized grazers, for they can live on hard, abrasive, dry plants. The grasses and herbs they pluck are often covered with dust and grit in the absence of snow. To counteract wear, sheep, like most grazers, evolved very long and broad molar teeth which are pushed out throughout life. These teeth are termed subhypsodont, because they do not retain an open pulp cavity throughout the animal's life as do the hypsodont incisors of rodents. The structure and ontogeny of sheep teeth has received little attention to date. Sheep also have a larger rumen than deer of equal size, which indicates that the tough grasses and dry plants are subject to a relatively longer period of digestion by bacteria than are the softer browse plants on which deer feed (McMahan 1964; Ullrey et al. 1964). More primitive ruminants, such as deer (*Odocoileus*) or moose (*Alces*), live on softer vegetation, while some living fossils, like the tragulids or even duikers (*Cephalopinae*), may vary their diet with animal matter (Kurt 1963). Young, succulent plants are of course nutritious even to us or to bears and do not need to be digested in a highly specialized system. By being able to live on dry, dusty plants, sheep can exploit a reserve of poor forage and thrive where many other herbivores cannot.

One factor in the success of sheep must be that they are a pioneering species. Having evolved in the Villafranchian under conditions which few ruminants mastered, they spread and reoccupied repeatedly glaciated areas. Since glaciations covered continents, every meltoff left a huge area ready to be occupied, and early Pleistocene species could spread at once into them and fill them. Sheep may well have reached their wide distribution and diversity because of the lucky accident of being pioneers. In general, those species which were quick to evolve and adapt to pleistocene conditions early in the ice ages, closed the door to other groups which might have adapted had they not faced the competition of an ecological equivalent.

The sensory equipment of mountain sheep has not been well investigated. Their eyesight is marveled at by hunters, and a popular myth circulates in North America that sheep vision is equal to that of a man aided by 8-power binoculars. However, little is known definitely. Sheep can probably distinguish colors just like their close relative, the goat (Backhaus 1959a), and they do have a fair capacity to distinguish shapes. Domestic sheep can distinguish a circle from a square, but not from a hexagon (Seitz 1951). Like other ruminants, sheep probably have astigmatic eyes and see vertical lines better than horizontal ones. They can discern detail less well than we do (Backhaus 1959a). More is not known, but from my own experience with tame or habituated sheep in the wilds I can add a few comments.

In general, I was able to spot sheep with the unaided eye before they noticed me. After some training I spotted them readily at 2,000 yards on slopes, and up to four miles away if they were moving on snow. Sheep indicated that they had seen me by looking at me from about 1,000 yards away. When I moved in the company of sheep which were tame or habituated, I noticed them paying attention to coyotes on open snowfields which were at least 1,000 yards away. The distances are only approximate since they are map measurements. Sheep spotted wolves or coyotes vastly better than I did, particularly if the predator was in shrubbery. I saw the coyote or wolf only if I happened to look at an opening he chose to cross. Sometimes it was a long time before I saw the object which attracted the attention of sheep. I saw coyotes before the sheep did only when the coyotes were about a mile away on a snowfield. If an animal was further than 400 yards away (a distance at which I could identify it at a glance), sheep usually looked at it for 10–20 seconds before returning to feed, even if it was another sheep. Their vision and ability to recognize appears to be different from ours, much better in spotting moving objects in obscure terrain, but not very good in resolving lines or shapes.

The sense of smell is well enough developed in sheep to scent a man at about 350 yards under favorable conditions. Nothing is known definitely about their hearing. The sense physiology of sheep offers much promising opportunity for research.

Sheep are proverbially gregarious animals though, contrary to proverb, not particularly peaceful ones. They fight probably more than any other ruminant. They segregate into male and female plus juvenile bands. Males follow the largest-horned male during major movements, while females tend to stick to one older lamb-leading ewe. Sheep society appears to be designed to minimize dispersion of juveniles and appears to transmit home ranges as a tradition from older to younger generations. Sheep may even pass on habitat preference, as in the case of Corsican and Sardinian mouflons. These sheep prefer forest to open terrain and generally find it upon being introduced to a region. However, once urials were introduced to these populations, the mouflons soon adopted the open country habits of their Asiatic cousins (Türck and Schmincke 1965). The preference for forest by mouflons thus appears to be acquired, a response perhaps to millennia of hunting by man.

Typically, mountain sheep wander great distances between their seasonal home ranges, of which one ram may have up to seven, but are very predictable in their movements and most loyal to their home ranges. This predictability disappears once they are hunted. The rams have areas where they concentrate en masse in spring and again before the rut in fall, and where occasionally rams fight in groups. Their rules of social behavior may appear odd to us (chaps. 6 and 7), but they are highly functional and evolved for good reasons. Rams live in a society where predictability of social relations is insured via rank symbols, as in any army; rams judge dominance rank of other rams from their horn sizes. Homosexuality is normal and adaptive for rams, while the smaller ram has the right to be aggressive against the dominant. Rams mature slowly in their social behavior as well as body size and proportion for 5–7 years after their sexual maturation, and can be considered sexually mature juveniles throughout most of their lives. The adult female is similar in size and appearance to a young ram and when in heat acts like a young ram, otherwise she behaves like a juvenile. Consequently rams do not treat males differently from females, rather they treat all subordinates alike irrespective of sex; in sheep society one does not differentiate in one's conduct between males and females, but only between larger (dominant) and smaller (subordinate).

Since American sheep like all northern ungulates give birth in spring, they must rut late in the year due to their short gestation period. Rutting season tends to be in November and December. American sheep tend to give birth to one lamb only, but Asiatic sheep may twin regularly and even give birth to triplets (Heptner et al. 1961). The yearling, or lamb from the previous year, is not chased away by the female, but disassociates from its mother on its own 4–8 weeks before the new lamb is born. It wanders only if it does not find an older sheep to attach to. The lamb is weaned in early fall. If a female, it usually remains with its home band, but if a male, it moves off after sexual maturation to a ram band.

Mortality of lambs is high, but decreases for sheep which have reached yearling age. Sexually mature rams which have not yet reached full growth suffer almost no mortality, but they die off rapidly after reaching full maturation at 8–9 years of age. Few reach the age of 15 years. The oldest ram I knew was a 19-year-old living in the wilds. Females live somewhat longer, occasionally up to 24 years in the wilds.

Body and horn size, age at sexual maturation, behavioral vigor, as well as life expectancy, depend on the quality of a sheep population. The larger and finer the animals, the more vigorous the rams and the more fertile the females, the shorter is their life expectancy. We are faced with a paradox, but only an apparent one, that the "better" the sheep the quicker they die.

Predators are of little danger unless a sheep is very old, exhausted into physical bankruptcy after the rut, or has a broken leg, which happens surprisingly often. The major sheep predator appears to be the wolf. Coyotes, grizzlies, wolverine, and even lynx may take an occasional sick or incapacitated sheep, while the mountain lion may take a healthy one now and again, but these carnivores appear to play a very minor role in sheep mortality. The greatest and most ruthless predator which sheep face is man, and in modern times man's technological advances have outstripped the sheep's natural defenses. In the last century wild sheep fared badly and their ranges fell in part to the livestock industry while their populations suffered from diseases brought by domestic sheep and from indiscriminate hunting. In northern Canada and Alaska, thinhorn sheep are holding their own well, while in other parts of the U.S.A. and central Asia small sheep populations lead a precarious existence (Buechner 1960; Heptner et al. 1961). Their future will depend less on their adaptations than on the goodwill of man.

2 The Field Studies

Introduction

Of the ten races of North American mountain sheep, I studied three:
the Stone's sheep in the Cassiar Mountains of northern British Columbia, the Rocky Mountain bighorn sheep in Banff National Park of
southern Alberta, and the Dall's sheep in the St. Elias Range at Kluane
Lake in the Yukon. In total over three and a half years of fieldwork
went into the study—twenty months with Stone's sheep, twenty months
with bighorns, and two and a half months with Dall's sheep. In addition, I observed rutting California bighorns for one week in 1963.
The study began in 1961 and ended in December 1966, although I
have visited the bighorn population since then, primarily to record the
survival and home range fidelity of marked individuals, and I spent a
month studying Stone's sheep on the Kechika River, British Columbia,
in November and December 1968.

Sheep habitat in North America has been described in many good
reports. Murie (1944), Viereck (1963), and Jones (1963) described
the habitat of Dall's sheep in Alaska; Smith (1954), McCann (1956),
Wishart (1959), Flook (1964), and Berwick (1968) described habitats
in which Rocky Mountain bighorns are found. California bighorn
ranges were described by Sugden (1961), Blood (1963, 1967), and
Demarchi (1965) in southern British Columbia, and by McCullough
and Schneegas (1966) in California. Desert bighorn ranges (*mexicana*
and *nelsoni*) were described by Jones (1950), Russo (1950), Robinson and
Cronemiller (1954), Welles and Welles (1961), and Bradley (1964).
Cherniavski (1967) described the habitat of snow sheep in eastern
Siberia. These studies contain a wealth of information on plant
communities, climates, and land forms that mountain sheep are
associated with, and enable us to form some generalizations. Mountain
sheep live in open, mountainous terrain, usually close to cliffs. The
plant communities are usually climax communities with few tall shrubs
and trees, but with an abundance of low growing shrubs, herbs, and

15

grasses. Temperatures and availability of water vary greatly. Desert sheep may live in mountains where temperatures soar to 120° F (49° C) in the shade and go without drinking water until they look dehydrated (Welles and Welles 1961), while Dall's sheep survive in the darkness and cold of the arctic night.

In principle the three study areas I worked on did not differ from other sheep ranges; yet they are examples of extremes. The outskirts of the St. Elias Range in the Yukon represents optimum, periglacial sheep country. Here Dall's sheep roam in large bands over dry, dusty mountain slopes in sight of the huge glacier that stretches for hundreds of miles and fills the interior of the range (fig. 2). This is a landscape much as it probably existed in the Alaska-Yukon refugium during the Wisconsin glaciation. The Cassiar Mountains in British Columbia, the Stone's sheep study area, represent the opposite. The glaciers, except for a few minor remnants, have melted away. The climate is wet and cold. The slopes are largely overgrown by dwarf birch and alpine fir, and sheep habitat is sparsely distributed over the mountains. Few sheep live here and one sees them usually in small bands, often only as singles. Their extinction may not be far off, unless the climate becomes dry. The bighorn study area in southern Alberta is similar to the Stone's sheep study area in that the mountains are largely over-grown by forest and that sheep habitat is patchy. Here, as in the Cassiars, sheep exploit the high country above timberline, the patches of grasslands that are found on exposed, windswept slopes, and the cleared areas along avalanche gorges. However, the forest cover is here subject to burning which creates long-lasting subclimax grasslands that are open to exploitation by sheep. I saw the same along the Kechika River (plate 10). These grasslands could be called secondary sheep habitat. The density of bighorns was at least fifteen times greater than that of Stone's sheep on my study area in the Cassiars. The three study areas appear to represent evolutionary stages through which sheep habitat can pass after glacial withdrawal; hence they reflect how sheep populations change with climatic changes and how sheep cope with the different habitats.

On the two main study areas, in the Cassiars and the Rockies of southern Alberta, sheep were found to live in stable populations. The sex ratio was about 90 rams to 100 ewes, while the proportion of fully grown, mature rams in excess of 7 years of age was about one-third of all rams. The Stone's sheep were the most vigorous and, qualitatively, the best population I studied. The juveniles grew rapidly and attained

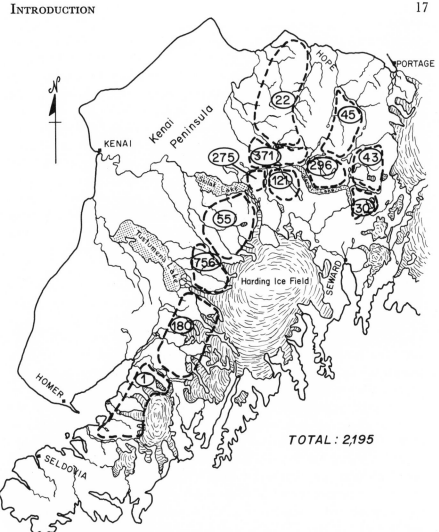

AREAS COVERED BY KENAI MOUNTAINS SHEEP INVENTORY SURVEYS , SUMMER, 1968

Fig. 2. Distribution of glaciers and Dall's sheep groups on the Kenai Peninsula, Alaska, summer 1968. (Courtesy of Lyman Nichols, Alaska Department of Fish and Game.)

sexual maturation early, reproduction was high, and the rams were vigorous in their social interactions. The bighorn and Dall's sheep populations showed the converse to this; the Dall's rams in particular were listless.

The Stone's sheep study was probably the most important one since it set the pattern which the other studies followed. Because it was poor sheep country with few sheep present, and because Stone's sheep vary greatly in color, I was able to get to know many sheep individually. Sheep were observed almost daily, weather permitting. Here the quantitative methods for recording behavioral data were worked out, the first film taken, and the first experience gathered in habituating sheep to my presence. A number of mountain goats (*Oreamnos*) lived side by side with Stone's sheep, and in observing these peculiar, distant relatives of sheep, I gained insight into the evolution of sheep behavior. In Banff I worked in part with bighorn sheep which were tame. Sheep readily tolerate harmless humans in their midst. The bighorn study yielded 16 mm film, some of which has been published and is referred to occasionally in footnotes. The Dall's sheep study lasted only one fall and I concentrated on documenting the behavior of sheep on film; there was no time for a quantitative study. Although chronologically this was the third study I carried out, I describe the Dall's sheep following the Stone's sheep since they are both of the thinhorn species.

THE STONE'S SHEEP STUDY

The study began in the early summer of 1961. I built and furnished a small log cabin close to a nameless little lake near timberline in the virgin wilderness of Eagle Nest Range, British Columbia (plate 4). These steep, rugged mountains are part of the Cassiar Mountains and lie in the triangle of land formed by the Klappan, Stikine, and Spatzisi rivers. The lake is situated at 4,250 ft elevation, surrounded by mountain peaks rising 7,000–8,400 ft. Five valleys radiate out from the lake, two lead a short way to little cirque glaciers, two lead to passes, and one holds the creek that drains the lake's water, which eventually flows to the Spatzisi River. The outfitter who guided hunting parties in that country had named the lake "Gladys," and I adopted that name for it and used it as my radio call when communicating with Prince George in winter.

Gladys Lake is frozen over for almost eight months of the year. Its clear winter water is flushed out annually by the murky meltoff, which gives it a chocolate color in summer and raises its level by almost three feet. In summer the docile little streams, which one could safely wade in fall and early spring, turn into torrents. The meltoff is heavy enough to cut new stream beds into mountains annually. Water is abundant in the country for it comes down heavily—as rain in summer and fall and as frequent and long snowstorms in winter. The longest consecutive period of rain was 22 days starting on 1 August 1962. Similarly, it could snow for days with little interruption while fog blanketed the mountains and hung low over the valley. Cloud cover was so frequent that most of my films have a dull appearance.

The excessive moisture and the high snow blanket have put their stamp on the plant communities which grow around the lake and rise on the mountains to about 7,000 ft elevation. Dwarf birch flats (*Betula glandulosa*) of variable height and alpine fir (*Abies lasiocarpa*) dominate the scene (plate 5). Tall willow bushes (*Salix* spp.) grow on alluvial flats around Gladys Lake or mingle in moist sites with dwarf birch. The south-facing, steep slopes of the many moraines left by departing glaciers are covered by stands of often small quaking aspen (*Populus tremuloides*), while some well-drained patches grow bunch grass (*Festuca*). On the north-facing or lee slopes of moraines and mountains, where the snow stays longest, the plant communities change abruptly to a tangle of tall dwarf birch and willows interspersed with spruce (*Picea engelmannii*) or lodgepole pine (*Pinus contorta*) at low elevations and dense alpine fir thickets at high elevations. Tall timber grows at the foot of the mountains and rises on north slopes to 6,000 ft elevation. The conifer stands were cut down in wide ribbons by annual avalanches and on these avalanche cuts grow dense stands of willow.

The south-facing slopes are largely bare of conifers except for a few scattered clumps of low alpine fir which are usually severely hedged by mountain goats. At elevations below 4,500 ft a few stands of aspen grow, but the higher elevations appear to be free of shrubs. A closer look, however, reveals that the south slopes are largely covered by dwarf birch, which grow so low and dense at high elevation that grasses easily protrude above them. True grassland is confined to warm, well-drained, often windblown sites and there are few of these. Large fans of shale and rubble come down from the cliffs. Many ridges are relatively barren of vegetation. Above the slopes rise ragged, broken cliffs.

Besides Stone's sheep, large moose (*Alces alces andersoni*) live about Gladys Lake and along the creeks, concentrating in the willow thickets on alluvial flats in early winter. A few moose leave these valleys in late fall and early winter to return in late May and June when most of the snow has gone, but many others remain year round in the high country. I found them all winter along moraines and on the south slopes or alluvial flats where the snow blanket was thin. In summer the moose live in the alpine fir thickets where their deep trails, soft droppings, and beds in the lush herbaceous vegetation reveal their presence. Caribou (*Rangifer tarandus osborni*) are infrequent wanderers through the valleys, but a number of cows come in spring and give birth to their calves on the very highest ridges of the mountains. Mountain goats (*Oreamnos americanus columbiae*) are seen at all seasons in the cliffs and the interspersed small slopes. Black bear (*Ursus americanus*), grizzly bear (*Ursus arctos*), and coyote (*Canis latrans*) are infrequent visitors, while wolves (*Canis lupus*), wolverine (*Gulo luscus*), and lynx (*Lynx canadensis*) are seen or tracked regularly. In 1961 and 1962 snowshoe rabbits (*Lepus americanus*) were unusually abundant, but almost absent in the fall of 1965. Clouds of willow ptarmigan (*Lagopus lagopus*) and white tailed ptarmigan (*Lagopus leucurus*) winter about the lake and feed on the red buds and twigs of willows, while in summer the high, lush meadows ring with the calls of willow ptarmigan broods. A few blue grouse (*Dendragapus obscurus*) are encountered along the valley bottoms, and a few ruffled grouse (*Bonasa umbellus*) live in the tall willows about the lake. Spruce grouse (*Canachites canadensis*) are common. The wildlife resident to the area is most conspicuous in winter when it crowds around the small lake, while the high valleys turn into a silent, snow-covered, landscape.

The most spectacular events at Gladys Lake are the sudden, warm, and violent chinook storms that howl in from the Pacific in winter. Temperatures could rise from $-40°$ F to $+40°$ F in a few hours. Snowmelt sets in. The gales tear off clouds of snow from the slopes, ridges, and trees in their path. In one night I have seen up to three feet of snow cover disappear leaving large puddles of water on the ground. During such storms I could go out on the frozen lake in light clothing and not feel uncomfortable. These chinooks are impressive natural spectacles, which seem to follow only certain valleys and hit only certain slopes and ridges. Stone's sheep winter on the slopes and ridges regularly cleared by chinooks. Without the rather frequent chinooks I cannot conceive how sheep could survive, for after some snowstorms they stood belly deep in snow, imprisoned on their tiny wintering area until a chinook hit. It may be that in some years the chinook comes too late for many sheep.

September brings a colorful, crisp Indian summer, a season of woefully short duration. In October the sheep arrive, soon to be followed by the first severe snowstorms and the all too common cloudy, foggy weather. For a few weeks the sheep are found low on the slopes, often in the dwarf birch zones feeding on frozen herbaceous vegetation. Sometimes they move out along creeks to some gravel fans where they crop the seed heads of cow parsnip (*Heracleum lanatum*). In November the rams disperse to their respective rutting grounds. Gladys Lake soon freezes and the eerie sounds of breaking, working ice reverberates in the canyons. The snow piles up. Dwarf birch and many willows bend under its weight and soon the birch flats are covered. Wolf packs begin to pay visits to the valley. The days grow shorter till by mid-December the sun shines for only two hours between two mountain peaks. First mountain goats and then sheep enter the rutting season. Around the New Year the last large rams return thin and exhausted from the breeding ranges, and winter holds its icy grip on the land.

Then the days lengthen gradually, the sun shines longer, the snow grows a little firmer in the open. While moving on showshoes is still a chore, one can now travel longer distances. Icy cold periodically descends on the land and the temperature can drop low indeed. Since my thermometer only read to $-45°$ F, I rarely knew how cold it was. But there were days so cold my tame whiskey jacks (*Perisoreus canadensis*) refused to be active and sat like little gray feather balls in the tall spruce beside my cabin, their nasal feathers crusted by frost and ice crystals glistening on their eyelashes. The nights are cold, clear, and often brightly lit, the silence broken only by the great horned owl or the calls of timber wolves.

In March the sun commonly shines and the snow grows harder still, allowing goat and sheep to walk on its surface. Their midwinter confinement is over and they begin to expand their ranges. A man can hike far on the hard snow, but for moose it is a time of crisis. The hard crust is a hindrance to them, and they confine themselves to the steep moraine slopes or high south slopes where the snow is absent or thin. I could rarely force them to leave these patches of thin snow. They stood defiantly and faced me. Those that ran floundered pitifully in the deep, hard-crusted snow which would not support their weight.

In April and May sheep make numerous travels between mountains. During the warmth of the day the snow melts but freezes hard at night. In the cliffs much of the snow disappears, and from here the meltoff proceeds gradually onto the slopes. On warm afternoons in May the first avalanches come thundering down the deep gorges, rolling along like yellow mud. The lake is still frozen and the creeks carry clear water in the morning, but by night their water becomes murky from the meltoff. As the water level rises, the ice becomes loose at the edges, develops dark spots, and begins to disintegrate. The creeks soon turn to torrents.

After the avalanches come the frequent but unpredictable rockslides. I saw one boulder the size of a boxcar hurl from the cliffs, bound down the slopes, and shatter on a rock platform sending chunks of rock whirling and spinning low over the slopes. On warm evenings in May one can hear a steady, distant rumble of descending rockslides as the mountains are slowly disintegrating.

During spring the rams concentrate in a large group and the clash of horns rings out morning and evening. When June comes the females begin to withdraw for lambing, soon to reappear with small, gray off-spring and form maternity bands. Mallards come to the lake for short visits, the juncos (*Junco hyemalis*) and varied thrushes (*Ixoreus naevius*) sing, and the whiskey jacks who have courted since April are nesting. The first mosquitoes indicate that summer is not far off.

In late June sheep and mountain goats are seen less and less often about the lake. They look scruffy as they begin shedding their old fur. Goats concentrate about salt licks. Then in early July sheep come to Gladys Lake a last time and are not seen there again till September. A warm summer, green and lush but thick with mosquitoes, follows. Caribou bulls fatten and grow antlers in the high valleys or seek refuge from flies by running on the snow or standing in shallow water. When white neck manes grow above their dark coats, when their antlers show red patches and bits of hanging velvet, one can sense that Indian summer is not far off. Such is a yearly cycle at Gladys Lake.

Stone's Sheep

Stone's sheep are dark-colored, thinhorn sheep (plate 6) which were named in honor of their discoverer, A. J. Stone of Missoula, Montana. Characteristically they vary greatly in color and patterning. They may be black, dark gray, silver gray, dark brown, yellowish brown, or almost pure white. At close range, black sheep have a brownish tinge in their hair. One band may contain individuals of various colors. At Gladys Lake black and dark gray sheep predominated; white individuals comprised less than 3% of the population.

Stone's sheep are not uniformly colored. The head is lighter than the body; frequently the neck is also gray, occasionally even white. A dark band usually runs across the nose (plate 7), and sometimes the eyes are ringed by dark hair. There is always a patch of light hair between the horns on the front, and the muzzle is white. The white rump patch, smaller than that of bighorn sheep, is sharply set off from the dark fur as is typical of all American sheep. A broad band of dark fur usually connects the black tail with the dark fur of the body. There is a dark middorsal streak in light-colored individuals. The white trimming on hind and front legs is larger than in bighorn sheep and is not lost in old rams as it often is in bighorns. The belly is white, but rams often form a dark band across or partially across the belly with age (fig. 3). Light-colored sheep have a broad dark margin where the darker body fur meets the white belly fur.

Fig. 3. Variations in coat pattern and horn form among Stone's rams of the Cassiar Mountains. Note the belly band on lower ram. Individual differences in coat pattern permitted identification of individuals.

The horns are dark amber or brown and vary greatly in size, shape, and spread among individuals. The age rings on Stone's sheep (plate 7) are more clearly set off than in bighorn or Dall's rams (plate 8). At Gladys Lake rams usually had closely curled horns, often with broken horn tips, but a few had graceful, wide-spreading ones. The longest-horned ram I shot was 10 years old. His undamaged right horn measured 45$\frac{2}{3}$ in (115 cm) while the left was broomed down to 42 in (106.7 cm); basal circumference was 13$\frac{3}{4}$ in (35 cm). His dry upper skull and horns weighed 20 lb (9 kg). I saw only one ram with larger horns during the study. The poorest-horned ram I encountered was 14 years old, yet his undamaged horns measured only 32$\frac{1}{2}$ in (82.5 cm) in length by 12$\frac{1}{2}$ in (31.7 cm) in basal circumference. This ram was a dwarf in body size. The ram with the most massive horns was also the largest-bodied ram I encountered. His horns were heavily broomed, 36 in (91.5 cm) long by 14$\frac{1}{4}$ in basal circumference. His dried skull and horns weighed 19 lb (8.6 kg) with each horn weighing 6$\frac{1}{2}$ lb (3 kg). These 3 rams span the extremes in horn size encountered at Gladys Lake. T. A. Walker kindly supplied the horn measurements of Stone's rams from the Eagle Nest Range which are shown in table 1. The average basal circumference of horns from 28 of these rams older than 7 years was 33.8 cm (13$\frac{1}{2}$ in), minimum 31.2, maximum 36.2 (12$\frac{1}{4}$–14$\frac{1}{4}$ in). The heaviest set of horns and dry upper skull weighed 20 lb (9.1 kg), and the lightest, 16 lb (7.3 kg).

TABLE 1

Horn lengths of twenty-eight Stone's rams killed by hunters in the Eagle Nest Range, 1955–62 (In mm)

				Age (yrs)			
	7	8	9	10	11	12	14
	(N = 5)	(N = 6)	(N = 2)	(N = 5)	(N = 5)	(N = 4)	(N = 1)
Average	867	905	913	972	978	975	825
Minimum	840	795	902	890	932	915	. . .
Maximum	890	978	925	1,150	1,105	1,067	. . .

To date no body weights have been published for Stone's sheep. I weighed only three sheep at Gladys Lake in November 1965, a mediocre 6$\frac{1}{2}$-year-old ram (170 lb), an exceptionally large female (135 lb), and a smaller than average $2\frac{1}{2}$-year-old ram (117 lb). Body measurements for the first two are given in table 2. The larger ram was considerably

TABLE 2
Weight and dimensions of two Stone's sheep

	Age (yrs)	Live weight (lb)	Hind foot length (in)	Total length (in)	Tail length (in)	Ear length (in)	Shoulder height (in)	Chest girth (in)
Ram	$6\frac{1}{2}$	170	$17\frac{1}{4}$	58	4	$3\frac{3}{4}$	40	44
Ewe	16+	135	$15\frac{1}{4}$	51	4	$3\frac{3}{4}$	35	40

emaciated when shot during the 1965 rutting season; he had lost most of his fat and had apparently a low rumen fill. In early fall he would have probably weighed 180–85 lb. Since rams continue to grow in body size till about 9 years of age, I estimate that the largest rams at Gladys Lake would weigh in the pre-rut 220–30 lb (100–104 kg), with an exceptional one topping 250 lb (122 kg). The female's dimensions in table 2 must be considered an absolute maximum for Gladys Lake; most would weigh 10–15 lb less. I did not find the Stone's sheep appreciably smaller than the bighorns I worked with in Banff, but this needs to be verified.

Stone's sheep differ from Dall's sheep in cranial characters. They have larger horn bases, a larger and relatively wider skull, and somewhat heavier horns (Cowan 1940). Indications are that Stone's sheep run somewhat larger than Dall's sheep but decisive evidence is lacking.

The Population

Size. Three wintering areas impinged on Gladys Lake and two others lay within eight miles of the cabin. Ghost Mountain was a female wintering area (see plate 4), Sanctuary Mountain was primarily a concentration area for rams in fall and spring, but rams and a few ewes also wintered here. Lupin Hill and Cliff Mountain were roamed over by the same small ewe band, and a few rams wintered on the latter. During midwinter, after the rut, Shady Mountain served as a wintering area for a few rams. Some wintered also at McMillan Creek, but I was not able to determine the size of that group. It is evident that the number of sheep around Gladys Lake varied seasonally; most sheep were present in spring, fewer were present in fall, and fewer still in midwinter.

The number of females and juveniles which were present at Gladys Lake in October 1962 is shown in table 3. The sex ratio during the

TABLE 3

Composition of female home range groups at Gladys Lake

	♀	♀y	♂y	L
Ghost Mt.	18	7	4	9
Sanctuary Mt.	5	2	2	2
Cliff Mt.	5	1	1	2
Total	28	10	7	13

NOTE: ♀, ewes; ♀y, yearling ewes; ♂y, yearling rams; L, lambs.

rut of rams older than 2 years to females older than 2 years was 88:100. Since 28 ewes were present in October there must have been 25 rams present. This calculation comes close to actual, for in November 1962, I counted 28 different rams in the Gladys Lake area. Hence, the total population of ewes, yearlings, lambs, and rams was about 86 in the fall of 1962. In addition, about 30 goats were present, divided into one major band of about 18 individuals on Ghost Mountain and two smaller bands of 5–7 animals each. In fall 1961 the sheep population had been the same size, or a little smaller.

Density.   Within an 8-mile radius of the lake there was only one small wintering ram band in addition to sheep on Ghost, Sanctuary, Cliff, and Shady mountains. This band at McMillan Creek contained at the most 12 rams; so there were approximately 98 sheep in an 8-mile radius of the lake, that is, 98 sheep in 200 square miles (512 km^2). I found no sheep when I moved beyond this 8-mile radius, hence the density of sheep would be even less than 1 per 2 square miles as indicated above—probably 1 per 4–6 square miles. The 200-square-mile area includes of course areas uninhabitable to sheep; sheep habitat makes up only a small, though undeterminable fraction.

Composition.   The rams of mountain sheep can be divided into horn size classes (see pp. 54–57 and fig. 6), which correspond to 18 months old (yearling), 2–3 years (class I), 3½–6 years (class II), 6–8 years (class III), and 7–16 years (class IV). Adult Stone's rams (classes I–IV) were present in the proportions indicated on table 4 at the season

TABLE 4

Composition of adult ram population on Stone's sheep study area

Census period	Class				No. of rams counted
	IV	III	II	I	
8 Nov–31 Dec 61	24%	24%	35%	16%	194
20 May–30 June 62	21	24	39	16	164

specified. These dates were chosen because almost all rams have crossed to their rutting ranges by 8 November, where they remain until Christmas. The dates 20 May and 30 June encompass the major concentration time of rams; all rams that came to Sanctuary Mountain did so by 24 May, but they were sighted on other mountains earlier. The sets of figures complement each other. I consider the spring figures to be more representative, because in fall class III and IV rams roam considerably (see chap. 7) and one would expect to record them more frequently.

The rutting population at Gladys Lake could be characterized as follows: for 100 ewes over 2 years of age there would be 34 yearling females, 21 yearling rams, 64 lambs, 15 class I rams, 35 class II rams, 25 class III rams, and 25 class IV rams.[1] Of the 100 ewes about 20 would be 2½-year-olds entering their first fall as adults.

Since the age of living rams can be determined with fair accuracy by counting the age rings on the horns (Geist 1966c), I aged 40 Stone's rams during spring 1962. Five of these rams were examined and aged more accurately after they died. The age distribution as determined for spring 1962 is given in table 5.

The two 13-year-old rams died in their fourteenth year of life, one by wolves and the other by hunting. Their age was exceeded only by two ewes which I examined. One, killed by wolves, was at least 14 years old and the other was at least 16 years old when shot. These ages were determined by counting horn rings, a method which reveals minimum ages only.

1. Based on individually known rams, not on observed sex-age ratios.

TABLE 5

Age composition of forty Stone's rams living at Gladys Lake, spring 1962

	Age (yrs)												
	1	2	3	4	5	6	7	8	9	10	11	12	13
No. of rams	1	2	3	6	7	5	4	5	2	1	2	0	2

NOTE: Five rams, one each from age groups 8, 9, 10, and 13, were examined postmortem and checked for accuracy of aging technique. The 8- and 10-year-olds had been aged correctly. The 9-year-old had been judged 8 years when alive. Both 13-year-olds had been rated 11+ when alive.

Group sizes. At Gladys Lake sheep were thinly spread and were usually seen in small groups and frequently as singles. Ram bands were smaller on the average than female bands, and band sizes fluctuated seasonally. Table 6 shows average band size for Stone's and bighorn sheep during the rutting season, when bands are formed by adult sheep of both sexes. In midwinter, right after the rutting season, sheep were usually found in smaller bands than at other seasons of the year. The average group size for male and female sheep of both species during midwinter is shown in table 7. In late spring bands tend to be larger than in winter and as large or even larger than the bands in fall (see table 8).

TABLE 6

Group sizes in the rutting season

Period	Average band size	Maximum band size	No. of bands[a]
	Stone's		
21 Nov–31 Dec 62	3.7	21	108
27 Nov–10 Dec 65	3.7	14	58
	Bighorn		
20 Nov–30 Dec 64	5.4	31	152
20 Nov–18 Dec 66	7.8	52	143

[a] Bands include here all sightings, including single sheep.

TABLE 7
Male and female group sizes during midwinter

Period	Sex	Average band size	Maximum band size	No. of bands[a]	No. of sheep	Sheep seen single (%)
			Stone's			
28 Dec 61–28 Feb 62	♂	1.9	7	145	278	28.8
	♀	3.8	12	50	189	1.0
			Bighorn			
1 Jan–7 Feb 65	♂	5.2	20	115	604	3.8
	♀	9.5	24	48	458	0

[a] Bands include here all sightings, including single sheep.

TABLE 8
Male and female group sizes in spring and fall

Period	Sex	Average band size	Maximum band size	No. of bands	No. of sheep	Sheep seen single (%)
			Stone's			
2–31 May 62	♂	2.9	10	76	219	11.5
	♀	3.3	11	51	167	6.0
1–30 Oct 62	♂	3.6	9	37	133	6.0
	♀	5.1	19	24	122	0.8
			Bighorn			
9 May–5 June 65	♂	8.2	49	159	1,302	1.4
	♀	11.5	41	36	416	1.0
6 Sept–31 Oct 64	♂	5.5	33	138	763	5.8
	♀	9.0	23	33	296	0.7

NOTE: Female bands contain ♀, ♀y, L, ♂y, and class I♂.

The relationship between the average group size for ram bands and the percentage of rams seen single is shown in figure 4. It is evident that Stone's rams at Gladys Lake lived on the average in much smaller bands than did bighorn rams on the Palliser Range in Banff park. Also, once the average group size exceeds 8, the chance of sighting single rams is slim. Bighorn and Stone's ram data fall along the same line indicating that Stone's rams are not inherently more solitary than bighorn rams. It also appears that band size and the frequency with which one sees single rams (outside the rutting season) is a direct reflection of the density of rams on an area. In general, the more rams converge on an area, the larger the bands and less frequently one sees singles.

Female Stone's and bighorn sheep are more gregarious than males, which is reflected in tables 7 and 8, and in the lower frequency that

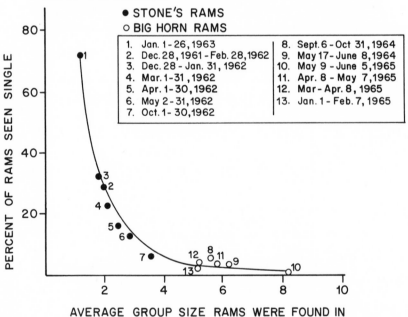

Fig. 4. As the average group size in which rams are found decreases, the frequency of sightings of single rams increases. The Stone's rams were found consistently in smaller groups than the bighorns.

they were seen alone (chap. 6). At Gladys Lake many females went about with only their lambs in winter or with an additional juvenile. Thus, in the periods of 28 December 1961 to 28 February 1962 and 1–27 January 1963, from 101 sightings of females 45 were single, 23 were groups of one female and her lamb, and 33 were of one female, her lamb, and a juvenile sheep. In essence then, in 56 out of 101 winter ewe bands only one adult female was present. These little groups had no counterpart on the bighorn study area; all of the 51 ewe bands I sighted there between 3 January and 7 February 1965 had at least two adult females, which could indicate that bighorn ewes are inherently some-what more social. The ewes at Gladys Lake, just like the rams, were dispersed widely and in small groups during midwinter.

THE DALL'S SHEEP STUDY

Sheep Mountain represented the best sheep habitat I encountered during my study. It lies on the eastern outskirts of the St. Elias Range at Kluane Lake, near mile 1,066 of the Alaska Highway in the Yukon Territory. I stayed there from 14 September to 24 November 1965, in order to describe and document the behavior patterns of Dall's sheep and to compare these with those of Stone's and bighorn sheep.

Sheep Mountain is a great contrast to the mountains about Gladys Lake in the Cassiars. It lies about fifteen miles down the valley from the huge Kaskawulsh Glacier, which with other interconnected glaciers fills the interior valleys of the St. Elias Range for hundreds of miles; the ice stretches continuously to the Pacific Ocean. In the last 50,000 years this glacier has made at least four major advances, the last only about 2,600 years ago. This advance ended the Slims nonglacial era that had lasted 10,000 years. Before it the Kluane glaciation had lasted 18,000 years beginning about 30,500 years ago (Denton and Stuiver 1967), which would probably be contemporary with Würm III of Europe. Today Kluane is in the neoglacial period, which is somewhat cooler than the preceding warm Altithermal period when bison, elk, musk oxen, and caribou were found at the foot of the range (MacNeish 1964; Goldthwait 1966).

The glacier feeds the Slims River which spills its muddy, silt-laden water into Kluane Lake. The valley is about a mile and a half wide, flat and overshadowed by big mountains. Its bottom is formed from loose glacial till, sparsely covered by windtorn grasses and clumps of low willow and dwarf birch. Stands of spruce grow at the foot of the mountains or climb the north slopes, while dwarfed aspen (*Populus tremuloides*) grow low on the south-facing slopes. The river meanders lazily in many channels along the valley floor, eroding the banks as it goes or filling them with yellow silt. Violent winds sweep the valley; in the evenings they could blast from the glacier, whirling dry silt in yellow clouds several thousand feet high down the valley and sweeping far over Kluane Lake. The mountains are skeletons of rock heaped over with dust and gravel. I used to sink ankle deep in the loose soil when climbing, and sheep went everywhere trailed by puffs of dust in their steps. Dust filled the air, covered the grasses and shrubs, discolored the spruce trees, clung to the cloth and hair, gritted between one's teeth, and muddied the drinking water.

The steep slopes of Sheep Mountain are of gravel and rock rubble, cut here and there by deep gorges which guide meltwater to the valley. Rocks protrude from the slope. The deep gorges, flanked by cliffs and spruce stands, are filled with snags and boulders. Mats of willows hug the slopes, and clumps of twisted spruce grow in depressions and on level areas. Above the slopes rise red, jagged cliffs.

The Kluane Lake area is sheep country as it probably existed during much of the late Pleistocene in the vicinity of large glaciers. We know that the flora of Alaska has changed very little from that of the Pleistocene epoch (see Viereck 1966). At the outskirts of the St. Elias Range, sheep dominate the scene and the mountains are laced with their trails and bedding sites. Sheep are the major ruminant here, goats are sighted closer toward the glacier, caribou are absent along the Slims River, and moose are not common.

Sheep Mountain is not virgin wilderness. The Alaska Highway cuts along its foot and a jeep road leads to small gold mining operations on two adjacent creeks. Sheep were hunted here legally before the area became a game reserve and the coyotes and wolves that live on the mountain are occasionally shot at from the highway.

In September when I arrived on the study area the land was gay, colorful, and dusty. In October snow fell and melted, mud formed on the slopes, and the white sheep carried soiled coats at times. When November rolled around the dust storms ceased and the slopes froze rock hard. Kluane Lake began to freeze. The bays formed ice first, while the outlets and center remained open. Winds produced waves, broke the ice, and drifted it about in large pieces. In the cold weather the open water steamed. Clouds lay several layers deep over the valley and ice crystals shimmered in the air if the sun broke through during the short winter day. Snow drizzled down, winds scattered it over the slopes, and packed it hard in hollows. On sunny days standing on the mountains, I could see the sun reflected in the valley. It was cold, bitter cold.

The number of Dall's sheep was large during the season I observed on Sheep Mountain, but I cannot give a population estimate or the density of sheep. The largest single gathering or band of sheep I counted was 106 animals, almost entirely females and juveniles. The largest ram band I observed numbered 51 animals. The average composition of female bands was as follows: for every 100 adult females over 2 years of age, there were 21 lambs, 11.5 female yearlings, 11.5 male yearlings, and 15 class I rams ($2\frac{1}{2}$ years old) (N = 117 sheep classified). A classification of 72 rams in November was as follows: class I, 19%; class II, 47%; class III, 18%; and class IV, 15%. The relatively low number of rams older than 7 years (classes III and IV, 33%) is surprising and may indicate poaching. Among Stone's sheep at Gladys Lake, rams older than 7 years made up about 46% of class I to IV rams, and among bighorn the corresponding figure was 47–52%.

Although sheep were numerous on Sheep Mountain, they were of lower quality than those at Gladys Lake and comparable in this respect to the Banff bighorns. The number of lambs and yearlings was low, much lower than for the Stone's sheep. The yearling rams (18 months old), however, were well grown since they often equaled adult females in body and horn size; furthermore, they showed some interest in females during the rut and dominated them. Some yearlings had large, clearly visible testes. The large rams were exceedingly lethargic. I saw only one short dominance fight between two class II rams and though I stood daily for several hours among rams after these arrived in the first days of November, I saw only seven clashes in three weeks. Among bighorns or Stone's sheep one can see that many clashes in an hour. Like the bighorns, but unlike the Stone's, Kluane rams huddled frequently (chap. 7); yet they interacted little and rarely fought. No data are available on the size and horn characteristics of Sheep Mountain rams.

THE BIGHORN SHEEP STUDY

The Eagle Nest Range where the Stone's sheep live is still wilderness in much the same form as it was in prior centuries. No new species have been introduced and no old ones eradicated. No cattle have been driven into the valleys; no domestic sheep have grazed the ranges; no mining, town building, or railroad construction has taken place. Banff National Park in Alberta's southern Rockies, where I studied bighorn sheep, unfortunately has a different history. By American standards it has had a long involvement with white man and is no longer virgin territory. It is, however, a wilderness where serious wounds inflicted in the past century are healing. The history of Banff park is reviewed by Banfield (1958) and more extensively by Byrne (1968).

In the past century several large fires have gutted valleys in the park. Bison became extinct, wolves were poisoned out twice, and black bear began to feed in garbage dumps and beg food from visitors along the roads until they were controlled. Elk, abundant a century ago, decreased almost to extinction and then after introduction of elk from Yellowstone National Park recovered to such numbers as to damage the flora along lower valleys. Horse grazing was permitted in some valleys. A power dam and power generating station were built in the park and a large artificial lake was created. What effects all this has had on the study population of mountain sheep no one will ever know completely, but these sheep certainly have not lived under conditions free from the influences of man. Probably no population of bighorn sheep in North America has. Despite this, my study populations had retained some features which were identical to those of the Stone's sheep at Gladys Lake, such as fully predictable seasonal movements through miles of timber and across rivers, while their migration timing was strikingly similar to that of Stone's sheep. Like the Stone's sheep they spent much of the winter at high elevations and searched out low slopes during storms or when green forage sprouted there in spring.

The study area lay within twenty miles of the locality where the type specimen of bighorn sheep was shot in November 1800 by Duncan McGillivray (Banfield 1958). It stretched from Stoney Creek along the Palliser and Bare Mountain ranges to Snowcreek Summit, a distance of about twenty-five miles. The main observation areas were the slopes of Grassy Mountain and the Palliser Range overlooking the Cascade River, as well as Bare Mountain and Panther Mountain, separated by the Panther River. I stayed on the study area from 5 May to 1 September 1963, 10 May 1964 to 7 June 1965, and 1 November to 17 December 1966. In addition I visited the study area for a week in July 1965 and eight days in spring 1968.

The Palliser Range (plate 9) lies on the eastern side of Banff National Park, where snowfall is lighter than on the continental divide. Along the Cascade Valley bighorns live largely on ranges which were created by forest fires. The grasslands are now slowly reverting to forests (Flook 1964). The silvery trunks of dead, partially charred Douglas fir

(*Pseudotsuga*) still stand or lie about the grassy slopes. Aspen groves stand on the southern exposures where there is often little soil and much exposed rock rubble. The lower margins of the grassy areas are rimmed by an open forest of pines (*Pinus contorta*) and fir; the younger trees at timber edge are often severely damaged by the hornings of elk and bighorn sheep. Alpine firs ascend the cool, moist northern slopes, while mature timber of Douglas firs alternates with old burn areas in the valleys. Sheep habitat is found on the slopes cleared of timber by fire, along avalanche gorges, on southerly exposed, steep, windblown slopes, on high ridges about 7,500 ft, and in the extensive cliff terrain. I found somewhat similar habitat for Stone's sheep in the Rockies at the northern end of the Rocky Mountain Trench. Here sheep exploited the upper reaches of extensive burns that were now characterized by some grassland and aspen (plate 10).

There were three home range groups of ewes on the Banff study area, whose ranges did not overlap. I will treat these as three different populations. These were the populations on Grassy Mountain, the Palliser Range, and Bare Mountain. These sheep, although coming very close to each other or even living in sight of each other during winter, had different movement patterns. The Grassy Mountain sheep, ewes and rams, arrived in early fall from Flint Mountain and went there again in late spring. Palliser sheep went south toward Lake Minnewanka as well as north along the range in early summer and arrived from the north in fall. The movements of Bare Mountain sheep are not known to me in detail, except those of rutting rams.

Grassy Mountain Sheep

The group on Grassy Mountain was the smallest of the three populations. The females came in September and left for Flint Mountain before the lambing season; the rams left a little later and concentrated about a large salt lick just east of Flint Mountain. Some rams came from the Palliser Range during late fall and returned to the range during spring.

The size and composition of this population in spring 1965 is shown in table 9. These estimates were obtained by direct counts, which, however, give only a minimum population estimate since some sheep are likely to be missed during each census, or by reconstruction of the population by noting the maximum number of each class of sheep sighted. Thus in spring 1965 I counted 145 class IV rams, 80 class III, 172 class II, 81 class I, 32 ♂y, 255 ♀, 20 ♀y, and 32 lambs. Estimates

TABLE 9

Estimates of the size and composition of a bighorn sheep population

	Class							
	IV	III	II	I	♂y	♀	♀y	L
a. Estimate if 2 L were present	9	5	11	5	2	16	1	2
b. Estimate if 3 ♂y were present	14	8	17	8	3	25	2	3
c. Estimate if 19 ♀ were present	11	6	13	6	2	19	1	2
d. Maximum count of each class	11	8	9	5	3	19	1	2
e. Most probable composition	11	6	13	6	3	19	1	2

a, b, and *c* in table 9 are based on these relative totals. Estimate *d* gives a minimum population of 55 sheep on Grassy Mountain in spring 1965, while the most probable estimate, *e,* gives 61. Table 10 gives the spring populations on Grassy in three consecutive springs and two falls, derived by the maximum count method.

TABLE 10

Composition of Grassy Mountain population in three consecutive springs and two falls

	Class								Population size	No. census trips
	IV	III	II	I	♂y	♀	♀y	L		
Spring										
9–19 May 63	...	37	...	4	2	16	3	8	66	7
13–20 May 64	11	9	12	4	0	15	3	4	58	6
18 Mar–18 May 65	11	8	9	5	3	19	1	2	55	33
Fall										
31 Oct–30 Dec 64	5	3	5	3	2	15	2	3	38	13
1 Nov–17 Dec 66	6	4	7	3	3	14	3	7	47	24

It is evident that the size of the population changed only a small amount between years; in particular, the number of adult ewes fluctuated within narrow limits. The same appears to be true for other populations. Wishart's (1959) study population fluctuated between 57 and 65 sheep in four consecutive years, while the number of adult ewes fluctuated between 24 and 26.

Bare Mountain Sheep

The female group from Bare Mountain ranged south eight miles to Bighorn Valley and north four miles to within two miles of Snowcreek Summit. It was a rather large home range group (Hunter 1962). In fall 1966 after twenty-four census counts of this group, I arrived at the following estimates: about 30 ♀, 3♀y, 3♂y, 20 L, and 2 rams 2½ years of age. This estimate is based on a maximum count of 28 ewes and 20 lambs in one day; the 6 yearlings and the 2 young rams I recognized individually. The population fluctuated little in size during the interval of spring 1964 to fall 1966, for on 30 June 1964 I counted 30 ewes older than 2 years, 12 yearlings, 7 newborn lambs, and 4 2-year-old rams. A few large rams could be encountered during every month on Bare Mountain, while a group of rams was found just north on Snowcreek Summit during summer and midwinter.

Bare Mountain was a lambing area to which ewes moved in late May. Here the females stayed with the small lambs till the beginning of July. Thereafter females with lambs were seen infrequently on the mountain; they appeared to roam considerably. These females almost met the Palliser female band to the south, but there was little exchange between these groups. Many Palliser females were tagged by the late E. J. Stenton, warden at Bankhead. No tagged female was ever seen among the Bare Mountain females either by myself or the wardens at Windy Station. One 2½-year-old female from Bare Mountain did follow a 2½-year-old ram to the Palliser sheep in October 1964. This is the only evidence that some exchange of individuals did occur between these groups. However, two tagged rams from the Palliser ram band did rut at Bare Mountain.

Palliser Range Sheep

The largest concentration of wintering bighorn sheep in Banff National Park are found on the Palliser Range between Stoney Creek and Bighorn Valley. This is a concentration area of rams in fall before the rutting season and again in late spring before dispersal to summer ranges. The number of rams on the Palliser fluctuates seasonally, from a maximum of about 90 rams in late May (1964 census) to none in late July and August. The spring concentration is about twice as great as the fall concentration; after the rut there were only 16–20 rams present in midwinter (1965). The female and juvenile population appears to move about in two bands; both are present on the south-west-facing slopes of the range apparently only during adverse snow conditions. Since only these slopes are open to census, my population estimates are less accurate than those for Grassy Mountain sheep. Counting the maximum number of sheep in any one class, I arrived at the following population estimates for the springs of 1964 and 1965 and the falls of 1964 and 1966 (table 11).

TABLE 11

Composition of Palliser Range sheep in several years in spring and fall

Period	Class								No. census trips
	IV	III	II	I	♂y	♀	♀y	L	
13–31 May 64	29	17	37	12	11	21	5	19	14
14 Apr–31 May 65	22	16	32	11	11	35	6	10	26
27 Oct–30 Dec 64	...	...	...	5	1	12	1	1	13
1 Nov–18 Dec 66	...	...	...	3	5	35	4	18	18

In 1964 I arrived too late at the study area to see the maximum concentration of females on the range, and the 21 females cited for 1964 is an underestimate. In fall 1964 only part of the female group frequented the southwest slopes, but the entire group was present in fall 1966. During midwinter the females often were absent from the southwest-facing slopes for days, but a few could be seen on the skyline, which indicates that they were in the high cliffs as well as in the broken, ragged terrain on the east-facing side of the range. The females occupied the southern end of the range and the rams the northern end (see chap. 3).

Part of the female group went south in summer to the mountains bordering Lake Minnewanka. They visited the tourist facilities at the shores of the lake where many were tagged by E. J. Stenton between the summers of 1949 and 1965. These sheep were largely tame and many others became tame during the course of study.

The Palliser females raised most of the rams from the large male group that frequented the Palliser Range, but it is likely that other female bands such as the Bare Mountain or Grassy Mountain females contributed as well. There were striking differences in horn, body size, and coloration among the rams, suggesting that this was a collection of rams raised in various regions. Rams tagged as juveniles at Lake Minnewanka, and therefore raised by Palliser ewes, did go as far north as Snowcreek Summit and crossed to Grassy Mountain and the Cascade mountains, while some were shot outside the border of the park. The rams spread and intermingle; the females hold more restricted home ranges.

The Palliser Range served primarily in my investigation of habitat behavior and in the collection of quantitative social behavior data. Most photographs illustrating this volume were taken there. The temperature investigations (see chap. 9) were made at the south end of the range above Stoney Creek.

Population Density and Composition

Table 12 shows the number and class composition of bighorn sheep present in the three female home range groups on the Banff study area. Since the ratio of rams (including ♂y) to females (including ♀y) was 90:100 and there were 90 ewes present, there were about 82 rams present. From 81 rams, 11 were ♂y and 8 class I ♂; hence, there were 62 rams older than $2\frac{1}{2}$ years of age present. The total number of sheep between Stoney Creek and Snowcreek Summit, east of the Cascade fire road, was estimated to be 225 individuals in late fall 1966.

TABLE 12
Composition of female home range groups, November and December 1966

	♀	♀y	♂y	L	Class I ♂
Grassy Mt.	14	3	3	7	3
Bare Mt.	30	5	3	20	2
Palliser R.	35	4	5	18	3
Total	79	12	11	45	8

The study area in late fall encompassed an area lying east of the Cascade road, one to three miles wide and running for about twenty-five miles along the road. Thus the study area encompassed 40 or 50 square miles. Since it contained around 225 sheep, the density of sheep along the Palliser and Bare Mountain ranges was 4–6 sheep per square mile in early winter.

I calculated density on a general area which contained a relatively small fraction of sheep habitat and not on the basis of area of sheep habitat. Cherniavski (1967) gives densities of snow sheep in the Koryak highlands of eastern Siberia. It is not clear from his paper if these figures are valid for the whole mountain range, including valley bottoms, or only for sheep habitat. He found 9–18 sheep per 1,000 hectares; this compares with a maximum of about 2 sheep/1,000 ha for the southern Eagle Nest Range within which my Stone's sheep study area was located, and about 20 bighorns/1,000 ha on the Palliser Range. Cherniavski also reports density figures for ibex populations as determined by various authors, which run from a low of 27–32 ibex/1,000 ha in the Terskei Alatau to 40–110 ibex/1,000 ha in the Pamir, to a high of 115.7–149.6 ibex (tur)/1,000 ha in the Caucasus mountains. Crude as these estimates are, they do indicate sparse populations of snow and Stone's sheep in a large area of mountainous terrain. The conclusion is entirely supported by impressions I gained while traveling in northern British Columbia and the Yukon, and it is also emphasized by Cherniavski for Siberia.

The class composition of bighorn rams varied a little seasonally and annually as shown in table 13. The reconstructed population

TABLE 13

Composition of bighorn ram populations in various seasons and years

Location and period	Class				Total sightings
	IV	III	II	I	
Palliser, Grassy					
1–30 Apr 65	29%	17%	40%	15%	477
1–15 May 65	29	18	35	19	586
16–30 May 65	31	19	34	16	739
Grassy, Bare, Palliser					
15 Nov–15 Dec 64	34	17	30	19	187
10 Nov–18 Dec 66	39	26	26	8	613
Reconstructed cohort[a]	32	21	35	12	

[a] Based on 77 rams found dead in the field.

based on dead rams found in the field compares favorably with the ones determined by actual counting. The mortality data on which the reconstruction is based are found in chapter 10. The composition of the bighorn ram population can also be expressed by including yearling rams in the count. This can only be done during rutting season, for then rams and ewes are found on the same ranges. Outside the rutting season class II–IV rams tend to be away from ewes. Hence only during the rut are the ratios of class I and yearling rams to older rams likely to be representative. Table 14 shows the percentage composition of rams during two rutting seasons on the study area.

TABLE 14

Composition of bighorn ram populations during rutting seasons

Period	Class					Total sightings
	IV	III	II	I	♂y	
15 Nov–15 Dec 64	28.2%	13.6%	24.8%	16.0%	17.5%	227
10 Nov–18 Dec 66	33.7	22.6	22.6	6.1	14.8	719

Working with Tame Mountain Sheep

It is hard to imagine a wild animal more readily tamed than mountain sheep. They habituate readily to man if not hunted and will accept him as a two-legged salt lick if he so wishes. Sheep will habituate to a person if they see him daily and within a few months allow him to approach closely. A close association between the investigator and his study animals is, during at least part of the study, a most desirable situation, as it allows him to gain insights unobtainable in any other way.

In general, bighorn sheep did not accept me as one of their own and came to me for salt only. There were exceptions, all unpleasant ones. Once the majority of sheep had accepted my presence, they acted in the following manner when I approached them. When I was about three-fourths of a mile from them some individuals stood and scrutinized me. More sheep raised their heads as I walked closer. Then one would move a few steps toward me, hesitantly, which tended to draw another animal forward. If a ram started to move toward me a slightly larger one might race ahead and block its way in a display, with a threat jump or clash. The animals always seemed to wait for someone to make the first decisive move.

Once the sheep were on the way down the slope, I could observe dominant rams cutting off smaller ones, racing ahead and turning, thereby stopping the whole troop. Such social interactions could hold up the progress of a ram group considerably; ewes usually came at a full run once committed.

The first sheep to approach came cautiously. However, once it licked salt, the others came in quickly, pushing and butting their way in. If the salt was placed on the ground, the rams would kneel or even crawl to reach the salt between a companion's legs. Large rams had priority over small rams when licking salt, a priority they often established by force. The most careful of all were the lambs, which often remained alone on the slopes and crags, while their dams came to me.

The purpose of attracting the animals was to read the small marking tags inside their ears. This could be accomplished by freeing the small ear tags of obstructing hair while allowing the sheep to lick salt. It usually took many tries before this was accomplished. At first it was necessary to condition each sheep to the touch. Hence the moment it licked salt, I placed my fingers on its rostrum and rubbed along the hairline. Gradually I worked my hand over to the side of the head, below the eye, and then to the ear. Usually the sheep jerked away once I reached the ear but returned to lick the salt after sniffing and licking my fingers (plate 11). They came readily to people and though I suspect that they could recognize persons individually, there was no certain indication of it. They followed persons readily along the mountains, and sometimes even followed as far as a quarter mile into the timber.

They had a tendency to return to the locality where they had first received salt and to search for it by sniffing along the ground. However, they soon learned to abandon this activity and follow the observer instead. Sheep usually did not follow at once, but only after some minutes of hesitation, and I generally had a head start of several hundred yards before the band caught up with me on the run. Thereafter they trailed me.

Sheep could be a nuisance by sticking their snouts into my pocket, grasping my jacket or packboard and tugging on it, licking across the camera lens, pushing their noses into open cine and still cameras, and occasionally placing their front legs on my chest. One had to be careful not to receive an occasional butt which was aimed at sheep but missed the mark. A few old rams, eager to get salt but experiencing difficulty in reaching me through a crowd of sheep, became aggressive against me also—a potentially dangerous situation. On one such occasion I was attacked by a ram. The big rams appear to become irritated on two counts. First, if they are engaged in slugging matches, and second, if they have access to the salt lick for only a few seconds. The pressure of a number of sheep pushes the observer downhill. I used to disengage successfully from such large crowds by suddenly turning and bounding down slope. On rare occasions a ewe galloped beside me and then swung around in front blocking my way with her body, or attempting to push me off course. Such ewes acted toward me in the same manner that lambs used to halt their dams to suckle. During one such escape a large ram pounced forward and hit my packboard with a glancing blow. He charged again as I ran on and again hit my parka and board. Since timber and safety were still about 400 yards away, there was no alternative but to stop and push a piece of salt sideways into the ram's mouth. Fortunately the piece of salt was small enough to enter the mouth but large enough so that the ram could not spit it out. The ram remained standing, occupied with the salt; I departed.

Some of the psychic adaptations of sheep became evident during our contacts. They appeared to have excellent memories, for sheep which were gone for months came to me unhesitatingly, occasionally over great distances. The behavior of sheep when I hid from their sight was most illuminating. They did not go to search for me where I disappeared but rather where I should have appeared. They seemed to form hypotheses about my movements and attempted to intercept me by going where I should and would have been had I continued in a straight line. Failing to find me, the rams became excited, some clashing followed, and then either they abandoned their attempts at finding me or they searched—against the wind—and once tracked me down by sniffing the footsteps.

If I placed myself motionless beside a tree, the sheep would recognize me and come. Once I climbed a tree and sat motionless on a branch in full view. The sheep milled about the tree in confusion and excitement. Some ran short distances into the forest and stood alertly, looking and listening. They must have been able to smell me, but none looked up at me even though their horns almost brushed my boots. If I climbed a tree in their full view (usually to load a camera), the sheep stood and watched me. They had seen me previously in trees; yet on this occasion they failed to locate me. Eventually the band moved uphill from sight. At that point I had to cough. At once a ewe came sprinting, ran past the tree, then stopped to look and listen. After about a minute of looking around, the animal left.

The tame bighorns provided a number of unique observations. Whereas in fall and spring, when little or no snow covered the ground, the rams came from considerable distances often crossing deep gorges, they failed to do so when the snow was deep. They faced me across a gorge and then returned to feeding. However, if I crossed through the deep snow and left a trail, the rams followed behind me back across the gorge. They used me as a snowplow. Their avoidance of deep snow becomes understandable once one has seen sheep struggle to free themselves from snow three feet in depth or more.

They were particularly frightened of odd, uncommon actions of their own companions. It is not the shot that frightens sheep as much as the sight of a rolling, kicking companion in its death throes. A sheep which bounded about erratically in an attempt to rid itself of a paper bag it held in its teeth, first caused the others to bolt and then return cautiously and watch it curiously, ready to bound away. It may be that the aggression of sheep toward ill or mutilated companions is in part triggered by the uncommon, odd, and unfamiliar actions of the latter.

Since one could touch sheep with impunity, it was possible to discover various oddities. First, not all sheep had a black mucous lining of the nose, palate, and tongue. Many had pink or pibald surfaces. One ram had a cataract on the right eye and kept it without any change of the milky spot for five years. In spring, when the new horn began to grow, clashes caused drops of blood to ooze from the junction of horn and skin on the forehead. The horn surfaces of rams were covered by broken bits of hair after a fight, and the noses cut open.

It was surprising to discover how inept the bighorns were at biting. Often I held my hand in their mouth while they chewed my fingers, and licked them, with a velvety, warm tongue. Only if they managed to get a bit of skin pinched between their incisors on the soft, upper palate were they able to cut my skin.

The rams and ewes differed in personality. Some tamed readily and became pests; ewes more so than rams. They did not mind if I touched their bodies, parted the hair, and extracted ticks from their backs. Most sheep are extremely sensitive to being touched anywhere except the head. One could make most sheep bound up straight by sticking one's finger gently into their ribs just behind the front leg. In general the sheep were more ready to come, even search for me, in spring than in fall. It appeared that their demand for salt was greatest in spring, although they took it willingly at any other season. Some rams that had not seen me for years were at first cautious in their approach, others came at a gallop.

One advantage of tame sheep is that they can be easily marked by clipping a tag into an ear while the animal licks salt, or the lambs can be caught and tagged when their mothers are licking. E. J. Stenton caught lambs by hunching down, stretching his hands past the licking female's front legs, and grasping the lamb by one front leg once it came close. These marked sheep provided information on home ranges, on longevity of individuals, and on the validity of the horn segment count as an aging technique (see Geist 1966c). Plate 17 illustrates the horns of a ram of known age.

Such a group of tame bighorns offers some advantages but they are few compared with sheep which are only habituated. Tame sheep can be a nuisance and a dangerous one at that, while habituated sheep can be approached almost as closely and usually ignore the observer. The fact that mountain sheep—and not only mountain sheep—can be readily tamed in the wilds offers undreamt of possibilities for management of native ruminants, as well as such research in which psychological adaptations or the effects of various oral drugs or supplemental feeding is to be investigated. It also offers opportunity to follow closely the life history and reproductive performance of individuals and obtain data on their weight gains and growth performances. It can be safely stated that any unhunted population of mountain sheep can be tamed, investigated, or harvested, cured of parasites and diseases—if that is desirable, and its migratory routes can be altered to suit management needs. It is not at all surprising that sheep and goats are probably the oldest domesticated animals next to the dog.

Comparison of the Banff Bighorns with Other Races and Populations of Sheep

Rocky Mountain bighorns (*O. c. canadensis*), particularly those from southern Alberta, are regarded as the largest race of American sheep. Our concepts about their size and dimensions, however, are based on a few exceptionally large individuals as Blood et al. (1970) correctly pointed out, and we assume bighorns to be larger than they actually are. To date several representative samples of Rocky Mountain bighorns have been weighed (Blood et al.; Taylor 1962), as well as some of Nelson's sheep (Aldous et al. 1958). These data together with the few weights available for Dall's sheep (Ulmer 1941), snow sheep (Heptner et al. 1961; Cherniavski 1962b), urials and Tien-Shan argalis (*O. a. karelini*) (Heptner et al. 1961), present a clearer picture of the size and sexual dimorphism in sheep than has been possible previously.

Body size. Fully grown bighorn rams 7 years of age or more, from southern Alberta, average in spring about 225 lb (102 kg), and fully grown females 159 lb (72 kg) (Blood et al.). Only a few rams will reach 300 lb (135 kg) in weight, less than one in one hundred, because the standard deviation from mean weight, for rams and ewes, is about 12 lb. Since sheep from southern Alberta and British Columbia are reputed to be large, it is likely that rams from further north and south along the Rockies would average less in body weight. Bighorn rams from captive, high-quality herds such as those from the National Bison Range in Montana may grow larger and reach 260–302 lb when more than 6 years of age (Taylor 1962). By comparison, a large argali ram (*poli*) from the Russian Pamir shot in early summer when devoid of fat weighed 265 lb (118 kg) (Clark 1964). Tien-Shan argali rams weigh at $3\frac{1}{2}$–$4\frac{1}{2}$ years of age 220–30 lb (101–5 kg) and about 290 lb (130 kg) when fully mature, while females weigh about 130 lb (60 kg). Only exceptionally do these rams grow larger than 400 lb (180 kg) (Heptner et al. 1961). From these data it is evident that bighorn rams are a little smaller than the medium-sized argali rams, whereas bighorn females are of similar size or a little larger. This was also my impression when confronting Kara-Tau argalis (*nigrimontana*) at the Frankfurt Zoological Garden. It was also striking that the argali ram compared to the females was proportionately larger than bighorn rams. This is also brought out by the data cited above; bighorn females are about 0.67 times the ram's weight. The sexual dimorphism appears to be greater in argalis and urials than in bighorn sheep, and not smaller as suggested by Heptner et al. (1961).

The Nelson's bighorn is reputed to be the smallest of the bighorn sheep, which is borne out not only by cranial dimensions (Cowan 1940; Bradley and L. R. Baker 1967) but also by body weights (Aldous et al. 1958) and a comparison of horn dimensions of record size. Aldous et al. unfortunately did not publish the ages of rams weighed, but they did publish hind foot lengths. For 12 rams which were fully grown since their hind feet exceeded 15 in (37 cm) in length, the average weight was 164.5 lb (134–90 lb) or 74.5 kg (61–86 kg); for 15 females the average weight was 96.5 lb (74–114 lb) or 43.5 kg (33.5–51.5 kg). Hence weight of females is about 0.59 times that of males, and as Blood et al. pointed out, the sexual dimorphism may be greater among these sheep than among bighorns from the north, not smaller as had been erroneously assumed.

Nelson's bighorns appear to grow considerably faster than Rocky Mountain bighorns, for the rams and ewes may reach proportions at

12 months of age which their northern counterparts do not reach till 18–30 months (see Hansen 1965). Nelson's sheep are not only smaller than Rocky Mountain bighorns, but also smaller than Stone's sheep, Dall's sheep, and Kamchatka sheep (*O. n. nivicola*). Four old Dall's rams weighed 173–85 lb (70–84 kg) (Ulmer 1941), but this may not be representative since a 5-year-old ram from the St. Elias Range in the Yukon weighed 226 lb in October. The weights of snow sheep from Kamchatka indicate that it is not a small animal but rivals our bighorns in body size. Four rams older than 6 years weighed 190–281 lb (86–128.4 kg), while 8 females weighed 102–20 lb (46.5–54.1 kg) (Heptner et al. 1961); 3 rams 6–14 years of age from Koryak highlands of northern Siberia, representing the race *O. n. lydekkeri*, were smaller than Kamchatka sheep and weighed 154–67 lb (70–6 kg) (Cherniavski 1962*b*).

Horn size.   *Records of North American Big Game* (Baker 1964) contains measurements of most of the very large rams shot or found on this continent. These measurements are useful as they give us the maximum dimensions achieved by various races of American sheep and serve as a standard with which to compare various populations. The Rocky Mountain bighorns excel other races in horn size by far. The average horn length of the first 50 rams listed by Baker, using the longest horn of each ram only, is 42.5 in (108 cm), while the average basal horn circumference of the first 30 rams is 15.6 ± 0.11 in (14.3–17 in) or 39.5 cm (36.3–43.2 cm). Since the horn tips of almost all large bighorn rams are broken, at least 8 in (20 cm) should be added to the length measurement to achieve a true picture of their horn size. The longest horn length recorded officially for a bighorn ram is 49.5 in (126 cm), although a lost head of a ram shot in 1882 in the East Kootenays of British Columbia and illustrated in Baillie-Grohman (1900, p. 145) measured 52½ in (133 cm) by 18½ in (47 cm) basal circumference.

To obtain maximum horn dimensions of Nelson's bighorns, I selected from the records all rams recorded as desert bighorns which were shot in Nevada (N = 37). Their average horn length was 35.4 in (90 cm) and the maximum horn length was 41.3 in (105 cm). The average horn base circumference of the first 30 rams listed was 14.2 ± 0.15 in (12.0–16.0 in) or 36 cm (30.4–40.5 cm). Clearly Nelson's bighorn rams are much smaller than their northern cousins. The horns of 6 Nelson's rams, 8–12 years old, measured by Welles and Welles were 25–33 in (63.5–84 cm) in length, 10–14 in (25–35 cm) in circumference, and weighed only 8.2–18.5 lb (3.7–8.4 kg), averaging 16.5 lb (7.5 kg).[2]

The average horn length of the 50 best Stone's rams on record came to 43.8 in (111 cm) with a maximum horn length of 51.6 in (131 cm). The basal horn circumference of the first 30 rams was 14.5 ± 0.11 in (13.8–15.8 in) or 38 cm (35–40 cm). As in bighorn and Nelson's sheep the true maximum for horn length will lie a few centimeters higher than indicated because Stone's rams also break horn tips, although not as frequently as bighorns. For Dall's rams horn length averaged 44.3 in (112 cm) with a maximum of 49.5 in (126 cm), while the horn circumferences of the first 30 rams listed in the *Records* was 13.7 ± 0.11 in (13.0–15.7 in) or 34.8 (33–40 cm). Since Dall's rams rarely broom horns, the true horn length maximum runs very close to 44.3 in (112 cm), whereas in Rocky Mountain bighorns it would be close to 50 in (127 cm) and in Nelson's rams about 42 in (107 cm).

Blood et al. weighed bighorn ram skulls and horns from various localities of the Canadian Rockies. Fully grown, mature rams (8 years or older) had on the average an upper skull and horn weight of 25 lb (11.3 kg); however, the spread was considerable, from 17 to 28 lb (7.7–13.1 kg). The largest head from the Banff National Park study area which I measured weighed 32 lb (14.5 kg) dry, with horn dimensions of 43.5 × 13.5 in (110 × 34 cm); the horns were unusually massive throughout their length. Clark (1964) reports a maximum horn weight of 44 lb (20 kg) for a bighorn. Large bighorn rams with horns of average record dimensions, 42.5 × 15.6 in (108 × 39.6 cm), would average about 30–32 lb (13–14 kg) in horn weight. Nelson's rams with horns of average record dimensions, 35.4 × 14.2 in (90 × 36 cm), would average about 20 lb (9 kg) in horn weight. Average record horns of Stone's rams, measuring 43.8 × 14.5 in (111 × 37 cm), would weigh 24–26 lb (10.9–11.8 kg), and the average horns of Dall's rams, measuring 44.3 × 13.7 in (112 × 35 cm), would weigh 19–21 lb (8.6–10 kg). These horn weights are estimates, based on my experience in weighing a good number of dry skulls and horns of Stone's and bighorn sheep, but data rather than estimates would be more desirable.

On the Banff study area 36 rams that died natural deaths at 8–17 years carried horns measuring on the average 92.6 ± 1.1 cm (36.5 in) in length (see table 15) while 32 of these averaged in basal circumference 36.6 ± 0.2 cm (14.3 in) with a range of 34–39.2 cm (13.3–15.5 in).

2. See also Bradley (1967) for an extensive analysis of *O. c. nelsoni* horns.

Plate 1. A Rocky Mountain bighorn ram. Note the stocky body, short legs, and sharply set off rump patch characteristic of American sheep. This is a 10-year-old class IV ram.

Plate 2. Urials and bighorn sheep have different preorbital glands: *a*, the gland in
mouflons and urials appears externally as a horizontal slit from which flows a waxy
substance; *b*, in bighorns it is a vertical, half-moon-shaped skinfold which projects
beyond the facial hair.

Plate 3. Nelson's rams. Note the *dalli*-like flare of the horns, the relatively small rump patch, and the complete stripe of dark fur connecting the tail with the dark body hair. These rams hide from a helicopter. (Photo courtesy of Jim Jett, Arizona Game and Fish Department.)

Plate 4. Ghost Mountain, the location where most observations were made during the Stone's sheep study. It contained small patches of primary sheep habitat. Gladys Lake in foreground.

Plate 5. McMillan Mountain, a wintering area of Stone's rams. It illustrates the rugged terrain favored by American sheep, as well as the extensive cover of small alpine fir typical of the study area. The gravel fan in the center was searched out by sheep and mountain goats in late fall; there they fed on the seed heads of cow parsnip.

Plate 6. A band of Stone's sheep from the lower Kechika River of British Columbia. Shown are an old ram, two adult ewes, a yearling ewe, and two lambs. The white spot behind the first ewe's shoulder is not an uncommon mark in Stone's sheep.

Plate 7. A 10-year-old Stone's ram. Note the distinct horn segments typical of thin-horn sheep, the grizzled front, and dark band across the nose, much as described for Siberian snow sheep. This is the typical dark ram common to the Cassiars.

Plate 8. A class IV Dall's ram from Sheep Mountain at Kluane Lake in the Yukon. The dark shading above the eyes and below the preorbital gland is due to dirt deposited by young rams horning his face.

Plate 9. The Palliser Range above Stoney Creek. The open slope in foreground was termed the *End* unit; adjacent to the left, beyond the first draw, is the beginning of the *Mid* unit.

Plate 10. Stone's sheep on patches of grassland formed after forest fires. Aspen and juniper are invading the old burn. Kechika River, British Columbia, November 1968.

Plate 11. The tag numbers of tagged bighorns could be read while the animals licked salt held in the observer's hand.

Plate 12. The skulls of an old Stone's ram (*left*) and a bighorn ram (*right*). The pointed horn cores typical of thinhorn sheep are shorter and taper more quickly.

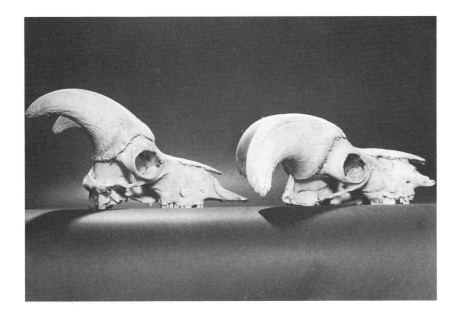

Plate 13. Six-week-old bighorn lamb.

Plate 14. Yearling female, about 19 months of age. Note the juvenile face and perfect, short horns. The dark area below the tail is formed from urine-soaked hair surrounding the vulva, which courting rams frequently taste.

Plate 15. In Dall's and Stone's sheep well-grown yearling rams in their second fall and winter are very hard to distinguish from adult females. The yearling ram is on the right.

Plate 16. A class I bighorn ram in June. The growth of the new, light horn sheath has lifted the old horn more than an inch above the hairline. This ram is 3 years old.

Plate 17. Bighorn ram 624, tagged as a lamb in 1960, photographed May 1968. The first two years of his horn growth has been broomed off, as is the rule for Palliser bighorn rams. Age 8 years.

Plate 18. Sheep on open, southwest-facing slope on which grasses form a dominant part of the flora. The opposite shady northeast-facing slope is characteristically grown over with conifers.

Plate 19. Bighorn rams at high elevation on a sparsely vegetated, wind-blasted ridge. This sheep habitat is found in Banff Park above 8,000 ft elevation. December 1964.

Plate 20. Sheep in May on well-vegetated slopes at 6,000 ft elevation, eating from a snow bank. Snow is the principal source of water for mountain sheep living in cold climates.

Plate 21. A group of six yearlings in early June gathering behind and following a 2-year-old female.

Plate 22. Rams follow the largest-horned ram in a band.

Plate 23. The stiff head-erect and ears-back posture of the alarmed sheep.

Plate 24. An alarmed mule deer assumes a posture similar to that of an alarmed sheep.

Plate 25. A group of young bighorn rams and ewes in the attention posture. Note large size of the Mount Norquay yearling rams compared to ewes. The yearlings are the three longest-horned sheep in picture.

Plate 26. A bighorn ewe horning a small aspen tree. The twisted twigs of the plant show evidence of previous horning.

Plate 27. Small pines were often chosen for horning by rams and in consequence sustained extensive damage.

Plate 28. Subordinate, senile female on left looks away from dominant as the latter approaches.

Plate 29. During the post-clash present, the subordinate ram may close his eyes.

The weight of such a head is about 24 lb (10.4 kg), of which 5–6 lb (2.2–2.7 kg) is the weight of the upper skull. For Stone's rams from Gladys Lake the horn weights of 5 rams older than 8 years averaged 17.5 lb, of which about 5 lb is the mass of the upper skull. The horn dimensions of a ram with such a horn and skull weight were 39.5 × 13.5 in. Although the average horn dimensions of my Stone's sheep and bighorn populations were far below the record average, the largest rams in both populations reached record dimensions; from 45 Stone's rams, 2 would place within the record average, as would 2 out of 36 measurable bighorn ram heads from Banff National Park.

Data on the horn dimensions of snow sheep are scarce. Heptner et al. (1961) report maximum horn dimensions for Kamchatka sheep as 43.2 in (111 cm) for length and 14.2 in (36 cm) in basal circumference. Clark (1964) in his patient search uncovered a good many measurements of Kamchatka sheep. Maximum horn length was 41.5 in (105 cm), maximum circumference at the horn base was 14.5 in (37 cm), while the largest head with horns measuring 41 in weighed only 15 lb. This is not surprising; Kamchatka sheep have horns which are thick at the base but taper rapidly toward the end. They are similar to the horns of Dall's sheep, but less massive and somewhat more wide spreading. Clark emphasized that the thin, long horn tips were not broken, and Heptner et al. made no mention of horn tip breakage, which is occasional in Dall's sheep, common among Stone's sheep, and the rule for all bighorns. Whereas the horns of Kamchatka sheep will average smaller in size than those of Dall's and Stone's sheep, this is not necessarily so for the sheep from the Stanovoi and Djugdjur ranges (*O. n. alleni*). The only photo I ever saw of a snow sheep was of a ram killed in the Djugdjur Mountains. It was a massive animal with heavily broomed thick horns, the image of a massive old Stone's ram. This animal had a pure white belly and large white trimming on the front legs. Heptner et al.'s description of *alleni* would fit for most Stone's sheep equally well. The study of snow sheep is likely to reveal some surprises yet.

On the Banff National Park study area, rams which died between 8 and 17 years of age had remarkably similar horn length. Table 15 shows that the longest horns were not carried by the oldest rams but by rams that died at average age. This is not surprising since rams with poor horn growth can be expected to reach old age, whereas rams with vigorous horn growth are not (chap. 10).

The growth rates of horns vary as much within populations as

TABLE 15

Horn lengths of bighorn rams found dead along the Palliser Range, Bare Mountain, Grassy Mountain, and Snowcreek Summit (In mm)

	Age (yrs)									
	7	8	9	10	11	12	13	14	15	17
	(N=3)	(N=3)	(N=5)	(N=5)	(N=5)	(N=8)	(N=4)	(N=3)	(N=2)	(N=1)
Average	889	906	873	907	918	962	969	933	918	1,015
Minimum	815	838	815	825	864	915	890	865	885	...
Maximum	955	965	925	1,030	975	1,105	1,040	1,015	952	...

among populations. Figure 5 shows horn growth rates of bighorn rams from two high quality Montana populations compared with those of bighorn rams from the Palliser Range. The Montana sheep are characterized by high growth rates of horns in the early years of life, which

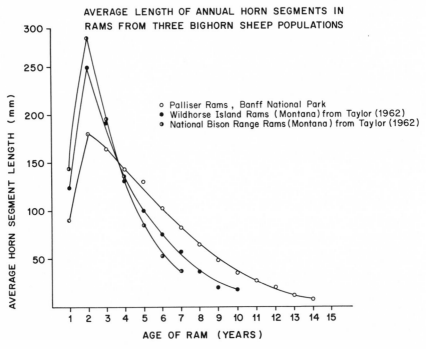

Fig. 5. In comparison to the Montana rams, the bighorn rams from the Palliser Range distributed their horn growth over the later rather than the earlier years of life. The Montana rams came from an expanding (●) and a captive population (◑); the Palliser rams (○) from a stable, low-quality population.

appears to be typical of expanding sheep populations of high quality but short life expectancy of rams. On the National Bison Range bighorn sheep appear to live with a superabundance of forage and hence mature rapidly and soon reach exceptionally large body size. The bighorn rams from Banff can be divided into those which died before average life expectancy and those that died after (fig. 6). The rams which were last to die had the poorer horn growth rate in their earlier years of life (see Geist 1966b). The same was shown for ibex by Nievergelt (1966a). Males from expanding ibex populations had a better horn growth and shorter life expectancy than males from stable populations. These are most important considerations in the evolution of mountain sheep as will be shown in chapter 11.

The skull. Skull dimensions of various races of bighorn and thinhorn sheep can be found in Cowan (1940), Baker and Bradley (1966), Bradley and L. R. Baker (1967), and for snow sheep in Heptner et al. (1961) and Cherniavski (1962a). Bighorns have the largest and widest skulls with the longest and thickest horn cores and a relatively large rostrum. Table 16 gives skull measurements of old bighorn rams found dead on the Banff study area. Snow sheep have smaller skulls, shorter and thinner horn bases, and short, small rostra. Skulls of thinhorn sheep are intermediate. Thinhorns have pointed horn bases which taper rapidly, whereas those of bighorns remain broad (plate 12). A detailed discussion of cranial differences between various races of North American sheep is given in Cowan (1940) and Bradley and L. R. Baker (1967). Berwick (1968) found that various populations of the race *canadensis* could vary greatly in skull dimensions. He, as well as Baker and Bradley (1966), showed that the skull of rams does not reach ultimate dimensions till the animal is 7–9 years of age, and in females 4–5 years. A discussion of the functional significance of the ram's skull structure is given in chapter 6.

Recently it was shown by Hemming (1967) that Dall's sheep from the Brocks Range of Alaska had an identical tooth eruption sequence as did the snow sheep which Cherniavski (1962b) studied on the Koryak highlands.[3] In these sheep the second premolar erupts after the third and fourth premolars. Taylor (1962) found that the premolars of the bighorn sheep he studied erupted in the sequence P_2, P_3, P_4, which was confirmed by Wishart (personal communication, 1968).

3. Bighorns may occasionally have upper canines. See Bradley and Allred (1966).

TABLE 16

Skull measurements (after Cowan 1940) of bighorn rams from the Cascade Valley, Banff National Park

	Sample size	Mean (mm)	Standard error of mean (mm)
Basilar L	9	272.0	$\pm$ 02.3
Nasal L	5	105.0	04.3
Nasal W	17	56.0	02.5
Orbital W	18	121.0	01.5
Zygomatic W	14	128.0	00.7
Maxillary W	17	89.7	01.0
Mastoid W	18	91.6	01.0
Palatal B (M3)	16	52.8	00.8
Palatal B (Pm2)	14	34.4	00.5
Postpalatal W	17	36.4	00.1
Palatal L	11	98.0	03.0
Upper molar L	18	82.0	00.9
Lower molar L	5	79.8	00.6
Prealveolar L	9	84.2	01.6
Postdental L	18	94.1	01.0
Basioccipital W	19	31.5	00.5
Premaxilla W	6	33.6	00.1
Length horn core	9	320.8	15.5
Horn core circumference	13	295.6	08.4
Horn spread	9	444.2	45.8

NOTE: Data courtesy of D. M. Shackleton.   L = length, W = width, B = breadth.

Taylor (1962) also found that the bighorns he studied shed their milk teeth and grew a permanent dentition at an earlier age than that reported typical by Cowan (1940) and Deming (1952). Whereas Cowan reported that bighorns had a permanent dentition by 48 months of age, Taylor found that his study animals had a complete dentition between 30 and 40 months of age. This discrepancy is easily explained. Cowan examined primarily the skulls of bighorns from native, and presumably stable populations, while Taylor's study animals originated from two small high-quality populations. Both the National Bison Range and Wildhorse Island populations lived below carrying capacity at the time of Taylor's study. The Bison Range sheep were in a fenced enclosure and held down in numbers. The Wildhorse Island population had been expanding and sheep from both locations were characterized by relatively large body size and rapid early horn growth. It appears from this that sheep which grow exceptionally well because of a favorable forage regime not only reach a large size and mature early, but also grow a permanent dentition earlier than sheep in stable or declining populations (see chap. 10). Thus Hemming (1967) found that Dall's sheep from the Brooks Range in Alaska had completed their dentition by 45–48 months of age, at the age indicated as typical by Cowan and by Deming. Bradley and Allred (1966) and Allred et al. (1966) showed that the second premolar was missing in a significant number of rams and ewes of Nelson's sheep. The condition was more prevalent among females. Similar studies are missing from other sheep races.

The coat. The differences in color and coat patterns of bighorn and Stone's sheep were given earlier when Stone's sheep were described. Northern bighorn sheep differ from southern desert sheep in having larger rump patches; the dark stripe of fur running from the tail mid-dorsally to the dark body fur tends to be complete in *nelsoni* and *californiana* but is usually broken in Alberta bighorns. A scrutiny of 95 bighorns from Banff park showed that in 70 the tail stripe had been lost or was partially interrupted; hence the rump patch is not usually bisected by the dark tail stripe. It almost always bisects the rump patch on Stone's sheep. Lydekker (1913) and Clark (1964) report that in Kamchatka sheep the rump patch is small, going no further than the root of the tail, while the tail is the same color as the body. These sheep are colored rather uniformly brown and like bighorns have a white muzzle. Their dark body hair may grade gradually into the white belly hair, which is also true for most bighorn rams and some Stone's rams, but not the females. The rump patch sizes of various sheep can be seen in figure 46.

Ears. Cowan (1940) noted that snow sheep appear to have shorter ears than thinhorn sheep. Heptner et al. (1961) report the ear length of Kamchatka sheep to be 9–9.5 cm for rams and 8–9 cm for ewes, which is the same as that for Stone's sheep. The longest ears are carried by the desert bighorns and the shortest by the northern races including thinhorn sheep.

SEX-AGE CLASSIFICATION OF SHEEP

Sheep were classified on the basis of horn size, body size, and sex into distinct classes, of which I recognized seven in the Stone's and Dall's sheep study and eight during the bighorn study. The classes are lambs, female yearlings, adult females, male yearlings, and adult rams of horn size classes I–IV (fig. 6). For Stone's sheep I combined classes I and II into a single class II, because 2½–3-year-old Stone's rams were not always quickly distinguishable from 3½–4-year-old rams. Such a classification is essential if variation in behavior due to sex or age is to be discovered. The bighorn sheep classes are arranged in order of resemblance in figure 6.

Lambs (L).   These are the smallest sheep in body and horn size, age 1 day to 1 year (plate 13). The lambs of Stone's and bighorn sheep are born mouse gray, except that Stone's lambs have a black tail. Cherniavski (1962*b*) gives an excellent description of newborn snow sheep from the Koryak highlands. These lambs appear to be similar in color to newborn Stone's lambs, being ash gray on the sides, dark gray on the neck, chest, and anterior parts of the front legs, and having a black tail and dark middorsal line. The belly, groins, rump, and dorsal margins of front legs and hind legs are white. Lambs shed the woolly juvenile coat between August and October and replace it with a coat similar to that of adults. At 6 months of age the Stone's and Dall's thinhorns and the Rocky Mountain bighorns that I studied had rather short horns compared to equal-age desert bighorn lambs as described by Hansen (1965). The lambs grow little between 6 and 12 months of age as is well illustrated by the data of Blood et al. (1970). In this, Rocky

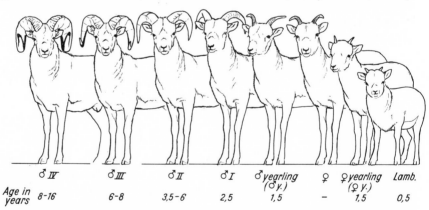

Fig. 6. The sex-age classes of bighorn sheep recognized in this study. Note that the animals form a cline in body and horn size and that the adult female is very similar in external appearance to the yearling ram. (Reprinted, by permission, from Geist, "On the interrelation of external appearance, social behaviour and social structure of mountain sheep," *Zs. Tierpsychol.* 25:199–215.)

Mountain bighorns and thinhorn sheep again differ from desert sheep, which appear to suffer no growth stoppage (Hansen 1965). During winter the lambs become lighter in color just like adults. The 11–13-month-old lambs are termed "yearling lambs" (see plate 21). This class was not differentiated by sex, since male and female are exceedingly similar in appearance. Lambs grow from 8–10 lb (3.6–4.5 kg) at birth to about 70 lb (31 kg) after 6 months of life when they are weaned and maintain this weight with little or no gain till the following spring (Blood et al.). It is likely that birth weights and growth performance will vary greatly between populations. The data by Blood et al. are representative of a better quality population than the one I studied in Banff National Park.

Yearling females (♀y). This class includes females 14–24 months of age (plate 14). They are larger than lambs in horn and body size but not as large as adult females, and they retain a juvenile short face. Their horns have usually perfect tips. Bighorn yearling females grow from about 60 lb (27.2 kg) to 110 lb (50 kg) in weight during their second year of life (Blood et al.), but the variation is great. A poorly developed female from the Palliser Range with a crippled front leg, weighed 50 lb (22.7 kg) at 23 months in May 1965, while a normally developed 24-month-old female, which was killed on the road, weighed 95½ lb (43 kg) in perfectly lean condition. Occasionally yearling females in good populations or in captivity become mature at 18 months of age (Woodgerd 1964; Deming 1955). There is danger of confusing exceptionally well developed yearling females with poorly developed yearling males.

Adult females (♀). This is the most common class of mountain sheep. The ewes reach their final adult proportions by 4–5 years of age, but even at 2½ years of age they differ little from older members of the class. Their horn growth is negligible during adult life and they maintain a constant appearance. Bighorn females from southern Alberta have an average weight of 159 lb (120–200) or 79 kg (54.5–91) (Blood et al.). I estimate that Stone's ewes average about 40 lb less on the Gladys Lake study area.

Yearling rams (♂y). This class, including males 14–24 months of age, is difficult to distinguish from adult females among Dall's, Stone's, and northern bighorn sheep, but not apparently among Nelson's bighorns

(Welles and Welles 1961; Hansen 1965). At 14 months of age males can be distinguished from equal-age females by larger body size and slightly longer and wider horns. The male continues to grow and in fall has reached a striking resemblance to adult females, at least in populations of normal or above normal quality. They are of similar size and weight as adult females (Blood et al.), have similar horn size, and carry a coat of identical color and distribution of white fur (plate 15). They differ in having slightly wider horn bases and more divergent horns. The hair on occiput and neck is slightly longer than that of females which gives the head a more chunky appearance, and their faces are a little more lamblike. In exceptionally well developed yearling rams the testes may be visible at 18 months of age, and they may participate in the rut. They differ behaviorally from females in using the ram urination posture, courting females and lipcurling over the urine of females, and using the low-stretch more frequently.

Class I rams.   These rams are 26–36 months old (plate 16). They differ from adult females and yearling rams by larger horns, and in normal populations equal or exceed adult females in body size (Blood et al.). Except for two class I rams I observed on Bare Mountain in the rut of 1966, all class I rams were sexually mature and participated in rutting activities. The testes of the two rams which were not yet mature were conspicuously smaller than those of normal class I rams. Class I rams are not yet markedly darker than females and their bellies are still white, although the white belly area appears to be decreasing. In a few rare cases a poorly developed ram 3–4 years of age was included in this class. In the Stone's sheep study, I included these rams with the next larger class.

Class II rams.   This class includes rams 3–6 years of age (see plate 38). The horns have formed over half but not three-fourths of an arc. Usually 6-year-old rams carried large enough horns to be included in the next larger class. The horn tips of class II rams are still complete and undamaged. These rams in bighorn sheep weigh about 180–200 lb (82–91 kg) live weight (Blood et al.); they are markedly larger than class I rams, but more lightly built and more tall-legged in appearance than older rams. It appears that such rams have reached nearly ultimate skeletal growth as indicated by hind foot growth (Blood et al.), but they still have more skull, horn, and body growth ahead.

Class III rams. These rams are 5–8 years of age, rarely 5 and exceptionally 9 (see plate 32). The horns form three-fourths of an arc. These are the "three-quarter curls." Their horn tips are often still intact, but show the first signs of splintering. The horn bases have reached nearly ultimate thickness, and the ram's facial features are similar to those of older rams. It appears as if the skull has also reached its ultimate size, although I suspect that it grows denser with age. These rams are close to their ultimate body weight, weighing in excess of 200 lb (91 kg) if they are bighorns from a good-quality population (Blood et al.). These rams are darker in body color than younger ones and have lost some or most of the white fur on the belly and the rear margins of their front legs. The muzzle is now clearly set off from the dark facial hair. These rams have almost reached behavioral maturation and they participate heavily in the rut, carrying in some populations a large part of the reproductive load. They fight more intensely with rams of equal size than do rams of different classes, and are more frequently engaged in dominance fights than other rams (chap. 7).

Class IV rams. These rams are usually 8 years of age (rarely 7 years) and older (plate 17). If the horn tips are still intact, they protrude well beyond eye level. If the horns are broomed, the broken tips must reach at least eye level if the ram is to be included in this class. The horns are heavy throughout their length and form a near perfect circle in side view. This category also included old, heavy-horned rams whose horns were badly broken. These rams have reached ultimate skull and body size, external characteristics, and are fully mature behaviorally and psychologically. In body size they are somewhat heavier than class III rams, but the difference is not conspicuous. Old rams, exceeding 13–14 years, may develop a sagging belly and back. These are the darkest rams, and often no white hair is left on the belly, front legs, or occasionally even the lower hind legs. These rams are the leaders of bands, do most of the breeding, and are the most dominant sheep. A comparable slow maturation and change in external appearance has been described for wild goats (*Capra aegagrus*) by Schultze-Westrum (1963) and is probably also true for ibex.

DATA COLLECTING

Data collecting had several objectives. First the behavior patterns of sheep had to be described and documented on movie film, still photographs, and occasionally by means of a sketch. The behavior patterns were to be recorded quantitatively so that the reasons for behavioral differences between classes and races of sheep could be investigated. The migratory and home range characteristics of sheep were to be investigated; individually known animals were to be képt track of. The behavioral adaptations of sheep to their physical environment or habitat were to be investigated, as was the population dynamics of sheep.

At first it was necessary to determine which actions of sheep were behavior patterns to be documented and recorded quantitatively. This became evident after observing sheep for several weeks. Filming was not begun until spring 1962, almost one year after I began with observations. Documentation on movie film and recording behavior patterns quantitatively require different techniques. In the first case one has to get close to sheep and remain with them without disturbing the animals while one is operating and handling cameras, lenses, and tripods or moving about. To be effective one must habituate the animals to one's presence. In the second case, I attempted to get far enough from the animals so that I remained unnoticed and followed them with the aid of a spotting scope.

When collecting quantitative data, I selected a locality 600–2,000 yards from the sheep which allowed a maximum of terrain to be viewed, so that I could follow the movements of sheep visually for hours. At first a tripod-mounted, 25-power single barrel spotting scope was used, but it caused eye strain and was replaced by a 15-power double spotting scope. This scope proved to be comfortable during long use and I made observations from the valley floor. During my second winter with Stone's sheep, I converted the cabin into an observatory, which allowed far more efficient gathering of data since there was no discomfort during cold weather. Previously, at $-40°$ F it was difficult to keep my extremities warm when sitting behind the scope; the glass fogged frequently and once fogged could not be rubbed clean; and the binoculars and scope froze and could not be focused. In addition, I could not write down observations fast enough. This changed once I observed from the cabin, which was located within 1,600 yards of one wintering area of sheep and within 800 yards of another.

The following was recorded: (1) the number and class of sheep under observation within a band; (2) after each 5-minute observation period, the number of feeding, standing, moving, and resting individuals; and (3) every interaction between two sheep. The last included noting: (a) the class of sheep initiating the interactions, and the class of sheep it interacted with, (b) the kind and sequence of behavior patterns used by both sheep (see chap. 6), (c) the number and classes of sheep which were in the immediate vicinity of the sheep which initiated the interaction (to determine what class of sheep the initiating sheep preferred), (d) the special situation, for instance, if the interaction took place in a huddle or in the presence of an estrous female.

Each of the social interactions so recorded was numbered and later transferred to a computer card. On it were recorded date, number of the interaction, class of sheep initiating, class of sheep chosen, numbers of sheep of other classes present, the first and second behavior pattern performed by the initiating sheep, the number of behavior patterns of each kind performed by the smaller and by the larger sheep during the interaction, the response (withdrawal or not) of each sheep to being kicked or mounted, whether the female urinated or not, whether she urinated before or after the courting ram reached her, whether or not the ram lipcurled, and the special situation.

In recording behavior I adopted a shorthand form. By breaking down behavior into patterns and recording these, subjective evaluation is reduced to deciding whether or not a pattern had occurred. I did not record if a ram had "lost" or "won" a fight, but only which behavior pattern he had used and in what order he used them. The decision whether he had "lost" or "won" would come from the frequencies and types of behavior patterns used.

At first it was not easy to decide with some behavior patterns when a pattern began and when it ceased. For instance, the low-stretch is a long-lasting display of horns. If a ram displayed first to one ram, then changed orientation and displayed to another, had he performed one low-stretch or two? I counted it as two. If the ram followed a female in a low-stretch, held his display steadily, but stopped and advanced n times, I counted $n + 1$ low-stretches. Should the ram interrupt the display even for a moment and resume it, I counted two displays.

Horning, rubbing, and nuzzling presented similar problems. If a ram horned another, but interrupted this activity n times, I counted $n + 1$ hornings, but if he continued horning uninterrupted it was counted only as one horning irrespective of how long it lasted. In this study the temporal differences between behavior patterns had to be ignored since the sophisticated machinery necessary for such recording was not at hand.

The second method of collecting data was to get close to sheep to photograph or to look and listen for behavior not noticeable at long distance. When filming few notes were taken and these were excluded from the quantitative data to counter the argument that my presence adversely affected the behavior of sheep (I detected no such effects). Such notes were used to describe various behavior patterns more accurately.

On the Stone's sheep study area I used a pair of white overalls and a white towel wrapped around my head when approaching sheep or mountain goat. The camera was mounted on the tripod and held away from the sheep. I often walked on "all fours," which in the steep Cassiars was not an uncommon means of locomotion even when not stalking sheep. It was best to climb up out of sight of the animals and then approach them from the top. Periodically I sat down and waited in full view till the animals paid little attention and advanced again. It was important to move slowly, to pause, to avoid hasty movements, and to have the wind blowing from the sheep toward me. This method works with mountain goats only if one does not show oneself completely and approaches from the top. Sheep habituated to my presence, but mountain goats showed no signs of doing so. However, it has been shown by Holroyd (1967) that mountain goats will habituate to humans.

The migratory habits were investigated by recording the number and classes of sheep on various mountains during frequent census trips and by noting the movements of individually known mountain sheep. At Gladys Lake, 36 Stone's sheep were recognized individually by differences in coat patterning, color, and horn shape (see fig. 3). Each sheep was identified by a letter (e.g., D-ram) and a record was kept of where and when it migrated.

In Banff National Park sheep were recognized either by the number of their tags or by their personal features, one method as reliable as the other at short distance. At long distance, however, I found bighorns more difficult to identify than Stone's sheep, and hence recorded the locality of a known individual only when I climbed about on the range and met it. The home range investigations are reported in chapters 3 and 4, where methods of investigation are discussed further.

Frequent trips along the valleys, during which all mountain sheep seen were classified, provided some of the data on population dynamics of sheep. Second, the gorges were searched for the remains of dead sheep whose horns provided data on the growth of the sheep and the age at death. The age of rams was determined by counting horn segments, a method whose reliability could be demonstrated by tagged sheep (Geist 1966c). The horn segments of Stone's and Dall's sheep (plates 7 and 8) are much more clearly visible than those of bighorns (plates 1 and 17). On a clear day without mirage, using the tripod-mounted, 25-power spotting scope, the horn rings on Stone's rams could be seen as far away as 600 yards. One can usually age rams less than 8 years old accurately at 400 yards. Since horn segments decrease rapidly in length after 7 years of age, the horn rings of older rams tend to be below the hairline on the head or they are camouflaged by deep grooves on the basal part of the horn. Even on old rams a fairly accurate estimate of age could be achieved by this method as is shown by table 5.

The horns of dead rams found in the field yielded the following data: length of horn, circumference of horn at the base, length of each annual horn segment measured from groove to groove along the frontolateral keel or ridge of the horn, and age of ram at death. Females could not be aged accurately by their horns, frequently because the lower part of the horn sheath was weathered and frayed. Moreover, there are indications that females may not lay down an externally visible horn segment when old and the horn segment count reveals only minimum age. A female that was tagged as an adult at Lake Minnewanka died ten years after tagging; yet at death she had only ten externally visible horn segments.[4]

The manner in which habitat adaptations and the temperature characteristics of a mountain sheep range were investigated is discussed in chapter 9.

4. The skull of this female and that of a bighorn ram, age known, are deposited with the Osteological Museum of the University of British Columbia, Vancouver.

3 Home Ranges and Migrations

INTRODUCTION

The home range is defined by Calhoun (1963) as the area to which an animal confines itself in its day-to-day activities. This definition, useful for small, short-lived mammals, has shortcomings if applied to mountain sheep or to moose as Houston (1968) discovered. These animals live not in one home range but in several seasonal ones. Moreover, rams change their home range, and therefore their migratory patterns, when they leave the female group which raised them and join ram bands instead. The ram's pattern of movement during his first two to three years of life is different from that of his later years.

The number of seasonal home ranges a sheep may occupy may be as high as six or seven if it is a ram or a maximum of four if it is a ewe. A minority of sheep have as few as two seasonal home ranges, the classical winter and summer home ranges. The home ranges can be anywhere from a half mile to twenty miles or more removed from each other and are usually separated by at least one deep, timbered gorge. They vary seasonally in size. In midwinter when deep snow fills the gorges and covers most of the slopes, sheep rarely roam over a larger area than a half mile across, but in spring, summer, and fall, they roam over most of the mountain block they happen to be on. Even when snow is no longer a hindrance, individuals or groups of sheep confine themselves to specific regions of the mountain; a home range is only a measure of an animal's habits, not an area with rigid boundaries, although for convenience' sake we treat it as such.

Sheep are loyal to their home ranges and return to them in the same season year after year. Occasionally deep snow prevents rams from performing the expected movements, or a young ram fails to appear where he was found the preceding year because he followed some old ram elsewhere. However, on the average about 77% of the rams will be where they were found a year ago. Sheep have in rare instances immigrated from their accustomed ranges, for reasons largely unknown, but

62

occasionally such a move has coincided with a catastrophic deterioration of the habitat. Normally one observes on a given mountain different sheep at different seasons of the year, but the same sheep at the same season in different years. The females in particular tend to live in "home range groups" in which a band shares one home range; for rams this concept is less useful.

The yearly migratory cycle of rams can be described as follows: sometime in late September rams appear on their fall, or pre-rut, home ranges. They gather in large bands, stay 2–5 weeks, then disband and disperse to different rutting grounds, where they remain till the end of December. Thereafter some rams return to winter on their pre-rut home range, some rams move to a distinct midwinter home range, while most young rams and a few old ones remain with the females on the rutting area, the latter being a wintering area of ewes. When the snow cover grows hard in late winter, from mid-March on, the rams not already on the former fall concentration area begin to return. Almost all rams which visit the fall concentration area are also found there in spring, but some additional rams also show up, so these animals have a separate spring range. After the usually massive spring concentration, rams disperse to their summer ranges, but may also move first to a salt lick and remain there for a few weeks. Therefore, a ram may have at the most a pre-rut range, a rutting range, a midwinter range, a late winter/spring range, a salt lick range, and a summer range. Not all groups of rams will follow this movement pattern, but the major ram bands on both my Stone's sheep and bighorn study areas did.

Ewes tend to arrive later on wintering areas and depart earlier than rams, spending 240–68 days on wintering areas compared to 271–303 days for rams. They remain most of the winter on the home ranges they occupy in fall. Once the snow cover hardens sufficiently to support their weight some females move to a separate late winter/spring range. Some give birth on the wintering area, while others move off to separate lambing areas. Hence a ewe may have a winter home range, a spring range, a lambing range, and a summer range.

It is commonly assumed that mountain sheep make two major movements a year, one to the wintering area and one to the summer range. This is a half-truth. There are five major periods in the year when sheep move long distances: (1) late September, early October—rams and ewes move to the wintering areas (pre-rut home ranges in the case of rams); (2) last week in October, first week in November—rams move to their rutting grounds; (3) last half of December, first week in January—

rams move from their rutting grounds; (4) late March, April—rams
and ewes move to late winter/spring home ranges; (5) late May, June,
beginning of July—females move to lambing areas, rams move to
salt licks, then rams, barren females, and juveniles move to the summer
ranges, usually in late June, early July.

My observations of individually known rams reveal one, at first
puzzling, feature of the home range patterns of rams: the home ranges
are laid out contrary to efficiency and logic. What sense was there in
the annual movement of bighorn ram 303 from Palliser Range 15 miles
to Bare Mountain where he spent the rut? This ram left the females
he lived with on the Palliser Range; he ignored the female band on
Grassy Mountain only a half mile from the Palliser Range and the
females living two miles away on the Cascade Range just across from
the Palliser. After the rut, ram 303 moved right back to his Palliser
pre-rut range, crossing the Panther River and climbing over 15 miles
of high, rugged mountain country. Yet, this kind of action, where rams
move past or through several female groups before reaching a particular
group of females, is not the exception but the rule. Of 16 known
Stone's rams living with females on Sanctuary Mountain, 12 left to rut
elsewhere. Of 48 bighorn rams, 40 left the Palliser Range and its females
to rut elsewhere, while a set of strange rams took their place. Rams
evidently do not establish home ranges to serve expediency; rather,
they inherit them from older rams they happen to follow in their
younger years. Once a ram forms the habit of moving at a specific
season to a specific locality he sticks to it. This is the most plausible
explanation of the home range idiosyncrasies of sheep. Females usually
inherit their home range pattern from the ewe band in which they were
born and raised (chap. 4).

METHODS OF INVESTIGATION
The home range and migration characteristics of sheep can be investigated directly by observing individually recognizable sheep, noting the
localities they occupy at various seasons and their dates of arrival and
departure, or indirectly by recording the seasonal fluctuations of sheep
on the areas. For the latter recording, the wintering areas are particularly suitable since sheep remain here for a maximum of 303 days, or
10 months, of the year. I studied such wintering areas in the Cassiar
Mountains in 1961/62 and in Banff National Park in 1964/65, and
simultaneously gathered data on known rams and ewes.

In Banff National Park a census was made of sheep every second or third day on the Palliser Range and Grassy Mountain, two separate but adjacent wintering areas. Figure 7 illustrates schematically their position. The west slopes of the Palliser Range from Stoney Creek $3\frac{1}{2}$ miles north to the third ridge past the elk trap constituted the first wintering area. This range was divided into three major census units.

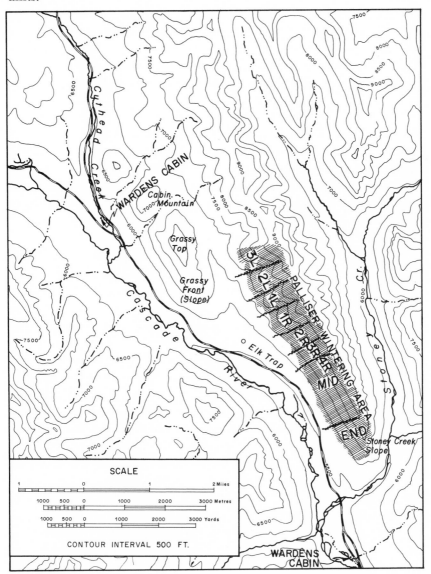

Fig. 7. Diagram of census units dividing the Palliser Range.

The northern seven ridges, each separated from the other by an avalanche gorge, was the first unit. These grassy ridges projected from the rugged cliff mass of the range (plate 9). The northernmost of these ridges, being the third left from the elk trap, was termed third left or 3L. The last ridge, lying to the right of the elk trap, was termed fourth right or 4R. Thus the seven ridges were called 3L, 2L, 1L, 1R, 2R, 3R, 4R. South from 4R stretched a long grassy slope that fell off steeply from the cliffs. This second census unit was termed *Mid*. It was about one mile long and terminated in a grassy knoll that dropped off to Stoney Creek. The grassy knoll was termed *End* and represented the last unit. The Palliser wintering area was about 3.7 miles (6 km) long from 3L to *End* and was an almost continuous piece of sheep habitat.

The second wintering area was Grassy Mountain. It was a huge ridge that rose sharply from the floor of the Cascade Valley and had its own population of sheep. It was also divided into three census units. The open, south-facing grassy slope was termed *Front*, the steep, rugged west slope with good sheep habitat in its upper reaches was termed *Top*, and a small mountain behind Grassy and separated by a very narrow gorge was termed *Cabin*.

Census counts of sheep were always made from the same localities along the road running parallel to the Palliser Range and Grassy Mountain. This insured that the area of mountainous terrain scrutinized remained constant and that variations in sheep counts were not due to variations in the size of area censused.

During each census the number and classes of sheep were recorded by census unit and, in the case of the Palliser Range, by the ridge. From March 1965 onward, the number of sheep on open, grassy slopes as well as in the cliffs was recorded separately. The fluctuations of sheep numbers on the Palliser wintering area is shown in figure 8. For each point the number of rams or ewes recorded in 6–8 census trips in two weeks was averaged. The fluctuations of ram and ewe numbers on Grassy Mountain are shown in figure 9.

On the Stone's sheep study area only Sanctuary Mountain, a wintering and concentration area of rams, was divided into census units. These were ecological units, based on terrain characteristics and elevation. The grassy slopes below 4,800 ft elevation, the steep cliff regions between 4,800 and 6,000 ft elevation, and a rubble slope above 6,000 ft elevation comprise the three units. None of the wintering areas were as large as those on the Banff study area.

Stone's sheep, unlike bighorn sheep, were easily recognized at a long

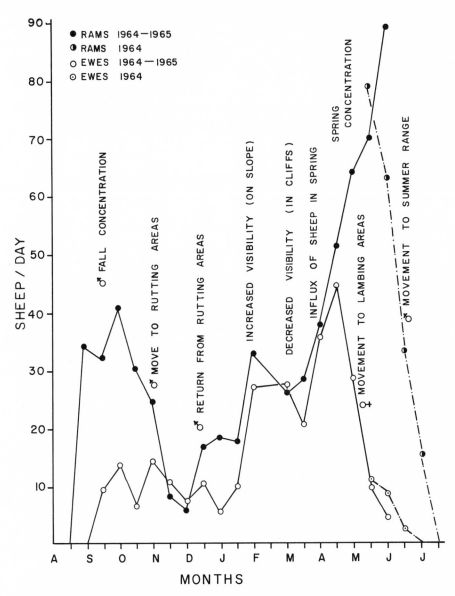

Fig. 8. The temporal occupation pattern of the Palliser Range by bighorn rams and ewes.

distance, thus making it a simple matter to record when known rams and ewes appeared, moved, or disappeared from the study area. My attention was focused primarily on the rams and, unfortunately, in

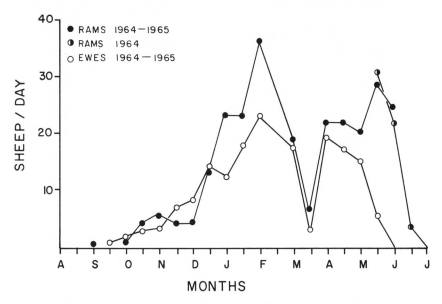

Fig. 9. The temporal occupation pattern of the adjacent Grassy Mountain by sheep.

this pioneering study I paid less attention to the ewes. During the bighorn study I did not find that I could consistently recognize individuals at a long distance, although at a short distance this was possible and reliable; so I recorded which known, usually tagged, sheep were present on the range whenever I climbed to them. Since my purpose during those visits was to document behavior patterns on film, I only noted in my records which ram or ewe made its appearance and the date of my last seeing it. Climbing various mountains and watching for known sheep allowed me to document where known individuals went and where I could expect to see them and check on them in successive years. I used the indirect and direct method to study home range and migration characteristics of sheep to supplement each other.

OCCUPATION OF WINTERING AREAS
Dates of arrival and departure of sheep. On all three study areas, in the Cassiars, at Kluane Lake, and in Banff National Park, the first sheep to arrive and stay on the wintering area came in September or early October. A few lone sheep or small bands passed through the wintering area earlier but did not occupy it. The last sheep to leave the wintering areas moved by the end of June. Specific dates for three wintering areas in the Cassiars and two at Banff are shown in table 17. On

TABLE 17

Arrival and departure dates of sheep bands on five wintering areas

Location	Fall arrival		Spring departure	
	♀	♂	♀	♂
Stone's				
Ghost Mt.	29 S	rut	18 Je	...
Sanctuary Mt.	14 O	2 O	20 Je	30 Je
Cliff Mt.	16 O	rut	...	...
Bighorn				
Palliser R.	22 S	6 S	18 Je	8 Jl
Grassy Mt.	27 S	8 S	25 My	20 Je

wintering areas occupied by large rams as well as ewes, the rams arrived earlier than ewes and departed later. On wintering areas of ewes (i.e., Ghost Mountain in the Cassiars, and Sheep Mountain at Kluane Lake), the rams arrived for the rut from late October onward; most rams older than 3 years left by the beginning of January and the rest by spring, while the ewes remained. Sheep stayed the greatest part of the year on the wintering area; ewes stayed 240–63 days and rams 271–303. They arrived before snow covered the ground uniformly and left long after it melted in spring.

Movement to wintering areas. The movements of sheep to their wintering areas are best described as slow drifts along mountain ranges, interrupted by hasty crossings of valleys. I first noticed this drift in fall 1962 when observing Stone's sheep return to Sanctuary Mountain and documented it later for bighorn sheep returning to the Palliser Range. Since the latter was subdivided into census units the advance of rams and ewes along the range could be recorded (see table 18). In 1964 rams appeared on the northern rim of the Palliser Range wintering area in the first two weeks of September. From 152 rams sighted between 6 and 16 September, 46% were on the northernmost ridge. Between 17 and 29 September, most rams shifted to the next ridge; 52% of 222 rams sighted were seen there. The table shows that rams and ewes

TABLE 18

Distribution of bighorn rams and ewes on the Palliser Range

Period		3L	2L	1L	1R	2R	3R	4R	Mid	End	Total sightings
6–16 Sept	♂	(46%)	14%	8.5%	7%	6.5%	0	0	14%	4%	152
	♀	0	0	0	0	0	0	0	0	0	0
17–29 Sept	♂	13	(52)	23.5	7	1.5	0	0	2.5	0.5	222
	♀	[100]	0	0	0	0	0	0	0	0	66
1–11 Oct	♂	25	(37)	11.5	6	0.5	4.5	2.5	0	13	245
	♀	5	[40]	21	18.5	6.5	8.5	0.5	0	0	81
17–31 Oct	♂	21	19	(29)	16.5	2.5	0	0	2.5	9.5	239
	♀	0	0	16	[41]	39	0	0	0	4	49
1–15 Nov	♂	24[a]	10.5	6.5	2.3	5.5	2.3	0	17	(32)	112
	♀	0	0	2	0	0	0	0	[72]	26	57
19–29 Nov	♂	0	0	2	0	0	23	4	23	(48)	49
	♀	0	0	0	0	0	26	1	21	[46]	65

Notes: Parentheses enclose the highest concentration of rams for each period; brackets enclose the highest concentration of ewes for each period.

Distance 3L to End = 3.7 miles.

[a] For the first period in November there was also a high concentration of rams at the southern end of the range (3L).

formed floating centers of activity which moved south along the range at a slow rate. In the first week of November, the rams separated into two groups, one continuing south while the other reversed and went north. Hence two centers of activity were recorded in that time period. When I returned in the first days of November in 1966, the same phenomenon had occurred; one group of rams was moving north and one had reached the southern tip of the Palliser wintering area, the Stoney Creek slope (*End*). It can also be seen in table 18 that the females came a little later than the rams and that the activity center formed by females drifted down the Palliser and arrived on the Stoney Creek slope by the end of November.

In contrast to the slow progress along the wintering area, rams moving to their rutting grounds walked rapidly and determinedly, as would sheep during an unseasonal return to their wintering area if surprised by a snowstorm while departing (Wishart 1958). Departure from the wintering areas is also leisurely.

Distribution of rams and ewes. Large rams and ewes tend to stay on separate wintering areas and if they do winter together may prefer different parts of the same area. The Palliser wintering area exemplified this well. Rams preferred the northern end and ewes the southern end of the wintering area as can be seen in table 19. This preference remained throughout the winter and from year to year.

TABLE 19

Distribution of bighorn rams and ewes on the Palliser wintering area between January and April 1964

	Census unit									Total sightings
	3L	2L	1L	1R	2R	3R	4R	Mid	End	
Rams	1.6%	9.5%	32.8%	15.2%	4.0%	20.2%	4.8%	7.3%	4.6%	1,219
Ewes	0	0	0.1	1.0	0.5	4.0	0.7	40.2	53.5	971

On Grassy Mountain rams and ewes moved over a common wintering area in separate bands, but there was less preference for a particular area by either sex. Between 1 January and 1 March the following distribution was recorded: *Front* was used mainly by rams (from 318 sightings, 97% were rams); *Top* was used mainly by ewes (from 503 sightings, only 31% were rams); *Cabin* was used equally little by both sexes (from 176 sightings, 60% were rams). Between 16 April and 15 May the ewes moved more frequently onto the open, south-facing *Front* slope. From 162 sightings, 62% were ewes compared to 3% ewes in midwinter.

On the Stone's sheep study area during late winter 1961/62 segregation by sexes was not complete, but nearly so. On Ghost Mountain there were about 30 sheep, including 2 rams over 3 years of age. On Sanctuary there were 11 rams plus 2 ewes, 3 yearling females, 1 yearling ram, and 2 lambs. On Shady and Cliff mountains there were 3 rams, and on Lupin Hill 2 females and 1 lamb.

Fluctuations in number. On no wintering area that I studied did the number of sheep remain constant all winter. There were predictable, marked numerical changes which coincided with major movements by sheep. Figures 8 and 9 show the fluctuations of ram and ewe numbers on the Palliser and Grassy Mountain wintering areas. There was one major concentration of rams on the Palliser Range in fall and a much larger one in late spring; during the rut only a few rams were present. One can recognize the seasons of movements: rams moved onto the range in September, in late December, and in late March, April, and May. They moved out in late October and beginning of November and in late June. The apparent increase in number of rams in February and decline in March are not changes in population size but visibility; during soft, deep snow conditions (February) sheep moved onto the open slopes and became highly visible, but when the snow crusted over hard and sheep moved into the cliff terrain (March) they became less visible. That these major fluctuations were caused by movement to and from the range was evident not only from the sighting of migrating sheep, but also from my records of individually recognizable sheep.

I recorded an almost identical fluctuation of sheep in the Stone's sheep study area on Sanctuary Mountain. Rams concentrated here in fall and again in spring, with the spring concentration being almost twice as large as that in the fall. In 1961, 12 out of 17 rams left Sanctuary in November to rut elsewhere; 6 of them returned in late December and early January; then no more rams came till 18 March. From that date onward rams arrived throughout April and May until 24 rams had gathered by 24 May. They were last seen on 30 June and did not return till October.

The fluctuations in numbers of bighorn ewes on the Palliser Range and Stone's ewes on Sanctuary Mountain were also similar. Figure 8 shows ewe numbers on the Palliser Range. On Sanctuary Mountain only one old Stone's ewe, her lamb, and a female yearling were present during early and midwinter. In April a second female with lamb joined her. On 4 April, most of the Ghost Mountain females reappeared after being absent since the rut; more females followed. Unlike the Palliser Range bighorn ewes, the Ghost and Sanctuary Stone's ewes gave birth to lambs on the wintering area.

Sheep numbers do not fluctuate in the same pattern on all wintering areas. On Grassy Mountain (fig. 9) there were no concentrations of rams in fall. No conspicuous increase in numbers occurred from the end of the rut onward; the fluctuations in numbers of sheep seen in February and March correlate with those on the Palliser Range and again appear to be the result of changes in visibility.

After considering the home range and migration patterns of sheep it will be apparent that the fluctuation pattern of sheep on wintering areas differs between ram and ewe winter ranges and that these are not predictable a priori on any range.

SEASONAL MIGRATIONS

There are five major periods of movements for rams. The following data on the dates and duration of migration periods were obtained from individually known Stone's rams in 1961 and 1962. I could not get data on the dispersal of rams from Sanctuary in early summer.

1. Rams return to Sanctuary: fall 1962, 12 rams, first arrival 2 October, last arrival 30 October.
2. Rams leave Sanctuary for rutting areas: fall 1961 and 1962 combined, 18 rams, first departure 27 October, last departure 15 November.
3. Rams return to Sanctuary after rut: fall 1961 and 1962 combined, 16 rams, first arrival 16 December, last arrival 12 January.
4. Spring movement of rams to Sanctuary: spring 1962, 15 rams, first arrival 18 March, last arrival 24 May.

Rams left and returned to Sanctuary in 1961 and 1962 on nearly the same dates. For movement no. 2 above the data break down as follows: in 1961—9 rams, mean date 3 November; in 1962—9 rams, mean date 8 November. For movement no. 3 above: 1961—8 rams, mean date 31 December; 1962—8 rams, mean date 26 December.

I obtained for the same Stone's rams the dates of movement to and from the rutting areas in consecutive years (table 20). Taking only rams which returned at once after the rut to their separate wintering areas one gets 11 pairs of dates. The discrepancy between departure or arrival dates in consecutive years varies from 0 to 11 days, and averages 5.7. Two rams (D and E, table 20) returned from the rut on exactly the same date in 1961 and 1962. (Since I was absent from the study area in early October 1961, the first sightings of known rams in 1961 are not directly comparable with their first sightings in 1962. Nevertheless, the data indicate that rams return at much the same dates in consecutive years to their fall range, a conclusion also reached by Spencer [1943].)

Observations in 1966 indicated that the Palliser bighorn rams moved to and returned from the rutting grounds at the same time as in 1964. However, as figure 8 indicates, movements in late spring and early summer are less accurately timed. Furthermore, rams from Grassy Mountain left earlier than their counterparts on the adjacent Palliser Range, but the ewes left at similar times.

The foregoing data suggest that the accuracy of the rut movements by rams is related to the accurate timing of the rut itself (see chap. 7),

TABLE 20

Dates of movements of individually known Stone's rams to and from Sanctuary Mountain

Name of ram	Age[a] (yrs)	Appears on pre-rut area in		Moves to rut area in		Returns after the rut of	
		1961	1962	1961	1962	1961	1962
C	8	26 Oct	9 Oct	4 Nov	10 Nov	13 Apr 62	....
D	13	16 Oct	9 Oct	27 Nov	8 Nov	28 Dec	28 Dec
E	9	14 Nov	9 Oct	14 Nov	4 Nov	30 Dec	30 Dec
G	8	26 Oct	2 Oct	....	X	30 Dec	X
H	7	....	14 Oct	....	X	6 Apr 62	X
J	6	16 Oct	2 Oct	....	....	22 Dec	26 Dec
L	5	16 Oct	....	15 Nov	....	31 Dec	....
LT	5	16 Oct	14 Oct	X	10 Nov	28 Apr 62	16 Dec
O	6	16 Oct	30 Oct	30 Oct	10 Nov	7 May 62	....
P	7	4 Sep	9 Oct	7 Nov	4 Nov	28 Dec	18 Dec
R	5	....	30 Oct	....	12 Nov	7 May 62	....
S	9	24 Oct	2 Oct	27 Oct	3 Nov	7 May 62	16 Dec
SO	8	....	14 Oct	....	12 Nov	17 May 62	30 Dec
Fc	12	28 Oct	....	1 Nov	....	11 Jan 62	....
F	7	....	....	27 Oct	....	18 Mar 62	....
M	8	....	....	....	....	9 Jan 62	12 Jan 63

NOTES: X indicates that the animal did not move that season and remained on the area.
[a] Age in 1962 is given for all rams except L, Fc, and F, for which age in 1961 is given.

but that the dates of late winter, spring, and summer movements are less predictable. It may be that the annual cycle of rams is synchronized by the timing of the rut, and events outside the rut, except lambing, are less accurately timed. However, this hypothesis must await further work on the timing of sheep movements before it can be verified or rejected.[1] Ewes are almost certainly synchronized in their behavior by lambing.

SEASONAL HOME RANGES

A seasonal home range is an area to which an animal confines itself between two seasonal migrations and which it occupies at the same time in successive years. By definition, an animal which has one seasonal home range must have at least one other some distance away. Why not consider the area over which a sheep roams in its yearly cycle as one

1. Confirmed by a study of R. Petocz during the winter of 1968/69.

home range? I reject this for the same reason as I would the view that a man who dwells in summer in a cottage and in winter in a city mansion lives in only one house year round.

How many seasonal home ranges can we recognize for mountain sheep? For rams the maximum is: (1) the fall or pre-rut home range, (2) the rutting ground or rut home range, (3) the midwinter home range, (4) the late winter/spring home range (1–4 on wintering areas), (5) the salt lick home range, and (6) the summer home range (5 and 6 off wintering areas). For ewes there may be: (1) the winter home range, (2) the late winter/spring home range, (3) the summer home range, and (4) the lambing home range (tentative). Not every ram and ewe possesses every one of these home ranges, but a few individuals do. Most sheep stay for several seasons on one area; but all sheep I studied had at least two seasonal home ranges, the classic summer and winter home ranges. The evidence for the existence of these various seasonal home ranges was obtained from observations of individually known sheep. Let us look first at the Stone's rams from Sanctuary Mountain.

1. Of 16 rams which arrived in October, 4 remained all winter and spring on Sanctuary; so these rams had one winter home range and at least one summer range.

2. In 1961 and 1962, 12 and 11 rams respectively left Sanctuary to rut elsewhere. Of these, 6 and 7 respectively returned right after the rut to Sanctuary Mountain and remained till late spring. Hence these rams had two winter home ranges plus their summer home ranges off the wintering area.

3. Of the 12 rams which departed in fall 1961, 6 returned in April and May 1962. These rams were absent from the rutting range after the rut, going elsewhere in midwinter. Therefore these rams had the same fall and spring home range but a rutting home range different from the midwinter range. Hence they had three winter home ranges plus their summer ranges.

   I never saw any of the missing Sanctuary rams on their midwinter home range, but I did see other Stone's and bighorn rams occupy such an area. They arrived on their midwinter home range in successive years after the rut and left in late winter once the snow grew hard enough to permit easy dispersal.

4. Seven rams came in late winter and spring 1962 to Sanctuary Mountain. I had not seen them the preceding fall and winter;

nor did I see them the following one. Since rams are very loyal to their home ranges, I conclude that these rams came to Sanctuary only in late winter and spring and hence had a distinct late winter/spring home range. I did not remain till spring 1963 and as a result could not check if these rams returned to Sanctuary when expected.

Observations on tagged and tame bighorn rams in Banff National Park revealed nothing new in principle. I observed rams in winter 1964/65 and early winter 1966 on the Palliser Range:

1. Seven known rams remained from September till June on the wintering area.
2. Three known rams came only in fall.
3. Seven known rams came only in late winter and spring and stayed till early summer.
4. Twenty-seven known rams which were present in fall came also in spring.
5. An unknown number of shy, strange rams came only during the rut.

These observations from the wintering areas demonstrate the existence of the following home ranges for rams: pre-rut, rut, midwinter, late winter/spring.

I inferred the salt lick home range by observing bighorn rams from Grassy Mountain. These moved to ridges surrounding a large natural lick in Flint Park, a subdivision of Banff National Park. Here they stayed in June and early July and then disappeared till mid-September.

The summer home range is the least known home range type to me. I only observed one band of Stone's rams in 1961 on their summer range. However, this summer range also served as a concentration area in fall since rams were to be found there till at least the first week of October. This indicates how complex the home range patterns can be. Unfortunately, heavy snowfalls prevented me from following up observations in October 1961; also, hunters spooked the band in late September 1962 and it never returned that fall and early winter.

Length of stay. I have accurate data on how long rams remained on their seasonal home ranges only for individually known Stone's sheep:

1. Twelve rams remained on the average 25 days (11–32 days) on the pre-rut range.
2. Thirteen rams remained on the average 50 days (35–70 days) on the rutting range.

3. Five rams remained on rut and midwinter home ranges between 154 and 191 days.

4. Two rams remained on their midwinter range about 58 days; a third remained about 75.

Since during meltoff in spring I was cut off from Sanctuary Mountain, I could not determine exactly when each ram vacated this wintering area.

The evidence for seasonal home ranges in ewes also comes from observing individually recognizable animals, as well as from observing conspicuous increases and decreases of ewe numbers on wintering areas. The bighorn female group wintering on Grassy Mountain arrived in September and left prior to lambing. These females left in the direction of Flint Park and I recognized several well-marked individuals there. The same individuals were seen day after day on Grassy Mountain indicating that the females did not leave Grassy in the winter. Hence these females had only one wintering area and in addition a summer home range and maybe a separate winter home range. On the neighboring Palliser Range there was a marked increase in the number of females in spring 1965 (fig. 8). This increase was real since strange females appeared which I had not seen previously. In fall 1964 the ear tags of 10 females were read; in spring I read 10 additional ones. These newly arrived females evidently occupied different home ranges in fall and early winter from those they occupied in late winter and spring.

On the Stone's sheep study area, the old N-ewe and her two subadult followers stayed from fall till early summer on Sanctuary Mountain. A second female with subadults joined N-ewe in April. Both females followed by the same subadults plus two lambs were back on Sanctuary in the following fall and remained on Sanctuary's south slopes and cliffs until I departed from the study area in late January 1963. The second female had therefore either (1) alternate home ranges for fall and early winter (the seasons of soft, often deep snow), or (2) the heavy snowfalls in fall 1961 prevented her from reaching her accustomed home range.

It is likely that ewes disperse somewhat right after the rut and concentrate again in late winter and spring if the range they inhabit is extensive and allows it. About two-thirds of the Stone's sheep females from Ghost Mountain left it after the rut and returned in late April. On the Palliser Range, most females stood at high elevation in midwinter and on many days I saw none at all. In mid-December 1966, the Bare Mountain females in Banff also began dispersing through the high, wind-swept ridges. This phenomenon is still in need of verification.

Size of seasonal home ranges.   The seasonal home range of a sheep covers part of, or the whole of, one mountain. The area over which a sheep roams depends primarily on the depth and hardness of snow but also on the amount of forest and cliff terrain on that mountain. When the snow is deep and soft as it usually is in January, February, and early March, sheep confine their activity to small areas. I could not entice tame rams in February and March to cross a gorge filled with deep snow, but once I crossed it and broke a trail, they followed readily. Many times sheep were seen to wade into a field of deep snow only to retreat in their steps. From January till 24 March, the 9 Stone's rams wintering on Sanctuary confined their activity to the steep, rugged west slope of that mountain, an area barely a half mile across. Similarly, 3 Stone's rams stayed from January to 18 March 1962 on a small, wind-blown area on Shady Mountain; then 2 of them left and joined the Sanctuary Mountain rams. The bighorn rams on the Palliser Range confined their activity to the seven northernmost ridges (3L–4R) in midwinter but roamed the length and breadth of the range in late winter and spring. During the rut, assuming snow conditions permit it, rams roam over a wide area. Thus, the minimum size for home ranges is about one-half mile in diameter in midwinter, and the maximum about 3.7 miles in spring and fall.

Distances between seasonal home ranges.   For many sheep one seasonal home range is only one valley removed from the next, but there are exceptions. The Stone's rams from Sanctuary Mountain which rutted on Ghost Mountain crossed only one mile of valley, and so did the ones moving off to Cliff Mountain and Lupin Hill. The two rams wintering on Shady Mountain crossed also about one mile of timber and lake ice to join Sanctuary rams, but the two McMillan rams which appeared in May on Sanctuary moved about 8 miles along a mountain chain. Bighorn rams which spent the fall on the Palliser and rutted on Bare Mountain moved about 15 miles; in 1966 there were 7 of them. Two Palliser rams moved even further and were seen heading toward Mount White, a distance of 22 miles from their pre-rut home range. Grassy Mountain rams, which crossed to Flint Park and stayed at the salt lick there, went about 4.5 miles over lightly forested low hills, as did the Grassy Mountain females which lambed somewhere on Flint Mountain.

I have no information on how far any of my known Stone's or big-horn sheep went to reach their summer home ranges. Blood (1963), who observed California bighorns in southern British Columbia, found that ewes moved about 6–7 miles across timbered terrain between their winter and summer ranges; rams moved up to 15 miles. It was reported by Smith (1954) and Wishart (1958) for bighorns, Sugden (1961) for California bighorns, and Jones (1963) for Dall's sheep, that their study populations moved 15–40 miles between summer and winter ranges. Heptner et al. (1961) report that urials may travel up to 100 km (60 miles) from their winter to their summer areas.

Loyalty to seasonal home ranges. Mountain sheep are very loyal to their home ranges; their movements between seasonal home ranges are orderly and predictable. Let us assume we observe in spring almost daily a large ram on a certain mountain. What are the chances that we will see him again there in the following year? Assuming that he survives, what are the chances that he will visit this very mountain in spring? The answer to the last question is a measure of the ram's fidelity to his seasonal home range. Both questions can be answered if three pieces of information are available: (1) the number of sheep living on a seasonal home range in year one (N_1); (2) the number of sheep which return to that home range next year at the same season (N_2); (3) the number of sheep which die before they can visit the home range in question in the second year.

For instance, in spring 1964 I identified 49 individually known big-horn rams on the Palliser Range in Banff National Park. In spring 1965, 38 of these returned. Rams from this population had an overall mortality of about 11%, so that 5 (5.4) rams out of the 49 were most likely dead. Of the original 49 rams, 38 or 77.5% showed up. Of 44 (43.6) rams expected alive in the second year, 38 or 87.1% visited the mountain. For convenience' sake the first expression (77.5%) will be termed *return* and the second (87.1%) *fidelity*.

In fall 1964 I identified 45 known rams on the Palliser and Bare Mountain. Two years later, in fall 1966, I found 31 of them where expected. The return over two years was 69%. To calculate fidelity, two years of mortality must be subtracted from the number of rams seen in 1964: 45 − (4.9 + 4.4) = 35.7. Fidelity is then (31/35.7) × 100, or 86.8%.

Of the 45 rams, 40 were seen on the Palliser Range, and 34 of these were alive in the spring and summer of 1965. In fall 1966, 27 of the 31 rams resighted were Palliser rams. It is most probable that the 34 rams alive in spring and summer 1965 were also alive in fall 1965, which allows one to calculate a return of $(27/34) \times 100$, or 79.2%. If we assume for the 34 rams an 11% mortality in the winter of 1965/66, then we get a figure for home range fidelity of 89.1%—the calculations being $34 - 3.7 = 30.3$ and $(27/30.3) \times 100$. However, if one deducts two years of mortality, which is the same as $40 \times (0.89)^2$, resulting in 31.6 rams expected alive, then home range fidelity is $(27/31.6) \times 100$, or 85.4%.

In the Stone's sheep study I obtained the data for calculating home range fidelity by following a small number of rams in successive years and observing directly each departure from the expected movement pattern. Since there was no need to calculate how many rams had probably died, the data show the actual deviations that living rams performed from their movement pattern of the previous year (table 21). Furthermore, it was possible to record how many rams not present in 1961 made their appearance in 1962. In 1961, 52 appearances by known rams were made on certain mountains at specific seasons. If the same rams had made appearances on the same mountains at the corresponding seasons in 1962, there would have been again a total of 52 appearances. However, only 38 took place, or 73% of the expected.

TABLE 21

Home range fidelity of Stone's rams

Location	Season	Known rams present 1961	1961 rams present 1962	Strange rams present 1962	1961 rams alive 1962
Sanctuary Mt.	fall	14	12	4	12
	rut	3	0	4	2
	winter[a]	8	6	4	6
Ghost Mt.	fall	1	1	0	1
	rut	15	11	3	12
	winter	6	4	0	6
Shady Mt.	winter	3	2	1	2
Cliff Mt.	rut	1	1	0	1
Lupin Hill	rut	1	1	2	1
Total		52	38	18	43

[a] Winter refers to the month of January only.

This figure is the same as the *return* calculated for bighorns. However, 3 of my known Stone's rams were dead in 1962, and the remaining rams, if they had done exactly as in 1961, would have accounted for 43 correct appearances. They accounted for 38, or 88%. That is, they showed a home range *fidelity* of 88%, since they appeared in 38 out of 43 cases where expected.

In fall, rut, and early winter 1962, 18 strange rams appeared where they had not been in 1961. Hence, the rams observed in 1962 on specific mountains at specific seasons were made up of $[38/(38 + 18)] \times 100 = 68\%$ of rams present in 1961. In other words, the 1962 ram population was only 68% the same as that in 1961. In 1961 the study area was under an exceptionally heavy snow blanket, whereas little snow lay in the early winter of 1962. Rams were able to roam more in 1962, and I saw them in places they had not been in the previous year. The influx of strange rams, particularly in the rutting season, was favored by the low snow cover. These "strangers" were probably rams which I would have seen in 1961 had the snow conditions been less severe.

One can now answer the two questions posed earlier: What are the chances of seeing a given ram on a specific mountain within a prescribed season in consecutive years? Between 73 and 79.2 times out of 100. What are the chances that the ram, if alive, will revisit the same mountain at the same season in consecutive years? Between 86 and 89 chances out of 100.

The return and home range fidelity values of Stone's and bighorn rams are very similar; the differences between them are not significant. The direct and the indirect method of determining home range fidelity gave almost identical results, which indicates that the annual mortality value of about 11% for bighorn rams, derived from rams found dead in the field, is very nearly valid. How well do these figures predict the return of rams? In spring 1968 came the chance to test them. The number of rams one can expect to see t years after first seeing them on a given mountain is predicted by the formula: $N_t = N_0 U(1 - m)^t$ where N_0 is the number of rams seen in year 0; N_t is the number of rams expected t years hence; U is the fidelity constant, which on the average is 0.87; m is the mortality per individual per year; and $(1 - m)$ is the survival.

In spring 1965 I knew 44 rams individually. The overall mortality as calculated from the ram mortality data (chap. 10) is about 11%, so $m = 0.11$. Therefore, for spring 1968, or 3 years hence $(t = 3)$, one would calculate that $N_3 = 44 \ (0.87)(1 - 0.11)^3$, or 26.9 rams back on the range. The predicted number is 27; the number actually found 26. Similarly, from 38 known rams seen in spring 1964 on the Palliser Range one would expect back $N_4 = 38 \ (0.87)(1 - 0.11)^4$, or 20.6 rams; 19 were found. From the foregoing it is evident that the number of known rams which will appear on a given area in consecutive years can be predicted fairly accurately.

In the previous calculations $m = 0.11$ was used. Since the mortality of rams differs with their age, can one predict the return of rams of various age classes? Rams between 2 and 7 years of age had a mortality of 3.9% ($m = 0.039$), while those between 8 and 17 years had a mortality of about 23.0% ($m = 0.23$). Predictions using these mortality figures for six groups of individually known rams are compared with actual or observed returns in the following:

1. Spring 1964, 19 Palliser rams, 8–16 years. Expected return in 1965 is $N_1 = 19 \ (0.77)(0.87) = 12.7$ rams; actual return 14 rams.
2. Spring 1964, 19 Palliser rams, 3–8 years. Expected return in spring 1965 is $N_1 = 19 \ (0.961)(0.87) = 15.8$ rams; actual return 17 rams.
3. Spring 1965, 20 rams, 8–16 years. Expected return in spring 1968 is $N_3 = 20 \ (0.77)^3(0.87) = 7.9$; actual return 10 rams.
4. Fall 1964, 17 rams, 8–16 years. Expected return in fall 1966 is $N_2 = 17 \ (0.77)^2(0.87) = 8.7$; observed return 12 rams.
5. Fall 1964, 23 rams, 3–8 years. Expected return in fall 1966 is $N_2 = 23 \ (0.961)^2(0.87) = 18.2$; observed return 16 rams.
6. Spring 1965, 24 rams, 3–8 years. Expected return in spring 1968 is $N_3 = 24 \ (0.961)^3(0.87) = 18.9$ rams; actual return 16 rams.

Evidently the formula, using mortality data derived from rams found dead in the field and fidelity data as established previously, slightly underestimates the returns. The rams were hence either more loyal or had a little lower mortality than calculated.

For ewes the data are more limited. From 11 bighorn females seen in fall 1964, 9 were seen in spring 1965 and were probably also alive in fall 1965, and 8 of these were found in fall 1966. On the Stone's sheep study area, all 13 known females seen in fall and winter of 1961 returned at the expected season to the expected areas in 1962. These are small samples and I take the liberty of lumping them together. Of 31 females (Stone's and bighorns) seen on a seasonal home range, 28 were resighted in the following year. This is a return of 90%. Home range fidelity cannot be calculated since no reliable mortality data are available for ewes. The 13 Stone's ewes confined their activity to the same areas as in the previous year. Only one female made an unexpected departure by crossing the timbered valley to the next mountain, but she returned after a few days. This female lived in spring and early summer 1962 on the southwest slopes of Sanctuary Mountain. She was not present there in the previous fall and early winter, but in fall 1962 she appeared and stayed on those slopes. These observations as well as those cited below indicate that ewes occasionally shift about and visit areas neglected in the previous year. Such deviations are negligible, however, compared with the great loyalty these animals show to their home ranges.

In late November 1965, almost three years after I had left my Stone's sheep, I returned again to the study area. After the aircraft had left, I raised my binoculars and scanned Sanctuary Mountain. There were sheep in the cliffs and I quickly put the spotting scope on the tripod and aimed it at the sheep. The first one I saw was G-ram. There he stood and looked down into the valley, within 200 paces of where he had fought M-ram on 19 and 20 March 1962, and where he had rutted in the same year. Next to him was old N-ewe, Nanni as I called her, the ewe he had bred in 1962 and which he also bred a few days after my arrival in the same cliff as in 1962. Further up on the mountain was Blackneck, now an 8-year-old with three-quarter-curl horns. As a class II ram he had given G-ram some trouble in the 1962 rut. On Ghost Mountain I found Black-ewe and Spot-ewe, and the ram who was wandering to the cut separating Ghost from Lick Mountain was O-ram. For a moment I felt I had never left but had been transferred into yesterday and was still watching my familiar animals. All told, I found 7 of 20 rams and 6 or 10 ewes during my two-week stay. Had deep snow prevailed, forcing the sheep to lower elevations and restricting their movements, I would have probably found more. Except for one ram, they were there where I expected them to be. The exception was a $2\frac{1}{2}$-year-old ram in 1962, who had come to Sanctuary and stayed on after the rut. I discovered him on Cliff Mountain opposite Sanctuary in 1965, about two miles from where expected.

The day after I arrived I saw Bonni on Sanctuary. She was only a little yearling female when on 9 November 1961, she followed C-ram across the valley from Ghost to Sanctuary Mountain and attached herself to Nanni and her lamb. In spring 1962 a strange dark female yearling came to Sanctuary and also followed Nanni. Blacki, as I called the stranger, formed a dominance pair with Bonni; that is, Blacki dominated Bonni, butted her periodically, and followed her wherever she went. In fall 1962 both young ewes followed Nanni back to Sanctuary, but separated shortly thereafter, for I saw only Blacki in the following rut. When I spotted Bonni in November 1965 on Sanctuary, she was not alone. Blacki stood beside her and, as I found out later, still followed Bonni, who now had a lamb at heel. Such observations on individual sheep speak more forcefully for the loyalty of these animals to their home ranges than any quantitative data.

The figures indicate that females may show a higher return than rams (90% versus 75%). However, the difference is not statistically significant with the small sample sizes at hand (31 ewes seen in year A, 28 in year B; 140 rams seen in year A, 105 in year B; $\chi^2 = 3.4$ N.S.). Nevertheless, I believe that the difference is real and that ewes which do not show up at the expected season are dead more likely than not.

Deviations from Seasonal Movement Patterns

Several factors reduce sightings of individually known sheep in consecutive years and cause real or apparent deviations from expected movements. Some sheep die, some rams under 4 years of age take up residence elsewhere at the expected season, some sheep delay or skip a migration because of climatic factors or unknown causes, or some sheep visit the area at the expected time but are missed by the investigator. The latter variable I consider inconsequential.

Movement deviations by young rams. In 1961, LI-ram at $3\frac{1}{2}$ years of age remained on Sanctuary Mountain during the rut. In the following year he moved with other Sanctuary rams to Ghost Mountain for the rut. Here I expected him in November 1966 and that is where he was. In late fall 1962 a small $2\frac{1}{2}$-year-old gray ram came from McMillan, via Cliff Mountain to Sanctuary, and stayed on after the rut. There was a good chance that he would be on Sanctuary in the 1966 rut, but he was on Cliff Mountain, 2 miles away.

The best example for movement irregularities is given by a bighorn ram from Banff park. In summer and early fall 1964 I became familiar with a $2\frac{1}{2}$-year-old ram from Bare Mountain. On 4 October I met him and a $2\frac{1}{2}$-year-old female from Bare Mountain on the Palliser Range about 13 miles from Bare Mountain (I photographed them to ascertain their identity with the aid of older photographs). Both animals disappeared thereafter but in early June 1965 the ram reappeared on the Palliser Range. In 1966 I saw him again on Bare Mountain on 9 November. He left on 11 November and did not return to Bare Mountain till the rut was almost over, on 8 December. He was last seen on 12 December, at which time he carried a deep cut on his right front leg and limped badly. It was not possible to state where that ram could be expected in the fall of 1966. If I were to look for him again, I would expect to find him on Bare Mountain prior to the rutting season or shortly after the rut.

From the eighteen unexpected appearances by Stone's rams in the fall and early winter of 1962, six were made by rams $2\frac{1}{2}$ and $3\frac{1}{2}$ years of age.

Deviations by older sheep. The two Stone's rams, S and SO, 9 and 8 years respectively in 1962, are good examples of movement deviations apparently caused by climate. Both moved in November to Ghost Mountain (see table 20), but S soon left the Ghost ewes and rutted somewhere beyond Ghost. After the 1961 rutting season both rams returned to Sanctuary in May 1962. S-ram came on 7 May and SO on the 17th. As noted earlier, there was deep snow on the ground in early and midwinter of 1961. After the 1962 rut, both rams returned at once to Sanctuary; S-ram came on 16 December and SO on the 30th. It is quite possible that both would have returned at once to Sanctuary after the 1961 rut if snow conditions had permitted.

In the 1961 rut, G-ram and H-ram were absent from the Sanctuary Mountain slopes visible to me, but both were present in 1962, and G-ram was there in 1966. (G and H were $7\frac{1}{2}$ and $8\frac{1}{2}$ years old respectively in fall 1962.) In 1962 the $4\frac{1}{2}$-year-old Blackneck was present on Sanctuary, and again in 1966, but not in 1961.

In 1961 C-ram moved from Sanctuary to Ghost on 4 November, returned on 9 November, and disappeared thereafter. In 1962 he moved straight to Cliff Mountain, where he had probably been in 1961 as well, and did not go to Ghost Mountain at all. (C-ram was $7\frac{1}{2}$ years old in fall 1962.)

Old bighorn rams in Banff also showed some irregularities. In the spring of 1964 I often saw and photographed an old small ram with thin, tightly curled horns. He did not appear in spring 1965, and I left in early June without seeing him. In fall 1966 I saw him again on the Palliser Range, where he had also been in fall 1964. It could be that this ram, whom I saw in 1964 during all of May, arrived later in June of the same year. Some rams were still coming to the Palliser when I left on 5 June 1965, and one 10-year-old ram (519 red), whom I had also seen in early May 1964 regularly, returned on 28 May 1965.

I had seen a rather tame 19-year-old ewe (819 blue) regularly in May 1964 on the Palliser. In 1965 she did not return; however, in that year Warden Stenton identified the then 20-year-old animal at Lake Minnewanka, about 8 miles from the Palliser Range.[2] It is quite possible that old and young sheep are less predictable in their movements than others.

Old, barren ewes remain longer on the winter ranges and need not go to specific lambing areas. There is no point expecting a barren ewe to come to a mountain where she lambed in previous years. One can expect to see her on her normal summer range. Some old ewes, however, behaved abnormally. Two bighorn ewes were frequently seen in the company of rams, and if not with rams then on the areas frequented by rams. One of them, female 894 blue, even played with rams in spring by joining in their running and frolicking games (see plate 4). It is possible that some old females become hormonally disturbed, begin to associate with males, and change their previous home range patterns.

Peter's excursion. I have emphasized the great order and predictability of sheep movements, but it must also be mentioned that sheep do not adhere unvaryingly to a movement pattern. A careful scrutiny of the data presented in this chapter reveals the frequency of these deviations from the expected. However, tabular data are never as convincing as individual episodes, and I shall relate one here of a ram who moved unexpectedly elsewhere, and yet "proved" the rule.

Peter was a Sanctuary ram nearing his seventh birthday in spring 1962. On 28 April, he and the 4-year-old LI-ram were in company of the large, 8-year-old F-ram. The latter had come to Sanctuary on 18 March, and was about to leave Sanctuary for the Cliff and Shady Mountain complex. As rams commonly do in spring, the three started to play, frolic, and dash, and before long F-ram raced downhill closely followed by the others. When they ran into the timber at the foot of Sanctuary Mountain, it became evident that the rams would cross Gladys Lake on the ice, and I hurried to its shores. Soon the rams ap-

2. Report by E. J. Stenton filed with the Warden Service, Banff, Alberta.

peared on the ice marching in single file, F in the lead, followed closely by LI, with Peter some distance behind the two. F-ram walked steadily on, the small 4-year-old LI followed unhesitatingly, but not Peter. He hung back, stopped frequently, and looked back at Sanctuary; finally he raced after his two companions after looking back at Sanctuary a long time. By that time they had crossed the half mile of lake ice and began to ascend Shady Mountain on the hard snow of an avalanche. All three soon disappeared from sight.

Peter's actions indicated that he was on a trip away from accustomed ground, but the stimulus of two companions walking away appeared to be greater in determining his actions than the urge to return to familiar ground. Peter did not remain away from Sanctuary long. Four days later he reappeared on Shady Mountain. Frequently he interrupted grazing and looked for long periods of time across to Sanctuary, a behavior typical of sheep about to embark on a major move. Peter did not leave Shady that day but went to rest overlooking the route he was to take. During the early afternoon of the following day he crossed Gladys Lake and when I saw him next he was busily courting Nanni. Then he rounded a corner in the rugged cliffs of Sanctuary and I lost sight of him for that day. The loyalty of an adult to its home range is great, but not absolute.

Human disturbance. One factor causing sheep to desert home ranges is disturbance by humans, in particular, hunters. This was brought home to me vividly in fall and winter of 1962. Eight miles from my Stone's sheep study area was a wide mountain that served as a home for about 20 rams in summer and fall. I had gathered data from these individuals in August and October 1961 and revisited the mountain in March 1962. This was not a wintering area of sheep, although a few goats were present. Indeed, sheep were absent even in June 1961 and 1962. These rams were of interest to me in 1962 since I hoped to age each one of them to obtain an age structure of this group. In September 1962 a hunting party shot at least two rams from that band. I visited the area shortly thereafter, but found no rams. I went the following week— still no rams. I went once every week from the end of September till the second week of December 1962 and saw one single ram. The band had deserted the terrain it had frequented previously.

I had similar designs on a second band of rams. I had seen them at a distance in fall and winter 1961 and visited them on a number of occasions in late winter and spring 1962. In September 1962 the rams returned. On 26 September a hunting party arrived and shot two rams the following week. The band left this area for the rest of the fall and early winter. I visited the area once every week from early October till the first week in December. I found only two rams, which had just crossed to this home range and were apparently searching for their companions, on 11 October. The fresh tracks in the snow showed where they had crossed the valley from Mount Will to McMillan Mountain. They were gone the next time I came and I saw none thereafter.

By good fortune I was able to visit the Stone's sheep study area in the first two weeks of September 1965. My first trip took me again to McMillan Mountain. It had been hunted intensively in 1964, as I had heard and as new pack trails and a new campsite indicated. During three visits I spotted not one band of rams, only scattered pairs or single rams, which is contrary to the normal condition and therefore significant. A few rams visited the mountain, but the typical groups clustered about one or several large horned rams were clearly absent. It is noteworthy that Grubb and Jewell (1966) found that disturbance provoked feral sheep to leave their home ranges.

The matter of disturbance from hunting is a delicate one, but one that must be faced nevertheless. If hunting causes sheep to vacate their accustomed areas and seek refuge on terrain where they would normally be rarely found, then we can expect deleterious effects on the sheep population as a whole. It means the loss of habitat to an animal. If this is wintering habitat, it means a decrease in population size. Clearly, if hunting could be confined to the summering areas, probably less harm would be done. Since there is every indication that sheep pass on home range knowledge from generation to generation, if sheep avoid areas where they are hunted, they will not pass on these parts of the range to their offspring. Only if the population is already compressed onto one mountain and cannot escape to an undisturbed region will hunting not lead to a loss of habitat.

The Inefficiency of Home Range Patterns of Rams

The home range patterns of rams and the timing and distance of movements between their home ranges run as a rule so contrary to efficiency that had a human engineer designed them he would have been fired. Efficiency would require conservation of body energy by the rams in winter, reduction of chances of mortality, and maximization of reproduction. Yet the migration dynamics particularly of rams in winter is at loggerheads with these requirements.

Take the case of bighorn ram 303 from the Palliser Range. Except for the rut, his winter home range was the Palliser Range, particularly the northern rim. This ram had three easy choices of where to rut. He could stay with the females which shared his home range, cross the half-mile-wide gorge to Grassy Mountain and rut with the ewes there, or cross the valley to the Cascade Range and rut with the ewes living there. Ram 303 did none of these. He went 15 miles north along the mountain range and crossed the Panther River to rut with the Bare Mountain females. Only two Palliser rams surpassed this, for they went 7 miles further to Mount White, staying only a few days with the Bare Mountain females.

When the rut ended in December, 303 could have stayed on the wintering areas on Bare Mountain, but instead he returned to his home range on the Palliser wintering area. He was reported to be on Bare Mountain in 1963; in the 1964 rut he came to me when I was filming there; in fall 1966 when I was again in Banff, I saw 303 as expected on the Palliser and during the rut on Bare Mountain; in January and February I expected 303 on Palliser, since he was there after the 1964 rut. I could not test this expectation till early February 1968. The first two rams to meet me ascending the Palliser in January 1965 were 303 and 555, and the first two rams to meet me in February 1968 were 303 and 555.

The long movements by rams away from, past, or through female groups to habitual rutting grounds, and their returns through perfectly good wintering areas to their accustomed winter home ranges, are not the exception but the rule. From 38 Palliser rams that I knew, only 11 were spotted with Palliser ewes during the rut; in 1961 out of 16 Sanctuary Mountain Stone's rams, only 4 remained with the Sanctuary Mountain ewes, and in 1962, 2 of 13 did the same. Yet while the others left the Palliser and Sanctuary respectively, strange rams moved in. An exchange of rams had taken place.

It would be tedious to enumerate the nonsensical movements performed by Stone's and bighorn rams which I knew. The animals appeared to be blind to the real opportunities they encountered. Instead they went on to a specific piece of ground at a specific season. They wasted resources during the critical midwinter period in moving long distances after the strenuous rut, rather than rutting or wintering at the closest opportune locality. They took the chances of getting stranded after a heavy snowfall, or drowning in a river as apparently happened to ram 616, whose body was found at the mouth of the

Cascade River in Lake Minnewanka. He must have suffered the fatal mishap when he crossed the river trying to get back to the Palliser from the Cascade Range in spring.

What reason is there in such wasteful movement patterns? One might suggest that not the individual ram but the population benefited from his actions. But if the rams were indeed acting altruistically—to reduce inbreeding, to remove their presence from critical ewe winter ranges, or to reduce competition—then sheep are capable of insights of sobering depth and must perform the feat of calculating how many and which rams can retain an efficient home range pattern and which not. A more logical reason for the idiosyncratic movement patterns is that they follow from the manner of home range establishment of rams. A ram appears to inherit his various home ranges from the different older rams he happened to be following during his age of home range fixation. The irrational element in the home range patterns is the chance element of *which* old ram the young ram fancied to follow during a particular migration period. Since young rams often and readily switch from following one ram to another, one young ram could adopt parts of the home range patterns of several rams.

In addition, dispersal by males from the maternal female band and breeding females other than those of the band that raised them might be greatly selected for, as experiments with reindeer in Russia have indicated. Preobrazhenskii (1961) showed the following: When reindeer does ($N = 511$) were inseminated from bulls of the same herd (the bulls and does were closely related), 4.5% of the does remained barren, 5.5% of the calves died shortly after birth, and the average live weight of calves at birth was 6.85 kg. By contrast, among 326 does from the same herd, inseminated by bulls from different herds and of distant relationship, there was only 1.5% barrenness, 2.8% loss of calves at birth, and the calves had an average weight of 7.05 kg. This result suggests that caribou bulls, and probably rams, which move to distant female herds have a consistently better chance of contributing to the next generation than those that do not. The increased viability of their offspring is probably due to their larger birth weight, which in turn is probably due to hybrid vigor. The pre-rut dispersal and long movements of rams during the rutting season might be selected for, not only because the individual male might breed more females, but also because his reproductive success increases by breeding females of distant genetic relationship.

Home Range Groups

Each sheep, of course, shares its seasonal home range with other sheep. That is, one can recognize the same individuals on a given area on consecutive days, and in consecutive years at the same season. Such groups of sheep, living on one area to which they restrict their movements without any obvious need to do so, were called home range groups by Hunter (1964). He found that several home range groups of domestic female sheep formed within one large flock on a pasture, and that individuals from any one home range group were very loyal to their home grounds. Grubb and Jewell (1966) made similar observations on feral Soay sheep. If one can recognize sheep individually, the home range group phenomenon is very apparent in mountain sheep, albeit not nearly as simple as that of domestic sheep. Mountain sheep rams live only seasonally in the same company and hence are members of not one but several seasonal home range groups. Grubb and Jewell found this to be true of Soay rams. Females may also live in more than one home range group, although their home ranges are more limited. The reality of such home range groups in bighorns has been shown by tagging. Every year from 1949 till 1965, the late E. J. Stenton, warden at Bankhead in Banff park, tagged sheep which came to Lake Minnewanka during summer. His tagging showed that these sheep ranged about 17 miles north, as this is the northernmost point I or anyone ever saw a tagged female sheep. A few tagged females mixed with sheep that came to Aylmer lookout, the next ridge beside the mountain range on which the tagged sheep lived. I never saw any of the females tagged by Stenton among the Bare Mountain females which lived next to the Palliser ewe group north on the *same* range. However, two of the rams tagged did visit this female group during the rut. No female tagged by Stenton was sighted among the females from Mount Norquay, although females from these groups lived on ranges separated by a river and approached each other to within one mile as was reported to me by J. C. Holroyd, then assistant chief warden in Banff National Park. The concept, however, that maternal home range groups develop because the association between mother and daughter persists for several years, as proposed by Hunter (1964) and accepted by Grubb and Jewell (1966), does not appear valid (see chap. 4).

SHIFTS TO DIFFERENT HABITATS IN WINTER

Daily observations in winter indicated that sheep used three different habitats within the home range: (1) the open, grass-covered, smoothly contoured slopes (plate 18); (2) steep, broken cliffs and projecting rock; (3) the sparsely vegetated rubble slopes and ridges at high elevations (plate 19). After heavy snowfalls in early winter (November through February), sheep moved to the grassy slopes and remained there as long as the snow was deep. Once winds had swept the upper elevations free of snow and exposed mats of sparse vegetation on the rubble slopes, sheep selected this habitat. These up-and-down movements of sheep were quite predictable and resulted in increased or decreased sightings of sheep depending on snow depth, as is illustrated by my sightings of Stone's rams on Sanctuary Mountain in January 1962 and 1963.

In January 1962, deep snow blanketed the study area. This is entirely a subjective evaluation, but it refers to a most tangible reality nevertheless. For instance, I could not climb mountains, which I could do with ease in the following year when the snow was rather low. In January 1962 I made 143 sightings of individually recognizable rams from Sanctuary Mountain. Had I seen every known ram on each census, I should have made 208 sightings. Furthermore, in 20 of the 143 sightings the rams were located on high rubble slope, above 6,000 ft elevation.

In January 1963, when little snow covered the mountains, I made only 60 from 179 possible sightings of known rams; in 19 of the 60 sightings, rams were seen on the high rubble slopes. Hence, my sighting efficiency during deep snow had been 69% in 1962 and 35% in 1963. During deep snow, only 14% of all rams were seen at high elevation, but 32% during low snow. These census counts were made on the same mountain, from the same localities, and on the same individuals.

In March and April, sheep began to vacate the open grassy slopes and move to steep, broken cliffs. This was a conspicuous shift, shown by Stone's and bighorn sheep alike (tables 22 and 23). It resulted in a

TABLE 22
Vertical distribution of rams on Sanctuary Mountain, 1962

	Low grassy slopes (4,500–800 ft)	Cliff regions (4,800–6,000 ft)	High rubble slopes (6,000–500 ft)	Total sightings
Jan	46%	40%	14%	123
Feb	52	30	18	131
Mar	21	61	18	156
Apr	25	66	9	60
May, June	51	41	8	85

TABLE 23

Distribution of bighorn sheep in cliff regions on Palliser wintering area, 1965

	Cliff regions	Total sightings
10–14 Mar	79%	156
26 Mar–5 Apr	60	146
8–12 Apr	50	193
18–23 Apr	12	256
24–29 Apr	22	329

high proportion of sheep sighted in cliffs—up to 80% of all bighorns in March 1965—and a low overall sighting. Thus a glance at figures 8 and 9 shows increased sightings in late January and early February and a sharp decrease in sightings in early March. This change in number of sightings is explained by the hypothesis that sheep move to open slopes during conditions of deep, soft snow, where they are rarely seen, and to cliff terrain during late winter, where they are often hidden or hard to spot.

What causes sheep to favor cliffs during late winter? I suggest that sheep go there to feed since it is the only habitat in which forage is readily available at that time. On the open slopes, blankets of dense, hard-frozen snow cover the forage and make it temporarily unavailable to sheep. Deep, but soft snow is no major obstacle to them for they readily paw through it. Soft snow is found in early winter but by March the snow begins to change. Figure 37 shows that in March maximum daily temperatures reach 32° F (0° C), whereas the average mean temperatures are only a little over 20° F ($-6°$ C). Under such conditions the snow melts on the surface during the day, then compacts and freezes rock hard at night. In the morning the snow is often so hard that sheep may run on it without breaking through (see plate 75). On some steep slopes, the hobnails on my climbing boots would slip off the icy snow surface. I noticed a few times that an ice pan had formed well below the surface crust, apparently a few inches above the ground. Under such conditions one cannot expect sheep to paw through the snow for forage.

In the cliffs on south-facing slopes another development takes place. Cliffs shed snow more easily than other terrain, and rocks are everywhere exposed to the increasingly intense sunlight in late winter. I found such rocks warm to the touch on cold but sunny days. The snow melt begins about such exposed rocks and the snow blanket creeps away from cliff areas. Hence, vegetation becomes exposed, and sheep flock in because it is the only terrain where they can easily reach food (plate 75). Once the slopes lose some of their snow cover in April and the grassy ridges become exposed, sheep desert the cliffs (table 23).

Hard snow crusts in March and April benefit the sheep in one way: they are able to disperse. From mid-March on sheep begin to move about, as is indicated not only by the steady rise in sheep numbers on the Palliser wintering area (fig. 8) but also by observations of wandering sheep. They move to areas where the snowmelt is most advanced and a maximum of vegetation is exposed—the south-facing slopes—and consequently sheep concentrate there in late winter and spring. Conversely, as long as the snow is soft and sheep can easily remove it, which is true for early and midwinter, sheep are sighted frequently on north slopes. South-facing cliffs are an important foraging area for about 6–8 weeks in late winter for all sheep I studied.

These observations on sheep wintering on the Palliser Range and at Gladys Lake may not be valid for all sheep populations. There may be many populations which descend a mountain in fall and remain on one wintering area till early summer, performing none of the distinct, long seasonal movements shown by the sheep I observed, or returning to high elevations. Such a pattern of range exploitation has been suggested for several small populations, for instance, the California bighorns studied by McCullough and Schneegas (1966) and Sugden (1961) or the bighorns studied by Smith (1954) in Idaho. These cases may be relict populations whose traditional movements and home range patterns have been mutilated by the activities of man.

On the whole the feeding actions of wintering sheep, ibex, or mountain goats conform to the laws of least effort and highest return. They move where forage is most easily available, where snow has been removed by wind, sunlight, avalanches or gravity, or where little snow fell on the ground in the first place. Nievergelt (1966a) found ibex to prefer more precipitous, snow-shedding slopes in winter than in summer, while McCullough and Schneegas (1966) report that California bighorns in the Sierra Nevada concentrated in steep, rugged canyons after heavy snowfalls and generally preferred the elevations below the permanent snowline in winter. There is some evidence also that mountain bovids avoid exposure to strong winds, for Nievergelt found that ibex moved to sheltered areas, particularly if the sun was not shining, and Munro (1962) as well as Grubb and Jewell (1966) noted that domestic and Soay sheep responded to strong winds by resting behind shelters and generally altered their daily activity with the weather. Although I did not observe any conspicuous effort by mountain sheep or mountain goats to shelter themselves from strong winds, their daily activity and habitat selection was such that they were active primarily during the warmest parts of the winter day on the warmest areas of the mountains (see chap. 9), while during the coldest times of the daily cycle, the night, some rams crowded together in caves. That all these actions would reduce heat loss, and consequently the amount of forage needed for survival, is indicated by the experiments of Joyce et al. (1966) and Joyce and Blaxter (1964a). Domestic sheep exposed to controlled wind speeds and low temperatures, or deprived of their coats increased feed intake as they increased heat production to compensate for heat loss. Mountain sheep are exceedingly hardy, for they can live through the icy polar nights north of the Arctic Circle, as Dall's sheep do in the Brooks Range of Alaska.

CAUSES OF MAJOR MOVEMENTS

Mountain sheep can show three kinds of major movements: local shifts within home ranges, seasonal migrations between home ranges, and the rare mass emigrations. Local shifts appear to be caused by environmental factors such as snowstorms or availability of forage. Sheep can respond dramatically to snowstorms as has been observed or commented on by Murie (1944), Smith (1954), Wishart (1958), McCullough and Schneegas (1966), Heptner et al. (1961), and myself. Sheep may pour in single file from several directions into a sheltering basin or broken mountain face and remain there as long as the snow is deep and soft. Grubb and Jewell (1966) found that feral Soay sheep would vacate their established home ranges after exceptionally heavy snowstorms.

In spring sheep appear to follow the retreating snowline probably feeding on the fresh sprouting vegetation (Murie 1944; Smith 1954; Wishart 1958; Blood 1963), which Nievergelt (1966a) also suggested for ibex. In late winter hard snow encourages dispersion, which explains the shifts and migrations of sheep, on which many investigators speculated, and whose views are reviewed by Blood (1963) and Heptner et al. (1961). The causes of seasonal migrations have been sought in weather and forage factors, but I agree with Murie (1944) that such movements are not simply a response to snow, forage availability, or insect pest, but are more complex phenomena. For instance, if sheep came to their wintering areas in fall because heavy snowfall forced them to, the following is expected:

1. Sheep must arrive during or shortly after a major snowstorm and never before. However, sheep do arrive before snow blankets the ground.
2. Sheep should arrive en masse and stay on the wintering areas. However, sheep drift in and out of the wintering areas, and build up numerically over weeks.
3. Sheep should move rapidly to wintering areas. However, sheep drift in slowly.

If sheep follow the retreating snowline they should move up in early summer and onto the north slopes and should not leave the mountains they are on, but they do. Moreover, environmental factors appear incapable of accounting for the rutting migrations, or the late winter movements between home ranges.

It is more probable that sheep are internally motivated to migrate but are synchronized by external environmental factors. The animals migrate not because of weather, forage availability, and insect pest but in spite of them. It is reasonable to assume that migratory movements are synchronized by the seasonally changing light regime just as much as the rutting season in sheep or other ruminants (Bissonette 1941; Yeates 1949; Hafez 1952; French et al. 1960). The timing of rutting movements in Stone's rams (table 20) is very accurate in consecutive years. However, movements by rams from the wintering area are apparently not quite as predictable from year to year (fig. 8). In Soay rams the only major movements coincided with the beginning and end of the rutting season, indicating that the rutting season, timed by light, was also timing these movements.

The seasonal departures of females to their respective lambing grounds argues also for an internal motivation for migration. These movements would be synchronized by the rutting season and the gestation period. The late winter and spring movements of rams coincide with their greater tendency to socialize at that season (see chap. 7), while the exhausted, large rams are the first to return from the rutting grounds. Both argue for an internal motivation for migration. Nevertheless, at present a comprehensive theory accounting for all sheep movements is not possible, but the proposed hypothesis accounts for more events than the traditional ones.

Mass emigrations by American sheep have not been reported,

although they do occur rarely, but they have found attention in Russian literature. Asiatic sheep, like their American counterparts, have constant, predictable migrations, but occasionally deviations are noted which coincide with a deterioration of the habitat. Severe droughts appear to have been responsible for massive emigrations by urials, in which some individuals moved up to 500 km (300 miles) from their original range. In Alaska, a group of Dall's sheep disappeared from a relict range and apparently reappeared 40 miles away along a river bank (D. R. Klein, Alaska Cooperative Wildlife Research Unit, personal communication). In Colorado a group of introduced bighorn sheep moved 25–30 miles to a new locality (C. Moser, Dept. of Fish and Game, personal communication).

The American mountain sheep share a good many similarities in their home range and migratory characteristics with domestic or feral sheep as is evident from the work of Hunter (1964), Hunter and Davis (1963), Hunter and Milner (1963), and Grubb and Jewell (1966). Apparently, artificial sheep can still act like real ones if given a chance.

For an informative account of migration and movement of another large ice age ungulate, I refer the reader to Kelsall's (1968) monograph on barren ground caribou. This is a nomadic animal, whose seasonal exploitation of its habitat is much less predictable than that of mountain sheep and is characterized by major shifts of populations, sometimes over hundreds of miles. While sheep live in a habitat with stable plant communities that change almost solely with changes in climate (see below, chap. 5), caribou may (1) lose large tracts of wintering habitat through forest fires, (2) be more severely affected by seasonal or annual variations in snowfall than are sheep, and (3) exploit a habitat of low productivity which is highly susceptible to overuse (Scotter 1964). To a caribou, habitat and sustenance are subject to sudden disappearance, a chance element which may be counteracted by the nomadic habits of the barren ground caribou.

4 Sheep Society and Home Range Formation

The manner in which mountain sheep establish home ranges is closely related to their social system. They inherit home ranges from their elders, by acquiring the movement habits of the latter; individual exploration plays a subordinate part. Females in general adopt the home ranges of the female group that raised them, but a few inherit the home ranges of another female group. Females have a critical period between one and two years of age in which they may switch to another female band if they happen to meet one, or follow a ram to another area and join females there. Young sheep may only follow individuals of their maternal band because they meet no one else.

Young rams desert the maternal "home range group" of females some time after their second year of life and join ram bands. They establish individual patterns of seasonal home ranges by acquiring the home ranges of various older rams they happen to follow. Young rams also have a vestigial dispersal period in their third summer, in which they may wander out of the normal range of sheep distribution. Most, however, join the closest band of rams at hand.

Sheep society has all elements essential for smooth passage of home range knowledge, while minimizing dispersal by young sheep. Lambs are not driven off by the females after weaning or prior to bearing another lamb; rather, the juveniles desert their mothers and follow adults of their own choice. No social bonds are broken suddenly; separation of female and child is gradual and the juvenile is never forced from the band to wander on its own. The result is that young sheep are rarely alone. They are tolerated by whomever they follow—adult females, subadults, or mature rams. During lambing time the yearlings often cluster behind a barren female while the majority of females are dispersed through the cliffs. The females retain the juvenile tendency to follow others throughout life; the rams gradually become more independent of companions in the course of 7 to 9 years. Females follow some older, usually lamb-leading female, while rams follow the largest-horned ram in their bands. When rams mature and become independent they are followed by younger rams and passively pass on their habits to them. The seasonal home range pattern of a ram appears to be fixed when he reaches $4\frac{1}{2}$ years of age.

The consequence of these actions is that sheep maintain their area of distribution as a living tradition and rarely depart from it. How and why this method of home range establishment evolved in sheep and not in moose or deer is discussed in the next chapter. Below are some observations of individually known sheep that reveal how sheep acquire habits of going to and staying at specific localities at specific seasons.

SANCTUARY MOUNTAIN FEMALES AND SUBADULTS

On 9 November 1961, I saw a small yearling female (18 months old) and a yearling ram alone in the lower cliffs of Ghost Mountain. The two youngsters had apparently undertaken a small excursion on their own, not uncommon behavior of subadult sheep. They were joined by C-ram, a 7-year-old class III ram, who first courted both yearlings and then proceeded to cross the mile-wide valley separating Ghost and Sanctuary mountains. The little yearling female followed him and half an hour later both emerged from the timber and climbed up Sanctuary Mountain. Here the female yearling attached herself to a large 12-year-old ewe and her lamb, and this trio remained together from then on. They were the only female group on Sanctuary Mountain in early and midwinter.

The old female was called "Nanni," the yearling female "Bonni," and the ram lamb "Buster." I did not see them every day for they roamed through the vast, broken crags of Sanctuary, whose south and west side only were open to census. Between 1 January and 6 June 1962, I saw Bonni on 52 days.

On 26 February only Bonni followed by Buster came to the west slope; on 28 February they were still without Nanni and had attached themselves temporarily to T-ram, a 6-year-old class II ram. However, Nanni reappeared on 28 February, and the trio reformed. It was the first indication that Buster was separating from his mother.

On 14 April, two strange yearlings appeared on Sanctuary. They were with Nanni, Bonni, and Buster at the entrance of a cave below the cliffs. The two strange subadults were restless and attempted to scale the cliffs. However, they became hopelessly lost in the small overhangs and got nowhere. Nanni ignored them, and Buster stood and watched them while Bonni followed the two, then waited as the yearling female out front attempted to find a way up. The path up the cliff used by Sanctuary sheep lay about 80 paces away, and in future times these new sheep used it without exception. Their abortive attempt to scale a cliff identified them, among other evidence, as strangers to the area.

When the two strangers were stuck in the cliffs, Bonni turned and hopped down to the cave entrance, which caused the strangers to run after her. The running subadults scared Nanni and she bolted, and the subadults bolted after her. Twenty paces further all three stopped and looked around, following a rule applicable to sheep—run first, look later.

Again the two strangers went for the cliff, and again they got lost. Again Bonni followed them. At this point Nanni walked away along the cliff. Buster stood, looked at the subadults in the cliffs and then at his departing mother. He moved a few steps in the direction of Nanni and then a few steps back in the direction of Bonni. He apparently could not make up his mind whom to follow. Then, after looking back and forth between Bonni and Nanni, Buster began plucking some grass. Soon he started to walk after Nanni, at first hesitantly, then at a trot, and finally at a gallop till he caught up with her. His gallop triggered the subadults into jumping down the cliff to follow Nanni. This was the second indication that Buster was soon to leave Nanni and follow other sheep instead. I called the new yearling female "Blacki," and the male "Bumper."

On 25 April three more newcomers appeared, an older ewe and her lamb plus a yearling female. This trio was named "Nuju," "Nuel," and "Browni." There were now two adult females, two lambs, and four subadults on Sanctuary Mountain. The subadult females Blacki, Bonni, and Browni soon formed a linear dominance hierarchy, in that order. Blacki and Bonni formed a dominance pair, that is, everywhere I saw Bonni, Blacki was close by, often butting her. The subadults stuck rather close with the old ewe they first joined on Sanctuary or came with to Sanctuary. Browni followed Nuju and Bonni, Blacki and Bumper preferred Nanni, but all joined some other sheep occasionally (table 24).

As the spring progressed toward early summer, the lambs Buster ($\male$) and Nuel ($\female$) followed their dams less and less often (table 25). Even when they were close enough to their dams to be counted as being with them, they appeared more interested in the subadults, while these were not infrequently roaming Sanctuary on their own or in company of rams. The old ewes tended to stand alone and

Table 24

Association of four subadult Stone's sheep with other sheep

	Period observed	Sighted with N-ewe	Sighted with U-ewe	Sighted without adult company	Sighted with rams	Total sightings
Bonni (♀)	1 Ja–6 Je 62	36	4	6	6	52
Browni (♀)	28 F–6 Je 62	4	9	3	3	19
Blacki (♀)	14 Ap–6 Je 62	11	2	3	3	19
Bumper (♂)	14 Ap–6 Je 62	8	1	1	5	15

Note: Subadult sheep are 1½–2 years old.

showed little interest in each other. Buster left Nanni for good by 22 April, about five weeks before Nanni gave birth to her lamb Bim (♂) on 30 May. Nuel left Nuju much later, by 20 May; Nuju gave birth in early June to Baml (♀).

When Nanni descended from the cliffs with her newborn lamb on 6 June, the subadults at once joined her and stuck to her from then on. The lamb appeared to be a center of attraction as new lambs tend to be. Nuju had joined the crowd with her lamb by 20 June, which was the last time I saw them before they moved to their summer ranges.

On 15 October 1962, the females and subadults returned to Sanctuary. Nanni appeared, followed by Bim, Bonni, Blacki, and Buster, while Nuju had Baml, Browni, Nuel, and Bumper in tow. The preferences

Table 25

Association of two known Stone's lambs with their dams during winter and spring

Month	Total sightings	Sighted with dam
Jan	9	9
Feb	6	4
Mar	15	15
Apr	19	12
May	21	9
June	7	0

for a specific female expressed by the subadults in the spring (table 23) had remained till fall. In addition to the subadults mentioned, there were three others with the females, two yearling females and one yearling ram. Nanni and Nuju had obviously picked them up in summer. They were not alone in this respect.

On 16 October the three Cliff Mountain females returned followed by two lambs and one yearling female. Since during the previous fall only one lamb had been present, which did not survive the winter, the yearling female must have been a pickup from the summer range or from the migration to Cliff Mountain.

The Sanctuary females did not retain the new yearlings that they brought to Sanctuary. One yearling female disappeared. On 28 December 1962, I saw Nuju and Baml on Ghost Mountain. Since previously Nuel and one yearling female plus a strange yearling male had followed Nuju about, it is likely she took them to Ghost Mountain with her. Only Nanni with Bim, Buster, Blacki, and Bonni were seen in the following weeks on Sanctuary.

I did not see what happened to Bonni, now 2½ years old and mature during her first rut. She separated from Blacki and was not present on those parts of Sanctuary I could easily census. Most of the time Blacki and 7-year-old H-ram were together in the cliffs, separated from other sheep. Blacki was resting or feeding, while H-ram stood behind her in a horn display. After the rut she and Bonni were together again; however, I have few sightings since in January 1963 little snow covered the ground and the sheep were at high elevation, roamed far, and were rarely seen. I left on 27 January 1963.

I returned almost three years later on 27 November 1965. The first ewe I saw on Sanctuary was Nanni. She was alone and had no lamb. In the following days I discovered Bonni and Blacki, and as in earlier days, Blacki followed Bonni. Bonni had a lamb at heel. One day a ewe with lamb crossed Sanctuary; it was Browni. One further ewe I saw several times was a young adult female which closely resembled Nuju not only in body marking, color, and head marking, but even in stance and facial expression. It was almost certainly Nuel, but I am not certain. I never found Nuju. Even if I had seen Buster, Bim, Baml, and Bumper, I would not have recognized them for they would have changed greatly in the preceding year.

The only other animal that must be mentioned is Schmudface, a 2½-year-old ram in 1962, whom I first saw 8 miles from Sanctuary on 13 November 1962. I spotted him next on Cliff and Shady on 27

November, then on Sanctuary on 28 November where he stayed for the rut, and where I last saw him on 26 January, a few days before my departure. There was a good chance of finding him on Sanctuary in early December 1965, but instead he turned up one mile across the valley from Sanctuary Mountain on Cliff Mountain, on 4 December 1965.

This case history of sheep on Sanctuary Mountain illustrates many important points in the home range establishment by sheep, as well as in their social life. These will now be examined in greater detail.

DISASSOCIATION OF MOTHER AND YOUNG

The disassociation of the two Stone's lambs Buster and Nuel from their mothers is shown in table 25. The lambs began to act independently 7–8 weeks before their mothers gave birth and were on their own 2–5 weeks before their first birthday. How representative were their actions of mountain sheep as a whole? This was investigated by indirect means, using the behavior of Buster and Nuel as the model to be tested.

On Ghost Mountain, across from Sanctuary, I consistently noticed the following from the middle of April onward:

1. Individually recognizable females entered ewe groups with a lamb at heel but left without.
2. Some individually known ewes would be followed by a lamb on some days but not on others.
3. Some ewes that I observed without a lamb in winter were suddenly followed again by a lamb.
4. One old, barren female often had from 2 to 6 lambs following her. Not only are twin births in sheep a great rarity, but this particular female had no lamb at heel till early spring. This animal could not have been the mother of any of the lambs.
5. Rams and subadult ewes were followed by lambs.
6. Lambs banded together into groups and often moved about on their own, quite independently of adult ewes.

These six points are compatible only with the hypothesis that lambs desert their mothers from April onward to follow and associate temporarily with sheep of their own choice, as was illustrated by the actions of Buster and Nuel. The ewes were not observed to discourage or to accelerate the disassociation; unlike moose or deer they did not chase their young away, they ignored them. In three consecutive springs with bighorn sheep, similar observations were made. The ratio of short yearlings to adult ewes rose as the lambing season approached (since pregnant ewes withdrew into seclusion to give birth), and dropped again thereafter (as females with newborn lambs emerged again and were joined by other sheep) (fig. 10).

The first evidence that bighorn lambs were beginning to leave their dams appeared in mid-March, or 10 weeks before lambing season. Lambs were seen to follow adult rams on the Palliser wintering area. The frequency of lambs associating with rams rose and fell in a similar manner as the ratio of yearling lambs to adult females (fig. 10). Among feral Soay sheep lambs began leaving their dams shortly after weaning (Grubb and Jewell 1966).

On both the Stone's sheep and bighorn study areas, a few barren females adopted groups of yearling lambs. Not infrequently they bounced and frolicked with the youngsters over the snow-free slopes, a behavior not engaged in by pregnant females. One old female licked and nuzzled the heads of a few yearling lambs, and one called after some yearling lambs that were deserting her. It may be that barren ewes experience an upsurge in maternal behavior in spring, but this has as yet to be demonstrated. The behavioral reasons for this association of generations are not known.

The consequence of the foregoing is that yearling lambs are almost

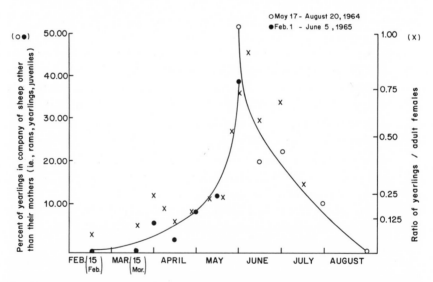

Fig. 10. The percentage of yearlings which follow sheep other than their mother increases from late February on and reaches its peak during the lambing season. After the lambing season, yearlings follow adult females more frequently. The ratio of yearlings to adult females undergoes a similar fluctuation.

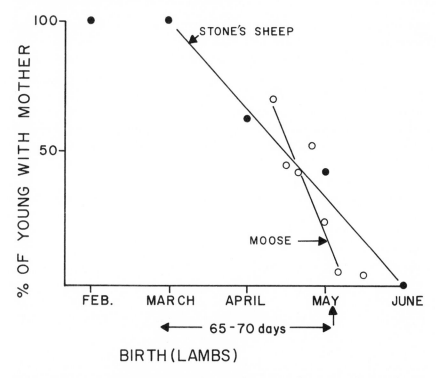

Fig. 11. Moose yearlings disassociate from their mothers faster than do Stone's year-lings from their dams. Stone's lambs began disassociating 65–70 days before the birth of the first lamb. (Moose data from Wells Gray Provincial Park, B.C. 1960)

constantly in the company of some older sheep. From 283 bighorn yearlings seen between 15 May and 30 June 1964 and 1965, 76% followed adult ewes, 15.5% followed adult rams, 5% followed 2-year-old ewes (plate 21), 3.2% associated with other yearling lambs, while only 1.05% were seen alone.[1]

Although it is not known how mother and young separate in most mammals, we do know that mountain sheep and moose (*Alces*) or deer (*Odocoileus*) differ greatly in this process. Cow moose and calf separate violently in the course of a few days, after which the yearling is entirely on his own. The cow moose becomes intolerant of other moose as calving time approaches and finally she turns on her own calves and chases them off. The calves attempt to follow but are chased off again, until they move off to join fellow sufferers or attach themselves temporarily to bulls. Figure 11 shows graphically that cow moose and calf separate

1. The sociology of young sheep can be seen in the Encyclopaedia Cinematographica film E 1336.

during a shorter period of the year than sheep, while table 26 shows the complex sociability patterns of moose during the calving season as observed in Wells Gray Provincial Park, B.C., in spring 1960. The following appeared to be happening: as the yearlings were forced from their mothers they associated often with adult bulls. However, when calving time approached closely, as indicated by relatively fewer sightings of cows, the frequent attacks by cows on bulls led to a breakup of bull groups (and increased sightings of single bulls) as well as of bull-calf associations. These associations re-formed after the height of calving. In summer the yearlings were very much on their own, indicating that bull-calf associations were not lasting.

TABLE 26

Social dynamics of moose during the calving season

Period	No. of bulls seen	No. of cows seen	No. of yearlings seen	Yearlings			Cows as % of adults ($♀/♀ + ♂$)	% of bulls seen alone
				% alone	% with cow	% with bull		
5–10 May	90	123	93	16	70	4	56	29
11–15	95	117	54	20	45	26	55	24
16–20	92	89	69	22	43	24	49	37
21–25	81	79	28	32	53	15	49	46
26–30	144	33	11 ⎫	76	24	0	18.5	61
1–5 June	213	102	28 ⎭				32	53
6–10	130	49	46	44	6.5	29	27	52
11–15	124	38	74	36	5.4	46	23	55

White-tailed deer (*O. virginianus*) and mule deer (*O. hemionus*) also appear to chase off yearlings at calving time; however, the females do tolerate the company of yearlings again in later summer (Servinghaus and Cheatum 1956; Lindsdale and Tomich 1953; Geist 1966*c*). The separation of mother and young need not be permanent as it apparently is in moose, although detailed observations on individually known deer as well as moose are needed to confirm this view. In some areas cow moose are frequently followed by a yearling in summer (Denniston 1956; De Vos 1956). Altmann (1963) suggests that cows which lose their calves shortly after birth may reaccept the yearlings. This is plausible, but in need of verification.

The separation in red deer and elk (*C. elaphus*) appears similar to that shown by mountain sheep, although the hard data on individually marked animals are scarce (Schloeth 1966). The yearlings tend to become independent 6–8 weeks before calving time and may be repulsed by the female once the new calf is born. The female yearlings tend to reestablish a bond with their mother, while the male yearlings are more independent. In the second and third years of life the females drift away from their mothers. Like mountain sheep, red deer females pass on their home range tradition to their female offsprings (Schloeth and Burckhardt 1961), as was determined from marked individuals. Lent (1966) shows indirectly that yearling caribou (*Rangifer*) separate from their mothers prior to calving, attach themselves to barren females, and are already on their own when the herds arrive on the calving grounds. There is little evidence of violent mother-young separation for red deer, caribou, and mountain sheep; females may, however, butt or slap away yearlings that get too close to the new calf. The significance of this to the biology of these highly social ruminants will be discussed in chapter 5. It is noteworthy that in the highly social zebras (*Equus quagga*) from the African plains, Klingel (1967) found no violent separation of mother and young either. The young mare remains in her family group till her first estrous period at which time she is abducted by stallions and becomes a low-ranking member in some other family group or the sole female in a young stallion's possession. The young stallion gets separated from the family group when he finds equal age playmates elsewhere, even though his father may search for him and return him temporarily to the family group (Klingel 1967).

Why should there be such differences in the mother-young separation of ungulates? The biology of free-living ungulates is too poorly known to permit a certain explanation; nevertheless, it is possible to explain what selective forces formed the differences in mother-young separation in mountain sheep and moose (see chap. 5). It appears that if ecological selection forces ungulates into social life, mother-young separation is gradual and not violent.

Loss of Subadult Females from Maternal Home Range Groups

The studies of Hunter (1962) and Hunter and Milner (1963) on domestic sheep in Scotland indicate that closely related sheep form home range groups, and that the home ranges of the mother are adopted by the daughters. Superficially, much the same appears to be true for mountain sheep. About two-thirds of all females in the Palliser group which I studied had been tagged by Warden Stenton during the period 1949–65. No tagged female was ever seen in the next group of females north of the Palliser, the Bare Mountain ewes, although females from these two groups came close to each other in Bighorn Valley. Only rarely was a tagged female reported from the Aylmer ewe group, which was observed daily at close range each summer for 15 years by Norman Tithrington from the Aylmer fire lookout tower. The Palliser and Aylmer females were as close together in summer as the opposite sides of the same mountain. Since Mr. Stenton concentrated on tagging yearlings and lambs, the observations indicate that juvenile females rarely leave the maternal bands. Yet, it does happen.

Bonni left the Ghost Mountain ewes by following C-ram to Sanctuary Mountain. Blacki appeared suddenly on Sanctuary Mountain on 14 April 1962 and, like Bonni, became a resident adopting Nanni's home range. The strange yearlings brought in fall 1962 by the Sanctuary and Cliff Mountain ewes were raised elsewhere. The same happened among bighorn sheep.

On 20 October 1964, I recorded two subadult bighorns from the Bare Mountain group, about 16 miles outside their home range on the Palliser Range. One was a 2½-year-old female, the other a ram of equal age. The female followed the ram. I had seen and photographed both on Bare Mountain on 4 October. I never saw that female thereafter; the partial history of the ram is recorded in chapter 3 with the discussion of deviations from seasonal movement patterns.

Another instance of a juvenile female following a ram outside the home ranges of her female group was reported by J. C. Holroyd, assistant chief warden of Banff park. On 4 July 1963, he noted a young bighorn male and young female on Mount Wardle, Kootenay National Park. These sheep were a considerable distance outside the limits of sheep distribution. These two sheep remained on Mount Wardle till 3 August, when they were seen by Mr. Holroyd crossing the Vermilion River and moving off in a direction where other mountain sheep were found.[2]

The behavior of the subadult females on Sanctuary Mountain indicated that in their second spring and third summer they could well have been lost to another home range group had the opportunity arisen. Although they showed some preference to follow a particular ewe, they did switch to the other available female, went off by them-

2. Warden Observation cards, 4 July and 3 August 1963, Kootenay National Park, District no. 2.

selves, or moved about with adult rams (table 24). It is possible that this time period in the life of females determines which home ranges they adopt; if on a minor excursion they meet sheep traveling elsewhere they may well follow. Once they are 3 years old they have probably fixed their home ranges as is indicated by the great loyalty with which females return to their seasonal home ranges. Females only rarely adopt home ranges other than those of their maternal band because of a residual loyalty to the female that raised them, and also because of lack of contact with strange sheep during the subadult stage of life.

HOME RANGE ESTABLISHMENT AND THE SOCIETY OF RAMS

Whereas the female generally remains on the home range of the maternal female group, the male leaves the female group some time after his second birthday—sooner only exceptionally. The changeover from female to male company is a gradual process which takes years to complete, since rams up to 6 years of age still show more tendency to be in female company than older rams do (fig. 12). The process of the

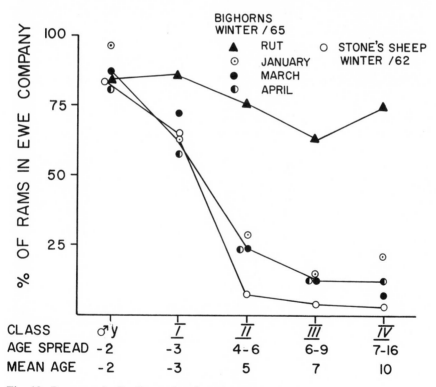

Fig. 12. Rams gradually disassociate from females with age.

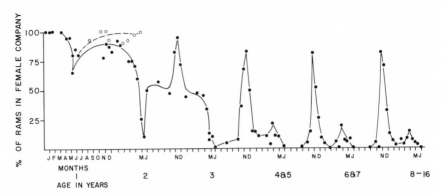

Fig. 13. The association pattern of bighorn rams with females in the yearly cycle throughout the life of the ram. The open points show the association pattern of females up to 2 years of age. At each lambing season (May and June—*MJ*) there is a low in the frequency of rams seen with ewes as the latter withdraw for lambing. The peak of association occurs during the rut (November and December—*ND*). A second peak appears in April, but this may be an artifact of rams and ewes crowding onto the slopes free of snow in early spring.

ram's disassociation from females is best shown by the graphs in figure 13. In general the yearling male is seen somewhat less frequently than yearling females in female company. The lambing seasons cause a marked drop in the frequency of males sighted in female company. In his third summer the ram is in the changeover process, but after his third birthday he acts similarly to older rams. He moves after he thoroughly dominates females (chap. 7).

The age at which the young ram moves to the females may differ between different populations as Nievergelt (1967) found for ibex. He showed that ibex males from young, expanding populations tended to grow larger and leave females earlier than males from older, stagnant populations.

During their third summer, young rams increase their chances of moving far from their maternal band not only by following rams but also by wandering off on their own. This wandering phase is indicated in the frequency with which $2\frac{1}{2}$-year-old rams were seen alone or in company of an equal-age companion (fig. 14). Rams older than 3 years are seen most frequently alone during the rutting season, whereas rams between 2 and 3 years of age are seen alone mainly in summer and early fall. Thereafter they are almost as social as yearling rams (table 27). It appears that most sheep seen outside their normal range of distribution are such young rams. Yet they could not act as colonizers.

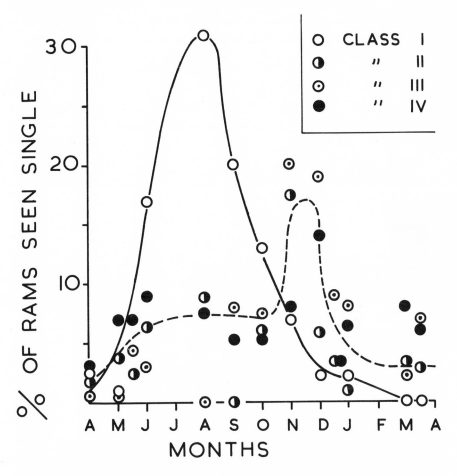

Fig. 14. Percent frequency of bighorn rams seen as singles throughout the year. Whereas rams older than 4 years are seen alone mainly in November and December, during the rutting season, rams at 2–2.5 years are seen alone primarily in summer and fall. They stray somewhat in their third summer of life.

Table 27 shows that young rams outside the short wandering phase in summer stick closely to other sheep; they are less independent of other sheep than older rams (table 51). From this alone one could infer that young rams once alone will soon attempt to find companions. The few wandering rams I observed moved from elevation to elevation, scanning the slopes and calling as lone sheep often do. It appears that a good habitat without companions is an unattractive environment to a young ram, and he cannot be expected to remain. Moreover, dispersing

TABLE 27

Frequency with which single rams were observed

	Class				
	IV	III	II	I	♂y
	Bighorn				
Average age (yrs)	11	7	5	2.5	1.5
Total individuals observed	1,796	985	1,880	366	401
No. seen single	116	56	71	9	7
% seen single	6.5	5.7	3.8	2.4	1.75
	Stone's				
Average age (yrs)	10+	7–9	4–6	2–3	1–2
Total individuals observed	39	178	159	34	54
No. seen single	19	35	15	0	3
% seen single	49	19.5	9.3	0	5.5

rams may also gain a reproductive advantage as discussed in chapter 3 (p. 90).

LEADERSHIP

After joining a band of rams, the young rams follow the largest-horned ram. By following various large rams during the yearly cycle the young ram presumably establishes a home range of his own. Leadership among rams is closely related to horn size. The larger a ram's horns the more bands follow him, the larger the bands he leads, and hence the more sheep follow him.

I recognized as a "leader" the first sheep in a moving band; only exceptionally is the first animal in front of a moving band not the one that is followed. Leadership was recorded quantitatively when bands of sheep crossed from one range to the next and when sheep fled from disturbances.

There were other leadership situations but they were too rare to be recorded quantitatively, such as lambs bolting suddenly and drawing the whole flock after them in a short flight or, at lambing time, barren females serving as leaders to bands of juveniles.

The following was noted for every band on the move: the sex and size of the leading sheep, the number of sheep in the band, and the

Plate 30. During normal, long movements sheep walk in single file.

Plate 31. A band of bighorn ewes and subadults in panicked flight. The animals bunch; a yearling lamb leads the way.

Plate 32. The low-stretch, performed by a class III ram while passing a class I ram. This is the most common signal of dominant rams.

Plate 33. Two full-curl rams in a present horn display during a dominance fight. The dark ram on left is the loser. Note his backing off from his larger rival.

Plate 34. Occasionally a ram crouches when performing a low-stretch toward a female, which suggests that this behavior pattern is homologous to the low-stretch of the mountain goat.

Plate 35. The twist. It is performed toward rams and ewes, primarily by dominant rams.

Plate 36. The front kick. Dominant ram kicks at subordinate.

Plate 37. Vestigial neck fight. A large class II ram places his chin over the neck of his smaller, class I opponent. This behavior, rarely seen in mountain sheep, is a common fighting behavior in primitive caprids.

Plate 38. A class II ram mounts a class I ram. Note that the smaller ram arches his back in lordosis.

Plate 39. Ejaculation posture of ibex and true goats, here performed by a markhor.

Plate 40. The lipcurl.

Plate 41. A ram sniffs and nuzzles the vulva of a urinating ewe. Note the hair structure of the coat in early winter.

Plate 42. A class II bighorn examines the rear of a yearling male after low-stretching to him. Note the small size of testes on the yearling.

Plate 43. Contact patterns. (*a*) A class II ram (*right*) rubbing on and nuzzling the horns of an old class IV ram. (*b*) The class II ram switches to horning the face of the old ram.

Plate 44. Young bighorn rams and an old ewe playing in early summer. The ram in the center shows a threat jump.

Plate 45. The butt. The ram on left propels himself flat over the ground and delivers a blow with the left horn edge.

Plate 46. The subordinate ram in a dominance fight (*left*) charges at dominant, while the latter rises to meet the onrush.

Plate 47. Ewe during clash. (*a*) After making contact the ewe continues to press down on her opponent by pivoting the rigid body and neck about the shoulders and jumping up in the rear. (*b*) Here a different technique is used to continue the force on the opponent. The ewe collapses the front legs and pivots the body about the acetabulum.

Plate 48. A miss. The full-curl ram fails to connect the blow and catches himself. Note the downward motion of the blow. The smallest ram evades the full-curl by jumping aside; the larger ram (*left*) throws his horns forward defensively in a horn threat.

Plate 49. A clash during a severe dominance fight. It was initiated by the smaller ram on left.

Plate 50. A clash in which the rams slipped off each other's horns and pitched head-first into the snow. This is no rare occurrence.

Plate 51. The rush charge.

Plate 52. Effect of the clash. The ram on left is telescoped by the clash.

Plate 53. Combat damage on the horn and face of an old ram. A large chunk of horn has been knocked out of his right horn; the horn tip is broken off. Some hair butted off the body of an opponent sticks to the horn tip and covers the horn surfaces.

Plate 54. Combat damage to the coat of the ram. Note the streaks left primarily by the broomed horn tips of the aggressor.

Plate 55. Splintered horn tips are one effect of the clash.

Plate 56. A class I ram about to butt a ewe, which is preparing to catch the blow.

Plate 57. Cross section through the skulls of an old thar (*top*) and an old bighorn ram (*bottom*). Note the extensive pneumations above the brain and the thickness of the skull bones. Bighorns have probably the most solid skull construction among sheep.

sex and age of each follower. Ninety-five ram bands and 23 ewe bands were so classified (see tables 28 and 29). The results indicate that:

1. During migration or disturbance, bighorn ewes and juveniles follow one mature ewe.

2. Rams follow one of the larger-horned rams (usually the largest-horned ram) in the band. Such rams led (a) almost every band they were present in (2 exceptions from 73); (b) more sheep than smaller-horned rams; (c) larger bands than those following smaller-horned rams.

3. Rams change their leadership preference as they advance in age from following ewes to following rams. The changes occur gradually between 2 and 4 years of age.

4. Although some ewes associated with and followed *large* rams, the converse was not observed.

During movement sheep either follow single file or, during disturbance, usually cluster behind the lead sheep (plate 22).[3] The lead sheep maintains its front position against those that attempt to pass it either by butting sideways at offenders or running forward while displaying in low-stretch. This behavior is not typical of lead sheep alone but is done by all sheep toward those attempting to pass. The result is a rather

TABLE 28

Leadership in bighorn rams

	Class			
	IV	III	II	I
No. of bands in which the designated class was present (A)	73	59	82	33
No. of bands in which the class was leading (B)	71	15	7	2
% of bands in which the class was present and led ($[A/B] \times 100$)	97.5	25.0	8.5	6.0
No. of rams led by the class (C)	437	81	20	5
Average size of band following a leader of this class (C/B)	6.1	5.4	2.9	2.5
% of all moving sheep found in bands led by this class ($[C/543] \times 100$)	80.4	15.0	3.7	0.9

NOTE: Data based on 95 ram bands containing 543 rams, Banff, 1963–65.

3. See also film E 1334.

TABLE 29

A comparison of ram and ewe leadership in bighorns

	Class							
	IV	III	II	I	♂y	♀	♀y	L
No. of sheep that followed rams in class (A)	100	82	205	48	4	8	1	0
No. of sheep that followed ewes in class (B)	0	0	3	16	14	65	9	32
% of all sheep on the move being led by ewes ([B/(A + B)] × 100)	0	0	1.4	25	78	89	90	100

NOTE: Data based on 95 bands led by rams and 23 bands led by ewes, Banff, 1963–65.

stable march order if sheep move in single file; the attempts to discourage passing appear to be effective and lasting.

Observations of individually known sheep indicated that old, senile ewes were not followed by other sheep, except by yearlings at lambing time, and that no one sheep consistently acted as leader. In areas with few sheep this appears to be different, for Welles and Welles (1961) observations of desert bighorns indicated that the female bands were rather stable and one female was consistently followed by all others. Normally, sheep on their seasonal home ranges move about in small groups or pairs rather than as one unit. The sparse population of Stone's sheep I observed was seen usually as very small groups. The female groups tended to split into units of one female with her lambs plus subadults and occasionally a female without lamb. These units moved about without too much attention to each other. To see sheep in marching order proceeding as one unit is not common.

Beninde (1937) and Welles and Welles (1961) suggest that leaders are the most independent members of a group. For rams this appears to be so. Independent animals are those that follow others least and are hence also found more frequently alone than others. The larger rams grow the more often they are seen alone (see table 27). Frequency of being sighted alone (table 27) and leadership (average size of band led, on table 28) are positively correlated for bighorn rams ($r = 0.95$, $t = 4.5$, $p < 0.05$). For ewes this hypothesis remains to be verified.

Often the question is posed whether dominance and leadership are related (Stewart and Scott 1947; Scott 1958; Beilharz and Mylrea 1965; Welles and Welles 1961). The question cannot be answered as such for mountain sheep. In ram bands, dominance and leadership are positively related; the largest-horned rams are the most dominant and are also followed most frequently. However, the reverse is true for dominance pairs of rams, for here the dominant follows the subordinate (chap. 7), as is also commonly found in Grant's gazelles (Walther 1968). In female bands the most dominant animals are the 3–5-year-old rams, but these follow rather than lead females. Here dominance and leadership are not related. The question why female sheep follow one particular female and less frequently others remains to be answered.

When the young ram enters the company of older rams he could follow one ram to his summer home range, another to the pre-rut area, a third to his rutting ground, and a fourth to the spring home range. The fixation of the home range pattern appears to take place between 3 and 5 years of age. Thereafter the ram moves in a predictable fashion between his home ranges, and as he grows larger becomes more frequently a leader to younger rams, passing on his home range knowledge to them. Yet, if home ranges are inherited socially and the distribution of a population is the result of a living migratory tradition, how do sheep disperse into uninhabited areas? If the young rams cannot be expected to colonize new range during their migratory phase, who does? These questions will be answered in chapter 5.

How similar or different is leadership in mountain sheep to that found in other ruminants? The question is not easily answered for there are little tangible data on leadership in the ruminant literature. Walther (1968) showed that in Grant's gazelles, the smallest males are ahead of the larger, dominant males when on the march. In fact, the march order of bucks is inversely related to their horn size and dominance rank, the reverse of what one finds in mountain sheep. McHugh (1958) showed that a few female bison accounted for most leading in female herds, while in bull groups often, but not always, a large bull led the way. Field observations suggest that in species which form female bands some large female is followed, but little can be said beyond this (on red deer, Beninde 1937 and Darling 1937; on chamois, Knaus 1960; on mountain goat, Geist 1965; on giraffe, Backhaus 1961). A number of studies on penned ungulates tell very little of relevance to the biology of the animals, except for Gilbert and Hailman's study (1966) demonstrating that female fallow deer (*Dama*) tend to follow each other in a predictable order during flight. In species in which one male is permanently associated with a female group, as in hartebeest (*Alecelaphus*) (Backhaus 1959*b*), in the vicuna (*Vicugna*) (Koford 1957), or in the zebra (*Equus quagga*) (Klingel 1967), the male may regularly or often direct the movement of the herd either by leading or by herding. Little has been reported about leadership in all-male groups, such as is found among the males of many deer. Darling (1937) found no obvious leadership among red deer stags; Beninde (1937) stated that large stags controlled the movements of the group, but were not ahead of the band. Obviously, some room for critical investigation remains.

5 Traditions and the Evolution of Social Systems: Sheep versus Moose

INTRODUCTION

The past history of mountain sheep indicates that they are one of the most successful large Pleistocene mammals. They survived not only from the beginning of the ice ages and spread to most major mountain ranges in the northern hemisphere, but also maintained themselves up to recent times in the face of man's activity. Their distribution from Europe to Siberia and Alaska to Mexico is equaled by few mammals and implies that sheep are successful dispersers and colonizers. Yet, in recent times sheep have revealed some limitations, which virtually contradict their past performance.

Up to the last century, sheep appear to have been numerous in North America and Asia and to have occupied a greater range than they do today. Buechner (1960) in his survey of the history of sheep in the United States showed that sheep have been drastically reduced in numbers and now are usually found as small, scattered populations on small fractions of their once vast range. The major causes of sheep reduction appear to be a combination of competition from livestock, diseases introduced by domestic sheep, and indiscriminate hunting. One race of bighorn sheep, the Badland bighorns (*O. c. auduboni*) was eradicated. In Canada and Alaska, sheep have apparently suffered less from man as their present distribution indicates, except for the California bighorns of southern British Columbia, which according to Sugden (1961) have lost range and been reduced in numbers. In Siberia and central and western Asia, sheep suffered much the same fate as in America. Heptner et al. (1961) report that snow sheep, argalis, and urials have all been greatly reduced in number and eradicated from much, if not most, of their former range.

In the United States and Russia measures were enacted to either protect sheep, or control hunting where sheep were still common. Despite this, sheep made no noteworthy recovery on either continent. Protection of sheep has been locally in force in the United States since

117

the turn of the century, and in Russia since after the October Revolution, yet only exceptionally have sheep spread from the restricted areas to which they were confined. On the whole sheep have maintained their number and distribution at the level it was shortly after protection began (Buechner 1960). Some populations rose in numbers but crashed only to rise again without colonizing uninhabited mountain ranges close by. Occasionally a sheep is sighted in a region inhabited once before by sheep, but the hope that more will come and settle is usually in vain. From the descriptions of Buechner and Heptner, Nasimovitsch, and Bannikov it is evident that sheep had opportunity enough to recolonize sizable portions of their former range but failed to do so.

What kept sheep, which colonized continents in the past, from reoccupying uninhabited former habitat close by? By contrast, moose have vastly expanded their range in Asia, Europe, and North America in the last half century and colonized thousands of square miles of new terrain (Hatter 1950; Heptner et al. 1960); white-tailed deer (*Odocoileus virginianus*) have done almost as well in North America.

In British Columbia moose advanced into the southern half of the province since the turn of the century (Hatter 1950). They penetrated the coastal ranges and extended their distribution to southeast Alaska (Klein 1965). In eastern Canada moose expanded southward and white-tailed deer northward (De Vos 1962). White-tailed deer spread across the northern parts of the Canadian prairie provinces and are now advancing into the Peace River area of British Columbia. They made small but noteworthy advances in southern British Columbia also. The large range extensions of moose in Eurasia are discussed by Heptner et al. (1961), Heptner and Nasimovitsch (1968), Briedermann (1968), and Pielowski (1969).

Why did sheep fail to spread when moose and deer did? No physical barriers or anatomical limitations are apparent which would preclude sheep from going where moose or deer could. Sheep can cross rivers or lakes in summer by wading or swimming and in winter by walking on the ice (Cowan 1940; Smith 1954). Snow is a serious hindrance when it is soft and deep, but in late winter it freezes hard each night and becomes like a paved road allowing sheep to run and gallop on its surface without breaking through. I have often seen sheep cross valleys on the surface of hard snow, a feat that a moose cannot do, for it breaks through the crust and generally refuses to move under such snow conditions. Sheep can cross rubble and cliffs which moose or deer could not and generally perform long movements over much the same terrain as moose or deer. Single sheep do cross to uninhabited terrain (Buechner 1960); if these can do it, there are no physical reasons why the others could not.

At first thought a psychological factor appears to limit sheep dispersal. Sheep dislike entering timber. This is evident to anyone who works with mountain sheep intensively. The tame but free-living bighorn sheep from the Palliser would follow me at heel for miles as long as I remained on the open slopes or in the cliff terrain, but they would desert me soon after I entered the timber. On a few occasions I did lead a small band up to 400 paces into the timber, but usually the bighorns returned to the open slopes after following me from 50 to 150 paces down into the forest. During migration sheep tend to stick to the open spaces, avoiding timber or displaying caution when entering it. Similar observations have been made by Murie (1944) and Wishart (1958).

Yet such observations are hard to reconcile with the fact that sheep in natural populations, such as the ones studied in the Cassiars or Banff National Park, made long, regular movements through miles of forested terrain or fled into timber when disturbed. The Stone's rams I knew crossed through one to two miles of timber when moving between Sanctuary, Ghost, Cliff Mountain, and Lupin Hill. Bighorns wintering on Grassy Mountain went through about 4 miles of open forest to and from Flint Mountain in spring and fall. Palliser rams crossed the forested Cascade valley as well as the densely timbered gorge to Grassy Mountain. In southern British Columbia, California bighorns wintering east of the Ashnola River moved in excess of 6 air miles through timbered terrain to reach their summer range. These sheep regularly took flight into timber upon disturbance, as do all sheep occasionally if no cliffs are about. One is faced by the contradiction that on one hand sheep seem to avoid timber and on the other they cross it readily and take refuge therein.

Since this cannot explain why sheep have not reoccupied former habitat, perhaps the question itself is based on false assumptions, for example, that sheep habitat once vacated by sheep remains acceptable to sheep for decades after their extinction. Perhaps sheep are perfectly capable of dispersing but do not colonize the former habitat because it is changed and no longer sheep habitat. This possibility can be tested. Two predictions are implied: (1) Sheep will not prosper in areas of former distribution if reintroduced there. (2) Biologists studying sheep biology are poor judges of their animals' habitat and requirements.

Both predictions can be tested by letting knowledgeable persons select areas suitable for sheep reintroductions and then release sheep therein. If the sheep prosper, obviously the habitat is suitable even if it has changed since the days of earlier sheep occupation, and the person selecting the site for reintroduction knew what he was talking about. This experiment has repeatedly been done in the western United States. To discover how successful sheep introductions were I turned to the game departments of the states of New Mexico, Oregon, Washington, Colorado, Texas, Montana, and the province of British Columbia. In the spring of 1966 the score stood as follows: the first four states mentioned had made fifteen reintroductions in total of which two were judged failures; Montana made thirteen reintroductions of which four are definitely a success, three are definitely not, one is a probable failure, while the remaining five are too recent to be evaluated. In British Columbia three transplants were made of which one was a failure. Texas had sheep in a holding enclosure where they were thriving. Even if some reintroductions judged successful are too recent to be evaluated, I conclude that much sheep habitat formerly occupied by sheep is probably still suitable to sheep and that biologists are competent judges of mountain sheep requirements, although they may not have mastered reintroduction techniques to assure success on each try. The failure of some transplants may be due to factors other than unsuitable habitat.

At this point one fact must be considered: sheep are not unique in their ineptitude to spread to suitable terrain, but share this peculiarity with their close cousins, the goats and ibexes (*Capra*). The manner in which reintroduced populations of these species act is very similar. Ausser (1946) and Nievergelt (1966a) reported on the reintroduction of ibex in Austria and Switzerland, respectively. The introduced ibexes dispersed little, occupied only limited areas, and were loyal to these areas. Timbered valleys and glaciers appeared to be barriers to dispersal; if dispersal did occur, ibex colonized areas along the mountain block they were on but never an adjacent mountain range. Occasionally single males wandered off but returned again to the release site. The same can be said for bighorn sheep.

Feral goats (*Capra hircus*) which formed free-living populations on some of the Gulf Islands off the south coast of British Columbia after being introduced between 1880 and 1940 (Geist 1960) occupied only fractions of the available goat habitat. The ranges of the goats were quite small, limited to a ridge top in one case, to two adjacent mountains

in a second, and to a long cliff face in a third. The goats confined themselves to these areas although other habitat was close by. They spread
as far as the habitat was continuous. The choice where to live was made
less by the goats than by their former human masters.

The behavior of introduced bighorn sheep populations resembles
those of goats and ibex. No detailed history of introduced populations
was available to me, but the game departments of the states and provinces which had undertaken sheep reintroductions were kind enough
to supply some essential information. Except for one herd in Colorado,
sheep remained in the general vicinity of their release site (the exception
was a herd which moved as a unit to an entirely new location 25–30
miles from the original site). Introduced sheep remained limited in
distribution and colonized no new habitat in addition to that about the
release area. A few sheep strayed up to 30 miles from the transplant
areas. Except for minor altitudinal shifts, these sheep had not developed
habits of seasonal migrations so characteristic of sheep in relatively untouched wilderness. Only two Colorado herds provide an exception, for
they move seasonally 8–15 miles between high summer and low winter
ranges.

One caprid, the thar (*Hemitragus*) does not follow the pattern set
by the advanced sheep and goats. Introduced in New Zealand it is
dispersing capably (Anderson and Henderson 1961; Christie and
Andrews 1964).

This still leaves unexplained why sheep failed to extend their range
despite ample opportunity while moose and deer did. It appears that
moose establish home ranges primarily by individual exploration, whereas sheep transmit home range knowledge from generation to generation.
In the latter system, in which individual exploration plays only a small
role, the animals maintain the same area of distribution. Range extension is achieved by sheep in a manner different from home range
establishment, but in the same manner by moose. How and why did
these different systems of dispersal and home range establishment
evolve? It appears that the habitat forces a species into a given social
system.

FLUCTUATING HABITAT AND THE EVOLUTION OF MOOSE

Throughout much of its range in America, the moose is associated with
short-lived subclimax plant communities that follow in the wake of
forest fires. Once the climax coniferous forest is burned, herbs, shrubs,
and deciduous trees usually flourish on the burn for a number of years

and provide moose with an abundant food supply. Moose invade "burns" a few years after the fire and rapidly build up large populations. As the coniferous climax forest slowly reestablishes itself, the deciduous trees and shrubs are replaced and the moose populations decline and vanish, except for some stray individuals. This concept is borne out in principle by the studies of Hatter (1950), Edwards (1954), Peterson (1955), Lutz (1960), and Spencer and Hakalu (1964). The unstable, short-lived deciduous tree and shrub community that grows on burns may be called *transient* moose habitat.

Moose also live on patches of climax deciduous tree and shrub communities, which are maintained by such factors as alluvial soils, avalanches in mountains that often remove the conifers, or special climatic conditions. Such islands of *permanent* moose habitat are found along watercourses and in deltas where alluvial soils preclude the growth of conifer forests. Here willow, aspen, poplar, birch, and alder stands assure to moose a small amount of living space, whether or not fires burn off the conifer forests close by.

Another kind of permanent moose habitat are the dwarf birch and willow communities at timberline in the mountains of northern British Columbia. During my Stone's sheep study I found moose throughout winter on southerly exposed slopes grown over by birch, interspersed with willows on moist sites and aspen groves at low elevations. Although in late fall a few moose left the high valleys in favor of burns and river flats at lower elevations, many remained behind and could be consistently located. In summer moose occupied the alpine fir thickets on the north slopes.

The permanent and transient habitats of moose are superficially similar since both are formed by communities of deciduous shrubs and trees. Permanent habitat is less common and less conspicuous since few moose are found here, while burns with their large moose populations attract more attention. Yet both are important to moose evolution. Moose living in permanent habitat are the nuclei of future, large populations once mature stands of timber, hot summers, and thunderstorms set the stage for forest fires and large tracts of "burn habitat." We can visualize moose as expanding repeatedly in the course of centuries into fresh transient habitat and retreating slowly again into small patches of permanent habitat. Moose habitat is hence subject to irregular, rapid expansions and slow contractions, while moose are frequently thrown into the expanding phase of the population cycle. Forest fires are natural and common events; so moose as a species can depend on the appearance of new habitat, although they cannot know where and when it will appear.

In this situation yearling dispersal by moose appears to be a means of finding and exploiting transient habitat. The close mother-young bond is shattered when the cow drives off her yearling and forces it to roam about on its own. The yearling's movements appear erratic (Houston 1968). We do not know how far yearling moose roam or what clues they use to find living space and establish their own home ranges, but Houston discovered that they are loyal to their seasonal home ranges as has been shown for deer (Dasmann and Taber 1956; Michael 1958; Zalunardo 1965; Robinette 1966; Geist 1966d).

Passage of traditional home ranges from generation to generation as practiced by sheep would be useless to moose because of the short life expectancy of transient habitat. Assuming such traditions would exist then moose with home ranges on burns would lead their juveniles to increasingly deteriorated habitat with each generation, and finally to no habitat at all. A social inheritance of home range knowledge is possible only if moose were social, that is, lived in groups and followed one another constantly. However, social moose would be selected against on two counts: first, they would lead their offspring to deteriorating habitat as just pointed out. Second, herds of moose cannot be expected to survive on small patches of permanent habitat. Since moose are very large and need up to 30 lb of browse each per day in winter to sustain themselves (Heptner et al. 1961), a herd of moose would rapidly strip its immediate surroundings of food. This would matter little if moose could move rapidly to undepleted patches of habitat, but this is not possible in late winter and spring when the snow is deep and very hard. Moose have difficulty moving about in such snow, which is reflected in their great reluctance to run from humans and also in increased feeding on browse of poor quality (Heptner et al. 1961; Des Meules 1964). That is, in late winter moose feed on what is available and are less selective than in fall or early winter. Moreover, their food intake drops, they reduce activity to a minimum, and they lose weight (Heptner et al. 1961; Heptner and Nasimovitsch 1968). A herd of moose mired in deep, hard snow in late winter would soon strip the patch of permanent habitat of its limited resources and then suffer starvation. Yet a few moose might well survive where many would not. Houston (1968) studying Shira's moose came to a similar view.

At first glance it appears that the violent separation of mother from young is adaptive solely because dispersal of yearlings presumably increases random wandering by the young and the chances that transient habitat will be found. Since the young first to find suitable burns are the founders of large populations, cows which disperse their young have a greater chance of spreading their genes than cows that do not. Conversely, cows on burn habitat that disperse young increase their chances of finding and living on permanent habitat. Again this would spread the cow's genes. Nevertheless, there is a simpler explanation for the cow driving off its young.

The mother-young bond is very close in moose and remains so right up to calving time. This close association appears to be essential for the survival of the calf, for it depends largely on the cow for defense against wolves in late winter and spring. While the cow confronts the predators, the calf crowds in behind the cow. Mech (1966) observed that calves separated only a short distance from their dam quickly fell victims to wolves. In late winter when moose are confined to limited areas and greatly hindered in moving through deep, crusted snow, they have little choice but to stand and ward off wolves. Their terrifying defensive head-low threat (Geist 1963) and, among cervids, the unique ability to kick with the hind legs, plus the harsh, loud scare call, appear to be antiwolf adaptations of moose. Cows which watch and protect their young would maximize their reproduction and spread of genes. The need for maternal protection of the calf ends once the snow is melted, and then calving time is not far away. The only way to break the close bond between cow and calf is by violence. If the cow would tolerate the yearling during and after the birth of the calf, she would be selecting against herself on several counts.

During their first few days of life, calf moose are likely to follow any passing large object, not only their mothers. This can make them a great nuisance to biologists catching and tagging such calves, for they may be quite persistent in following their captors. It is likely that a calf would get up and follow any moose passing by were it not for its mother's determined effort to clear the calving area of all other moose. If the yearling was tolerated by the cow, it is likely that the small calves would follow it. Since yearling moose may meet other yearlings and play with them, chances are that the calf would be transferred to a strange yearling and be lost. Moreover, the calf may experience difficulty deciding whom to attach to permanently and may be forced to compete with the yearling for the same milk supply, much to its detriment. It appears, therefore, that a cow moose retaining her first offspring would select against her second.

STABLE HABITAT AND THE EVOLUTION OF SHEEP

The habitat of mountain sheep differs from that of moose in many ways, but the most important difference is that it is formed by stable, long lasting, climax grass communities. Grasslands regenerate themselves and do not vanish within a few decades as do "burn" habitats which moose inhabit. Sheep habitat appears to be displaced only gradually by other plant communities in response to climatic changes. Some grasslands occupied by sheep are exceptions, for they are created by forest fires, but even these grasslands revert slowly to climax forest. Such are the grasslands on the arid south-facing slopes of the Palliser Range in Banff National Park (Flook 1964). Although sheep habitat in North America is highly varied, stretching as it does from beyond the Arctic Circle to the hot deserts of California, Nevada, and Mexico, it is characterized by an open landscape and stable plant communities in which grasses or sedges predominate (Murie 1944; Russo 1950; Smith 1954; Sugden 1961; Blood 1963; Welles and Welles 1961; Demarchi 1965; McMahon 1965).

Sheep habitat is in my experience not continuous. It is patchy and the patches may be separated by miles of terrain unsuitable for sheep, such as dwarf birch flats, timbered valleys, glaciers, lakes, or rivers. On some mountains sheep habitat is confined almost entirely to southerly exposures, or a few well-drained, windswept slopes and ridges, while the rest of the mountain is covered by alpine fir, Engelmann's spruce, dwarf birch, rubble slopes, and aspen or willow groves. These dispersed patches are linked by the migratory routes of sheep into large units of range exploited by a population. In wilderness areas little disturbed by man, sheep move between these patches of habitat in a predictable manner as demonstrated in chapter 3.

The patchy distribution of sheep in the once glaciated regions of British Columbia, the Yukon, and Alberta indicates that once sheep inhabited a much larger area than they do today. The patches of sheep habitat would then be remnants of much larger grassland areas of earlier millennia. Sheep moved into the regions covered by the Cordilleran glaciers of the Wisconsin glaciation once the ice masses melted off about 10,000 years ago. During the Altithermal period it is likely that grasslands were more prevalent than today, but when a cooler, moister climate came, forests and brush flats spread along the valleys and ascended the mountains, thereby dividing and obliterating sheep habitat and restricting it to ever smaller patches at higher elevations. This was a slow process, and sheep continued their normal movement between mountains within a mountain range, despite the expanding forest. Hence, the present picture in relatively undisturbed areas shows sheep moving regularly through miles of timber between patches of habitat.

Under natural, undisturbed conditions, all patches of habitat are linked to a migratory net by sheep and all available habitat is exploited. There is hence *no* unexploited habitat close to a sheep population under *natural* conditions. In this situation no juvenile going out on its own could possibly discover new habitat. He can only find habitat patches already exploited by the population, but in striking out on his own, the juvenile wanders off into miles of unsuitable terrain where he could be easily lost or killed. Dispersing juveniles have nothing to gain and everything to lose. Therefore, selection would be against dispersing juveniles and in favor of those that stick with older sheep and follow them to distant patches of habitat. Selection would be particularly severe in relict populations that exploit few widely dispersed mountains, with much timber between them. Young sheep that follow adults adopt the habits of older individuals, habits which have been proved successful for generations and which allowed the leaders to grow old.

It is evident that any factor causing juveniles to lose contact with adults would lead to wandering and dispersal of juveniles, and would decrease their chances of survival. Thus a violent separation of ewe and lamb in which the lamb is chased off could well lead to aimless wandering of the disturbed lamb and to its untimely death. A female which made a practice of chasing her offspring away would select against her own genotype. Conversely, females that minimize disruptions in her offspring's following response would maximize the chances that her lamb remained in the company of older sheep. It is also evident that lambs which are closely attached to the female and fail to grow independent as spring approaches and the female gets ready for lambing increase the chances of a violent separation from their mother and the resultant consequences. A close association between ewe and lamb after weaning is of no significance to sheep, unlike moose, since ewes do not defend lambs against predators. Sheep are much too small to face wolves, and their only means of escaping them is to head for safer terrain. It is hence adaptive for lambs to separate from ewes after weaning and follow any adult. When the pregnant females move off into hiding to lamb, their yearling lambs are steadily in company of old barren ewes, subadults, or rams and are usually not left to roam on their own. That yearling sheep deprived of leadership in spring can get lost miles from their range is indicated by the remains of dead yearlings, found by W. D. Wishart in southern Alberta (personal communication). It appears that social inheritance of home ranges is adaptive to the individual sheep, but dispersal is not.

Now another paradox can be answered. It appeared that on one hand sheep avoided timber and on the other moved through miles of it on migration. Entering timber for no special purpose would increase the chances of juvenile sheep getting lost or succumbing to predators. Entering timber along a traditional migratory trail when moving to another piece of habitat in the company of elders is adaptive. Sheep hence appear to enter timber mainly when going to a known location, but there are exceptions to this as will be shown below.

Today sheep live in the western United States in an artificial situation. As a result of man's activity much sheep habitat has been cleared of sheep, and relict sheep populations now live close to vacant good habitat. This situation rarely if ever occurs under *natural* conditions. Normally, the slow disappearance of habitat, not man, brings about sheep extinction; so no vacant habitat lies close to any population. Sheep as a species have no meaningful response to this new situation but behave just as they must have done for the millions of years of the Pleistocene—by confining their activity to the limited areas they now happen to inhabit. They have no means of finding and incorporating distant habitat patches into a population's realm readily.

RANGE EXTENSION BY MOUNTAIN SHEEP

The foregoing comparison of moose and mountain sheep biology indicates why it is adaptive for moose to disperse yearlings and why it is not for mountain sheep. Sheep follow along predictable, traditional pathways which confine them to a given area, and they would never be able to escape from that area if their system of leadership worked at top efficiency. However, it does not, nor are the habits of older animals rigidly fixed, as has been discussed in chapter 3. Since sheep have made almost no range extensions in North America in the past decades, we can only speculate how sheep colonize new ranges; but we know enough about sheep to make some educated guesses.

Since we do know that introduced caprids, be they sheep, goats, or ibex, spread as far as the habitat is open and continuous, it is evident that sheep can spread to an adjacent mountain range once the timber has disappeared from the valley. Then the habitat is continuous from the inhabited to the uninhabited range and sheep can move in freely.

It was noted earlier that some old sheep departed from the normal route they took. It is hence possible that a group of younger sheep might follow some oldster to a new area and form a population there. This possibility I consider most unlikely.

We do know that sheep can perform sudden, erratic movements. These have been observed in Asia, where they were correlated with catastrophic events, such as droughts (Heptner et al. 1961). Some sheep moved as far as 500 km, which is a remarkable distance indeed, and stayed in one case three years in a new area. There is little doubt that erratic immigration by part of a population could lead to colonization of new range by sheep.

There is a further method. Assuming that grasslands expand and sheep populations begin to increase in size and density and that the distances between occupied and unoccupied habitat decrease, the following is certain to happen: the ram populations increase and form larger concentrations in spring. When this happens many old and young rams find themselves on the same range. Now frequently a segregation by age classes takes place: the mature rams are more sedentary, while younger rams roam in groups of their own. Such groups of playful, young rams periodically go on excursions into the timbered valleys. I observed this a number of times on the Palliser Range. The young rams return in a great arc back to the familiar range.

If the distance between a ram concentration area and some un-occupied range is not large, say one mile, and only a narrow belt of dense timber separates them, it is conceivable that young rams may penetrate the timber and find themselves on the other side in open terrain. To mountain sheep a habitat apparently is not home without a companion. Whereas the *single* young ram would not likely return to the patch of unoccupied habitat he found, the *group* of young rams may remember it as a habitat with companions and return again, stay longer, explore the new terrain, and incorporate it into next spring's excursions. Once some 2-year-old ewes follow rams across, they may well choose this terrain as a secluded lambing area, and eventually lead other sheep across. For the present this is no more than a plausible, but unverified, hypothesis of how sheep colonize new terrain.

The foregoing is a hypothesis of how the habitat molds and shapes the society of two ruminants. It does not explain all attributes of sheep society. Why, for instance, should males be less gregarious than females and roam about more frequently alone? This is explained in chapter 10. The present theory explains only why yearling sheep must stay with adults and follow them. However, once they are adult and possess fixed home range patterns, what advantage is there in staying in groups? One would suspect that there are other forces at work shaping sheep society, and indeed there are (see chap. 6).

The fluctuating habitat theory explains not only the social but also the reproductive characteristics of moose, and it correctly predicts the reproductive characteristics of caribou.

The theory presented demonstrates one important point. Traditions and the mechanisms responsible for them can be explained as arising from classical, individual selection rather than group selection as Wynne-Edwards (1962) postulates. Traditions are the result of the ability of animals to learn, form habits, and acquire the habits and idiosyncrasies of lead individuals, and it was shown what benefit befell those individuals that adopted the traditions in question.

6 The Social Behavior of Mountain Sheep

INTRODUCTION

The social behavior of mountain sheep must come as a painful surprise to anyone who applies our moral codes to animal behavior (as even ethologists may unconsciously do), for there is little in sheep behavior our society would condone cheerfully. It is a popular game today, as in the past, to scrutinize the actions of animals and exalt exemplary conduct, thereby justifying it for humans. The fiction that wolves will not kill wolves, that "dog does not eat dog" (Lorenz 1963; Barnett 1967) is a hapless example of this. Unfortunately for wolves and moralists, the former do kill and consume conspecifics just like other large carnivores—just as we did throughout much of our history as a species and still do sporadically. (For wolves, see Jordan et al. 1967 and Rausch 1967; for African lions, Schenkel 1966b and Schaller 1969; for mountain lion, Hornocker 1967; for black bear, Jonkel 1967; for grizzly bear, J. Craighead and A. M. Pearson, personal communication.) It is to the credit of the carnivores that they do not indulge in murder wholesale, as is eminently respectable in human societies. Nevertheless, they show an inhibition to kill conspecifics at best within their own social group, much as we do. Be that as it may, sheep are not likely to become symbols of moral conduct once their behavior is known, even though those actions we disdain make their society a lesson in social stability. Odd as sheep behavior may be to us at first, we must never forget that it is a time-tested, evolutionary success and illustrates one way in which highly aggressive animals can live together with a minimum of harm to each other.

There is no distinct "female form" in mountain sheep society as there is in our own since the adult female and the male at sexual maturation look much alike. The males are neotenous for they continue to grow and mature behaviorally for another 5 or 6 years after sexual maturation and segregate into herds of their own away from females and juveniles. This is a segregation by behavioral type, those acting like

130

sexually immature sheep stay in the female bands, those acting like "males" in male groups. The male groups are homosexual societies in which the dominant acts the role of the courting male and the subordinate the role of the estrous female. The dominant male treats all sheep smaller than he is, irrespective of sex and age, like females; it is his prerogative to act sexually, but it is the subordinate's prerogative to act aggressively. Most overt aggression is directed by subordinates at dominants, not vice versa. There is little danger for the dominant in this because he can catch and neutralize the clashes of a smaller ram with his massive, armored head. Male dominance and breeding success run parallel with horn size, and rams use their horns not only as weapons or shields but also as rank symbols. A ram can thus tell a stranger's dominance rank from the size of his horns. These rank symbols allow rams to live in a predictable social surrounding and permit sheep to live in an open society. The largest-horned ram in a band automatically becomes the leader of the band since small rams follow him.

In fighting, the ram combines the principle of the sledge hammer with that of the karate chop and smashes his heavy horns edge-first into the opponent. The latter catches the blow skillfully with his horns. Since the clashes are rendered harmless by the defense, rams can freely indulge in battles, which they do, and serious fights may be long and tedious but are rarely injurious. Social selection appears to be responsible not only for the structure of the skull and horns but also for the thick skin on the ram's rostrum which is exposed to horn blows, for the preorbital glands and their secretion which leaves an identifying odor on a subordinate, and for the pliable facial hair which can withstand horning by subordinates. Frequent minor fights allow rams to associate horn size with clash impact and hence to judge an opponent's combat potential from his horn size. Hopeless combat is thus avoided. Rams fight not for females but for dominance and do it year round. They primarily test rams of similar dominance rank (horn size). They take advantage of rivals occupied in combat by smashing into their sides and may persecute injured superiors. Unlike zebras (Klingel 1967), sheep appear to be egocentric and pay little attention to a sick and disabled member of the group, except for butting it. Under severe climatic conditions in winter females may even butt their lambs from exposed forage.

The female sheep has two behavioral phases. Normally she behaves like a juvenile, but during estrus she acts like a subordinate, *young*

male. Conversely, one can claim that the young male acts like an estrous female, mimicking her behavior and appearance, which allows
him to live side by side with larger males. The female is paedogenic,
representing throughout life the immature form of the male. Except
for old males all sheep are juveniles, some sexually mature, some not,
at various stages of development.

This thumbnail sketch of sheep society is based on analyses of
behavior patterns. There were seventeen behavior patterns I recognized
and thirteen were quantified, since they occurred frequently and were
conspicuous enough at long distance. Behavior patterns are signals—
postures and actions performed in a more or less stereotyped, distinct
manner before conspecifics and accompanied occasionally by emissions
of sound and odors. They are conspicuous acts which stand out from
the normal grazing, resting, or walking of the animal. Normal, everyday movements are usually slow and relaxed, never rigid; a rigid
stance is already an alarm signal and a most conspicuous one. Social
behavior patterns, the sheep's vocabulary, are characterized by unusual
body conformations, by faster or slower, jerkier or stiffer movements
than normal ones, by nonrandom orientation toward other sheep, and
by concomitant releases of sounds and odors. A man can quickly learn
to distinguish and identify these signals.

A few behavior patterns made up the bulk of the signals exchanged
by sheep (see table 31). Thus, the low-stretch and front kick accounted
for 87.2% of the behavior of dominant Stone's rams toward subordinates, while the replies of the subordinates were made up of 60.7%
rubbing and horning. The behavior of anestrous females and juveniles
contained 72.8–78% aggressive patterns (see table 29).

Behavior Patterns

Attention and Alarm Postures

The most common postures assumed by sheep are those of grazing,
resting, and walking, but none of these has social meaning in the
sense that a response is shown to them by other sheep. During normal
walking the sheep's head is held quite low, nose pointing to the ground,
while the ears are held back and droop down a little. If the sheep raises
its head and holds it up rigidly while walking, with tense steps, it at once
draws the attention of all others. This is the *alarm posture* (plate 23),
which in sheep, mule deer, and elk is almost identical (plate 24).

An alarmed sheep need not run away but may move at a stiff, tense walk uphill. It stops periodically, looks at the source of the disturbance, and struts on again. It appears to glance backward from the corner of one eye at the disturbance; sheep appear capable of watching something almost behind them without turning the head. On several occasions single rams carried the alarm behavior to extremes. They strutted about in tight circles in one place, stopping occasionally to look at me, and then slowly lay down facing me. Murie (1944) described a whole band of Dall's sheep doing this in front of a wolf.

In addition to assuming the characteristic posture, alarmed sheep may stamp the ground with a front leg and blow sharply through the nose. The latter is done by domestic goats and some Asiatic sheep (Walther 1961). Stamping with a front leg is rather uncommon among American sheep. I have seen it done by captive, excited bighorns and a few times by large rams confronting a coyote. It is more common to see excited, alarmed sheep perform several short hops with all legs bunched under before departing. This hopping is reminiscent of stotting in gazelles (Walther 1968; Estes 1967).

A sheep suddenly freezing and staring in one direction alerts others who then do the same. This is the *attention posture* (plate 25). The ears are perked forward and the animal may orient its body along the line of sight. A sheep in a rigid posture and looking steadily in one direction has very likely seen something of interest, such as a distant coyote, a bear, or another sheep. A sheep that frequently interrupts feeding and then, in a less rigid posture, looks steadily across a gorge or valley, indicates that it will soon move in that direction. With its gaze the sheep gives notice of its intent to travel and of the direction it will take. Schaller (1963) and Kühme (1965) described similar behavior of leaders of gorilla and African hunting dog groups (*Lycaon*). Sheep may remain several days on a ridge overlooking the valley before finally crossing over.

Horning

Sheep of all ages and sexes horn shrubs, grass bunches, or small trees (plate 26). It occurs frequently during dominance fights of rams, where it is performed by both partners with nearly equal frequency (see table 58). Some of the horning may simply be done to remove an uncomfortable clump of hair or other irritant from between the horns. Occasionally rams butted heavily against elastic conifer stems and let the backlash carry them back to the original stance. Other rams horned and nibbled juniper branches (*Juniperus*) alternatively and appeared to grow excited by doing this. Rams tended to select lodgepole pines (*Pinus contorta*) for horning, and the twisted, damaged stems of little pines at timberline gave ample evidence of this (plate 27). White-tailed deer (*Odocoileus virginianus*) also prefer conifers for horning (De Vos 1967). It may be that essential oils found in conifers stimulate sheep, deer, and elk to damage trees. In May 1964 I observed only once a yearling ram nibbling bark from a young pine and licking the sap. In April 1965 I saw a cow elk tear off bark from pines in sap, then rub her head and neck liberally in the tree's wound. Experiments by Gundlach (1961) on red deer (*Cervus elaphus*) showed the excitatory effects of pine oils on these deer.

Generally sheep horn during intense social interactions or prior to long movements through timbered valleys. Mountain goats also horn shrubs and grass bushes in antagonistic interactions. Horning is occasionally contagious, for several rams may start horning once one begins. Horning may be initiated with a butt, after which the horns are rotated or scrubbed under pressure over the grass bushes, shrubs, or small trees. The horning posture is tense and the tail may be raised. There is an aggressive overtone in this behavior.

Orientation toward the Conspecific

During grazing sheep are dispersed and no obvious orientation is apparent. However, Crofton (1958) found that grazing domestic sheep orient to fix a fellow sheep with each eye. Each sheep tended to graze in such a manner that its body bisected an angle of approximately of 110° formed by it and the two sheep it had a fix on.

During encounters sheep adopt certain positions toward conspecifics. A ewe calling her lamb orients toward the lamb and looks directly at it. Otherwise a direct stare of one sheep at another appears to be an aggressive posture, although the evidence for this is indirect. Subordinates look away from dominants when the latter approach (plate 28) and often turn their rear to them, exposing the rump patch. Even lambs do this. During the post-clash present the subordinate ram may close his eyes rather than look at the dominant's face (plate 29). Sheep tend to rest in such a manner as not to face each other directly (see plate 77). It appears that at short distances only dominant sheep are free to look in all directions; small sheep glancing at dominants were commonly butted in return. When sheep are close together they tend to face in the same direction, probably because this minimizes staring, and is hence the most peaceful group structure. In this sheep are similar to

rhesus monkeys, among which a stare is aggressive behavior, not indulged in by the subordinate (Altmann 1962).

When sheep are on the move they discourage others from passing by
butting at them, displaying in low-stretch, or by quickly running ahead
and cutting them off. This restores the original march order. Occasionally, small sheep attempting to pass a grazing dominant at close range
are butted back severely the moment they reach the shoulder level
of the dominant. Sometimes a large ram leading a band of rams walks
for long distances in a low-stretch. It appears that sheep in general
attempt to keep others behind them. However, this easily gives rise to
the illusion that a leading sheep defends its "lead" position, whereas
any sheep further down the line also discourages others from passing.
This results in a stable march order in single file (plate 30). During
flight, however, sheep may run off as a tight bunch behind the lead
animals (plate 31).

Behavior Patterns Used in Social Interactions

Horn displays: the low-stretch (Lo) *and the present.* The horn displays are
the most common social behavior patterns used by sheep. They are
present or display threats shown by dominant to subordinate sheep
(plate 32) and are comparable to the broadside displays of most mammals. In the low-stretch the horns are displayed from a lowered head
and in the present, from an elevated head (plate 33). In both displays
the horns are shown frontolaterally (fig. 15), and it appears that more
horn is visible to the opponent in this orientation, than in a frontal or
lateral one. If the size of the horns is the important factor in these
displays, then rams must be able to distinguish horns of different sizes
and must be able to respond correctly to rams with smaller or larger
horns. Both predictions are correct (chap. 6 and Geist 1966*b*). I quantified only the low-stretch since at long distances the present is not conspicuous enough to be recognized if performed at a low intensity. The
low-stretch is shown:

1. Between rams of equal or near equal horn size. Otherwise only
   the larger-horned ram displays (see fig. 19).
2. By rams, and occasionally females, when entering or leaving a
   group, when passing a subordinate sheep at close distance
   or a resting dominant one at greater distance, or when leading
   a band of rams. The low-stretch is used here almost like a
   salute in an army, except that it has the opposite meaning.
3. By rams courting ewes. In this situation the ram may crouch on

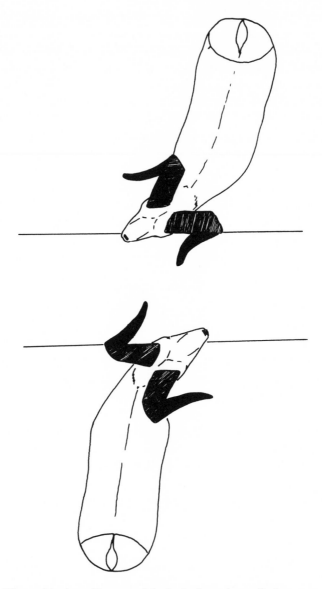

Fig. 15. The positioning of horns and body during a horn display.

occasions (plate 34) indicating the primitive origins of this behavior pattern as a rupicaprid courtship posture. I observed an extreme crouch by an old barren ewe which attempted to approach the first lamb of the year (chap. 8).[1]

1. See film E 1338.

4. By adult sheep attempting to displace a subordinate from his resting place.
5. By a ram passing several female mule deer. This I observed only once.

The low-stretch is shown primarily by rams and infrequently by females. Like other display patterns it is missing from the repertoire of young lambs. The youngest lamb I observed to perform a low-stretch was a 6-month-old Dall's lamb. As rams mature bodily and behaviorally, they perform the low-stretch, present, twist, and front kick more frequently.

The present is performed with a raised head. Displaying rams pull their noses slightly away from the opponent and it appears as if they look past each other. The head is also pulled back, so that the neck muscles bulge. The ears are folded back; the eyes of the subordinate ram may be shut (plates 29 and 33). The present is most conspicuous after a clash. The rams recoil back and freeze into a rigid present for a considerable time span. Unfortunately I never timed how long they stand in present but occasionally this appeared to exceed a minute. The present may also follow a threat jump or be in response to a move by the opponent during a dominance fight. It is virtually absent after clashes during vicious battles. It is commonly seen in huddles by rams and during courtship by the estrous female; the dominant rams present while subordinates, or females, rub or horn their necks, horns, or bodies (fig. 29).

The low-stretch and the present are almost identical in thinhorn and bighorn sheep. Both species occasionally flick the tongue during the low-stretch, the ears are laid back or pointed at an opponent, and the head may be rotated back and forth around its long axis. Thinhorns rotate less than bighorns and often tilt the nose more upward than bighorns commonly do. This makes the low-stretch of thinhorn sheep slightly stiffer than that of bighorns.

Twist (T). The twist is similar to an intensified low-stretch. The ram dips his head down, simultaneously rotates it sharply about its long axis, flicks rapidly with the tongue, and expels a harsh, loud growl. If he stands close behind the opponent or female, the ram may push his muzzle into the side of the social partner (plate 35). The twist appears in many variations. It may be coupled with a front kick, in which case the ram also pushes his opponent with his chest. The twist may terminate a low-stretch approach of a ram to a ewe, after which the ram freezes into a horn display. Twists may alternate with low-stretch as a ram stands behind or beside a resting subordinate and attempts to make the latter vacate his bed. During courtship of near estrous ewes, young rams may pounce toward the female, twist, and return to a nearly normal stance after retreating a couple of steps. The courting ram thus seesaws a few paces behind the ewe. A large, dominant ram may begin to disperse small rams from the vicinity of a near estrous female by approaching them in low-stretch, twisting and shortly freezing in present, then twisting and freezing in present repeatedly until the small rams leave or the dominant suddenly charges them. The twist appears to be a serious display threat. It is performed more frequently by bighorns than by thinhorns (see table 30).

Front kick ("Laufeinschlag" [Walther 1958]) (L). The kick with the extended front leg is performed mainly by dominant rams on all subordinate sheep irrespective of sex and age. The ram whips the front leg up and hits the opponent ventrally on chest, belly, haunches, and occasionally on neck and chin (plate 36). Sometimes a ram takes the opponent's body into a front leg-chin pincer. A ram often kicks several times in succession after raising the front leg. During intense social interactions, such as in dominance fights or interactions about the estrous ewe, rams growl loudly when kicking. They may solidly bump their chest into the opponent's side during each kick and even, although rarely, dig a horntip into his back. The latter behavior is more common to bighorn than thinhorn sheep. Large rams may combine the kick with so powerful a push with the chest as to dislodge an opponent and move him several steps downhill. Occasionally a ram kicks so high up on an opponent's haunches that it appears the ram is attempting to mount. Very rarely large rams about an estrous ewe will kick the front leg into the air when confronting an opponent. The dominant literally waves his front leg at the subordinate who stands a few paces away.

The front kick is less a kick than a push and is not painful. I experienced it more than a dozen times when inadvertently getting between two interacting bighorns. The front kick is rarely performed by ewes, and if it is, then by dominant ewes. Old rams kick more frequently than young ones. On rare occasions, the front kick is replaced by pawing if the opponent happens to be resting.

The front kick is a characteristic behavior pattern of many ruminants. It is absent in deer but present in the giraffids and many bovids (Walther 1960). In all species for which this behavior pattern was described, it is performed during courtship by the male often in a highly ritualized manner as, for instance, in the gerenuk (*Lithocranius*) (Walther 1958). At first glance mountain sheep appear to differ from this rule, since they kick male and female alike. But sheep do not distinguish between male and female in their behavior—only between "smaller" and "larger" sheep as shall be shown a little later. Rams treat all smaller sheep irrespective of sex and age like females. Hence, the front kick, a behavior shown by dominant rams toward all subordinates, follows the same rules as in other species. The front kick is linked to the display threats of sheep, such as the low-stretch, present, and twist; it is virtually a contact display threat.

Neck fight. The neck fight is a rare behavior pattern which in the few instances observed was performed by rams on males and females alike. The rams put their chins and throats over the withers of their opponents (plate 37); however, no pushing or wrestling followed. This behavior pattern, common and functional in the Barbary sheep (*Ammotragus*) (Haas 1958), is vestigial in mountain sheep.

Mount (M). Mounting is performed by dominant sheep on subordinates irrespective of the latter's sex and age (plate 38). It is not only the sexual pattern during which copulation occurs but also a pattern which is the privilege of the dominant to perform. Only if a sheep can mount another without being punished has it demonstrated dominance. Females mount rarely. Young rams mount spontaneously more frequently than older ones; spontaneous mounting is a behavior pattern which like overt aggressive patterns diminishes as a ram matures.

The mounting posture of mountain sheep is erect with the head held high and the nose pointed at the back of the mounted partner. Pelvic strokes are performed irrespective of the sex mounted. The penis may be partially extruded prior to mounting. I saw no conspicuous final thrust indicating ejaculation, but after some mounts the rams appeared listless, which suggests that ejaculation had occurred. Not only do dominant rams treat subordinates like females, but subordinate males may also react like females by showing lordosis when mounted (plate 38) or urinating to the larger rams.

In early fall when young rams begin to enter into dominance conflicts with females, they attempt to mount them. This need not be done from the female's rear; occasionally the young ram mounts from the side or front. These small rams often approach resting females in a low-stretch and then jump on top of them attempting to mount.[2] Most young lambs know only how to perform overt aggressive behavior —such as the butt, clash, and the respective intention movements—and how to mount. The display patterns appear during ontogeny.

Ejaculation. Rams may ejaculate spontaneously throughout the year during interactions with other rams, while courting estrous or non-estrous ewes, or after rising in the morning. The ram suddenly crouches in the rear, protrudes the penis sideways past the front legs, and staggers stiff-legged forward or steps around in a narrow circle (fig. 16). Then the ram slowly relaxes and returns to the normal standing posture. Ejaculation is not frequently seen. Usually nothing happens after such an act, but once a Dall's ram stepped forward and after nuzzling what was probably the ejaculate he lipcurled. One Dall's ram nuzzled his penis during ejaculation, a behavior uncommon in sheep but common to Barbary sheep (Haas 1958), ibex (Krumbiegel 1954), and markhor (see plate 39). A 2-year-old argali ram (*nigrimontana*), which I observed in the Hellabrun Zoo in Munich, ejaculated in the same manner as American sheep.

Fig. 16. Ejaculation: *left*, by bighorn; *right*, by Stone's ram. (From photos.)

2. See film E 1338.

Lipcurl ("Flehmen") (F). The lipcurl is normally performed by rams after they nuzzle and lick the urine of ewes be it on the ground, in the long hairs below the ewe's vulva, or as it is expelled from the ewe. After the ram nuzzles the urine he raises his head, opens his mouth slightly, retracts the upper lip and exposes the palate, droops the lower lip slightly, and often moves the head slowly back and forth (plate 40). It is probable that some urine passes through a special duct to the Jacob's organ (vomeronasal organ) for analysis (Knappe 1964). At the end of the lipcurl, the ram licks his lips and returns to a normal stance.

The lipcurl is characteristic of sexually mature rams, although it is performed rarely by adult females or yearling rams at 12 months of age and exceptionally by a lamb. Rams lipcurl not only on female urine but also on the urine of males, even their own. Now and again one sees a ram step back after urinating, nuzzle his urine, and lipcurl. There is no competition among rams for the urine of a ewe. Several rams may stand side by side and simultaneously lipcurl where a ewe, or one of them, had urinated. The probable significance of the lipcurl is discussed in chapter 7.

Sniffing of rear (Sv). After a ram approaches a ewe in low-stretch he frequently sniffs and nuzzles her rear (plate 41). At close range one occasionally sees his tongue dart out and lick the perianal region or his mouth open and close after touching the long hairs below the female's vulva. If the female responds by urinating to the approaching ram, the latter lets the urine run over his lips and subsequently lipcurls or examines the ewe's rear or urine on the ground. Rams will also sniff the rear of a subordinate male (plate 42). The significance of this behavior and the lipcurl have never been demonstrated although there is no lack of opinion about their function. Rams deprived of their sense of smell were not able to distinguish between estrous and nonestrous ewes by sniffing (Lindsay 1965).

The head shake. This behavior is shown almost only by small sheep, particularly subadults and females after being disturbed by a large sheep. Occasionally during the head shake the animal bounces forward, frolics, threat jumps, and runs on. A threat jump by a subordinate male may be initiated with a head shake. During play rams sometimes shake their heads before butting or clashing. Small sheep shaking their heads in response to a disturbance by larger sheep had on all occasions the rump turned to the dominant. Head shaking is not common.

Horning body (Hb), *rubbing* (Rb), *and nuzzling.*   These three contact patterns are the most commonly used behavior patterns of small rams on larger ones. After a small ram approaches a dominant he begins to lick and nuzzle the head of the dominant (plate 43*a*); to horn his face, neck, chest, or shoulders (plate 43*b*); or to rub his face on the face of the dominant.

Large Dall's rams carry distinct gray and black markings around their preorbital glands and eyes, whereas small rams show little evidence of this (plate 8). These markings are caused by the horning of young rams. Since small rams horn larger ones daily, the dirt from their horns and the secretion from the preorbital glands of the large rams would be spread about the eye region of the latter. It is most likely that small or subordinate rams impregnate their own horns and face with the gland's secretion. Hence, a band of rams would acquire a group scent from this horning. We can only speculate about the function of the preorbital gland. It may be that a subordinate ram gets an advantage by impregnating himself with the dominant's odor, for at night the dominant is then able to recognize him. This would reduce the subordinate's chances of being attacked and damaged, since the dominant can recognize him as one of the subordinate crowd and act accordingly. Sheep appear to be active at night, and the nights of fall and winter are longer than the days in the north.

The body hair of mountain sheep is brittle. This does not apply to the facial hair, which is tough and pliable. This toughness appears to be related to the facial hornings which rams receive almost daily throughout the year. If the facial hair were brittle, it would be quickly broken off and removed by the activity of the subordinate rams. The skin would thus be unprotected not only from the frequent butts and clashes but also from direct contact with snow and cold temperatures in winter. A small air space between snow and skin appears to be necessary for the protection of the skin, to keep it from freezing, as is indicated by the furred muzzle of caribou. It is evident that rams with brittle facial hair would soon be deprived of it by the horning of subordinate rams and would freeze their facial skin when foraging in deep snow.

Dominant rams usually accept the horning and rubbing of subordinate rams or estrous ewes while standing in present but will occasionally kick and growl at them.

Horn threat (Ho).   The horn threat is an intention movement to butt

and as such is a true weapon threat. It is frequently shown by subordinates toward approaching dominants, or by dominants chasing
away subordinates. The behavior pattern consists of lowering the head
and inclining the horns at the opponent (see plate 48).

Threat jump (Thj).   This is an intention movement to clash in which
the sheep rises on its hind legs in front of the opponent and inclines its
head toward the opponent (plate 44). Like the clash it is primarily
initiated by subordinate sheep toward dominant ones and is shown by
sheep of all sexes and ages. It occurs during dominance fights and during
play; in the former it is executed much more stiffly and is followed by a
present, while during play it is often preceded by a head shake and
performed while frolicking.

Butt and clash (B, Cl).   The sole weapons of mountain sheep are their
horns. In butting or clashing they deliver a blow with them onto the
opponent's body. The butt, which is the mildest blow a sheep delivers,
is a downward blow with the head, during which the chin is drawn in
and the horns thrown forward and down. The sheep puts the weight of
its rigidly held body into the butt and pushes the horns against the
opponent's body once contact is made. When butting the sheep keeps
its hooves on the ground, though it may crouch first and then hurl
itself forward into the butt (plate 45). The clash is a more sophisticated
and exaggerated form of the butt and differs from the latter in the force
of execution and in the means of achieving such force. Whereas the
butt is usually performed by one opponent only, both opponents participate in a clash. The sheep may jump into the clash from a four-
legged stance or after a bipedal run. Examination of movie film revealed
that the clash is more than two sheep banging together head on: it is a
sophisticated, specialized behavior which concentrates all the force
a ram can generate onto one narrow horn keel to achieve a hard blow.

The clash has several stages. In the preparatory stage the ram initiating the clash faces his opponent, lifts one front leg, and simultaneously
tilts his head sideways and crouches in the rear. If the head is tilted to
the left, the left horn will first make contact with the opponent. His
eyes are wide open and looking at the opponent; his ears are laid back
flat (see plate 88). The ram may rise on his hind legs and lift the front
legs off the ground. The front legs are then extended as shown in plate
46.

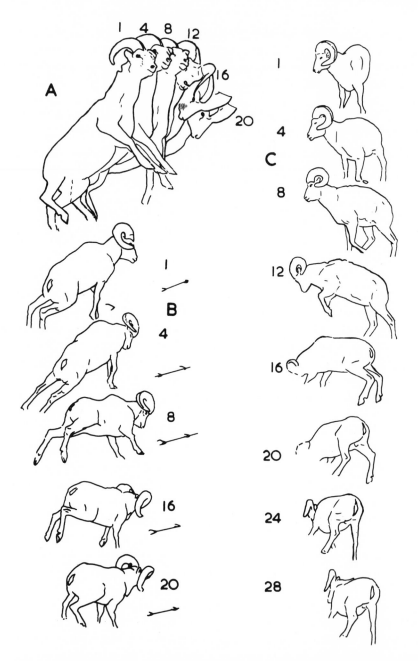

Fig. 17. Bighorn rams in successive phases of the clash. Numbers indicate frame number (film speed 24 frames/sec). *A*, a clash from the bipedal stance. Note rigidity of body. Contact is made with the left horn. *B* shows the propulsion of a clashing ram and how he catches himself. *C*, ram deals out a blow while spinning about.

Next the hind legs propel the body forward and up. The eyes remain fixed on the opponent. Then the body straightens out and begins to fall; head and neck are propelled down at a faster rate than the body; the chin is pulled in sharply, flinging the heavy horns forward and down. Hence, there are four forces which increase the forward and downward momentum generated by the ram: (1) the body propulsion achieved by extending hind legs and spinal chord, (2) the fall of the body due to gravity, (3) the downward propulsion of head and neck, and (4) the forward and downward propulsion of the horns. It appears that these forces should summate to produce a far harsher blow than if the ram clashed as a rigid body into the opponent (fig. 17). However, this is not all, for the ram hits his opponent with the narrow edge of one horn. The force of the blow is focused on that one narrow horn keel the way that a karate fighter concentrates the force of a blow on the edge of his palm. Momentarily he stiffens into the blow; then, after making contact with one horn, he rotates his head and brings the other horn into contact with the opponent. The ram performs in effect a double blow.

He continues the force of the blow in one of two fashions: (a) The ram kicks up in the rear and pivots his rigid body about the front legs, thereby "riding home" the clash. The upward throw of the rear would, in combination with a rigid body, increase the downward force with the head (plate 47a). Walther (1968) describes that Thompson's gazelles increase clash force in exactly the same manner. (b) The ram collapses his front legs, letting the rigid body pivot in the hip about the acetabulum, and then he quickly crouches in the rear, thereby maintaining the downward propulsion with his head (plate 47b). Ewes fight in the same manner as rams and illustrate both methods of continuing the clash force on the opponent after making contact with him.

After having made contact with the opponent, the clashing ram also begins to prepare his body for landing. He brings his legs forward into line with his descent. This is illustrated best when a clash misses (plate 48). During the clash the rams close their eyes (plates 49 and 52). All these actions, from the initial preparatory phase of the clash to the final landing after the clash, take place in little more than a second. The ram appears to maximize the clash force, even to the extent of using terrain in his favor, clashing downhill if possible (see plate 88).

There are many variations to the clash. Contact may be made when the ram's front legs are off the ground or when his hind legs are off the ground. The rams may slip off each other and crash head first into the ground, an occurrence which is not rare (plate 50). The clash occurs primarily during dominance fights but also in play. The butt is the most common manner in which conspecifics are displaced from a salt lick or put in their place. Subordinates defend themselves by butting, whereas the butt and its intention movement, the horn threat, are used by dominants and subordinates about equally often. The clash and threat jump are used primarily by smaller sheep toward larger ones. The rush with a lowered head, culminating in a butt, is an action I saw only dominant sheep perform (plate 51).

The Effects of Combat and the Defense Mechanisms

Both the great force of the clash and the rough, grooved horns leave their mark on the opponent. The ridges and grooves of the horn permit a grip on the opponent's body and tear out hair in the process. The horn surfaces of fighting rams are usually covered with bits of broken hair. The broomed horn tips often have sharp edges and may cause gashes on the opponent. Occasionally one spots a ram with blood-spattered horns. The effects of the clash are as follows:

1. Small rams are telescoped by the force (plate 52). However, I have never seen a ram knocked sprawling by a clash, for several reasons. First, most clashes are initiated by small rams on larger ones, and second, rams are able to control themselves during a clash even when being knocked downhill. They kick up the hind legs and sail backward propelled by the opponent, to land again on their legs in full control of their body, sometimes several yards below their original stance (compare parts *a* and *b* of plate 68).

2. Nose and orbital regions are cut badly (plate 53), nasal bones may be split (Allred et al. 1966), and hair is cut in streaks from the body (plate 54).

3. Horn tips get broken and splintered (plate 55). Small and sometimes large chunks are knocked out of the horn (plate 53). Occasionally, the greater part of a horn is broken off.

4. Rarely, gashes are opened on the body with broken horn tips and horn edges. One ram apparently received a broken shoulder in a fight; one dead ram I found had the left horn core snapped off. Considerable amounts of blood had accumulated subcutaneously, as was indicated by the dark red connective tissue on the left side of the skull. This ram was probably a fighting casualty.

5. Hair is torn out, occasionally in great clumps.

6. Blood is found on the horns of some rams. It may be the opponent's blood or his own. When horns are growing in spring and summer, blood may ooze in large drops from the contact line between horn and skin after a few clashes. This blood is spread over a ram's horns after he horns some shrubs or trees.

Mills (1937) observed bighorn rams in rut in Yellowstone National Park. He reports seeing rams with bleeding noses, splintered horn tips, and hurt legs; he found one ram dying of fighting injuries. I do not know what internal damage rams suffer from fighting. They accept some tremendous blows into their sides by rams interfering with a dominance fight. However, most damage which is observable centers about the head.

The simplest defense against a clash or butt is to jump aside (plate 48). This is commonly resorted to by subadults and females but rarely by rams. Observations in the field and of slow-motion film of fighting sheep showed that they constantly attempted to face the opponent and catch his blows with their horns.[3] In plate 56 a 2-year-old ram is in the process of butting a female. Note that the female is swinging her body around to face the ram. Her head is lowered and the horns are pointed forward to receive the blow. The downward blow by the ram would be caught against the tension of the neck and would force the head of the ewe down, but would hardly cause any damage. One function of the horns appears to be to catch an opponent's blow and neutralize it, hence shielding the animal from the butts and clashes. This function explains much of the sheep's head morphology.

The first line of defense against blows on the face is a thick, tough hide. In fact, mountain sheep have the thickest hide on top of the rostrum and face. Rams have a thicker skin there than females. Unfortunately, by the time I noticed the significance of this, I had only one Stone's ram and one female to examine. Therefore, I made corresponding skin measurements on males of domestic goats. Domestic goats are close relatives of sheep and possess similar fighting behavior; so they should have similar defensive mechanisms, which is borne out by skin measurements and skull structure. In figure 18 the skin measurements of domestic goats, Stone's rams, and male mountain goats are compared. Mountain goats do not fight like sheep or domestic goats with frontal

3. See film E 1334.

Fig. 18. Skin thicknesses (in mm) in a domestic goat (*Capra hircus*), a class III Stone's ram, and an old male mountain goat. The domestic goat, *top*, like its close relative the sheep, has the thickest hide on the head and neck; the mountain goat, on its rear end.

butts, but strike ventrally at the opponent's belly and haunches. Most blows exchanged by mountain goats land on rump and belly, since the antagonists are positioned antiparallel to each other (Geist 1965, 1967). Male goats have a "rump shield" of thick dermis, which in a 9-year-old male reached 22 mm in thickness. On the other hand the facial skin of mountain goats is very thin, which correlates with the absence of head-to-head fighting in this species. It appears that in mountain goats and sheep alike the skin is thickest where most blows land in fighting—on the head for sheep and on the rear for mountain goats.

The skull structure of mountain sheep, rams in particular, appears to be adapted to withstand heavy concussion. Like other ruminants or swine which collide head on in fighting, the skull of sheep is heavily pneumated. There are two layers of bone, up to 5 cm apart, overlying the brain. In the spaces between these bones are numerous cross connections of bone, acting like struts. The helmetlike double roof of bone extends from about 5–6 cm before the brain to the occiput. Here it fuses into one 2-cm thick, spongy-textured bone (plate 57). The bony horn cores, about 10–11 cm in diameter at the base, are formed from the upper skull roof. They are hollow and filled with a maze of cross connections. Some of these struts radiate out from the lower bony case encapsuling the brain and run upward in a nearly straight line for almost half the length of the horn core. The bone forming the horn cores is very hard and up to 6 mm thick. The nasal bones are also of dense, strong bones in rams and are solidly fused to the frontals. The mountain goat skull by contrast is surprisingly light and fragile. The brain is encapsuled in only one layer of light, spongy-textured bone, and the nasal and frontal bones are thin. A mountain goat's skull fractures easily and occasionally a goat which is shot and falls down a mountainside smashes its skull almost to pulp. The mountain goat's skull is clearly not adapted to withstand heavy blows, which correlates with the absence of head-to-head fighting in this species.

The spaces surrounding the lower braincase of sheep appear to be derived from the frontal sinuses. In mountain goats these sinuses are very small and located just anterior to the brain over the cribiform plate. Domestic goats, thar (*Hemitragus*), and primitive sheep like the mouflon or urials (see Pfeffer 1967) occupy a position intermediate between mountain goats and American sheep. The sinuses in the skulls of males in particular are greatly enlarged but do not continue past the horn cores. That is, the parietals are not split into a lower and an upper plate connected by cross struts as in some mature bighorn rams, but are one layer of spongy-textured bone. The skull of domestic goats is much heavier and sturdier than that of mountain goats but not as heavy or complex as that of mountain sheep. The skull structure outlined for mountain sheep is valid only for large, mature rams. Young rams have smaller sinuses and the parietals are one thick spongy plate, much as in primitive sheep or goats. Here ontogeny appears to recapitulate phylogeny.

Since the clash probably generates an enormous force, not only the skull but also its attachment to the neck vertebrae must be adapted to withstand the clash. How do sheep counteract the great torque on skull and atlas when a ram catches an opponent with only one horn instead of squarely between the horns? Schaffer (1968) addressed himself to this question in the Caprini. He showed that in *Capra* large muscle masses inserting on occiput and mastoid processes could counteract this lateral torque. Compared to *Capra*, sheep have only a small area for muscle attachment on occiput and mastoid process and could probably not counteract the lateral torque with muscle power. At this point Schaffer was led to believe that sheep struck with both horns and caught clashes squarely between both horns. Were this the case, then sheep would experience little lateral torque about the occiput. However, since sheep do strike with one horn during the clash, and all too frequently catch the full clash force with one horn only, the lateral torque about the occiput must be great indeed.

A comparison of the skulls of *Oreamnos* and *Hemitragus* versus *Ammotragus*, *Ovis*, and *Capra* shows that the last three genera have much larger and wider occipital condyles than the first two. The size and shape of condyles, mastoid processes, and attachment area for muscles on the occiput is almost identical in *Oreamnos* and *Hemitragus*. From this it appears that caprids which specialized in clashing have a broader, more massive atlas than rupicaprids or primitive caprids and can absorb some of the clash force by locking the skull against the atlas. This would prevent involuntary head twisting and would distribute the clash force or torque along the length of the spinal column. Since during the clash the spine of bighorn sheep appears to be S-shaped, much of the force could be absorbed against the tension of the spine.

An examination of photos and films shows that during the clash the ram's head is not rotated backward but forward. That is, the ram's nose is pushed down toward his chest. The clash force is apparently exerted below rather than above the level of the spinal column. An examination of the ram on the left in plate 52, and the rams in plate 49 makes this plain. The downward force on the skull may be counteracted by the broad mass of elastic-fibrous tissue which connects the occiput to the cervical vertebrae.

It appears that the head of mountain sheep has been formed less by selection pressures from the habitat than by social selection which formed skull, horns, hair, and skin to fulfill functions dictated by the social environment.

THE RULES OF CONDUCT IN SHEEP SOCIETY

Behavior Used by Dominant and Subordinate Rams and by Estrous Females

A dominant ram is defined as one who acts in the manner of a large-horned ram to a small-horned one. A large-horned ram treats a small-horned ram in a conspicuously different manner than a small-horned ram treats a large-horned one. Large-horned rams treat their subordinates, be they males, females, or lambs, in the same manner. Moreover, large-horned rams successfully chase away smaller-horned ones from estrous females and do most of the mounting (chap. 7). A dominant male hence courts his opponent and always acts as if he were the larger, even in instances where he is not.

Dominant rams primarily use horn displays and sexual behavior patterns toward subordinates (shown for Stone's and bighorn rams in table 30). Horn displays and the front kick alone make up 87.2% of the behavior of dominant Stone's rams, while the same behavior patterns make up 63.4% of the dominant bighorn ram's behavior (table 31). During harsh winters, however, one sees less of these patterns and more of butting and pushing during competition for forage. To court and display is the prerogative of the dominant. This has also been shown by Walther (1965) for Grant's gazelle (*Gazella granti*) and by Krämer (1969) for chamois (*Rupicapra*).

Subordinate rams primarily use contact patterns, that is, horning, nuzzling, and rubbing on larger-horned opponents. These behavior patterns account for 60.7% of the behavior of subordinate Stone's rams and 61.5% of that of subordinate bighorn rams (table 31). Although aggressive patterns made up only 22.9% and 24.0% of the behavior of subordinate Stone's and bighorn rams respectively (table 30), the subordinate rams were the ones who initiated most of the butts and clashes. To be aggressive and butt and clash on dominants was their

TABLE 30

Frequency of major behavior patterns among Stone's and bighorn sheep (In percent)

Pattern	Dom ♂ on sub ♂		Sub ♂ on dom ♂		♀ and ♀y on equals or subadults	
	Stone's (N = 1,549)	Bighorn (N = 976)	Stone's (N = 697)	Bighorn (N = 682)	Stone's (N = 228)	Bighorn (N = 64)
Display and sexual						
Low-stretch	39.0	40.0	11.5	11.3	12.5	19.0
Front kick	48.2	23.4	4.4	1.1	7.9	6.2
Twist	2.0	10.5	0	1.3	0	0
Mount	1.6	3.0	0.4	0.5	1.3	1.5
Sniff rear	1.0	2.6	0	0.3	0.4	0
Aggressive						
Clash	0.9	2.0	5.6	7.5	0.9	14.0
Butt	3.1	7.5	8.2	8.2	25.0	28.0
Threat jump	1.2	4.4	7.7	6.9	0.9	3.1
Rush	1.3	1.1	0	0	23.6	4.7
Horn threat	0.6	3.0	1.4	1.4	27.6	23.0
Contact						
Horning body	0.5	1.1	31.0	43.5	0	0
Rubbing and nuzzling	0.6	1.0	29.7	18.0	0	0

NOTE: N is total number of patterns observed and recorded.

TABLE 31

The two most common behavior patterns of dominants, subordinates, and females

	Patterns	%
Dom ♂		
Stone's	front kick, low-stretch	87.2
Bighorn	low-stretch, front kick	63.4
Sub ♂		
Stone's	horning, rubbing	60.7
Bighorn	horning, rubbing	61.5
Females		
Stone's	horn threat, butt	52.6
Bighorn	horn threat, butt	51.0

prerogative. Thus in 471 interactions of Stone's rams, subordinates initiated 115 butts and clashes and dominants only 44. This difference is highly significant ($\chi^2 = 32.0$, $p < 0.001$). Bighorn rams followed the same rule. In 258 interactions only 20 out of 69 clashes were initiated by dominant rams ($\chi^2 = 12.1$, $p < 0.01$). In harsh winters this can differ when dominants displace subordinates from feeding craters by butting. In dominance fights the smaller or losing ram is the one who deals out most clashes, for of 74 clashes in which I could determine who initiated them, only 15 were initiated by the larger and ultimately victorious ram ($\chi^2 = 26$, $p < 0.001$). In only one dominance fight did I see a larger ram quickly smash a smaller one into submission. The dominant stands, displays to, or courts the subordinate while the latter rubs his head on the dominant's face and horns; the subordinate occasionally butts and clashes while the larger takes the blows on his well-armored head.

A further way to demonstrate which behavior patterns are used by dominant and subordinate rams is shown in table 32 for Stone's and bighorn rams. The behavior patterns are ranked in order of use by dominant rams. Although dominant and subordinate use the same patterns, there are some almost exclusively used by the larger, such as the aggressive charge or the front kick, and others used primarily by the smaller, such as rubbing and horning. Stone's and bighorn rams behave similarly but not identically.

The behavior of subordinate rams greatly resembles that of the estrous female. This resemblance goes further than indicated by the quantitative data, for there are behavioral similarities between these classes of sheep too rarely observable or too inconspicuous to quantify. Estrous females at peak receptivity perform lordosis, and so may subordinate rams when mounted (plate 38). Females commonly urinate to the approaching courting male, a behavior pattern which appears to be ultimately destined to allow the female to withdraw and reduce harassment (chap. 7). Subordinate ewes may also urinate to a low-stretching adult ewe. In the case of the ram this leads to lipcurling by the dominant, much as in the true courtship sequence. A few times I observed dominant Stone's rams courting subordinates pull their heads low and lick the penis of the subordinate and lipcurl thereafter. The most convincing demonstration of female mimicry I have seen occurred at the Hellabrun Zoological Garden in Munich in October 1967; a 6-month-old male mouflon, confronted by a large, courting ram, urinated to the dominant while crouching in the typical female posture.

TABLE 32

Relative frequencies of behavior patterns used by dominant and subordinate rams

	Bighorn			Stone's		
	Rank	% use by dom	Number	Rank	% use by dom	Number
Rush-charge	1	100	12	1	100	60 (20)[a]
Front kick	2	96	236	4	96	795
Sniffing of rear	3	93	27	2	100	16
Twist	4	92	112	3	100	32
Mount	5	88	33 (16)	5	91	34 (25)
Low-stretch	6	84	468	6	87	698
Horn threat	7	74	39	8	41	35 (20)
Butt	8	56	129	7	48	113
Threat jump	9	48	90	10	20	93
Clash	10	28	71	9	28	54
Rubbing	11	8	132	11	4.3	207
Horning body	12	4	309	12	3.6	224

NOTE: Data for bighorns based on 336 interactions between dominants and subordinates; for Stone's sheep, 573 interactions.

[a] Number in parentheses shows the actual number of patterns observed while recording events quantitatively. Because of small sample size, events captured on film, photo, or while among sheep on the mountains were added to increase sample size, i.e., under normal circumstances I saw 20 rush charges by dominant rams at subordinates in 573 interactions. While observing rutting Stone's rams I saw rams charge 40 times, hence 40 + (20) = 60.

In the interactions of dominant and subordinate rams it is typical that the subordinate remains and only rarely withdraws. Previously, I have given data on the tendencies of subordinate Stone's rams to withdraw during normal, everyday interactions (Geist 1966a). In 136 interactions between rams of equal horn size, the subordinate turned and showed his rear to the dominant in 30 instances and walked away in 4. The tendency to withdraw increases if the subordinate is much smaller than the dominant. In 134 interactions in which one ram was one horn size smaller (i.e., class II is one horn size smaller than class III), the subordinate turned away in 37 instances and walked away in 21 of these. In 73 interactions of rams differing by two horn sizes, the subordinate turned away in 31 instances and walked away in 30 of these. This pattern does not hold when a large ram defends an estrous female. Subordinate rams then tend to get away from an antagonistic dominant as quickly as possible.

The behavior of the anestrous female toward sheep of equal or smaller size is characterized by aggressive patterns. The two most common patterns of Stone's and bighorn ewes are butting and the horn threat, which account for 52.6% and 51.0% of their behavior respectively (see table 31). Aggressive patterns account for 78.0% of the Stone's ewe's behavior and 72.8% of that of the bighorn ewe (from table 30). Adult ewes interact little with each other, but if they do it is likely that one chases away and butts another, although occasionally the females show a low-stretch or twist to one another. Even a front kick is on a rare occasion delivered by one female on another, and I have seen in a few instances a dominant subadult female mount its subordinate. The behavior of anestrous females is similar to that of lambs and subadults.

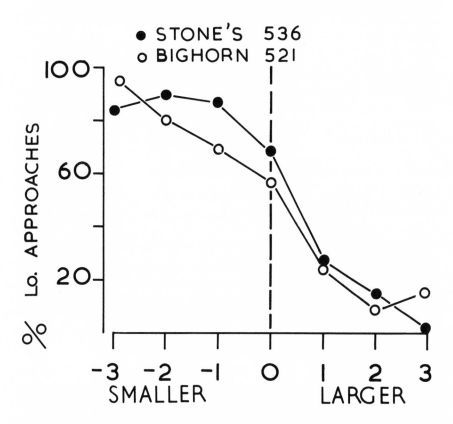

Fig. 19. The percentage of approaches initiated with a low-stretch by rams toward smaller-, equal-, and larger-horned companions. — 3 stands for 3 horn classes smaller. For example, a class I ram is 3 horn sizes smaller than a class IV ram. 0 stands for rams of equal horn size. Number of approaches recorded = 536 and 521.

The attacked female, subadult, or lamb usually departs, but occasionally it comes to a short exchange of blows.

Dominant and subordinate rams usually initiate interactions in a different manner. Rams approach companions with smaller horns in a low-stretch and those with larger horns in a horn threat, indicating their intention to horn and rub on the larger's face or to butt his horns. The exact relationship between approaches in low-stretch and horn size differences of the partners in the interactions is shown in fig. 19. Stone's and bighorn rams behave in the same manner. Thus rams approach rams of equal horn size in 55–70% of the interactions in low-stretch, while much larger rams are approached in low-stretch in only 4–20% of the interactions, and much smaller rams are approached in 85–95% of all interactions in low-stretch. Superimposed is the tendency of rams to approach equal-size companions more and more frequently in low-stretch as they grow older and mature, treating them as inferiors.

Ewes and subadults initiate few interactions with a low-stretch. Adult Stone's ewes did so in only 14% of the interactions (N = 157) and yearling ewes in only 10% (N = 58). The manner in which sheep start off an interaction depends on the size relation of both and on their sex.

Behavior of Rams toward Females, Yearling Females, and Lambs

When two sheep come together and perform behavior patterns toward each other, they are in an interaction, which is the unit of comparison used here. An *interaction* is the record of the kind and number of behavior patterns used by each of the two social partners. Since each sheep in an interaction is classified and since it is known which kind and how many behavior patterns were initiated by one individual on the other, how one class of sheep behaves toward another can be detected. It is only necessary to standardize procedures. Thus I recorded 596 interactions (N = 596) between adult Stone's rams (classes II–IV) and adult females. Thirteen behavior patterns were recordable.

It can be seen from table 33 that rams dealt out 162 low-stretches per 100 interactions toward females. Below the pattern frequency for females, is shown the behavior of rams toward immature yearling females. Thus, rams dealt out 35 front kicks (L) per 100 interactions with female yearlings. That is, about every third courtship the ram would kick a yearling female. It can also be seen that the rams acted rather similarly to adult females and yearling females, for those patterns

TABLE 33

Behavior of Stone's rams toward adult females vs. yearling females (In no. of patterns/100 interactions)

	Lo	L	T	M	B	Ho	Ru	Sv	F	Cl	Thj	Rb	Hb
Stone's ♂ to ♀ (N = 596)	162	26	21	8	4	1	8	49	30	0	0	0	0
Stone's ♂ to ♀y (N = 165)	140	35	25	12	3	2	5	37	28	0	0	0	0

NOTES: Lo = low-stretch; L = front kick (*Laufeinschlag*); T = twist; M = mount; B = butt; Ho = horn threat; Ru = rush; Sv = sniff rear; F = lipcurl (*Flehmen*); Cl = clash; Thj = threat jump; Rb = rubbing; Hb = horning body.
$r = 0.993$, $t_0 = 18.7$, $p < 0.001$.

shown often to adult ewes were also shown often to yearling ewes. It would be more satisfying to know how similar the behavior of rams is to ewes and yearling ewes. This can be achieved by correlating the two sets of figures. Then the correlation coefficient r tells us how similar the two sets of figures are. In the above instance, $r = +0.993$, indicating that the ram acts in almost identical fashion to adult ewes as to yearling ewes. In this instant r does not differ significantly from unity (1), but does differ significantly from zero ($t_0 = 18.7$, $p < 0.001$), so that the behavior of the ram toward the female yearling can be predicted from his behavior toward the adult female.

How do rams treat lambs? Do they act in the same way toward them as toward females or differently? Observations indicated the former, but we can be more exact (table 34). Since the correlation coefficient ($r = 0.958$) does not differ significantly from unity, rams treat lambs in the same manner as females. However, they perform fewer patterns

TABLE 34

Behavior of Stone's rams toward adult females vs. lambs (In no. of patterns/ 100 interactions)

	Lo	L	T	M	B	Ho	Ru	Sv	F	Cl	Thj	Rb	Hb
Stone's ♂ to ♀ (N = 596)	162	26	21	3	4	1	8	49	30	0	0	0	0
Stone's ♂ to L (N = 195)	88	34	8	9	7	6	2	18	10	0	0	0	0

NOTE: $r = 0.958$, $t_0 = 10.3$, $p < 0.001$.

per 100 interactions, indicating a lower preference for lambs than
females. Together tables 33 and 34 allow the conclusion that Stone's
rams treat females, immature females, and lambs in the same manner.

Table 35 shows that adult bighorn rams behave toward adult females
in the same manner as toward yearling females and lambs. Like the
Stone's rams, the bighorn males show little preference for subadults as is
indicated by fewer patterns per 100 interactions and the fact that so
few interactions between subadults and rams were recorded ($N = 29$).
It is safe to conclude that Stone's and bighorn rams treat adult females
and subadults in the same manner even though they may have little
preference for the latter.

TABLE 35

Behavior of bighorn rams toward adult females vs. yearlings and lambs (In no.
of patterns/100 interactions)

	Lo	L	T	M	B	Ho	Ru	Sv	F	Cl	Thj	Rb	Hb
Bighorn ♂ to ♀	138	23	79	8	2	1	3	82	39	0	0	0	0
(N = 205)													
Bighorn ♂ to ♀y and L	65	6	9	12	12	0	6	27	12	0	0	0	0
(N = 29)													

NOTE: $r = 0.882$, $t_0 = 6.1$, $p < 0.001$.

The correlation coefficient r is a useful measure of overall similarity.
If r is close to $+1$, then the classes compared behave in the same manner;
if r is close to -1, then the classes compared behave in diametrically
opposed ways, one class using frequently those behavior patterns that
the other uses rarely. This r does not measure the magnitude of frequency; it only says how closely pattern frequencies are related.

Behavior of Rams toward Subordinates

In the foregoing explanation of the method used to investigate the
social behavior of sheep, it appeared from the tables that rams acted
in a rather consistent manner. This is typical of mountain sheep. Thus
large rams treat subordinate rams in the same fashion regardless if
these are large or small. Table 36 compares the behavior of large class
IV rams toward subordinate class IV rams, and toward the much
smaller and younger class II rams. Small class II rams treat their

TABLE 36.

Behavior of Stone's dominant rams toward subordinate rams (In no. of patterns/ 100 interactions)

	Lo	L	T	M	B	Ho	Ru	Sv	F	Cl	Thj	Rb	Hb
Stone's IV to sub IV (N = 47)	189	264	15	0	8	0	0	0	2	2	0	4	6
Stone's IV to II (N = 82)	117	172	6	0	8	1	1	0	1	1	3	1	1

NOTE: $r = 0.990$, $t_0 = 32.9$, $p < 0.001$.

subordinates in the very same manner as large class IV rams treat theirs (see table 37). Table 38 shows that small class II Stone's and bighorn rams act alike toward subordinate companions. Similarly, large Stone's rams and large bighorn rams act almost alike when confronting subordinate rams (table 39).

Dominant rams treat subordinate males in the same manner as adult females and subadults. It was demonstrated that rams treat adult females in the same fashion as yearling females and lambs. Everyday observation indicates that rams treat their subordinate companions and adult females in a similar manner. Although their behavior to females shows a fair correlation to that toward smaller rams, the similarity is not very close. Table 40 shows this for Stone's sheep. Bighorn rams behave a little more similarly to females and subordinate males than do Stone's sheep (see table 41, $r = 0.72$), but the similarity again is not great.

TABLE 37

Behavior of Stone's dominant rams toward subordinate rams (In no. of patterns/ 100 interactions)

	Lo	L	T	M	B	Ho	Ru	Sv	F	Cl	Thj	Rb	Hb
Stone's IV to III (N = 63)	170	228	2	0	9	2	2	0	2	2	5	2	2
Stone's II to sub II (N = 66)	118	112	8	4	9	0	3	2	3	3	14	3	6

NOTE: $r = 0.979$, $t_0 = 16.1$, $p < 0.001$.

TABLE 38

Behavior of Stone's vs. bighorn dominant rams toward subordinate rams of same class (In no. of patterns/100 interactions)

	Lo	L	T	M	B	Ho	Ru	Sv	F	Cl	Thj	Rb	Hb
Stone's II to sub II (N = 66)	118	112	8	4	9	0	3	2	3	3	14	3	6
Bighorn II to sub II (N = 39)	88	33	18	13	10	0	0	14	5	0	5	0	3

NOTE: $r = 0.865$, $t_0 = 5.5$, $p < 0.001$.

TABLE 39

Behavior of Stone's vs. bighorn dominant rams toward subordinate rams of different class (In no. of patterns/100 interactions)

	Lo	L	T	M	B	Ho	Ru	Sv	F	Cl	Thj	Rb	Hb
Stone's IV to III (N = 63)	170	228	2	0	9	2	2	0	2	2	5	2	2
Bighorns IV to III (N = 64)	103	67	30	2	23	3	3	3	5	2	2	15	5

NOTE: $r = 0.883$, $t_0 = 5.9$, $p < 0.001$.

TABLE 40

Behavior of dominant Stone's rams toward females vs. subordinate rams (In no. of patterns/100 interactions)

	Lo	L	T	M	B	Ho	Ru	Sv	F	Cl	Thj	Rb	Hb
Stone's IV to ♀ (N = 176)	161	36	32	6	0	2	8	48	31	2	2	2	0
Stone's IV to III (N = 63)	170	228	2	0	9	2	2	0	2	2	5	2	2

NOTE: $r = 0.631$, $t_0 = 2.66$, $p < 0.05$.

TABLE 41

Behavior of bighorn dominant rams toward females vs. subordinate rams (In no. of patterns/100 interactions)

	Lo	L	T	M	B	Ho	Ru	Sv	F	Cl	Thj	Rb	Hb
Bighorn IV to ♀ (N = 70)	154	40	120	9	2	0	2	73	36	0	0	0	0
Bighorn IV to III (N = 64)	103	67	30	2	23	3	3	3	5	2	2	15	5

NOTE: $r = 0.720$, $t_0 = 3.8$, $p < 0.01$.

During daily observations of rams interacting with ewes and subordinate males, it is also noticeable that the females react differently than do subordinate rams. Whereas small rams stand and allow larger ones to display or kick and even mount them, nonestrous females withdraw. Hence it appears that if females would not withdraw but stand and take it, rams would treat them exactly like subordinate rams. This hypothesis can be tested. When the female is in estrus, she acts and responds very much like a subordinate ram to the courting ram (see below). Therefore, the behavior of a ram toward an estrous female and the behavior of rams toward subordinate males can be compared (see table 42 for Stone's sheep).

The correlation is now quite close, indicating that indeed the female's change in behavior at estrus enabled the ram to treat her like a small ram. Yet inspection of the data indicates that there are some serious

TABLE 42

Behavior of Stone's dominant rams toward estrous females vs. subordinate rams (In no. of patterns/100 interactions)

	Lo	L	T	M	B	Ho	Ru	Sv	F	Cl	Thj	Rb	Hb
Stone's IV estrous ♀ (N = 114)	88	292	58	130	2	5	8	20	3	0	0	0	0
Stone's IV to III (N = 63)	170	228	2	0	9	2	2	0	4	2	4	5	0

NOTE: $r = 0.881$, $t_0 = 5.9$, $p < 0.001$.

discrepancies. The estrous female is mounted much more frequently than a subordinate ram. However, this discrepancy disappears if the behavior of a ram toward a subordinate male in the presence of an estrous female is considered. This situation does occur normally. One large dominant ram guards the female and courts and breeds her, while smaller rams, barred from the female, interact among themselves. Table 43 compares the behavior of such rams, barred from the female but greatly excited, toward smaller male companions with the behavior of the breeding ram toward the estrous female. It is evident that in the presence of an estrous female, rams barred from that female treat their subordinates in much the same manner as the guarding male treats the

TABLE 43

Behavior of Stone's rams close to an estrous female: Large nonguarding ram on subordinate vs. guarding ram on female (In no. of patterns/100 interactions)

	Lo	L	T	M	B	Ho	Ru	Sv	F	Cl	Thj	Rb	Hb
Stone's large ♂ to small ♂ (N = 68)	78	175	6	69	13	5	8	3	0	0	0	2	0
Stone's IV to estrous ♀ (N = 114)	88	292	58	130	2	5	8	20	3	0	0	0	0

NOTE: $r = 0.971$, $t_0 = 12.9$, $p < 0.001$.

estrous ewe. The lesser rams appear to use their smaller companions as a substitute for the female, and it does happen that small rams attempting to escape their companions are occasionally chased through the cliffs just like an estrous ewe.

The foregoing demonstrated that given the chance dominant rams will treat subordinate rams and females in the same fashion. Since it was shown earlier that rams behave in the same manner toward adult females, yearling females, and lambs, it is evident that rams treat all subordinates in the same fashion irrespective of the subordinate's sex.

The Estrous Female's Male-like Behavior

The estrous female behaves like a subordinate ram toward males. Usually the female in estrus is followed by a group of rams and attempts to escape. However, if the female is alone with a ram, and this ram appears exhausted from breeding, the female may begin to court him

TABLE 44

Behavior of Stone's estrous females vs. small Stone's rams toward dominant rams
(In no. of patterns/100 interactions)

	Lo	L	T	M	B	Ho	Ru	Sv	F	Cl	Thj	Rb	Hb
Stone's estrous ♀ to IV (N = 114)	0	0	0	0	4	22	0	0	0	29	0	2	0
Small Stone's ♂ to larger ♂ (N = 68)	0	0	0	0	2	5	0	0	0	26	0	0	0

NOTE: $r = 0.88$, $t_0 = 5.9$, $p < 0.001$.

in turn (chap. 7). The female's courtship behavior greatly resembles the behavior of subordinate rams in that both use the same or similar behavior patterns with similar frequencies. Table 44 compares the actions of estrous Stone's females toward courting class IV rams with those of the small rams close by which are courted by other large rams that have been blocked from the female by the most dominant one.

What are the responses of the small males that are used as substitutes for an estrous ewe? Might they differ greatly from those of subordinate rams in normal interactions with large rams? Table 45 shows that they do not. Subordinate rams respond to the actions of dominants in much the same fashion irrespective of the situation.

The Anestrous Female's "Juvenile" Behavior

The anestrous female behaves like a sexually immature juvenile female or lamb. Only rarely do they butt back; usually they move off and do

TABLE 45

Normal reply of Stone's subordinates vs. reply with estrous female present (In no. of patterns/100 interactions)

	Lo	L	T	M	B	Ho	Ru	Sv	F	Cl	Thj	Rb	Hb
Stone's sub ♂ normal reply (N = 346)	13	4	0	0	15	2	0	0	0	65	11	4	5
Reply when close to estrous ♀ (N = 68)	0	0	0	0	2	4	0	0	0	26	0	0	0

NOTE: $r = 0.943$, $t_0 = 9.4$, $p < 0.001$.

TABLE 46

Behavior of Stone's females, yearling females, and lambs and of bighorn anestrous females to courting rams (In no. of patterns/100 interactions)

	Lo	L	T	M	B	Ho	Ru	Sv	F	Cl	Thj	Rb	Hb
Stone's ♀ to ♂ (N = 596)	0	0	0	0	1	1	0	0	0	0	0	0	0
Stone's ♀y to ♂ (N = 165)	1	0	0	0	2	2	0	0	0	0	2	0	0
Stone's L to ♂ (N = 145)	0	0	0	0	0	0	0	0	0	0	0	0	0
Bighorn ♀ to ♂ (N = 205)	1	0	0	0	0	4	0	0	0	1	0	0	1

not reply to the courting ram but feed intensely. It can be seen in table 53 that anestrous females and subadults including lambs respond in the same manner to the front kick. They jump away, and hence respond quite differently than rams or estrous females. Table 46 shows the response of adult Stone's ewes, yearling ewes, and lambs to courting rams, while the last line shows the response of the adult anestrous bighorn ewe to courting rams. Even without mathematical treatment it can be seen that these classes of sheep, be they bighorn or Stone's, hardly responded to the males.

In their social behavior, anestrous females and juveniles are very similar. Table 47 shows the behavior of adult females toward other adult females and compares it to the actions of yearling females toward equal or smaller sheep, namely other female yearlings and lambs. That

TABLE 47

Behavior of Stone's females vs. yearling females toward females of same class or lambs (In no. of patterns/100 interactions)

	Lo	L	T	M	B	Ho	Ru	Sv	F	Cl	Thj	Rb	Hb
Stone's ♀ to ♀ (N = 139)	16	8	0	0	36	43	37	0	0	2	2	1	1
Stone's ♀y to ♀y and L (N = 66)	15	10	0	6	47	27	9	0	0	6	0	1	1

NOTE: $r = 0.796$, $t_0 = 4.2$, $p < 0.01$.

Stone's and bighorn ewes behave similarly toward other ewes in social interactions is demonstrated in table 48.

For the present I have insufficient data on lambs 6–12 months of age to demonstrate conclusively that adult anestrous females and lambs behave alike in similar social situations. Lambs unfortunately interact even more rarely than females or yearling females. However, their lack of reply to courting rams, their tendency to withdraw if kicked (see table 53), their relatively frequent use of aggressive patterns, and the virtual absence of displays in their behavior are all characteristics in which they resemble anestrous females.

TABLE 48

Behavior of Stone's vs. bighorn females toward other females (In no. of patterns/ 100 interactions)

	Lo	L	T	M	B	Ho	Ru	Sv	F	Cl	Thj	Rb	Hb
Stone's ♀ to ♀ (N = 139)	16	8	0	0	36	43	37	0	0	2	2	1	1
Bighorn ♀ to ♀ (N = 70)	20	3	0	1	43	31	10	0	0	2	2	1	1

NOTE: $r = 0.850$, $t_0 = 5.3$, $p < 0.001$.

Social Preferences

Rams prefer to interact socially with adult females and rams of equal horn size, while juveniles and adult females interact primarily with sheep of equal or smaller body size. This preference is not strongly expressed, since rams interact with all classes of sheep, though adult females and juveniles only rarely choose adult males (Geist 1968a). Schloeth (1961) showed that cattle chose primarily those of similar rank to interact with.

Since I have previously reported on the social preference of mountain sheep, only a short sketch will be given here. If we were to take large, full-curl (IV) Stone's rams and assume that they had no preference whatsoever for any class of sheep, one would expect them to interact at random with the sheep in their vicinity. Hence the frequencies with which they approach various classes of sheep should be proportional to the frequencies with which these classes were present. It was noted which classes of sheep were present and how many individuals of each class were present whenever class IV rams interacted with a sheep.

TABLE 49

Preference index calculations for class IV Stone's rams

	Class						
	IV	III	II	♂y	♀	♀y	L
Individuals per class	196	393	649	251	947	400	509
No. of interactions observed	63	111	124	47	236	48	25
No. of interactions expected	38	77	127	49	194	78	99
Preference index (observed over expected)	1.64	1.44	0.97	0.95	1.27	0.61	0.25
χ^2 values	16	15	0	0	9	11	55
p	0.001	0.001	N.S.	N.S.	0.01	0.01	0.001

In 654 interactions between class IV Stone's rams and other sheep, there were 3,345 sheep in the vicinity of the class IV rams. The sheep split up into the number of individuals of each class as shown in table 49.

It can be calculated how many interactions class IV rams should have had with each class if each individual had the same chance of being picked. These results can be compared with the actual values obtained. Class IV rams picked large rams (IV and III) and adult females significantly more frequently than expected and juveniles

TABLE 50

Intensity of social interactions by Stone's rams on individuals of other classes

	Class						
	IV	III	II	♂y	♀	♀y	L
Class IV on other classes							
Patterns per interaction	5.0	4.2	2.05	2.2	4.1	2.5	2.4
No. of interactions	47	63	82	28	176	50	26
Class III on other classes							
Patterns per interaction	2.7	6.1	2.5	2.0	3.0	3.1	1.9
No. of interactions	49	32	56	14	124	48	25
Class II on other classes							
Patterns per interaction	1.9	1.9	2.8	1.9	3.2	3.0	1.9
No. of interactions	38	38	66	32	296	67	54

(♀y and L) less frequently than expected. From this one can infer that class IV rams prefer rams of similar size and adult females, whereas they ignore juveniles.

The same conclusion is reached when comparing the frequencies of behavior patterns dealt out per individual of the chosen class. Thus full-curl (IV) Stone's rams dealt out more patterns on rams of similar horn size and adult females than on small-horned rams and juveniles (table 50). Both of these methods are crude and appear to give reliable results only with large sample size (for details see Geist 1968a).

SOCIAL MATURATION: THE EFFECT OF NEOTENY AND PAEDOGENESIS ON SOCIAL BEHAVIOR AND STRUCTURE

When the classes of bighorn sheep are lined up in order of resemblance (see fig. 6), they form gradients in body and horn size as well as in skull structure, coat color, and patterning. The class IV rams at the end of the cline are the heaviest and largest-horned sheep; they carry the darkest coat and have lost the white belly and white trim on the rear margins of the front legs. A close look at the cline shows that the female and yearling male so greatly resemble each other that it is often difficult to separate these classes. Both may be of much the same size, carry horns of similar length and thickness, and have white bellies and ample white fur on the rear margins of the legs. One can consider the female as frozen in her development at the stage of a young ram, while the ram continues to grow and develop toward his ultimate, mature body form at 8 to 9 years of age. Male and female sheep pass through the same developmental stages, but whereas the female's development is stopped at sexual maturity, the male's development goes on. Since rams mature sexually usually at $1\frac{1}{2}$ to $2\frac{1}{2}$ years of age but do not reach ultimate size and proportions until 6 or 7 years later, they can be considered sexually mature juveniles, or neotenic. Since the females are stopped in development and never reach the ultimate growth form possible to sheep, they can be considered as sexually mature juveniles throughout their life, a condition termed paedogenic or paedomorphic. Consequently, the only fully mature or adult sheep are the class IV rams, while all other sheep are juveniles at various stages of development.

This hypothesis is fruitful if applied to the social behavior of sheep. Rams mature not only externally but also in their social behavior and psychological characteristics, while ewes act like young rams under the proper circumstances. Some parameters of social maturation are described in the following.

TABLE 51

Independence of bighorn sheep by class

	IV	III	II	I	♂y	♀	♀y	L
No. of sheep sighted	2,168	1,226	2,114	412	524	2,619	185	489
No. of sheep seen single	151	83	76	10	7	35	1	0
% seen alone	7.0	6.8	3.6	2.4	1.3	1.3	0.5	0

NOTE: Data from observations throughout the year, excluding the rutting season, at Banff National Park.

Independence. Mountain sheep grow increasingly independent along the cline from lamb to class IV ram. This is indicated by the increasing frequency with which sheep are seen alone (table 51). Large class IV rams, be they bighorn or Stone's are seen most frequently alone, whereas

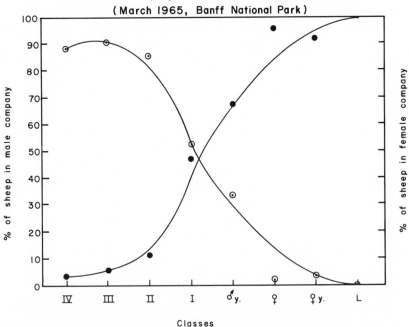

Fig. 20. The preference of sheep for ram company (○) increases gradually along the cline from lambs to class IV rams; the preference for ewe company (●) decreases. There are no sharp breaks in preference between classes.

young rams, females, and juveniles are least frequently on their own. Adult ewes, yearling rams, and class I rams did not differ significantly in this respect ($\chi^2 = 1.2$, N.S.), but did differ significantly from class IV rams ($\chi^2 = 98$, $p < 0.001$).

Companion preference. The tendency of sheep to associate with rams increased along the cline (fig. 20). The larger and more developed a ram, the more likely he is found in ram company outside the rutting season, and the more juvenile a sheep the more likely it is found with females.

Interaction preference. The tendency of sheep to interact voluntarily with class II–IV rams increases along the cline in the same fashion as their tendency to associate with males. This is true for bighorn as well as Stone's rams. As the rams grow larger, a greater proportion of their interaction is performed with large males, whereas females and juveniles choose them rarely (fig. 21).

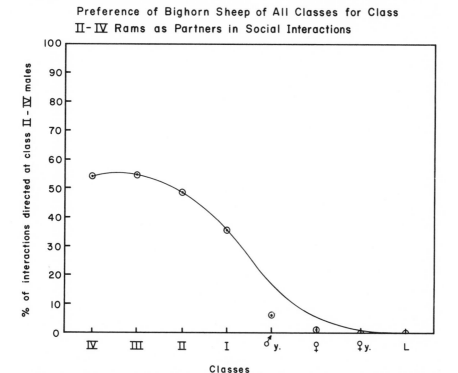

Fig. 21. The tendency of sheep to choose adult rams as partners in social interactions increases along the cline from lambs to class IV rams.

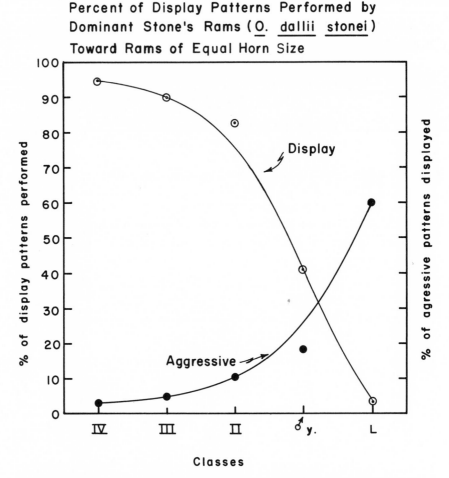

Fig. 22. The relative (and absolute) frequency of displays increases with the age of the rams, while the frequency of aggressive behavior patterns declines.

Aggressive and display behavior. As rams mature they use more horn displays and fewer overt aggressive patterns in their interactions with rams of equal horn size (fig. 22) and they butt and mount anestrous females less (fig. 23). The rams become more polished in their social behavior, less overtly sexual and aggressive. During the ram's ontogeny, the overt sexual and aggressive tendencies so typical of lambs fade simultaneously, as is shown by their close correlation (fig. 23). This indicates that the older rams grow, the less likely they will hurt females.

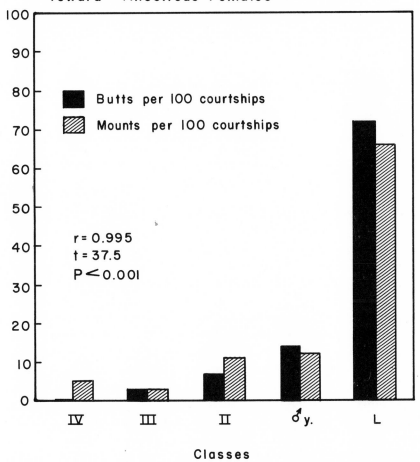

Fig. 23. The frequency of butting and mounting in the courtship of rams is closely related and decreases with the age of the rams. Overt aggression and mounting predominates in juveniles.

A psychological parameter. As rams mature, they treat other rams of equal horn and body size more and more frequently as inferiors. It was shown that rams approach subordinates in low-stretch. As rams mature, they approach equals more frequently in a low-stretch, one

TABLE 52

Relative frequency with which rams approached in a low-stretch other males of equal horn size

	IV	III	II	♂y
Total approaches	137	54	110	24
No. of approaches in horn display	92	36	52	12
% approaches initiated in horn display	67	66	47	50

NOTE: Bighorn and Stone's sheep data are combined on this table. For IV and III vs. II and ♂y: $\chi^2 = 11.7$, $p < 0.001$.

type of horn display (table 52), that is, treating them as inferiors. It appears that rams grow "brave" with age.

Rutting maturation. During early winter and throughout the rutting season, rams of different ages show a different pattern of association with females (fig. 24). It can be seen that young rams associated more closely with females than older rams; the latter spent less time with females during the rut. The tendency to associate with females during and outside of the rutting season appears to be subject to maturation.

Is the female mountain sheep the equivalent of an immature male? The hypothesis outlined above suggests that the female is frozen in her development at the level and in the image of a young male, and hence should not only look like one but also act like one. Indeed, adult females comply with this hypothesis in being as gregarious as young males (table 51). If the hypothesis is valid, females and young males should: (1) use the same behavior patterns in comparable social situations; (2) use these behavior patterns with the same frequencies or in similar rank order; (3) use the same behavior patterns in similar chronological order; (4) be treated alike by large rams, that is, females and young males should in general be courted similarly by large males and should respond similarly.

These predictions are not fulfilled if the female is not in estrus. The anestrous female behaves differently from the young ram. Although courted like any subordinate by large rams, the anestrous females do not reply with social behavior patterns as subordinate rams do and usually withdraw from rams. The anestrous female is similar to young

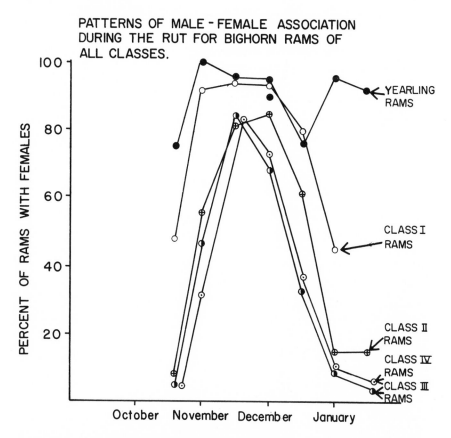

PATTERNS OF MALE - FEMALE ASSOCIATION
DURING THE RUT FOR BIGHORN RAMS OF
ALL CLASSES.

Fig. 24. The mechanism which synchronizes the arrival and departure of rams on the rutting grounds appears to be subject to maturation. Note that young rams associate earlier with females and depart later. During the rut, older rams spend less time with the females than do younger ones.

males only in her social tendencies as was shown in table 51. If the female is in estrus, however, she acts not only like a subordinate male toward the courting ram, but like a subordinate *young* ram. Table 53 shows the female's response to being kicked by a ram when in estrus and when not. The anestrous female's response is similar to that of juvenile sheep, whereas the estrous female does not differ quantitatively in her withdrawal response from young rams ($\chi^2 = 0.5$, N.S.). The estrous female does, however, differ significantly from the fully matured class IV rams ($\chi^2 = 27$, $p < 0.001$).

Estrous females, unlike anestrous ones, interact voluntarily with rams, follow rams (Banks 1964), and search out male company (Lindsay

TABLE 53

Relative frequency of withdrawal response to front kick for Stone's sheep by class

	IV	III	II	♂y	estrous ♀	anestrous ♀	♀y	L
No. of kicks received	161	175	242	63	327	276	110	43
No. which led to withdrawal	2	30	35	11	58	204	69	24
% of kicks which caused withdrawal	1.2	17.1	14.5	17.5	17.5	74.0	63.0	56.0

1966); and like young rams they prefer large-horned males over small-horned males. Young rams follow the largest-horned ram in a band (chap. 4); hence estrous females should do the same. Unfortunately, one cannot demonstrate that estrous ewes prefer to follow large rams, for if several rams are about the estrous female, they all follow her. Only occasionally when a single ram is with an estrous female and the former appears exhausted, can it be seen that the estrous female follows the ram if he moves off. This does not demonstrate her preference for large-horned males when in estrus—only a preference for males. However, the female does act differently toward large-horned and small-horned males when mounted. She jerks away significantly more frequently when a small male attempts to mount than when a large male attempts to mount (table 54). Although it cannot be demonstrated as yet, it appears that most of the long chases of estrous ewes through the cliffs are attempts by the ewe to escape from small males. They may

TABLE 54

Proportion of mounts accepted by estrous female from males of various classes

	Bighorn			Stone's		
	IV	III	II	IV	III	II
No. of mounts accepted by female	19	6	0	28	8	0
No. of mounts rejected by female	35	27	13	13	11	10
Total no. of mounts	54	33	13	41	19	10

NOTE: For Stone's and bighorn data combined: IV vs. III, $\chi^2 = 6.7$, $p < 0.01$; III vs. II, $\chi^2 = 7.6$, $p < 0.01$.

select large-horned rams because they are less molested in their presence than in the presence of a smaller defender and because large rams are less rough in their courtship.

It appears that the "male" behavior patterns of the females lie dormant for 363 days of the year till the hormonal change at estrus brings them out in the open. Male and female then have identical behavioral components whose expression appears to be dependent on specific hormones in adequate concentration in the blood stream. This hypothesis remains to be verified for sheep but has already been demonstrated to be valid for rats (Levine 1966).

The concepts of neoteny and paedogenesis explain the characteristic social groupings of sheep. Thus if one looks at figure 20, which depicts the slowly changing social preference of rams, it is evident that males must split into separate groups from females and juveniles. Similarly, if rams grow more "brave" with age as indicated in table 52, it is not surprising that they perform a greater portion of their social interactions with large rams as they grow older (fig. 21) and get into more serious fights with age (chap. 7). The exceedingly close grouping of female sheep as compared to older rams appears to be a function of their juvenile state, that is, females act like lambs by sticking closely together (table 51). They also act like lambs when preferring the company of females to that of rams (fig. 20). Maturing rams in following the largest-horned male continue in their juvenile tendency of associating with and following others.

One need not ask what advantage there is in females sticking more closely together than rams, not if this characteristic is the consequence of the female's juvenile state, nor is there any need to ask what is the adaptive significance of sheep forming into bands of males and females and juveniles. This social structure is also the consequence of the male's change in preference for males with sexual maturation. The ram's change in preference appears to result from the female's unsatisfactory social responses. The males leave females only after they thoroughly dominate them, a view strongly supported by Nievergelt's (1967) observations on ibex that poorly developed males leave the female bands at a later age than well-developed males. Hence young males dominating females cannot butt and clash with them since females withdraw. Young males can vent their aggression only on others of equal or larger body size. The reasons why aggression is highly adaptive for rams are discussed in chapter 11. The consequence is that young males move to males, but this shift is overlapped by their juvenile tendencies to go

with females as seen in figure 20. The social structure can be explained
therefore as the result of the male's social preference. The gregariousness
of sheep is explained by forces which select for neoteny (chap. 11)
and against juveniles that disperse on their own and females that
cause their young to disperse (chap. 5). Leadership in the ram bands is
simply a consequence of the most independent animal being followed
by more dependent ones. Conversely, independent animals are less
likely to follow and will be more frequently left behind, accounting
for the higher frequency of single class IV and III males being sighted.
It appears to me that living in groups has no significance in itself for
sheep once they have established a home range, and that their gregariousness is a logical outcome of the selection forces imposed on them by
the habitat they exploit.

THE SIGNIFICANCE OF HORNS
The functions and evolutionary significance of horns has been subject
to considerable discussion and speculation, most of which were reviewed
by Bruhin (1952) and Geist (1966a). The huge horns carried by mountain sheep in particular attract attention. What selection forces could
possibly be responsible for such outsized monstrosities? The first thought
is that horns evolved as weapons. There is little doubt that they function
as such. Rams smash their heavy horns edge-first into opponents, and
these severe clashes do leave some injuries. Since blood is drawn, hair
torn out, the body bruised or cut, and bones occasionally broken, the
horns must be considered as weapons, although more efficient ones
could be conceived. I have been butted by rams in the course of my
work and although their blows were not pleasant I remained unharmed.
Had a mountain goat done the same to me, I would have been fortunate
to survive. The small, light, sharply pointed horns of mountain goats
are deadly daggers as is evident from autopsies of goats which fought
(Geist 1965, 1967); one male I examined had 32 punctures on his
body including pierced rumen, lungs, and heart. The mountain goat
achieves with the small horns such severe damage that it is incredible
that rams must grow 65–90 times as much horn to achieve a lesser
effect. Although the horns are used as weapons by sheep, and the
lateral edge with which rams hit opponents is almost certainly an
adaptation to concentrate the energy during a clash, horns must fulfill
other functions as well.

Mountain sheep also appear to use their horns as shields as was
discussed already. Daily observations indicated that rams whirled or

Plate 58. A clash between a class III and IV ram. Note that the smaller ram attacked, as he is in a more advanced stage of the clash than his opponent. The class IV ram arches out sideways to catch the blow. The attack came from the side. (Reprinted, by permission, from Geist 1966a.)

Plate 59. Broken horns are not common. This old ram has exceptionally battered and cracked horns.

Plate 60. During feeding, rams are usually dispersed over the hillside. An erosion site is in the foreground.

Plate 61. Huddle formed by two class III rams in a dominance fight and two "spoiler" rams. The two rams in the rear are displaying to and kicking one of the two combatants, while the other combatant is approaching his feeding opponent in low-stretch.

Plate 62. Bighorn rams in a huddle displaying horns to each other. April 1965.

Plate 63. Rams playing in early summer. The two rams in foreground are jumping up and spinning about; the two rams in the background are about to clash.

Plate 64. During a vicious fight rams slug sideways. Ram on the left attempts to evade the blow.

Plate 65. Rams in a vicious fight pushing each other about with the horns, neck, and shoulders.

Plate 66. Two rams have accidentally locked horns.

Plate 67. An estrous ewe, which accepted mountings from a full-curl ram, evades a three-quarter-curl ram. Raping attempts of anestrous females are commonly performed by young rams.

Plate 68. A typical interaction about an estrous ewe. *a*, a large class III ram attacks the guarding class IV ram; *b*, the clash throws the old ram about six feet downhill; *c*, while the ewe escapes, the smaller ram attempts to push the old ram away with his side and block his way to the female; *d*, while the young ram attempts to cut the old ram away from the ewe, the old ram butts into the smaller opponent; *e*, the old ram gets ahead of the smaller ram, then whirls and clashes into him with full force. Note that he hits the small ram with his left horn edge; *f*, the smaller ram slips past the old ram and chases the ewe, followed closely by the old ram.

Plate 69. A large ram guards an estrous female, while subordinate rams cluster below, interacting with each other.

Plate 70. Young Alpine ibex male in low-stretch behind female at the Hellabrun Zoological Garden, Munich.

Plate 71. Ewes often terminate suckling by stepping over the lamb's neck with a hind leg.

Plate 72. Lambs spend much of the day with each other in juvenile groups such as this.

Plate 73. Mounting and butting are the two most common behavior patterns in the interactions of lambs.

Plate 74. Bighorn sheep foraging in loose snow. The principal method of snow removing is pawing. Note the identical belly markings of the adult female and the 20-month-old yearling male in the foreground. Both animals are pawing.

Plate 75. In late winter hard snow crusts will carry sheep and allow them to disperse.

Plate 76. An erosion site on the Palliser Range. A trail leads to the bedding area. Note the long, coarse grass below the open soil and the tall upper wall on which sheep rub off their coats.

Plate 77. Erosion sites are favorite resting areas of sheep. Typically, sheep rest in positions such that they do not look into any companion's face.

Plate 78. A shedding bighorn ram in May standing in an erosion site. Note the strands of hair and underwool rubbed off along the upper edge of the erosion wall. Two ground squirrel holes are visible in the foreground. The ram is well advanced in shedding. (Photo courtesy of Harold Carr.)

Plate 79. During coat shedding, matted underwool and guard hair can hang towel-like about the sheep.

Plate 80. Ram rubbing off fur during molt. The hair is bleached and of similar color as the rump patch.

Plate 81. This ewe opened up her withers with horn scratching. New, dark hair is growing on the areas freed of old hair. Circular spots are locations where ticks engorged. A tick is crawling on the old hair on the back. A few scabs are visible at the border of old and new hair.

Plate 82. Poor quality bighorn lambs 4 months of age which have just started to shed their juvenile coat. Bare Mountain ewes, October 1964.

Plate 83. Poor quality yearling rams. Note small horns (*inset*). *In center*, a 16-month-old ram who resembles in size and proportions a lamb 6 months of age from a high quality population. October 1964.

Plate 84. High quality yearling ram, age 22 months, from the Mount Norquay band, Banff National Park. Note long, thick horns and large testes (cf. plate 42).

Plate 85. An adult ewe, an exceptionally well-developed female yearling (*center*), and an average-size male yearling from the Bare Mountain sheep. July 1964.

Plate 86. A 5-year-old ram with a broken leg in spring. He vanished a few weeks after the picture was taken.

Plate 87. A ewe about three months after breaking the left hind leg. This animal continued to suckle a lamb. What effect a broken leg had on this animal can be judged from her emaciated body. She died in winter.

Plate 88. It appears that sheep evolution has been spurred by selection for the greatest possible clash force. Here a ram "falls" on his opponent by crashing into him from uphill, using gravitation to increase the clash force.

Plate 89. A typical urial ram. Note the goatlike pointed ears, the neck mane, throat beard, and inward-pointing circular horns.

arched sideways to catch the horn blows of opponents (plate 58). Most ruminants have this defense syndrome of catching an opponent's attack between the horns. If a horn or antler is missing, then the animal's defense is impaired and an attack can bring damage to the side not guarded by the horn or antler. Thus Harper et al. (1967) observed two wapiti bulls both of which carried a normal seven- or five-point antler on the left and a malformed spike or saber on the right. The combat damage sustained by these two bulls was, as expected, on the right side of the body. One bull had even lost his right eye, since no brow point was there to guard it. The hypothesis that ram horns function as shields, although valid, is insufficient to explain the size of horns. Cattle and bison also appear to use their horns for catching charges and yet their horns are quite small compared to those of sheep.

The suggestion that ram horns evolved to absorb concussion is not a fortunate one. Females fight just like rams but carry only tiny horns. Moreover, wart hogs (*Phacochoerus*) and giant forest hogs (*Hylochoerus*), which clash head on after taking a run at each other (Mohr 1960; Frädrich 1965, 1967), have no horns at all. It appears rather that the pneumation observable in the skull of bovids, giraffes, and hogs has evolved as a means of absorbing concussion and shielding the brain. McHugh (1958) suggests that the bison's thick hair mop on the forehead has the same function.

Taylor (1966) suggested that bovid horns function as thermoregulatory organs. He demonstrated on domestic goats that the horns vasodilate in response to exercise, that they vasoconstrict when the animals rest in a cold environment, and that there is a direct relationship between heat loss per minute per cm^2 of horn surface and the ambient temperature. A resting goat normally loses 3–4% of its heat production through the horns, while a goat heated up from running could lose as much as 12% of its heat production after stopping until it vasoconstricted. The horn cores and sinuses are covered by a rich vascular plexus, which is the means by which blood may be distributed for cooling. It was noted by W. D. Wishart of the Alberta Fish and Wildlife Branch that heavily exercised bighorn rams caught in traps had rather warm horns, while Ogren (1965) observed that Barbary rams (*Ammotragus*) covered their horns with moist sand or mud on hot days. Hence there is evidence that mountain sheep horns function to some extent in thermoregulation, but there is little evidence that they evolved as thermoregulatory organs. The rich vascular plexus appears to be necessary both for growing horns during the short summer and enlarging the horn cores. Both of these functions require a rich blood supply, for a bighorn ram who grows 20 lb of horn in eight years, given the typical growth rate, must be adding 3–4 lb of horns during some summers. Moreover, in enlarging bone cores, bone must be carried away on inner surfaces and added on outer surfaces, while the cross struts are enlarged. A good blood supply would certainly not be a liability to a ram whose horns function as weapons as Taylor (1966) suggests. On the contrary, a poor blood supply would probably result in small horns and horn cores, hence lead to a loss in dominance and breeding success by the ram. The thermoregulatory functions of horns appear to be by-products of the rich vascular plexus, in the same manner as thermoregulation by our legs, arms, or face is the byproduct of a rich vascular plexus. Yet, our legs and arms hardly evolved as thermoregulatory organs.

If horns evolved as thermoregulatory organs then one must expect a correlation between horn size and habitat and not the converse as Taylor suggests. If we look at mountain sheep in Asia, we find the small-est-horned sheep in the warm climates of the south and the largest-horned sheep in the cold mountains and plateaus of central Asia. In North America, the converse is by and large true. The smallest-horned sheep are in the north and the largest-horned in the warm or hot south. If rams grew large horns for thermoregulation, why not females? There are more arguments against the view that horns evolved as thermo-regulatory organs, although they probably function as such in more bovids than the goat.

That horns could function as rank symbols was demonstrated for mountain sheep by Geist (1966b). This hypothesis was first stated clearly by Beninde (1937) who felt that large-antlered red deer could intimi-date smaller ones and gain social advantages without fighting. That is, opponents could judge the fighting potential of opponents from their horn size. Hence the horns would act as symbols of dominance rank. If this hypothesis is applied to mountain sheep, several predictions are inherent:

1. One can expect a horn display, that is, a means of making horns conspicuous to opponents. Such a display is indeed present in mountain sheep, both in the low-stretch and present, in which the horns are displayed frontolaterally.
2. Rams must be able to distinguish horn size, for no horn display would be meaningful without this ability and horns could not function as rank symbols. By demonstrating that sheep pre-ferred companions of equal horn and body size it was made

evident that sheep could distinguish the sex-age classes (Geist 1966b, 1968a). This in itself did not demonstrate that horn size was the clue by which the distinction was made. Since the predictions based on the hypothesis that sheep distinguished the various classes by class specific sounds and odors were wrong, only visual clues were apparently used to distinguish classes (Geist 1966b). The main visual clues were body and horn size. However, since class III and class IV rams are of similar body but not horn size, and sheep were able to distinguish these classes, horn size was left as the most probable visual clue.

3. Large-horned rams should be dominant over small-horned rams. This implies first that large-horned rams should behave differently toward small-horned rams than small-horned rams do toward them, which is true. Second, large-horned rams should be able to displace small-horned rams and chase them away. This happens about the estrous female (chap. 7).

4. Young rams with vigorous horn growth should surpass older rams in dominance once they surpass these in horn size. I observed such a changeover among Stone's sheep, when C-ram in 1962 at $7\frac{1}{2}$ years of age became a full-curl and dominated all other full-curls from Sanctuary Mountain, one of which was 13 years old, the other 10, and the third $7\frac{1}{2}$ years of age; C-ram carried the most massive horns of the three. Similarly, S-ram became a full-curl and began dominating E-ram, a 10-year-old of equal horn size but smaller body size. The observation that young rams dominate smaller-horned older rams was not uncommon among both the Stone's and the bighorn sheep I observed; however, the demonstration that horn size of rams is more closely related than age to dominance is as yet outstanding.

5. Rams should be able to recognize a strange ram's dominance by the latter's horn size. That is, strange rams of unequal horn size should behave in accordance with their horn size. Rams with smaller horn size than the stranger should treat him as a dominant while he treats them as subordinates; rams with horns larger than the stranger's should treat him like any subordinate and he should respond like a subordinate in turn. Strange rams of equal horn size have no way of settling dominance except by fighting, for none can tell who will dominate whom prior to the fight. Hence strange rams entering

bands should interact extensively only with rams of equal horn size.

I was able to gather data on five Stone's rams which were strangers integrating into bands of rams. Figure 25 shows how many aggressive and display patterns these rams received from resident rams of various horn sizes. Rams of a horn size close to that of the stranger dealt out by far the most patterns. The most intense dominance fight I ever witnessed occurred between two strange class III Stone's rams and it lasted 25 hours. Of the 25 dominance fights I observed among bighorn and Stone's sheep, at least 15 were between strange rams, that is, rams which had not seen each other at least for several months.

6. If large horns evolved as rank symbols, rams with large horns should have a reproductive advantage over small-horned rams. Indeed breeding success is closely related to horn size (see chap. 7).

7. The loss of horns by a ram should lead to rams treating him as one of lower rank. I did not attempt to verify this prediction since it requires altering and mutilating animals, which was beyond the scope of this field study. However, there were rams that had lost a large part of their horns due to severe breakage (plate 59). I did observe one incident which is worth reporting. The very old "broken horn," as I called the ram in plate 59, returned in spring 1965 to the Palliser Range. Here he met ram no. 48, a 5-year-old resident ram. The old ram displayed in low-stretch to 48 but with the side on which the horn was broken. The young ram stood and faced the old ram for a little while then walked straight toward him and kicked him squarely on the chest. The young ram treated the old one as a subordinate. The old ram turned, walked back by about ten paces, then whirled, rose, and charged at the young ram. After the clash, the small ram at once began licking the face of the old ram, indicating he had submitted. This incident indicates that loss of horns may indeed lead to a ram misjudging the fighting potential of a larger ram.

8. This prediction is based on the following data: If one calculates the survivorship curves for Dall's rams from Murie's data (1944, table 4, based on 89 rams found dead), one finds that rams 2–8 years of age show a negligible mortality, whereas rams 8–14 years of age die rapidly. The same is shown by bighorn

sheep. A survivorship curve based on 77 ram skulls found in
Banff park (see table 67) indicated a mortality of 4.0% per
annum for rams 2–7 years of age, while rams 8–17 years died
at 23.0% per annum. Observations of Stone's, bighorn, and
Dall's sheep indicated that rams under 7 years of age did little
breeding. Breeding rams were 8–16 years of age. Therefore,

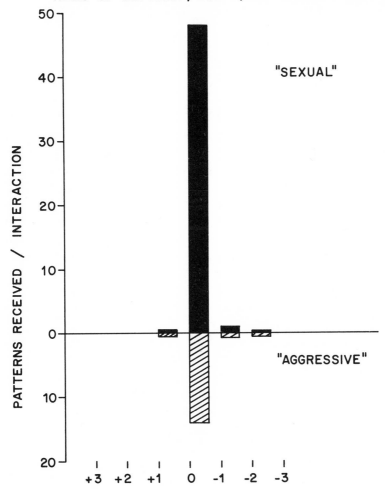

Fig. 25. Strange rams integrating into a band receive most patterns from rams of
equal horn size. (From Geist 1966*b*.)

it appears that "breeding" rams had a much higher mortality than "nonbreeding" rams.

Since a ram's dominance and breeding success depends on his horn size, then rams with vigorous horn growth should reach breeding status earlier than rams with poorer horn growth. Since breeding rams have higher mortality than nonbreeding rams, rams with vigorous horn growth should die younger than rams with poor horn growth. Therefore, if one measures the rate of horn growth of rams found dead in the field, one should find that rams dying prior to average age at death have a better horn growth than rams dying after average age at death. Thus 21 bighorn rams which died between 7 and 11 years of age grew on the average 4.6 cm more

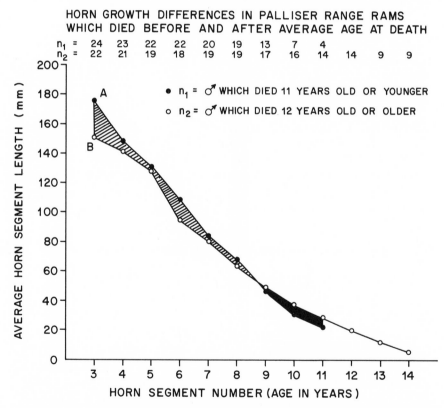

Fig. 26. The average horn segment growth for Palliser rams dying before average age at death (10.12 years) is greater between 3 and 8 years of age than for rams dying after average age at death. (From Geist 1966*b*.)

horn between 3 and 8 years of age than 19 rams which died between 12 and 17 years ($t = 2.34$, $p = 0.023$). The growth rates of the horns from both groups are shown in figure 26. These data indicate that horn size, breeding success, and decreased life expectancy are directly related.

How rams determine their own horn size: A hypothesis. The foregoing raises the question: How does a ram know his own horn size? The horns of a ram change in size with age, and yet the individual knows how to behave toward smaller-horned and larger-horned rams. The following hypothesis explains how rams achieve this. In growing from an 18-month-old yearling to an 8–9-year-old class IV ram, a bighorn ram increases body weight about 1.75 times, increases horn length about 4 times, and horn circumference about 2.5 times. However, his horn weight increases about 20 times. The major difference between rams of different classes is in horn mass (see Blood et al. 1970). It was noted earlier when describing the clash that four forces were involved. These were propulsion of the ram toward his opponent, drop of his body due to gravity, rapid lowering of his neck, and forward flick and propulsion of the horns just prior to contact. These forces are additive. Given two rams of equal body size and equal capabilities, but of different horn sizes, the one with the heaviest horns will deliver the harshest blows.

Right after a clash rams freeze into a stiff present. Hence each opponent first experiences a blow and is then shown the horns responsible for this blow. A ram can therefore associate at once the clash force with horn size. Since rams clash commonly throughout the year, gathering in huddles and play groups on the hillsides and ridges, they have ample opportunity to be reminded of what clash force goes with what horn size.

It appears that selection is for large horns because they allow rams to deal out more forceful blows when clashing than small horns. The larger the horns of a ram, the more companions he can subordinate and the more dominant he becomes. Vigorous horn growth allows a ram to reach high dominance rank and participation in breeding during the rut earlier in life than poor horn growth, but rams with vigorous horn growth have a shorter life expectancy than rams with poor horn growth. This inverse relationship of horn size and life expectancy is a most important factor in the evolution of mountain sheep (see chap. 11).

7 Behavior during the Rutting Season

INTRODUCTION

The rutting season in late November and December is preceded by a gathering of rams from late September to mid-October. The rams are then in their best physical condition, and they interact extensively, often while standing on top of ridges in a tight group or huddle. Their activity during daylight hours gradually increases and reaches a maximum during the rut. In early November the rams disband and move to their respective rutting areas.

When the rams meet strangers on the rutting grounds they may enter into dominance fights. These occur most frequently between class III rams and can be very long. They are the most spectacular social interactions of sheep. Not infrequently dominance fights attract other rams, which may take sides and clash on one or the other of the two fighters. In general both fighters court each other and clash till one submits, by acting like a female. The smaller of two combatants takes the initiative in aggression, but the larger may take it if the smaller "insults" him by courting or mounting him. As a rule the smaller does most of the attacking and the larger most of the displaying. The more equal two rams are in size and proportion, the more alike they act, and the longer the fight. The ram initiating clashes appears to use every trick at his disposal to increase the clash force. The dominance fights differ considerably from the unritualized, vicious brawls which occasionally erupt about estrous females.

As long as no female is in heat all rams have access to the females and court these. The females tend to withdraw and urinate, which appears to be an adaptation to get away from the ram, since the ram usually nuzzles the urine and lipcurls. However, no conclusive explanation of the female's urination can be given as yet. Anestrous females are courted but not guarded except occasionally by a young ram.

When a female comes into heat, the largest-horned ram consorts with her and drives off all competition. These other rams are not easily

184

discouraged, and they occasionally abduct the female and chase her off into the cliffs. A long chase may follow, spotted with fights, in which the dominant deals out most of the blows. Once the chase comes to a halt the dominant ram again holds the ewe. Although the largest-horned ram does most of the breeding his subordinates get in a few mounts, primarily the class III rams. The female appears to prefer large-horned to small-horned rams and is quite skilled at thwarting the mounting attempts of small rams. Occasionally a large ram is alone with an estrous female. In this case the female may begin courting if the ram is too exhausted and shows little interest in her. She behaves much like an aggressive subordinate ram and in so doing appears to stimulate the ram into mounting.

The rams remain with the females for about two weeks after the females have been bred, and then the larger and older rams move to their own wintering areas.

THE PRE-RUT

Fall Gathering of Rams

Some time between early September and early October the rams return to the wintering areas from the summer ranges. The animals have long since shed the old winter hair and have a dark coat, which in bighorns is spotted here and there by a patch of light fur (plate 56). The coat is not yet fully grown and will not reach that stage till early November. This is also the case for Siberian snow sheep (Heptner et al. 1961). The Stone's rams are at this time not quite as dark as they will be about two months hence, when the darkest among them are almost glossy black. The rams are now in the best physical condition. Their body contours are round for they are fat and they are quite spirited.

The early fall days go by quietly. The rams feed dispersed over the hillsides as is normally the case (plate 60), and they rest periodically. They engage in minor interactions just prior to resting and again after rising, prior to feeding. Rams of similar horn size in particular tend to interact. Occasionally a larger displaces a smaller one from the bedding site by displaying to him in low-stretch and pawing his back, then he paws the bed with a front leg and lies down. The rams rise periodically, urinate or defecate, then turn and lie down again. The bedding areas are well fertilized, therefore, and in spring the grass is usually greener and grows longer at the lower edges of the beds.

Occasionally some rams move from one end of the range to another.

During a temporary halt small rams often nibble the horns of a larger or rub their face on them. Rarely, the large-horned lead ram marches on in a low-stretch, an indication that if one of the followers attempts to pass, the leader will prevent it. Groups of rams mix with a minimum of strife. Rams entering another group frequently do so in a low-stretch (plate 61).

In the evenings and early mornings, and occasionally at other times of the day, the rams perform group interactions which I termed "huddles" (plate 62). The rams gather into a tight bunch on a level spot, usually on top of a hill or ridge, on a level rock projection from the cliff, or on a large erosion site on the slope. They face the inside of the gathering, their white rump patches facing out, and perform social behavior patterns in accordance with their rank. The large rams display and kick while the younger ones rub and horn the larger ones. Periodically the huddle erupts into threat jumping. Clashing rams freeze into rigid presents thereafter and then close in for more displays, kicks, twists, and rubbing. Rarely, one ram mounts another; only in huddles have I seen smaller rams mount larger ones. The behavior of the larger and smaller rams still follows the rules typical for their respective ranks, but the subordinates are much more vigorous in huddles and allow themselves certain freedoms. Thus they display much more than in normal interactions. Table 55 shows that dominant bighorn rams in huddles behave toward their subordinates much as they do outside the huddles. Table 56 shows that subordinate bighorn rams in a huddle use similar behavior patterns toward dominants as they do in normal circumstances; however, it is also evident that subordinates use many more patterns during a huddle. Class IV rams replied to dominants with 84

TABLE 55

Behavior of rams toward subordinates in and outside huddles (In no. of patterns/ 100 interactions)

	Lo	L	T	M	B	Ho	Ru	Sv	F	Cl	Thj	Rb	Hb
Bighorn IV to sub IV, normal (N = 42)	81	79	21	0	25	2	2	0	7	0	2	7	3
Bighorn IV to sub IV, huddle (N = 47)	165	100	19	0	28	0	0	0	0	13	9	4	4

NOTE: $r = 0.954$, $t_0 = 10.5$, $p < 0.001$.

TABLE 56

Behavior of subordinate rams toward dominants in and outside huddles (In no. of patterns/100 interactions)

	Lo	L	T	M	B	Ho	Ru	Sv	F	Cl	Thj	Rb	Hb
Reply of bighorn sub IV to IV, normal (N = 42)	2	0	0	0	5	0	0	0	2	5	2	16	52
Reply of bighorn sub IV to IV, huddle (N = 46)	52	15	10	0	19	2	0	0	0	35	10	42	124

NOTE: $r = 0.919$, $t_0 = 8.0$, $p < 0.001$.

patterns per 100 interactions in normal, everyday interactions, but with 309 patterns per 100 interactions during huddles. This difference is significant ($\chi^2 = 45$, $p < 0.001$).

The huddles have a playful nature; here subordinate rams are least inhibited. This is indicated not only by their increased interaction with dominants—frequent clashes and threat jumps accompanied by head shaking (which does not occur in dominance fights)—but also by their use of display patterns and even the mount. Occasionally a huddle disintegrates into a group of frolicking, clashing rams (plates 44 and 63).

Huddles were observed throughout the year among bighorns, but they occurred primarily in fall, spring, and early summer. In fall an occasional huddle became a raping party in which a group of rams focused their attention on a small 2–3-year-old ram and began mounting him. In all four such raping parties that I observed the small ram ran away, followed by the larger rams. Unfortunately, they soon disappeared from sight.

Groups of playing rams are more often seen in spring and summer than at other seasons (plate 63). Such plays often began after the rams rose in the morning and clumped into a huddle in the cliffs high above the slopes. One large ram would suddenly turn from the group, shake his head, and begin bouncing downhill. Others would follow and begin to frolic. Suddenly the lead ram would whirl and clash into the ram behind him and both would present. Other rams hurried to them and formed another temporary huddle around them till one ran off downhill. During such runs the rams would whirl about, bound high into the air, threat jump repeatedly, clash in rapid succession with several rams, and cut other rams off by barring their way.[1] I soon discovered that such play could be artificially produced if I could get the rams to run downhill toward me. This was not difficult to do since the rams were eager to lick the salt I always carried for them.

The Stone's sheep in the Cassiars huddled less frequently than the bighorns, but the Dall's rams on Sheep Mountain huddled extensively. The Dall's rams differed from the bighorns in that they hardly clashed. They displayed, kicked, and used contact patterns, but mainly they stood in tight knots doing very little. The Stone's rams were very active, however. Their play during the cool August evenings was the most extensive I saw. Rams went on long chases through the cliffs; they bounded and frolicked but clashed rarely in comparison to bighorns.

Mountain sheep are apparently unique among North American ruminants in performing huddles or extensive group interactions, although such behavior is not uncommon among African gazelles (Walther 1964, 1968), and also occurs among ibex (Schloeth 1961b; Nievergelt 1967). Huddles appear to help stabilize dominance rank among rams. In a huddle, rams have an opportunity to meet all potential opponents and engage in interactions without precipitating a dominance fight. They can acquaint themselves with the clash forces of all other rams and are repeatedly reminded of these as the days pass. It may also be that rams continuously impregnate themselves with the secretion from the preorbital glands of larger rams and acquire a group scent which might be useful during interactions at night.

The Move to Rutting Grounds

In late October and early November rams began to appear on the ewe ranges where the rut takes place. The ram concentrations had broken up and the rams alone or in small groups were seen wandering to their respective rutting grounds. The rams became increasingly more active. In October the Stone's rams were active about 65% of the daylight hours ($N = 93$ hours); in the first half of November, 67% ($N = 60$); in the second half of November, 73% ($N = 64$); in December, 83% ($N = 68$); in January, 71% ($N = 98$); and in February, 58% ($N = 114$). Overall activity increased to reach a maximum during the rut and subsided in the following months.

The rams often wandered about alone crossing between ewe bands

1. See film E 1333.

as well as from range to range. The large class IV and III males particularly were often alone on the move. In 1966, 62 out of 675 class IV and III bighorns were seen alone but only 6 out of 286 class II and I rams; the difference is significant ($\chi^2 = 16.5$, $p < 0.001$). These searching rams moved to projecting rock outcroppings and often stood and scanned the mountain slopes below. When on the move such rams proceeded at a walk along established trails, stopping here and there to sniff the ground or urinate and lipcurl. They frequently licked their lips and now and again called with a deep, loud "baa"; Dall's rams seem to have a higher voice than bighorns. Once I got to know the mountains in my Stone's sheep study area well, it became evident that searching rams systematically visited and looked over the localities favored by sheep. The evolutionary significance of this dispersal has been discussed (see chap. 3).

Once the rams appear on the rutting grounds, their common actions are courtship of anestrous ewes and interaction with other rams. One may also witness the few, but impressive, attempts by young rams to hold and guard anestrous females, and with good fortune one may see a dominance fight between large rams.

COMBAT AMONG RAMS

Dominance Fights

The most spectacular social interactions of sheep are the dominance fights of rams. They are by no means common, but they may occur at any time of the year when strange rams meet. If the strangers differ conspicuously in horn size, the smaller one at once acts like a subordinate, and a normal dominant-subordinate interaction results between them. If strangers of equal horn size chance upon each other, they have no means to judge each other's fighting potential except by fighting.

Most dominance fights are observable prior to the rut when rams meet on their various rutting grounds, or at any time of the year when rams congregate such as in late spring. I observed dominance fights at all seasons except during January and February, which are the coldest winter months. The severest fights are fought among 6–8-year-old three-quarter-curl rams, which are just reaching their ultimate body size and must contend for breeding status. Thus of the 26 dominance fights I witnessed among mountain sheep, 11 occurred between 8–14-year-old rams, 8 among 6- and 7-year-olds, 7 between 3–5-year-olds, and 1 between two 2-year-olds. And yet the 6- and 7-year-olds, which make up almost all of the class III rams, are less common than rams of either the IV or II classes (table 13). Moreover, class III rams interact more intensely in their normal interactions than do rams of other classes (table 57). Dominance fights may be very short and last only for several minutes, but they can also be very long, such as the 25-hour battle between two class III Stone's rams, described below. These dramatic fights are variable; no two I watched were the same, and they differ in Stone's and bighorn sheep. Despite this, a few generalizations can be made. Matched rams, usually strangers, begin to treat each other like females and clash until one acts like a female. This is the loser of the fight. The rams confront each other with displays, kick each other, threat

TABLE 57

Frequencies of behavior patterns of Stone's and bighorn rams in interactions between rams of equal horn size

	Stone's			Bighorn		
	IV	III	II & I	IV	III	II & I
No. of interactions	47	32	66	88	20	77
Patterns/interaction	6.2	7.8	4.4	3.9	5.7	3.1

NOTE: Stone's rams differ as a whole significantly from bighorns ($\chi^2 = 142.8$, $p > 0.01$). Class III rams perform significantly more patterns than class IV rams (in Stone's sheep, $\chi^2 = 7.0$, $p > 0.1$; in bighorns, $\chi^2 = 16.5$, $p > 0.01$).

jump, and clash till one turns and accepts the kicks, displays, and occasionally mounts of the larger without aggressive displays. The loser is not chased away. The point of the fight is not to kill, maim, or even drive the rival off, but to treat him like a female. The antagonists may remain together for a day or for weeks after a fight is settled. They may form distinct dominance pairs in which the subordinate is shadowed by the dominant and pestered (courted) up to six or seven times a day, if not more.

The longest dominance fight I observed occurred on 19 and 20 March 1962 between two Stone's rams, both 7 years old with three-quarter-curled horns. These rams, G-ram and M-ram, showed almost all the possible combat phases of Stone's sheep. G-ram was one of the nine resident rams from Sanctuary Mountain. M-ram appeared shortly after the rutting season, on 9 January 1962, on Shady Mountain, about a mile and a half from Sanctuary. On the morning of 18 March, M-ram crossed Gladys Lake to Sanctuary with F-ram. F-ram was also only 7 years old but was much larger in horn and body size than M. They did not meet the Sanctuary rams till the morning of the 19th. F-ram interacted shortly with two slightly smaller full-curls from Sanctuary, the 13-year-old D-ram and 8-year-old E-ram, and emerged as the dominant without a fight. Then G-ram came and noticed the strangers. He moved in low-stretch at F-ram and kicked his rear. F whirled and threat jumped. G-ram quickly turned his rear to F and, holding his low-stretch, moved straight to M-ram and kicked him on the chest. Both rams stood now shoulder to shoulder, their heads raised and cocked in present, and kicked at each other's chest and belly. Thus at 10:10 A.M. began a fight which was to continue till the following morning.

The behavior of Stone's rams in a dominance fight may be divided into several categories (fig. 27). Events occur in cycles: one ram approaches the other in low-stretch, twists and growls, then delivers a kick at the opponent's chest. This initiates the kick phase. The rams stand or turn about each other shoulder to shoulder and kick at each other's belly. Both display in present and growl on each kick they deliver. Occasionally one digs his horns into the opponent's back or butts sideways at his head. They may push each other with their chests. The kick phase may last for only one kick, but may run to 43 kicks and averaged 5.4 (90 kick phases). The rams reply to kicks in a tit-for-tat fashion.

The kick phase ends when one or both suddenly pull their heads down into the low-stretch and move past each other. Occasionally Stone's rams move apart without assuming the low-stretch. Sometimes one dips his head into a low-stretch, then turns around on the spot thereby pressing his rear against the opponent. After this both walk away several steps, then almost simultaneously whirl around and rise on their hind legs (threat jump). Sometimes they clash and present; sometimes they simply drop down again and freeze in a present. The rams may break off at this point and feed, or stand side by side, or again initiate a kick phase with a low-stretch and thus begin the cycle all over.

Bighorn rams differ from Stone's rams in that they kick far less frequently. Hence, one cannot expect a kick phase in the dominance fights of bighorns, and in fact it is almost absent. If the kick phase is absent, then no kick phases are initiated or terminated by an approach or withdrawal in low-stretch. The result is that bighorn rams fight quite differently from Stone's rams. When walking away from the opponent to initiate a clash, the rams hold their heads low, noses pointing to the

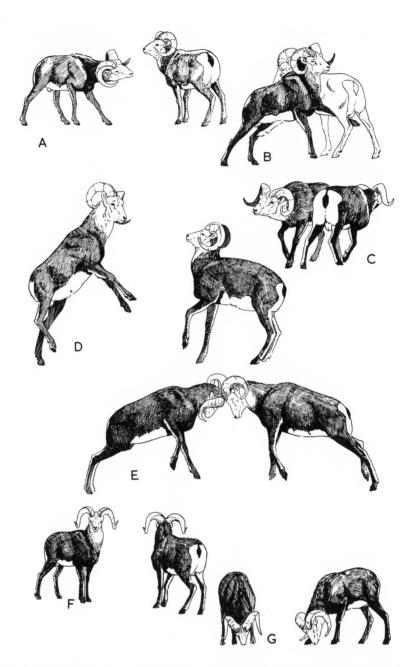

Fig. 27. The cycle of events in a dominance fight of Stone's rams. *A*, one ram approaches his opponent in low-stretch; *B*, the rams exchange kicks with the front legs; *C*, the opponents move apart in low-stretch to whirl; *D*, rise into a threat jump, and/or, *E*, clash head on; *F*, after the clash follows the post-clash present. Then the rams may repeat the cycle by one approaching in low-stretch, or they may interrupt the cycle and, *G*, feed side by side.

ground, not forward as is usual with Stone's sheep (see the illustrations in Welles and Welles 1961). After the clash and present, the rams often begin to feed. Then one, still feeding, turns his rear to the opponent and walks away, a sure sign that he is about to initiate a clash. On the other hand, both rams may suddenly rear up from feeding and clash head on, or one may follow a passing ewe and whirl to clash on his opponent the moment the other follows. Thus bighorn rams in a dominance fight are seen mainly to feed side by side, clash, present, and return to feed. Kick phases are not entirely absent but are very rare, and may change into a short slugging fight in which the rams will butt one another, dealing out horn blows wherever they can. After the fight the dominant may follow and kick the subordinate just as Stone's rams do. On the whole, a dominance fight among bighorns is more a show of brute force than is a fight among Stone's rams.

From the 25 hours which M- and G-rams fought, I obtained 8 hours of quantitative data. I recorded 92 kick phases; 36 kick phases were followed by a threat jump. Of these 20 led to feeding by the rams and 16 to a new kick phase. Seventeen kick phases were followed by a clash. Of these only 3 led to feeding by the rams and 14 to a new kick phase. It appears that a clash was more likely to lead to new exchanges of kicks and displays than a threat jump. In all, from 92 kick phases, 30 were followed at once by another kick phase and 62 led to feeding. Of the latter, 39 ended without a threat jump or clash; the rams simply moved apart and fed.

During these feeding pauses G- and M-rams were rarely more than a few paces apart, usually parallel to each other. They appeared to watch each other carefully. I kept note on how 78 feeding periods ended. On 38 occasions both rams suddenly jerked up their heads but froze rigidly into a present display. On 23 occasions they jerked up and clashed. On 15 occasions they rose into a threat jump, then froze into a present, and on 2 occasions one butted the other and the rams continued with the fight. A little more than half of all clashes observed in this fight were performed suddenly from feeding. None of the rams turned and moved away to initiate a clash as bighorns tend to do. From these 78 feeding periods ended by a present, clash, butt, or threat jump, 64 led to a kick phase and 14 to a new period of feeding.

Only in the beginning of their long engagement did M- and G-rams horn grass bunches and alpine firs extensively. In the first hour they horned 4 times, in the second 20, in the third 16, in the fourth 4; thereafter they horned between 1 and 6 times per hour. On the morning of the 20th, the tired rams had stopped horning. This suggests that horning is a sign of excitement and not necessarily a socially meaningful behavior. Both rams horned with the same frequency (table 58).

The rams did not butt each other as frequently during the first few hours of the fight as later. In the first $4\frac{1}{2}$ hours, the rams exchanged two butts, but in the next $3\frac{1}{2}$ hours they butted each other 27 times. It was evening now and the rams appeared tired and strained in appearance. They staggered to regain footing after some heavy clashes. In some clashes their horns slipped off each other and one of them piled up in front of the legs of the other. Occasionally one climbed a rock and hurled himself straight down at the other; neither lost his footing then. Once they hooked horns and began a short, violent struggle.

I ended observations at 6:50 P.M., as dusk fell. During the night I awoke several times and heard clashes, indicating that M- and G-rams were still at each other. The next morning at 7:00 I spotted both. They were resting a few feet apart in a stiff posture, still displaying horns to each other. At 9:00 A.M. the rams had engaged again. At 10:20 A.M. the last clash fell. Just prior, G-ram had entered into a violent kick phase. M-ram took these kicks while displaying stiffly. It appeared as if G-ram was desperately acting as dominant. Then both rams fed steadily.

At 12:15 P.M., M-ram whirled toward G and froze into a present. G did not flinch and fed on. M returned to feed. At 12:25 P.M. M-ram approached in low-stretch and began kicking G-ram. The latter turned his rear to M and continued feeding. He did not reply to M's displays, front kicks, or threat jumps. The fight was over. The dominance positions were settled. G-ram had lost.

Toward evening of that day, M- and G-rams moved out of my sight. M had celebrated an orgy of front kicks on G, a behavior commonly

TABLE 58

Behavior patterns by Stone's rams M and G during a dominance fight

	Lo	L	M	Cont	B	Ho	Cl	Thj	R	Hb
M-ram	318	60	0	0	5	0	1	7	0	33
G-ram	234	38	0	5	18	0	4	5	0	34

NOTE: Cont = contact, $r = 0.896$, $t_0 = 28.0$, $p < 0.001$.

indulged in by the dominant after a fight. The two rams fed close to each other during the day, M a little behind G. Periodically M interrupted feeding and went over to G in a low-stretch and kicked him a few times. When last seen, G-ram was moving away with M-ram following close behind him.

Occasionally opponents separate once a fight is settled, but more commonly the dominant follows the subordinate awhile. M-ram followed G only on the 20th, and did not search him out later. One 4–5-year-old Stone's ram followed his defeated opponent for three days after they first met. The 13-year-old D-ram from Sanctuary was strongly attached to the 7–8-year-old S-ram. In early November 1961 when I got to know D- and S-rams, D was following S, displaying, kicking, and occasionally mounting him. S-ram disappeared for the rut and midwinter and returned to Sanctuary on 7 May 1962. D-ram at once began following him steadily and again displayed, kicked, and mounted him. When the rams returned in October, D-ram and S-ram were again together with D usually following S and pestering him prior to and after feeding. I do not know if D- and S-rams ever fought, but they were the best and most predictable dominance pair I ever observed.

It appears that rams usually separate about a day or two after a severe dominance fight. From six dominance fights by bighorn rams in late fall of 1966, after which I was able to keep track of the opponents for several days, three pairs of opponents separated on the first day and three on the second day.

One behavior pattern not shown by M-ram and G-ram, but shown by other Stone's and bighorn rams during dominance fights, is pawing of the ground. This followed occasionally after the rams had disengaged from the kick phase. The ram walked a little way off, stopped, pawed the ground three or four times, or turned first and pawed while low-stretching at the opponent. Bighorns did this a little differently. They fed between clashes. Before feeding they pawed to remove snow from the vegetation. Some of the smaller rams destined to become subordinates pawed the snow away but did not feed. They stared at the opponent. Then they moved a little, pawed, lowered the nose, but again did not feed. Some turned and walked away (indicating intention to clash), then stopped, pawed the snow from the vegetation, lowered the nose shortly to the ground, whirled into a threat jump, and raced on their hind legs at their opponent. During this onrush they often growled loudly. Walther (1961) reported that a captive Marco Polo ram (*Ovis ammon poli*) pawed exuberantly prior to threat jumps in engagements with a urial, or against the observer. In American sheep this pattern appears greatly underdeveloped by comparison.

After the dominance fight the subordinate often accepts what can be considered insults—displays, front kicks, and mountings. Over the years I observed and filmed a number of instances in which subordinates used these patterns on dominants and were attacked at once. After a dominance fight the winner may move in front of the feeding loser, look squarely at him, and threat jump repeatedly. At all other times I would expect the subordinate to clash at once into the dominant but after a dominance fight the defeated rams kept on feeding and turned away from their opponents. It appears that turning the white rump patch to the opponent appeases him.

Dominance fights between ewes are exceedingly rare. In 42 months in the field, I observed only one such fight, and a short one at that. On 31 October 1964, three bighorn ewes were seen apart from the main group on the top of a ridge. Two of these were engaged in fighting. What appeared to be the smaller ewe butted the dominant five times, clashed four times on her, and twice nibbled her head for a noticeably long time. She received one clash and one horn threat in return. The third ewe clashed twice on the smaller one and mounted the larger one once. As in ram interactions the dominant animal can accept the aggressive behavior of the subordinate with little or no reply. A further report on what appears to be a dominance fight of ewes is found in Blood (1963).

Although dominance fights are variable, they do conform to certain rules. If two rams are of equal horn and body size, such as the Stone's rams M and G, they behave similarly in that they treat one another like a subordinate. Each assumes the role of the dominant. In comparing the frequencies of identical behavior patterns performed by M-ram on G-ram and vice versa (table 58), it is evident that those behavior patterns used frequently by M were also used frequently by G-ram. A correlation coefficient of $r = 0.996$, which does differ significantly from zero ($t_0 = 28.0$, $p < 0.001$), indicated that G's behavior could be predicted from M's, and vice versa. Therefore M and G acted alike. Furthermore, G and M each acted like a dominant. This can be demonstrated from the data in table 59. The actions of Stone's rams of large horn and body size toward smaller rams are expressed as behavior patterns per 100 interactions. Thus, in 100 interactions, large rams performed 141 low-stretches toward smaller rams, etc. If we compare the behavior of these large rams toward their smaller and subordinate rivals we

TABLE 59

Behavior of rams in dominance fights

	Lo	L	M	Cont	B	Ho	Cl	Thj	Ru
Large ♂ to small ♂ (*A*)	175	141	2	4	7	2	2	4	2
M-ram to G-ram (*B*)	318	60	0	0	5	0	2	7	0
A-ram to O-ram (*C*)	64	27	0	0	0	0	0	1	0

NOTE: For *A* vs. *B*, $r = 0.973$; *B* vs. *C*, $r = 0.878$.

obtain a correlation coefficient of $r = 0.973$, again not significantly different from unity ($t_0 = 11.7$, $p < 0.001$), indicating that M-ram acted like a large ram toward a smaller one.

The third line of data in table 59 shows the behavior of a 7–8-year-old class III Stone's ram (*A*) who was victorious in the fight with the smaller-horned O-ram. Correlating his behavior with that of M-ram we get a correlation coefficient of $r = 0.878$ ($t_0 = 4.8$, $p < 0.01$), indicating that he too acted like a dominant toward a subordinate; he displayed and kicked and accepted, but did not deal out blows and clashes.

The dominance fight between O-ram and A-ram differed from the one between M- and G-rams. It was much shorter and the rams were not matched; O-ram was noticeably smaller in horn and body size. Like G-ram O-ram started the fight by first courting and then attacking the larger A-ram. In this fight all behavior patterns were accounted for (table 60).

It is evident that O-ram did not behave at all like a dominant ram. In fact, there is no correlation between his behavior and that of his

TABLE 60

Behavior of A-ram vs. O-ram in dominance fight

	Pr	Lo	L	M	Cont	B	Ho	Cl	Thj	Ru	P	Gh
A-ram	11	64	27	0	0	0	0	0	1	0	0	4
O-ram	8	0	15	0	0	0	0	4	0	0	4	10

NOTE: Pr = present; P = pawing; Gh = ground horning. $r = 0.157$, $t_1 = 5.0$, $p < 0.001$.

victorious opponent since the correlation coefficient differs significantly from 1. Typical of subordinate rams, O-ram initiated all 4 clashes and displayed relatively little. However, he did not horn and nuzzle the body of the dominating class III opponent as is typical of subordinate rams.

The following account illustrates another extreme in the dominance fight among Stone's sheep. C-ram returned after an absence of almost five months to Sanctuary Mountain on 13 April 1962. He was then a tall, massive-horned 7-year-old ram whose horns formed about three-quarters of an arc. When I first saw him, he and P-ram had already engaged in combat. P-ram was a resident Sanctuary ram. He also was 7 years old and carried well-formed three-quarter-curled horns but was smaller in all dimensions, though stoutly built and always spunky. Just as I spotted the two, the first clash rang through the canyons and echoed within the rocky walls. C-ram and P-ram were frozen in a stiff

TABLE 61
Behavior of C-ram vs. P-ram in domi-nance fight

	Lo	L	B	Cl	Cont
C-ram	4	6	1	1	0
P-ram	0	0	3	6	6

NOTE: $r = -0.9$.

present. It was a very short fight (table 61), in which P-ram initiated 6 of the 7 clashes, while C-ram stood, took it, and displayed. The behavior of P-ram is virtually the converse of that of C-ram; P-ram did frequently what C-ram did rarely and vice versa; the correlation coefficient is $r = -0.9$. Here the subordinate's behavior (P) is the quantitative antithesis of that of the dominant (C). These data suggest some common sense rules of mountain sheep dominance fights. The closer the opponents are matched, the longer the fights and the more they treat each other as subordinates.

The dominance fights of bighorn rams differ in particular from those of Stone's sheep. Here too the smaller or subordinate ram deals out most of the clashes. In 11 dominance fights observed between 6 November and 3 December 1966, 43 out of 48 clashes were initiated by the smaller, subordinate, or losing rams. The makeup of the fight differs as was described above. When the ram about to initiate a clash moves off, he simply appears to walk away; yet the coming sequence of events can be correctly anticipated by the human observer as well as the opposing ram. The latter may get ready to receive the clash or also walk off, but in the opposite direction. The ram about to clash stops; he may paw the ground with his front leg and then suddenly whirl and charge bipedally uttering a loud growl. At the same time his opponent whirls and faces the attack bipedally. After the clash the rams freeze into a stiff present, just like Stone's rams, and then return to feeding. There are many variations, but in general the fighting rams feed, often paw the ground—occasionally looking at the opponent during pawing—suddenly rise to clash, or threat jump and present thereafter. Periodically one walks away, indicating intention to clash. The other may or may not move away in similar fashion. When the aggressor whirls and rises for the clash the opponent does the same, and a clash usually follows. Toward the end of the fight, the larger may approach periodically in a low-stretch and kick at the smaller. If the latter does not respond, the dominant may go into an orgy of kicking and sometimes mounting; occasionally a vicious fight results. In a few dominance fights the antagonists assumed a peculiar arching of the back, which was accompanied by extended hind legs during their low-stretch or present displays. These rams appeared exceedingly tense. The arched back can be interpreted as a relic behavior from the sheep's rupicaprid ancestors (see chap. 11).

Unfortunately, I have no quantitative data on the dominance fights of bighorn rams since it was my concern to document such fights on film first. Fighting Nelson's rams appear to fight much like bighorn rather than thinhorn sheep judging from the descriptions of Welles and Welles (1961). Dominance fights of bighorn rams may proceed as follows: the shortest dominance fight I observed occurred in late November 1966 on Bare Mountain, Banff National Park. The very old, heavy-horned Y-ram had just arrived from the distant Palliser Range. When he came to the group of sheep I stood by, an 8–9-year-old full-curl approached Y-ram in low-stretch and kicked him on the chest. The two rams exchanged kicks; then the full-curl separated from old Y-ram and began to horn a juniper and several aspen.

The second full-curl in the group was a ram from the Palliser Range, like old Y-ram. This ram, Peter, had continued feeding during the preceding interaction. He looked once at old Y-ram, but went on feeding. Suddenly, he approached old Y-ram in low-stretch and kicked him. Old Y-ram kicked back and vigorously pushed Peter with his chest. Then Peter turned from old Y-ram and walked downhill, and so did old Y-ram. The two rams walked almost nonchalantly parallel to each other, gradually drifting apart, till they were about seven to eight paces away from each other. Peter whirled into the bipedal stance facing old Y, and the latter did the same. It was old Y who charged and clashed (see plate 46). The rams froze into the present. Then Peter began kicking old Y in the face (see plate 36). The latter began horning and nuzzling Peter's head and horns, while Peter kicked vigorously. Then old Y walked past Peter up the slope, closely followed by Peter, who still kicked, twisted, and nudged at old Y-ram. After following old Y-ram uphill for about twenty paces, Peter left him and the rams ignored each other from then on. Peter was younger, larger in body size, but smaller in horn size. Old Y-ram was at least 14 or 15 years old in November 1966, and his body build indicated that he was very much past his prime (see plate 36, ram on left). He did not remain on Bare Mountain but went north the next day toward Snowcreek Summit, and I never saw him again.

Z-ram came to Bare Mountain from the Palliser Range on 20 November 1966. I saw him in the early morning within a huddle of four other rams, one of which was an 8–9-year-old full-curl. Z-ram was a very old ram, small in body size with the pot belly typical of his age group, but with large, slightly asymmetrical horns. Despite his age, he was a vigorous, lively animal.

The younger full-curl had been kicking at Z-ram within the huddle, and Z-ram turned away, pawed the snow from the ground, and horned some grass bunches. In the meantime the younger rams departed, leaving the full-curl and Z-ram behind. Z marched about, pawed, fed a little, horned the ground, and periodically faced the young full-curl in low-stretch. The latter appeared to be hesitant, but he too looked at Z-ram in low-stretch. The two antagonists faced each other over a distance of several paces. The young full-curl walked past Z-ram, Z followed, and both fed. Then Z-ram rose to clash, the young full-curl rose to meet him, and Z-ram hurled himself down the very steep hill. The clash threw the younger ram about four paces downhill, but he landed securely on his legs and froze into a horn display. After some feeding Z rose again. In this clash, Z slipped off the horns of his younger opponent and fell about three paces downhill. He staggered but caught himself and displayed, but then turned and began feeding. At this the young full-curl rammed him with his chest and began kicking. Z-ram horned back and began nuzzling the younger ram's head. Old Z-ram had lost. As in the fight described earlier, a very old ram had been defeated by a younger one that was larger bodied but smaller horned. In both instances, the old rams that had been challenged had just appeared on the rutting areas. However, it is doubtful that Peter and old Y-ram were strangers for they both spent the early fall on the Palliser Range.

Not all dominance fights are between strangers. On 3 December 1966, long after their appearance with the Bare Mountain females, two full-curls fell out with each other. The ram that was smaller in horns and body attacked and clashed five times with the larger. Each time he went above the larger ram and clashed downhill (plate 49). Between clashes the smaller displayed horns in an exaggerated fashion (plate 33). Then a small 5-year-old ram hurried to the two antagonists. He pushed past me on the trail, brushing me aside with his shoulders, and unhesitatingly charged the smaller of the two opponents. A short vicious fight developed between the dark full-curl and the small 5-year-old ram, in which the smaller clashed four times onto the full-curl's side; two other butts were caught by the full-curl with his head. Twice the dark full-curl charged with head low at the 5-year-old and chased him off, but the second charge was cut short when the larger, dominant full-curl fell into the side of the dark full-curl. The interaction between the two full-curls lasted about 40 minutes. The aggressive smaller ram was also the loser who later submitted to the kicks and twists of the larger.

The foregoing fight illustrated a not uncommon event, namely the interference of a third ram in a dominance fight. In the above instance only one ram interfered, but I have seen as many as six interfering. From 26 dominance fights I observed, 7 were persistently disrupted by one or more rams. Although I saw more bighorn fights disrupted, Stone's rams were also observed spoiling fights.

Rams spoiling dominance fights appeared to take sides if they were smaller or larger than the two combatants. Small-horned rams attacked the smaller of two fighters as in the above example, while larger-horned rams attacked or kicked and displayed to the larger of two fighters. Several large rams treated both fighters impartially. Large rams came and pushed the combators about with their chest, kicking at them, growling, and twisting. They smashed into the sides of the fighters the moment these rose to clash.[2] In a few instances the spoilers clashed with either

2. See film E 1334.

of the combatants, and clashes involving three rams resulted. They disrupted the normal clash sequence, for if one combatant rose to clash, a spoiler would rise together with the second combatant. This caused some indecision on the part of the first ram, distracting his attention from his opponent to the spoiler. Usually the rams did not clash but dropped to their legs and displayed. Occasionally spoilers stole a clash by quickly butting in and clashing with one of the combatants before the second one could. Some rams in a dominance fight used spoilers as barriers, across which they could safely display horns at the rival. Rarely, a spoiler was taken between two combatants and was kicked and displayed to by both.

Mountain sheep are not the only species in which males may take sides in fighting and gang up on one another. Schloeth (1961a) reported that in cattle several bulls grouped together, attacked the dominant bull, and kept him away from the female group from then on. McHugh (1958) reported that several bison bulls ganged up on one, while Buechner (1963) and Walther (1965) noted that Uganda kob (*Adenota*) and Grant gazelle bucks may interfere with the fight of others, bringing such fights to an end. Yet spoiling actions by rams are not always present, and I have seen combatants carrying on their fight while other rams rested or fed close by. Although spoiling actions can be observed in ruminant societies, they appear to be less common than among cercopithecine primates, in which dominants apparently regularly disrupt the fights of subordinates (Kaufmann 1967). Dominance fights may be contrasted with the violent, unritualized fights of rams.

Unritualized Fights

Such fights may occur between rams about an estrous ewe and rarely within a dominance fight. They may be provoked artificially by providing a band of rams with limited access to a piece of salt. I have observed and filmed a number of unritualized brawls in the latter situation, and have found them no less fierce than those about estrous ewes. The violent fights of rams are slugging and wrestling matches of brute force, lacking all ritual and finesse. Rams whirl about one another, try to keep their horns pointing at the opponent (as a defense measure), and attempt to crash into the opponent's side whenever possible. They hit out sideways with their heads (plate 64), push each other around with chest and shoulders (plate 65), butt each other wherever possible while trying to avoid the blows of the other. Occasionally horns get locked (plate 66), and the rams tug and wrestle or whirl around each other, attempting to free themselves; such rams appear to be blind to their surroundings. The fight may end with one fleeing and the other charging with lowered head after him (plate 51).

During the defense of an estrous ewe, a large Stone's ram slammed a class II ram into the snow with a blow to its side. The small ram recovered quickly. In another fight about the estrous ewe, the defending large class IV ram stumbled and fell into a snow bank. At once the next largest, a class III ram, pounced on him and held the struggling full-curl helpless on his side with the horns. A few times I saw Stone's rams try to push smaller rams off a cliff during the defense of a ewe. I saw this only in the stated situation and never during normal interactions among rams. However, I did see a 2-year-old female trying to push a yearling ram off a cliff face. In all instances the endangered sheep jumped to a lower ledge. The vicious fights of rams have little in common with dominance fights.[3]

Courtship of Anestrous Females

The Urination Response

Rams were observed courting females not only during the rutting season, but during every month of the year. In the idealized courtship the ram approaches the female from the side or rear in a low-stretch. Occasionally the ram shows a slight crouch (plate 34).[4] The ram licks the vulva and tastes the urine-soaked hair below the vulva while the female feeds. The female then crouches and urinates (plate 41). The ram dips his muzzle in the stream of urine or licks it on the ground and performs a lipcurl (plate 40). Thereafter he stands for a few moments, licks his lips and leaves the female.

There are many variations to this. The ram may approach in low-stretch, then twist and grunt or kick the female with the front leg, after which the female jumps away. The female may urinate before the ram reaches her, or she may urinate after being kicked. Young rams have a marked tendency to suddenly jump on top of the female whereas old rams rarely mount anestrous females spontaneously (fig. 23). The ram may begin courting again after lipcurling.

Occasionally a young ram shows an extended interest in one ewe and persistently courts the uncooperative female. He follows her in low-stretch, stops behind her, then bursts forward with a twist or kick which

3. See film E 1334.
4. See film E 1338.

makes the female jump forward again. In a few instances I observed such a ram stand several paces behind the female in a low stretch, then twist and kick the front leg high into the air waving it in the direction of the female. The young ram may also advance two or three steps, twist, grunt, and flick his tongue, then pull back to his previous position. With each twist-growl or kick approach the female jumps forward. A few young rams seesawed behind the ewe,[5] much as Walther (1961) described in the courtship of the *O. a. poli* ram.

Despite the variation, rams of all classes use much the same patterns in similar frequencies as was demonstrated earlier (chap. 6). The anestrous female is sensitive to being kicked or mounted and jumps away, interrupting further courtship. This behavior as well as her urination appear to be attempts to rid herself of the ram. It was noticed that several times female yearlings ducked down and urinated when approached in low-stretch by dominant ewes. Occasionally it could be seen that a small ram urinated to a large one when approached in low-stretch. Rams lipcurled on the urine of females as well as on that of rams (occasionally their own), and while rams lipcurled relatively rarely in the interactions with subordinate rams, they also lipcurled rarely in the interactions with estrous ewes. Hence it appears that sheep urinate to the dominant, who upon lipcurling, for some reason, leaves them in peace. Walther (1968) studying gazelles and Krämer (1969) studying chamois saw much the same and formed similar views.

Outside the rutting season, when rams courted less frequently, the females urinated more frequently than in the pre-rut and rut. Thus outside the pre-rut and rutting season Stone's females urinated in 43% of the courtships (N = 48 courtships), while during the pre-rut in November they urinated in only 20% of the courtships (N = 445 courtships). In December, when the rams courted primarily estrous females and paid less attention to the anestrous ewes, these urinated in 36% of the courtships (N = 270 courtships). For bighorn females, which rutted at much the same time as the Stone's sheep, the data are similar. Thus outside the rutting season bighorn females urinated in 30% of the courtships (N = 41), during November they urinated in 20% of the courtships (N = 141), and during December in 22% (N = 36). Nevertheless these data indicate that frequency of being courted and the urination response of the female are inversely related. The more often a ewe is courted, the less often she urinates, probably because she runs out of urine.

5. See films E 1338 and 1335.

I obtained a verification of this concept observing mouflons in Hellabrun Zoological Park in Munich. On 4 October 1967, one of the females in the herd appeared to be close to estrus, but not yet receptive. She was followed and courted constantly by one of the two large rams in the enclosure. The female attempted to escape by darting into the female herd, but the ram followed her constantly. He attempted to cut her off from other females by blocking her way while standing in a deep low-stretch, mouth open. Sharp chases developed whenever the female managed to get past the ram and dive into the herd until the ram had separated her again. Sixteen times the female turned on the ram and confronted him in horn threat. Twice she kicked at him with a front leg while keeping her horns lowered. When the ram pulled forward with a twist, the female horn threatened him in 19 out of 23 advances. The female was hard pressed by the ram and had little rest. At times both animals were panting. During 90 minutes of observation the female ducked down to urinate 25 times, but I could not see a drop of urine emerge, even though I was only two to ten paces from the pair.

The foregoing data and observations argue that subordinates gain some advantage from urinating to dominants. This is further substantiated by the observation of a large male lamb assuming the female's urination posture rather than the normal male urination stance, when confronted by a large ram. The anestrous Stone's female and yearling female urinate during late fall in 71% ($N = 671$ courtships) and 73% ($N = 227$ courtships) of the courtships respectively, which leads on the average to between 30 and 40 lipcurls per 100 courtships by rams. However, in 144 courtships of estrous Stone's females I saw no urinations by the female and only 7 lipcurls by rams. Again it appears that where male-female cohesion is permissible, as with the estrous female, urination and lipcurling are depressed. And yet, one cannot demonstrate that urination by the female appreciably alters the courtship of the ram.

It is true that when the female urinated before the ram reached her there was little courtship by the ram, for the latter among Stone's sheep performed only 1.8 patterns per 100 courtships ($N = 122$ courtships) and among bighorns, 1.9 patterns per 100 courtships ($N = 14$). If the female did not urinate till the ram reached her, then there were 3.7 patterns per 100 courtships shown to Stone's ewes ($N = 147$) and 3.7 patterns per 100 courtships shown to bighorn ewes ($N = 33$). The females were hence courted more intensely if they did urinate later, the difference being significant ($\chi^2 = 13.7$, $p < 0.001$). However, the females which did not urinate at all were not courted more intensely than females that did urinate. The average number of patterns shown toward females that did not urinate was for Stone's sheep 2.5 patterns per 100 courtships ($n = 643$) and for bighorns 3.1 patterns per 100 courtships ($n = 188$).

Perhaps females that do not urinate are treated more aggressively by rams than females that do. However, no such difference was apparent. In 264 courtships by Stone's rams of females that urinated, the females received 15.2 butts and threats per 100 courtships, while in 643 courtships in which females did not urinate, they received 17.0 butts and threats. The difference appears negligible.

The most that can be said about the urination response of the female is that females urinate less the more frequently they are courted, that rams do court females less if these urinate prior to the ram reaching them, and that subordinate males and females may urinate to dominants. At present, it cannot be demonstrated that courted females which urinate gain a real advantage from this act.

Guarding of Anestrous Females by Young Rams

Rams rarely show persistent interest in an anestrous female till shortly before her estrous period. Young rams have unobstructed access to anestrous females and may court these with impunity in the presence of large rams. If a female urinates several rams may come to lipcurl without antagonism.[6] Once an anestrous female has been inspected the ram usually leaves her. However, on the Stone's sheep study area in each of the three rutting seasons I spent there, I observed a few young rams guarding anestrous females.

In general, the young ram attempts to prevent the female from going anywhere. The moment she moves, the ram pounces in her way and chases her back. The ram can be positioned above or below the ewe. He does not feed but stands and watches her. A few times guarded ewes attempted to break out and join other ewes, but the rams gave chase and cut them off. Only once did I see a ewe escape into a female band. Guarding rams which stood above the ewe descended steadily while those below a guarded ewe ascended steadily, since with every chase the former ram chased the female down and the latter chased her up. The largest ram I observed guarding an anestrous ewe was a 6–7-year-old Stone's ram; the others were all 3–5-year-old rams.

In December 1965, I observed a most exceptional occurrence. A

6. See film E 1335.

5-year-old Stone's ram guarded a nonestrous female and defended her against two small rams as if she was in estrus. On three successive days I checked on this group. The guarding ram did not feed, rested little, and prevented the other rams from getting close to the group of females, consisting of one adult, one subadult female, and one lamb. These sheep stood on a large, rough mountain isolated from other sheep; I doubt that the young ram would have continued guarding had there been more females to distract him and larger rams to interfere with his guard.

Yearling Rams Gain Dominance over Ewes

When in October 1961 and 1962 Stone's sheep were returning to the study area, yearling rams frequently interacted with ewes. I noted the same among Dall's sheep in October 1965 but not among bighorns in fall 1964. The yearling males approached females often in a low-stretch, then suddenly butted them or attempted to mount with erected penis. They approached resting females, stood behind them for a little while, then jumped on them. They showed some preference for subadult females which were smaller and less capable opponents than full grown adult ewes. Whereas adult females and yearling ewes were present in the ratio of 100:34, they were courted in the ratio of 100:75 by the small rams (N = 173 courtships). The small ewes usually withdrew, but older females occasionally gave battle and in a few instances chased the yearling rams away. Females are less inhibited from striking back at yearlings than at older rams. Thus adult Stone's females replied to large rams with 3.7 patterns per 100 courtships (N = 596 courtships), but with 19.0 patterns per 100 approaches to yearling rams (N = 98); yearling females acted similarly as there were 5.4 patterns per 100 courtships in reply to large rams (N = 165), and 13.0 patterns per 100 courtships toward yearling rams (N = 75).

Table 62 shows the usual treatment handed down by Stone's yearling rams to adult females and the latter's reply. Female yearlings were treated by yearling males the same as adult ewes; but the latter responded with 19 aggressive patterns per 100 interactions while female yearlings responded with only 5. By the time the rutting season had come, all yearling Stone's rams I observed had become dominant over adult ewes and courted them with impunity.

On the bighorn study area in the fall, yearling rams were smaller than adult females. In contrast to the Stone's sheep I observed, the bighorn yearlings had small, inconspicuous testes and showed no interest in females during the rut. Some bighorn rams were not sexually

TABLE 62

Behavior of Stone's yearling males toward females and females' reply (In no. of patterns/100 interactions)

	Lo	L	T	M	B	Ho	Ru	Sv	F	Cl	Thj	Rb	Hb
Stone's ♂y to ♀ (N = 98)	89	13	5	12	14	9	18	39	20	0	0	1	0
♀ reply to ♂y (N = 98)	0	0	0	0	6	2	0	0	0	0	10	0	1

mature at $2\frac{1}{2}$ years of age since they lacked interest in estrous females and failed to participate in the rutting activities. Female bighorn sheep did occasionally manage to drive $2\frac{1}{2}$-year-old rams from a salt block. It appears, therefore, that only large, well-grown, and sexually mature yearling rams enter into serious interactions with adult females. In late fall, a yearling ram occasionally pursued, herded, charged, and butted a female as if enjoying the license of hard-won dominance. Schloeth (1961a) found that young Camargue bulls (*Bos*) began their ascent on the dominance scale by first subduing adult females.

THE RUT

Females in Heat

Toward the end of November the ewes begin to come into estrus. The timing of estrus appears to be controlled by photoperiodism (Bissonnette 1941; Yeates 1949; Hafez 1952), but it can be advanced by sounds and odors emitted by adult rams (Radford and Watson 1957; Watson and Radford 1960). It can also probably be advanced or retarded by the level of nutrition of the female, as is known from reindeer (Preobrazhenskii 1961). On the Stone's sheep study area, I observed the first ewe in heat on 25 November and the last on 16 December. In total, 16 Stone's ewes were seen in heat in the two complete rutting seasons of 1961 and 1962, plus the greater part of the 1965 rut (27 November to 10 December). On the bighorn study area in 1964 I saw the first female in heat on 19 November and the last on 4 December. In 1966 the first ewe in estrus appeared on 26 November and the last on 11 December. In the 1964 rut, 5 estrous females were observed and in the 1966 rut 16. Hence a total of 37 estrous females contributed to the observations and data recorded below. It is not known how much timing of estrus varies in individual ewes from year to year, but one Stone's sheep female, a 12-year-old in 1961, was in estrus on 4 December in 1961, on 2 December in 1962, and on 29 November in 1965. The rut lasts about two to three weeks, although the rams are on the ranges with the females for about eight weeks.

A number of signs indicate the approach of estrus in females. A few old rams begin to stick with particular females and block access to her for other rams. These smaller rams make no attempt to circumvent the guarding ram but move on to court other females. The females, despite the interest of the large rams, show no sign of heat. They withdraw if kicked like any anestrous ewe and permit no mounting. The ram guarding the female feeds and rests close to her; sometimes he courts or stands for several minutes or longer in a low-stretch behind her displaying the horns.

Another sign that a female is soon to enter estrus is the intense courtship and interest young rams may display toward her. The young ram stands a little behind the female, suddenly he pulls his head down into a twist, nudges the female or kicks her and pulls back again to his original stance while the female bounces forward with each twist. Let one ram show persistent interest in a ewe and others hurry by to investigate.

When a group of rams have gathered behind a female and follow her, it is a certain sign that the female will soon be in estrus. I have seen as many as nine rams behind a female. Closest to her is usually the largest-horned ram. He threatens subordinates and blocks their way to the female with the broadside of his body while pulling his head back in present. He may slam his chest into the broadside of a subordinate ram, push him downhill, kick him with the front legs, and finally butt and push him away with the horns. He may advance at the smaller in spurts in a low-stretch, twisting, grunting, and flicking his tongue, or suddenly charge and butt him. The subordinate rams begin to keep their distance from the dominant. Some walk backward when confronted by the twisting dominant, only to turn and bolt. Inevitably this triggers the dominant into a charge after the subordinate who may receive a parting blow on his rear. If the near-estrous female is still in a band, the dominant systematically begins to remove subordinates from the female's vicinity, sparing not even sexually immature yearling males. However, subordinate rams are not easily discouraged, and the dominant is repeatedly forced to intercept them and, occasionally, fight them off.[7]

7. See film E 1335.

If the female runs away from the rams and leaves the female band in favor of cliff terrain or forest, the largest-horned ram stays right behind her and discourages lesser rams from passing. He whirls toward them with lowered horns, makes rushes at them, or clashes on the ram following him. Then the large one quickly turns and hurries after the ewe.

Inevitably a young ram does succeed in getting past the guard of the dominant ram and behind the ewe, and a wild chase results. While the female flees, the smaller ram attempts to mount (plate 67). The dominant is usually right on his heels butting his rump. He crashes into the side of the smaller when the latter mounts the ewe and sends him sprawling. Short, violent fights erupt between the dominant and the lesser ram as the latter defends himself. Such fights are short-lived for some other small ram is by that time in hot pursuit of the female, and the dominant hurries after him. Sideways butting may develop between the dominant and the subordinate as the dominant gallops alongside the smaller ram and pushes him off course with his shoulders (plate 68). Once the dominant ram gets behind the female, the wild chase usually comes to an end, unless the female is not yet receptive. If this is the case and the female does not stand for the courtship of the excited dominant, the chase continues, and one may observe any of the following evasive maneuvers of the female:

1. She usually heads for cliffs or forest and preferably into forested cliffs. Thus much of the breeding takes place off the locations normally frequented by sheep, somewhere in the high cliff terrain or on the forested, broken north slopes of the mountains. In her attempts to shake the rams the female may run two or three miles away from the female band and her lamb.

2. If the ram is right behind her, the ewe may jump up, turn by 180°, and run past him.

3. She may run past a narrow spot on the trail in steep cliffs, then turn, step onto the narrow spot, press her side against the rock, and face the rams.

4. She may simply stop and press her side or rear against a rock face while the rams fruitlessly try to mount her.

5. She may jump off the trail onto a narrow foothold on the cliff face where there is only room enough for one sheep. This was also noted by Jones (1950) for desert bighorns.

6. She may come to a crevice in the cliffs, quickly turn, and back into it.

7. She may throw herself on the ground and, for a while, resist all attempts by the rams to get her on her legs.

8. She zigzags and dashes sideways every time a ram attempts to mount her.

9. Bighorn ewes, but not Stone's ewes, may become aggressive when a ram attempts to mount and will butt him on the side or haunches. The two animals then wheel about each other, the ram attempting to mount, the female butting him and evading mounts by jerking sideways.[8]

None of the female's evasive actions appear to be highly successful, for the rams inevitably dislodge her from the cliff face or crevice. They push, butt, and wedge her away from the rock till she dashes off. They may paw or butt her to her feet if she is on the ground, butt her rear when she zigzags, and find a way to her if she attempts to isolate herself in an inaccessible spot. After a while the female simply gives up. She does not withdraw if kicked or twisted to, but feeds and accepts mounts. Her tail is raised steadily. The female can now be considered in estrus.

After the female has submitted, the rutting group usually stands together somewhere on a high ridge or slope, or on a cliff platform. The guarding ram, usually a full-curl 9–12 years of age, stands between the female and the smaller rams. These may feed and rest, but often they stand in a tight group and interact with each other while looking at the breeding pair (plate 69). They form a huddle about the smallest ram and treat him like a substitute for the estrous female, by courting and mounting him, nuzzling his penis and lipcurling thereafter. Generally the smallest ram accepts this, except when being mounted excessively. Twice I saw a small Stone's ram being chased by a courting class III ram. Like any female, the small ram headed for the cliffs while the larger attempted to mount him. The larger ram ignored anestrous females he passed while following the small male. Alternately, one of the larger rams close to the estrous ewe may concentrate his attention on his closest subordinate, also a large ram, and court and mount him instead of the smallest ram present. If the guarding ram is an exceedingly large-horned, heavy ram, the subordinates may begin to drift off one at a time and look elsewhere for estrous ewes. The breeding pair is then left alone in the cliffs, but more commonly the subordinate rams periodically attempt to get at the estrous female.

The frequency with which rams court and mount estrous females

8. See film E 1335.

appears to depend on (1) how much copulating they did previously, (2) whether they just finished a fight, and (3) whether they had a long chase. On 7 December 1961, I observed a 12-year-old Stone's ram chase down and begin breeding a female that had just entered estrus. In one hour he mounted 11 times. Then he and the female disappeared from sight. On the following morning the old ram was markedly less vigorous in his defense of the female and did not mount. Then a 4-year-old class II ram managed to steal the ewe and got lost with her in some precipitous cliffs. In 3 hours he mounted the ewe 39 times. Then the old ram found the couple and took over the ewe again.

A 7-year-old class IV Stone's ram was very listless on the female's second day of estrus. He mounted her only 11 times in 5 hours and only after extensive courtship by the ewe. When I was observing single Stone's rams guarding an estrous female or when I was standing behind the camera close to a breeding pair of bighorns, it was striking how rarely such single rams courted and mounted. However, if a wandering ram comes and attempts to get at the ewe and engages the guarding ram in a short battle, then the dominant starts breeding the ewe at once. It appears that overt aggression and excitement stimulates overt sexual behavior as well. One can reach the same conclusion from data published by Lindsay and Ellsmore (1968) for domestic rams in breeding paddocks.

Whereas the guarding ram is commonly a full-curl, his largest competitor close by is usually a large 6–7-year-old three-quarter-curl. These rams have just reached ultimate body size, and they are the most vigorous class of rams as is indicated by their intense interactions with other three-quarter-curls, their frequent dominance fights, and their greater tendency to roam during the rut. Such rams need not be hesitant in their attempts to get past the guarding ram to the ewe. They can and do attack forcefully and attempt to push the guarding ram aside (see plate 68a). Now and again he will succeed in driving off the ewe (see plate 68f), particularly if the dominant appears exhausted or for some other reason is incapable of following. Now the smaller ram will assume the role of the dominant ram, breeding the female and warding off smaller rams, just as the larger ram did previously. Once the large ram does catch up with the smaller rams and the ewe, the smaller guarding ram leaves the female to the larger, uncontested. The smaller ram hesitantly walks away from the estrous female, while the larger ram begins courting and mounting the female. The smaller ram does not chase away the female when the dominant approaches, as he could easily do, but walks away after some stepping about and glancing back and forth between female and approaching dominant.

Twice a rather unusual interaction was observed. In both instances a large three-quarter-curl Stone's ram suddenly moved in present at the slightly larger guarding ram, slammed his chest against the latter's side, and proceeded to kick and display. The subordinate suddenly acted like a dominant. In both instances the dominant's response was to whirl around and clash into the subordinate. Once when the dominant turned, the subordinate quickly mounted. In both instances the revolt by the smaller ram was fruitless. After being hit by the dominant the subordinate dashed off, chased by the dominant over a short distance.[9]

TABLE 63

Normal behavior of Stone's dominant rams toward subordinates vs. behavior with estrous female present (In no. of patterns/100 interactions)

	Lo	L	T	M	B	Ho	Ru	Sv	F	Cl	Thj	Rb	Hb
Stone's IV to III, estrous ♀ present (N = 50)	36	34	10	0	38	2	40	6	0	6	0	0	0
Stone's IV to II, estrous ♀ present (N = 46)	67	17	15	0	11	6	52	0	0	0	0	0	0
Stone's IV to III, normal (N = 63)	179	228	2	0	9	2	2	0	2	2	0	2	2

The typical behavior of dominant Stone's rams toward their subordinates in the presence of an estrous ewe is shown in table 63, where it is compared with their behavior in the absence of an estrous ewe. A ram guarding estrous females displays (Lo, L, T) less than normal but charges (Ru) at his subordinates much more frequently than normal. The quantitative data showing the typical behavior of Stone's rams to estrous females and their reply, as well as the behavior of subordinates close to estrous females, was shown in tables 42 to 45.

The females remain in estrus for two to three days, as is indicated by the interest of the rams. The large ram guards continuously, unless a

9. The futile attempts of a subordinate to act like a dominant in a fight can be seen in film E 1334.

second female comes in estrus close by, a situation I only saw once. The second largest ram took over the second ewe. Then the largest ram went over and claimed the second ewe, and the second largest ram went over and guarded and bred the first ewe; they exchanged ewes several more times. Twice I saw an old Stone's ram leave the estrous female voluntarily and pay no attention to the next larger ram who now copulated and defended the female against smaller rams. In the meantime the old ram fed and rested and later claimed the female without a fight. Females disregarded by old rams were still chased by small rams, although these females would not stand for mounting.

The extensive long chases, the vigorous fights about estrous ewes, and frequent copulations are only typical of the first week of the rut. As the rut wears on it is more common to see large rams with a ewe standing dispersed in the cliffs. This implies that once the females are in estrus, most large full-curls participate in the breeding. Soon the rams begin to look thin and exhausted. Intruding subordinates are still intercepted by dominants, but neither acts spirited. It may happen, as was the case in 1964 on Bare Mountain in Banff, that toward the end of the rut many large rams may feed and ignore smaller ones chasing estrous females close by.[10] However, it is not a usual occurrence. Lungworm infestations may have brought about this unusual behavior (see below).

In general, the larger-horned rams do most of the breeding and fighting, and they are preferred by females, as is demonstrated by the quantitative data (table 54). Figure 28 shows the frequency with which Stone's and bighorn rams of various horn size classes mounted estrous females. Almost all rams managed to get on top of a female, if only during a chase, but the frequency of their mounting is related to their horn size. It can be seen from figure 28 that large Stone's rams were more successful in mounting females than large bighorn rams. Thus 13 class IV Stone's rams accounted for 41 copulations, but 11 class III rams for only 19. This difference is significant ($\chi^2 = 4.8, p < 0.05$). Twenty-two full-curl bighorns accounted for 92 copulations, while 13 class III rams accounted for 49, a difference which is not significant ($\chi^2 = 0.4$, N.S.). Therefore, class III rams were considerably more involved in breeding on the bighorn study area in Banff than on the Stone's sheep study area. This difference is no reflection of a species difference, but appears to have another cause.

The Stone's sheep I observed were very vigorous animals, which was true even for the oldest rams. The bighorn rams I observed differed in

10. See film E 1335.

that the old, large rams were not nearly as capable runners as their younger competitors. These large bighorns had great difficulty keeping up with the young rams when these chased off the ewes; in particular, they appeared to have difficulty breathing. While panting, with mouth wide open, some of the large bighorn rams followed the wild chase not at a run but at a walk. They had no difficulty in reclaiming the female once they reached her.

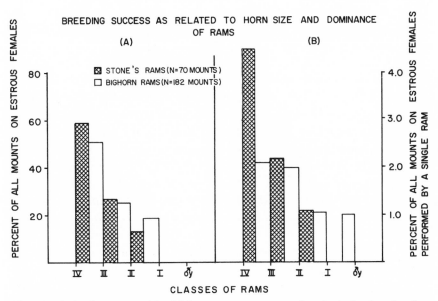

Fig. 28. *A*, the frequency with which rams mount estrous females is closely related to horn size. Most mountings on estrous ewes among Stone's and bighorn sheep were done by class IV rams. *B*, individual class IV Stone's rams mounted about twice as often as class III rams, while on the Banff study area, class III and IV rams mounted equally often. However, since there were more class IV than III rams, they accounted for a greater amount of the breeding (*A*).

Autopsies of 5 sheep killed on the roads in Banff and of one large ram who slid down the hard snow covering a slope and broke his back and neck in the process showed heavy lungworm lesions on the lungs. The lower portions of the lungs were hard and rubbery, indicating that such lungs could never expand to the maximum capacity of uninfected lungs. Evidently, heavy lungworm lesions bring about reduced tidal volume of the lung. Since age allows lungworm lesions to heal, old rams should have more sclerotized lungs than young, and hence should have more trouble breathing when on the run than young rams. This in turn should allow younger rams to stay longer with a female once they manage to break the guard of the old ram. For instance, on 19 November 1964, I observed for 88 minutes a group of bighorn rams about an estrous ewe. The guarding ram was exceptionally large and only a few short chases developed. In total, the three class IV rams present mounted the female 25 times, the class III ram 3 times, the class II ram 7 times, and the two class I rams 4 times; a yearling ram did not mount at all. Therefore 25 of 39 mounts attempted were made by class IV rams, and 20 of these by the most dominant ram. On 30 November 1964, I observed for 25 minutes a group of rams where a lot of chasing took place. The two class IV rams mounted 13 times, the lone class III ram 14 times, the three class II rams 15 times, and the lone class I ram 2 times. In this situation when a vigorous class III ram successfully chased off the ewe from an old guarding full-curl, the full-curls performed only 13 of 45 mounts. As these data and past discussions indicate, breeding in mountain sheep society is done by the dominant, by the aggressive who manages to cut the estrous female away from the dominant, by the lucky who manages to get lost in the cliffs momentarily with the female, and by the fast runner who chases the female far enough away and copulates before the dominant ram catches up.

It is also not surprising that most blows are dealt out by large guarding rams and received by class III rams. The distribution of butts and clashes received and dealt out by bighorn rams about an estrous female during the rutting seasons of 1964 and 1966 are shown in table 64. The 6–7-year-old class III rams attempt repeatedly to get past the guarding male and consequently suffer the attacks of the dominant. These received fewer blows than other rams and dealt out most. For Stone's sheep, the data is similar (table 64).

Although the dominant, breeding full-curl is most antagonistic toward the nearly equal-size rams that are his most serious competitors, he is also antagonistic to the sexually mature and immature yearlings, and occasionally even to male lambs. One old large ram threatened the female's lamb repeatedly, and finally butted it downhill.[11] On the Stone's sheep study area yearling rams were judged to be mature not only by their large testes, but also by their prolonged interest in estrous females. Not surprisingly, they were regularly chased away by large rams. The behavior of the bighorn indicated that they were aware of what was a male even if it was sexually immature.

11. See film E 1335.

TABLE 64

The distribution of butts and clashes dealt out and received by rams of various classes

	Stone's			Bighorn		
	IV	III	II	IV	III	II
B and Cl dealt out	39	17	2	68	13	5
B and Cl received	9	36	7	23	53	16
B and Cl dealt out per ram present	3.9	1.4	0.3	4.0	1.2	0.7
B and Cl received per ram present	0.9	3.0	0.1	1.3	4.8	2.3
No. of rams present	10	12	7	17	11	7

Courtship by the Estrous Ewe

Under very rare circumstances, when the estrous female is alone with a ram who shows little interest in breeding, the courtship behavior of estrous females may be observed (fig. 29). From 37 estrous females only 3 did some courting; all were Stone's ewes.[12] In the presence of several rams, the exhausted dominant would soon be relieved by eager subordinates, and there would be little reason for the ewe to stimulate an exhausted ram into courting and mounting.

I observed extensive courtship by a Stone's ewe on 4 December 1961. The female was in the company of a 7-year-old full-curl, who had been with her since late November. This old ewe, the ram, the female's lamb, and a yearling female were isolated from other sheep. On the morning of 4 December, the old ewe was well in heat and the ram appeared tired and listless. In the following 5 hours there were 26 courtship interactions, of which the ram initiated only 8, 5 on the lamb and 3 on the yearling female. All interactions between the old female and male were initiated by the ewe.

The behavior of the courting ewe is best described from a sample of my notes:

> N-ewe has been feeding. She now stands in front of F-ram facing away from him. She suddenly bolts, and F-ram almost by reflex bounds after her for a few paces and freezes in a low-stretch. N-ewe whirls and horn threatens him (fig. 29B). Then she comes and rubs her side along his

12. Recent observations by R. Petocz suggest that bighorn ewes from high quality populations court frequently.

body while he stands frozen in a horn display (low-stretch). Again she bounds away a few paces, turns, butts F-ram on the head, jumps backward, horn threatens and ducks under his chin, and rubs her side and haunches along his chest. F-ram turns slightly and assumes a position directly behind her and mounts three times in rapid succession. N-ewe moves forward a little and F-ram follows; she moves again,

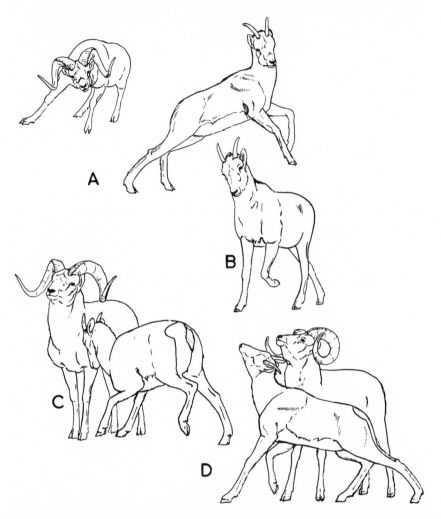

Fig. 29. Courtship by the estrous female of the ram. *A*, the female performs a sudden coquette jump, pulling the startled ram after her; *B*, the female turns and in a head-high horn threat prances at the ram; *C*, she horns and forcefully butts the ram on the shoulder, while the latter presents stiffly; *D*, the female rubs the full length of her body along the ram's chest while horning his chin.

but he remains standing. N turns her head and looks back at the ram, but he has begun to graze. The ewe turns and walks back to the ram. She grazes close to him and parallel with his body, almost touching him. This parallel grazing lasts a few minutes. Then N horn threatens F-ram, slips under his neck, and rubs her side along his chest. For a moment she stops, pressing her haunches backward against his chest and then steps forward. Suddenly F-ram rushes at her with lowered head, but she avoids him, quickly turns and butts him on the head. She slips in close beside him and assumes a low-stretch, as does the ram. Both move a few steps forward in low-stretch, apparently in body contact, and stop simultaneously. She turns from F-ram and trots several steps away, then turns and looks at F-ram. The ram just stands. Then he paws a bed in the snow and lies down; the ewe does likewise.

The behavior patterns of the estrous ewe include a sudden bouncing away from the ram, which the female terminates by turning toward the male. During her advance at the ram the female horn threatens and may prance a little. She horns and butts the neck, chest, shoulders, and head of the ram and rubs her body full length along his or across his chest (fig. 29D). The old N-ewe only twice nuzzled the ram's head in 26 interactions, but this behavior was shown more frequently by a $2\frac{1}{2}$-year-old ewe in her first heat period. In the 26 interactions, N-ewe performed the horn threat approach 17 times, horned the ram's body 10 times, performed the sudden running away 10 times, and butted the ram 3 times. The ram served her 11 times. In one respect he acted unusually. He charged N-ewe 7 times and the female yearling twice. Both ewes evaded him easily.

From the observations of Hulet et al. (1962), Banks (1964), and Lindsay (1966), it appears that domestic ewes in estrus act in principle similarly to female mountain sheep in heat. They search out rams (Lindsay 1966), look over their shoulders at rams, butt and nuzzle them, and may also wheel about with the ram in antiparallel posture. These ewes also interfered with the courtship of rams on other ewes, which was not done by anestrous females (Hulet et al. 1962; Banks 1964).

The behavior of the estrous female in courting the dominant male is remarkably similar to that of the small, subordinate ram toward a large one. Her behavior differs from the young ram in that the female rubs her whole body along that of the ram. Like any subordinate ram she uses contact patterns and aggressive patterns. The sudden dashes away, which are not used by young rams, can also be classified as an aggression-provoking pattern, for commonly a ram does charge head-lowered after a departing subordinate. (The only time I was attacked by a bighorn ram was after I dashed away from him downhill.) It appears plausible that in using aggressive patterns in her courtship the female rouses sexual behavior in the ram by arousing aggressive impulses. After all, rams do mount estrous females primarily after a battle or a spirited chase. There is always some scrapping involved with rams during such chases. It should also be noted that sexual and aggressive behavior are closely linked during the ram's ontogeny.

Dalton et al. (1967) observed that homosexual mounting increased in dairy bulls during and after periods of excitement. Lindsay and Ellsmore (1968) found that domestic rams did more mounting of ewes when in competition with other rams in the same breeding paddock than when working alone. Modha (1967) found that crocodiles (*Crocodilus niloticus*) courted after watching a severe fight between crocodile males. The hypothesis therefore arises that in her courtship the female mimics a battle and provokes a ram into mounting just as it happens after a real battle.

After the last females have been bred, the rams remain for about two weeks on the female ranges. Then the large, old rams begin moving back to their own wintering areas, while many 3–6-year-old rams remain behind with the ewes to return in spring (see fig. 13). On the Stone's sheep study area the old rams were more solitary than at any other season of the year but became more social as winter waned into spring (fig. 30). The midwinter following the rutting season is a quiet time on the sheep ranges. The animals stand dispersed if the ridges are blown free of snow or clump on areas with a dense cover of grass if a deep blanket of snow covers the ground. The rams generally interact little. Most old fellows look thin and haggard, and their coats take on a worn appearance which is increased by the many battle streaks in the fur (plate 54). The females move in small bands over the ranges. The main function of sheep activity now is simply to survive.

RUTTING BEHAVIOR: A COMPARISON OF SHEEP AND OTHER RUMINANTS
Several characteristics of rutting mountain sheep are striking. Rams do not herd harems (Cherniavski 1962*b*) as is typical of red deer or elk (*Cervus*). They form consorts with anestrous females only exceptionally, and hence rarely guard anestrous females as is typical of mountain goats (Geist 1965), moose, red deer, or caribou bulls. There is no competition for anestrous females, no competition for the female's urine, little serious aggression among rams when no female is in estrus,

and no dispersal of young males by aggressive old males as is typical of elk (Altmann 1952; Struhsaker 1967). Consequently rams remain together during the rut, and although some distribution of large rams over the ranges does occur, it is not as striking as that shown in ibex, in which males of equal size are as a rule not in the same band during the rut (Nievergelt 1967).

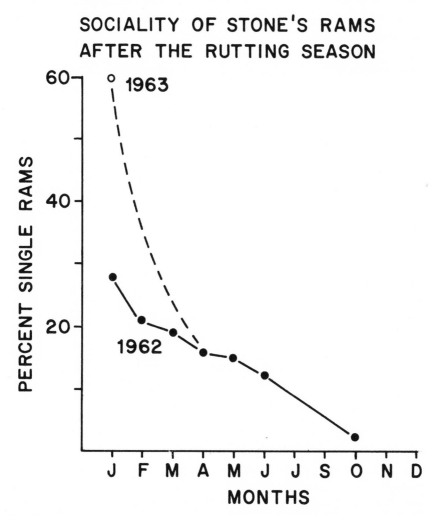

Fig. 30. Right after the rut, the Stone's rams were most solitary but became progressively less so as winter advanced. During 1962 a deep blanket of snow covered the mountains and forced sheep into closer contact than during 1963. A comparable change in the sociality of rams was not found in the high-density population of bighorn sheep.

Unlike some gazelles and African antelope, for example, the kob (*Adenota*) (Buechner 1963; Leuthold 1966), water buck (*Kobus*) (Kiley-Worthington 1965), Thompson's gazelle (*Gazella thompsoni*), Grant's gazelle (*Gazella granti*) (Walther 1964, 1965, 1968), or gnu (*Connochaetes*) (Estes 1966), mountain sheep form no breeding territory, where the males may court and copulate unchallenged. The breeding ram is hence subjected to frequent interference by other males; competition for the estrous female is intense. If a ram appears with horns larger than those of the breeding ram, he has unhindered access to the female, but then he must keep smaller rams away from the female by displays, threats, battles, and fast maneuvers. Since in this system young rams do get a chance to breed, small as this chance may be, there is a steady selection for quick copulation. The smaller ram, if successful in driving off the ewe, has little time to copulate before the large ram arrives and butts him off the female. The semen is administered in many small doses—a domestic ram only ejaculates about 2 cc at a time—rather than in one large one as is common in horses, cattle, or pigs (Foote and Trimberger 1968). The frequent mountings by rams appear to be a consequence of the mating system, the lack of a breeding territory, and the undaunted attempts of the subordinate rams to get at the estrous ewe.[13]

When a ram is alone with an estrous female his courtship becomes strikingly cautious. He displays behind the female, avoids body contact, and following each courtship advance, he retreats to the original position. However, the ram is not unique in this, for the cautious courtship is strikingly shown by its close relative, the ibex, and still more so by red deer. Ibex males may stand for hours in display behind the female and twist occasionally. Moreover, the female ibex readily butts the males or even chases them away (Burckhardt 1961), something not done by female mountain sheep. The principle seems to be to make the female receptive without making her leave the area. The courting red deer stag acts similarly. He approaches the female in a specific posture, which is the antithesis to the herding posture he used to get stray females back to the group. In courting the stag trots directly at the hind, keeps his ears out, and flicks with his tongue. Since he at once begins licking the female, his tongue-flick approach apparently signals his intention to lick. He licks the female on the rump, back, withers, neck, sides—in short over most of her body. He very carefully

13. For a good comparative treatment of courtship behavior in mammals see Ewer (1968).

attempts to mount, balancing on his hind legs and putting little if any weight on the female. A sambar stag I observed (*C. unicolor*) did not even clasp the female with his front legs; rather, his legs hung loose from his body. If the female moves, the stag dismounts and continues licking. He repeats those careful mounts till he suddenly bounds upward driving the penis into the vagina and ejaculates.

The historical or evolutionary reasons for the cautious courtship are not difficult to visualize. Since rams, stags, and bucks are not equipped physically to grab and hold on to the female and copulate with her despite her struggles, copulation can come about only with the female's cooperation. If a stag or ram courts roughly, what does he achieve? The female withdraws and, if followed by the ram, attempts to escape. In the case of the ram such a chase will invariably catch the attention of other rams and they will hurry to intercept the female. Competition for the female is increased; the chances that a larger ram than the original one will be drawn to the chase is also increased, and the original ram's chances of siring offspring is reduced. In the case of ibex and red deer, a female courted by a rough male has only a short distance to run before she is in the domain of other larger males. Again the original male loses out in the breeding. The very elaborate courtship of Uganda kob males, so well described by Buechner and Schloeth (1965), evolved probably for the same reason. The males hold small breeding territories clumped in leks, and the female makes a choice of which male she will associate with. Rough courtship decreases a male's chances to sire offspring, for the female will simply step into the next territory. If breeding territories are large as in Thompson's gazelle, a buck's herding of the female, by which he prevents her departure from the territory, still has some utility; however, kob breeding territories are so tiny that a few jumps bring the female into another male's domain. Consequently, we do not observe cutting and herding in kob as we find it in Thompson's gazelle. In general, it appears that a male who mistreats the female, thus making her leave, selects against his own genotype.

The peculiar switch of the female into male-like behavior at estrus is not confined to mountain sheep but appears to be widely spread among ruminants. I found signs of this switch in estrous mountain goats, for one female dug rutting pits when in heat, while another courted her 18-month-old son in the low-stretched, crouched courtship posture so typical of mountain goat males (Geist 1965). Walther (1965) noted that female Grant's gazelle in estrus displayed to the male in male fashion and were promptly mounted. Schloeth (1961*a*) found that estrous cows chase off other cows. Females of various old-world deer which I observed during the fall of 1967 in Hellabrun Zoological Park, Munich, also showed this marked behavior reversal. Typical male components of behavior during the rutting season include wallowing in urine-soaked mud, pawed-up wallows, rubbing the neck on trees, horning the wallows and trees, roaring, courting, and mounting females. Males of some primitive deer, like the barasingha (*C. duvauceli*), also indulge in horning and rubbing on dominant larger males. Estrous hinds of various species showed these behavioral components during estrus. They not only licked and rubbed their faces on the male's body, but also butted him while one female fallow deer confronted the stag with lowered head and performed the weaving motions, which had she had antlers would have brought her weapons in contact with the stag's. Estrous hinds attempted to mount other hinds, although I never saw them court these hinds. One red deer female wallowed, pawed, and horned the stag's rutting pit, while a female fallow deer rubbed her neck on a tree trunk in male fashion. The rubbing and nuzzling by females has apparently no counterpart in the behavior of the males in fallow deer, red deer, or elk. Nor is this to be expected since large males of these species are highly intolerant of other males during the rut, but it is part of the male's behavioral repertoire among barasingha. The large stags, though aggressive, are more tolerant of youngsters, a trait which appears to be present in other South East Asian deer, to judge from my observations at the zoo. Like estrous hinds, the two young barasingha stags I observed horned and nuzzled the body and head of the larger one. All female old-world deer appear to have the same submissive posture in which females lower the head, nose pointing forward and ears flattened. In extreme situations, the females make rapid chewing motions with the mouth, flick up the rostrum rhythmically, and even vocalize. If the female is resting, she may flatten herself on the ground. It appears that young stags may use the same posture. I did see young, fallow stags assume the female's submissive posture, though not the chewing motion. Burckhardt (1958) saw young fallow stags lie flat on the ground in female fashion when approached by the large stag. Even though the female's behavior in estrus is not nearly as complete a reversal as in Stone's sheep, there may be a tendency in the ruminants for the female in estrus and males (or perhaps just subordinate males) to show the same behavioral components. Hence there is the potential for the evolution of female mimicry shown by subordinate males in the presence of larger ones.

The rutting behavior of American sheep appears to follow much the same rules as that of other ruminants. Gazelle, deer, and caprid females all urinate to the courting male, attempting to "buy time" or get a breathing spell while the male lipcurls on the urine, as Fritz Walther (1968) fittingly stated in his book on gazelle behavior. Today we are able to visualize at least some of the evolutionary forces which altered or maintained the basically similar courtship behavior of ruminants. Not unexpectedly, the courtship of mountain sheep resembles that of other caprids and the ancestral rupicaprids. The courtship behavior of one argali and a urial ram have been described by Walther (1961), the behavior of domestic sheep by Banks (1964), of feral Soay sheep by Grubb and Jewell (1966), of ibex by Steinhauf (1959), Walther (1960), and Burckhardt (1961), of markhor by Walther (1961), of Barbary sheep by Haas (1958), Katz (1949), and Ogren (1965), of rupicaprids by Geist (1965) for *Oreamnos*, and Walther (1961) and Krämer (1969) for *Rupicapra*. One finds bits and pieces of incomplete observations on the activities of various caprids in many papers. I also observed captive rutting mouflon and ibex in fall 1967. For the present I find no evidence to contradict the hypothesis that courtship behavior is exceedingly similar in all sheep and differs little among the caprids as a whole. In other words, the various races of sheep use the same behavior patterns with minor alterations but at different frequencies. Other caprids use behavior patterns similar to those of sheep but somewhat altered, resulting in similar courtship behavior throughout the tribe, which is not, however, the case with fighting behavior.

The published data on rutting caprids allows at present no detailed comparisons, for most observations are either inexact or incomplete, or made on a small number of captive animals and insufficiently illustrated. No detailed quantification, essential for detailed comparisons, has been published. The only sheep I can compare with authority are bighorn, Stone's, and Dall's sheep. Their differences in courting were small and even these could be reduced to a few minor differences in the use of aggressive, display, and sexual patterns. Bighorns were more overtly aggressive and sexual, displayed relatively less than thinhorn sheep, and were more juvenile or neotenic in their behavior (see chap. 11). For that reason, bighorn rams were more rough and unpolished when courting estrous ewes than Stone's rams. The latter preceded each copulation with a series of front kicks, while bighorn rams tended to mount more often spontaneously; they twisted and kicked, but not frequently. The courted bighorn females just before and right after

estrus protected themselves from the advances of the rams by turning
on them and butting, a behavior in line with their aggressive nature
which I never saw Stone's females do. How much our sheep differ in
their rutting behavior from their tall-legged European and Asiatic
cousins is hard to tell. Fritz Walther's (1961) exacting verbal description
of a courting argali ram (*O. a. poli?*) does not reveal any difference,
except that the ram he saw did not flick the tongue during the twist,
which our American sheep as well as domestic ones do (Banks 1964).
The movements to and from rutting grounds of Soay rams described by
Grubb and Jewell (1966), their short consortships with ewes just prior
to estrus, and the grouping of rams behind the estrous female (Boyd et
al. 1964), indicate in principle a rutting behavior similar to that in
mountain sheep. The reference by Heptner et al. (1961) to harems in
argalis requires verification.

As we move to more distantly related caprids such as the true goats,
including the ibex and markhor, or to *Ammotragus*, the sheep-goat of
North Africa, the animals begin to show a few marked differences in
their behavior patterns. The ejaculation posture of the true goats, as
well as those of *Ammotragus*, differs from that of sheep in that the penis
is taken into the muzzle (plate 39). *Ammotragus* performs a curious intermediate behavior, for Haas (1958) writes that the male protrudes his
penis past the front legs, whips it up and down and against his belly
(in sheep fashion), and attempts to get it into his mouth. In ibex,
ejaculation is a smooth, quick operation in which the male puts the
penis quickly into his mouth, maybe using the cheek cavity as an artificial vagina. *Ammotragus* has not been reported to use front kick, whereas courting ibex often lift the dangling front leg and paw toward or on
the female. I did see feral domestic goats use a true front kick in courting.
Ammotragus rams vocalize loudly when simultaneously twisting and
nudging the body of the female (Haas 1958), which is also done by
sheep; ibex buzz during the twist. The low-stretch of ibex (plate 70)
is more extreme than even that of thinhorn sheep and is much more
tense than in the latter; ibex males raise the tail but rams do not. The
copulatory postures of males of sheep, goats, and *Ammotragus* appear to
be identical. Unfortunately, we know nothing about courting thar
(*Hemitragus*).

Of the rupicaprids, the tribe ancestral to the caprids, we know only
about the behavior of the most aberrant forms, the mountain goats
(*Oreamnos*) of North America and the chamois (*Rupicapra*) of Europe.
The behavior of the latter has been well described lately by Krämer

(1969), and the former was observed and reported on by Geist (1965). We know nothing of the behavior of the most primitive and old genera, like *Noemorhedus* and particularly *Capricornis*. Mountain goat males happen to be subordinate to females when adult and their cautious courtship behavior, including the flat, depressed low-stretch approach is a reflection of this. Yet, this crouched low-stretch is occasionally seen in mountain sheep. I saw an old Stone's female in great excitement virtually crawl on her belly toward the first newborn lamb of the year. Rams crouch occasionally when courting females (plate 34), and it is well seen in film E 1337 when a 2½-year-old Dall's ram does it toward a ewe. This crouched, low-stretched posture is used by chamois as the female's courtship posture and as the young male's or juvenile's submissive posture (Walther 1961; Krämer 1969). This low-stretch, including tongue flicking (used by *Oreamnos*), appears to be the homologue of the caprid low-stretch. Mountain goat billies use a front kick but no twist. When approaching in low-stretch and flicking the tongue into the female's fur, they may buzz softly, much as ibex do. Their copulatory posture is different from that of the caprids, since the males bury their noses in the dorsal hair of the female. The cautious courtship in mountain goats, as well as the inconspicuous courtship in chamois, are probably due to the small degree of sexual dimorphism in these species rather than to the ability of females to escape overtly aggressive males. A female mountain goat is a respectable antagonist who can fatally injure billies (Geist 1967); caution is adaptive on the part of the male.

The main aim in studying courtship behavior is to elucidate the factors governing its evolution by reducing complexity to fewer denominators and then exploring the historic reasons for these denominators. An ungulate committed to a breeding territory must develop more elaborate courtship than one who searches out and follows the female wherever she goes, and a species committed to a small territory must court differently than one who has a large territory. The same applies to sexual dimorphism and how capably armed the partners are, for a dangerous female poses different selection forces to courting males than an utterly harmless one. Similarly, the group formation by rams about the estrous female can be explained as an effect of the relatively undamaging weapons and good defenses of the rams; a small ram can afford to take a butt trying to chase off the female. Most butts he can evade or catch with his horns and the few that land are usually harmless, for to deliver full-power blows a ram must get a long way back and charge. Over a short distance the butts are not potent and the young ram chances at best a few bruises. If rams carried sharp horns like mountain goats, a young ram's attempt to get at the female would be suicidal. In mountain goats we find that males pair off with females if possible, but if it is not, they stay out of each other's way (Geist 1965). The same behavior by thar bulls (Anderson and Henderson 1961) implies that thar bulls, like mountain goats, are damaging combatants. Therefore, the frequent quick mounts by breeding rams appear to be a consequence of the intense competition for the ewe as explained earlier; intense competition is a consequence of good defenses and ineffective weapons coupled with the lack of a breeding territory; the reasons for the mountain sheep's weapon system can be explained (see chap. 12), but the lack of a breeding territory is as yet mysterious, although the sheep's ancestors were probably territorial rupicaprids. It can, however, be pointed out that breeding territories appear to be typical of ungulates in which adult males look alike, so that the rank (fighting potential) of each cannot be predicted from his horn or body size. The breeding territory can serve in this situation as a rank symbol (Geist 1966a). In sheep, a horn size gradient fulfills that function and breeding territory would be redundant. The territorial behavior described by Pfeffer (1967) for mouflon rams appears to have little to do with the defense of a geographic area, a piece of real estate, as is typical for gazelles. Localization by a male to a ridge or mountainside during the rut is not evidence for territory.

It appears that the weapon system plays a dominant role in the evolution of ruminants, so much so that it overshadows the evolution of threats, displays, courtship, the body proportions, skin thickness, coat patterning, color, and even maternal behavior of the animals.

INTRASPECIFIC COMBAT IN RUMINANTS AND THE NATURE OF
AGGRESSION

The study of social behavior in mountain sheep and ruminants in general offers some insights into the nature of aggression that have received little consideration to date. Intraspecific combat tends to be very dangerous in the majority of ungulates since these are large, agile animals often armed with lethal weapons and quick to fight. Such fights end more commonly in serious injury or even death of one opponent than is generally appreciated, particularly in the large periglacial species of late Pleistocene origin although less so in the older evolutionary forms exemplified by African antelope. The extent of mortality inflicted by intraspecific fighting on the males of a species is usually hard to determine since it is rare to find carcasses fresh enough in the field to diagnose the cause of death. Nevertheless, some such data has been accumulated and it does allow one to estimate the order of magnitude of combat losses. In the Woronesh sanctuary in Russia, of 208 red deer stags found dead over the course of 20 years, 13% had been victims of fighting; in the Krim sanctuary 10 of 33 stags found had suffered the same fate (Heptner et al. 1961). Combat losses in the Eurasian moose of the race *alces* are of a similar extent. Of 50 bulls 4 years and older shot and autopsied at Petschora-Ilytsch, the famous Russian moose experimental station, 6 had fresh antler punctures. Bulls killed in fighting are found there almost every year, and wounded bulls are no uncommon sight after the rutting season. In a second sanctuary, 7 of 14 bulls found over 9 years were casualties of fighting (Heptner and Nasimovitsch 1968). In an introduced, expanding moose population in Poland reported on by Pielowski (1969), among 37 adults of both sexes that died naturally there were 4 bulls killed in fighting. Unfortunately, it is not reported how many of the 37 adults were bulls. However, since Pielowski documented the growth of the moose population by sex, one can calculate a rough estimate of the chances a bull has to be killed each year in the rut. The sum of the numbers of bulls present during each rut from 1955 to 1965 was 105 and the number dead was 4; this amounts to a chance of about 4% per bull per year. It must be mentioned that the race *alces* differs substantially in antler form from the American-type moose which includes also the East Siberian moose. Bulls of the race *alces* typically carry very small antlers, often devoid of palmation, and armed with only a few, but long and massive, points. Such antlers appear to be poor shields in combat compared to the massive palms of American moose. I am not familiar with the hide of Eurasian moose, but that of American bulls, particularly those in the rut is up to $\frac{1}{2}$ in (10–12 mm) thick and very tough, probably evolved as a defense in fighting.

McHugh (1958) described severe combat damage and death in bison (*Bison*), and found upon autopsy that 23% of bison bulls over 4 years of age had broken ribs. Similar injuries and combat death are reported for European bison from Russia (Heptner et al. 1961). Saiga antelope appear to suffer a higher casualty and wounding rate in intraspecific fighting, as bleeding or dead males are a common sight on rutting grounds (Bannikov et al. 1961); unfortunately the Russian workers failed to report how common. During observations of mountain goats in two rutting seasons I found 4 males seriously wounded in intra-specific fighting, 2 mortally. Since there were only 8–10 different males on my study area each year, the chances of a male being injured in fighting appears to be high. Of 21 individually known mule deer bucks over $2\frac{1}{2}$ years of age which I observed at close range at the end of a rutting season, 4 had been wounded. More literature pertaining to intraspecific combat and injury in ungulates is reviewed elsewhere (Geist 1966a).

These figures and earlier observations on fighting injuries in rams should give one pause, since they suggest that ethology's conventional wisdom, that animals rarely kill or maim each other in intraspecific fighting, has been overstated. Ewer (1968) has also cautioned against its overenthusiastic acceptance. At first glance it would seem that a bull moose whose chances of getting wounded in a rutting season is 10% and getting killed 4% has little to fear from intraspecific combat. On the contrary, he is living a very dangerous life. In 10 rutting seasons his fraction of a chance to escape unhurt is only $(0.9)^{10} = 0.35$, and to escape with his life is $(0.96)^{10} = 0.62$. At this rate of injury and death a group of 100 bulls would be reduced to 62 in 10 years by murder alone, while only 35 of 100 bulls that lived through 10 rutting seasons would escape unhurt. If the above figures are reasonable estimates, and they appear to be on the basis of the data cited, then the prospects for a European bull moose are not rosy. Moreover, intraspecific combat can lead indirectly to the death of the participants through exhaustion and the consequent inability to cope with environmental extremes, as is well documented for Saiga antelopes by Bannikov and his colleagues (1961), or by becoming predation prone as Estes (1969) has convincingly argued for in the gnu. Even a minor injury could eliminate a combatant from the population given the predation pressure of the African plains.

Nevertheless, in all fairness to that wisdom, it is largely valid as a statement of fact for ruminants. One must, however, reject its loose and uncritical use and the consequent human implications. Furthermore, the explanations advanced for its existence and evolution leave some-thing to be desired.

It is not my intention to review in detail a subject as lengthy and passionately discussed as intraspecific combat, nor to detract from the theory of aggression as elaborated by Lorenz (1963) which I believe to be largely valid. It is, however, necessary to point out that in the writings of Lorenz (1963), Eibl-Eibesfeld (1963, 1966), Barnett (1967), and Tinbergen (1969) it is strongly implied or stated outright that the onus of not injuring lies with the combatants. That is, although well-armed animals are capable of carnage, they will not practice it. Eibl-Eibesfeld states: "The opponents assess their strength without injury to the weaker. The selection pressure which leads to such ritualized combat is easily understood: It acts as species preserving if the weaker opponent is chased off and excluded from reproduction for the present. However, he should live on so that he may be victorious later" (1963, p. 723). These are curious statements. Why, one could ask, should the stronger only drive off the weaker instead of killing him outright? Of what disadvantage is a dead opponent? What has a victor to gain from sparing a rival whom he will confront again and thus chance injury, loss of status, or death? The inescapable conclusion is as repugnant as it is correct. Moreover, the above quote illustrates one other common course of action. The necessity to maintain a species is invoked, as an explanation, as if some cosmic force dictates that species must survive. Paleontology teaches to the contrary. What is necessary are hypotheses, testable at least in principle, that show how ritualized combat and agonistic behavior are shaped. One can explain why intraspecific combat is usually noninjurious with mechanisms known today, as well as how it evolved without invoking group selection. This also goes for the "epideictic displays" of Wynne-Edwards (1962), which coincide largely with what the Germans call *Imponierverhalten*, and which is referred to here as bravado displays or indirect threats.

Fighting in most horned ungulates is in principle so similar to fencing that it might be useful to examine this form of human combat. An uninitiated observer would note that the fighters assume a specific, rather peculiar, and uncomfortable posture, that they rush hither and thither with loud clashes of their lethal blades, and that the fight wears on and on without either opponent receiving a wound. On the face of it, fencing is the very image of a "ritualized" "comment" fight. Yet he who has wielded the blade knows that each motion, stance, or rule of fencing is dictated by deadly necessity, and that it would be suicidal to deviate from them in a duel. Fencing welds together actions essential to avoid being pierced by the opponent's saber, while allowing one to pierce the opponent. The low, spread-legged stance is highly functional; it permits the quickest possible retreat as well as advance and reduces the target area to the opponent. The blade is moved so as to block the opponent's blade, or bypass it. The rapid dashing back and forth, the drawn-out fight and blade clatter are the consequence, not aim, of two fighters skilled in defending themselves with a blade, and it continues as long as both are alert and on guard. Much the same can be said about the intraspecific combat of many ungulates, and we know from a good many careful observers that often it is woe to the combatant who slips and loses his defenses in a serious fight (see Geist 1966a).

The reason why bloodshed is rare in severe intraspecific combat is not that the opponents disdain it, but that they usually protect themselves with a variety of defenses. An attack may be neutralized against an armored skull or body shield as mentioned earlier for mountain sheep or goats; the opponent's weapons may be caught or held, rendering them useless. This can be done by means of hornlike organs, or in carnivores by grasping the opponent's jaws or snout as Schenkel (1967) described for wolves. An attack can be evaded by quick maneuvers as is beautifully described by Estes (1969) for gnu (*Connochaetes*); an opponent's weapons may be rendered useless by assuming an orientation to him in which he cannot use them. This evasive technique needs a little elaboration, however, since I failed to recognize it when I wrote my earlier review of combat techniques in ungulates (Geist 1966a). An example of it is provided by rhino bulls (*Ceratotherium*) as observed by Schack (Backhaus 1964). In a fight the small opponent remained constantly side by side, shoulder to shoulder with the larger opponent and followed each of his turns. This was interpreted by Schack as a defensive action which prevented the larger bull from ramming his horns into the smaller one's side. Klingel (1967) provided a further and quite different example of evasive techniques from zebras (*Equus quagga*). Fighting stallions bite each other's legs. The opponents deny each other a target by squatting on the ground and covering their legs with their bodies. Consequently they shuffle about one another on their carpal and tarsal joints, each trying to bite the other's legs. The obvious inference from these considerations is that bloodshed must follow in serious combat if the defensive mechanisms are impaired, accidentally or experimentally.

It has been amply discussed in the ethological literature that elaborate displays and threats precede, or often substitute for combat, and that these displays aim at the same gains but not the same consequences as combat. These agonistic behavior patterns fall readily into two classes, the direct threats and the implied or indirect threats. The direct threats again fall into three categories, the rush threats (mimicking a rapidly approaching large object), the weapon threats (presenting the weapons against the opponent in a position ready for striking, i.e., exposing fangs and opening mouth), and the scare threat (a combination of all possible deterrent stimuli while directly confronting the opponent). These types of threat are not used haphazardly. In its pure form the rush threat is the prerogative of the dominant as demonstrated for mountain sheep. Moreover, I have not recorded, nor can I remember, any deviation from this in any ungulate species that I have observed for any length of time, be it mountain goat, elk, red deer, fallow deer, moose, mule deer, or caribou. The weapon threats are used by dominants and subordinates. The scare threats, known to me among ungulates only in moose, but common in carnivores, were shown in former species by subordinates, or by moose confronting carnivores or humans (Geist 1963). The direct threats are signals which allow conspecifics (and not only conspecifics) to correctly predict the consequences of interacting with the sender and which serve as a warning to be respected. The indirect threats or bravado displays (display threats, Lent 1966; present threats, Geist 1965) are behavior patterns of a different nature and in humans analogous, if not homologous, to "showing off" in its widest sense. These displays are the prerogative of the dominant and a characteristic of males that are, or act as if they were, the larger. Whereas lambs are born with threats already formed, bravado displays are subject to maturation. These displays emphasize size and height, hence the common broadside orientation, the erectable hair ridges or long hair pants in some ungulates, and the color patterns, spots, localized quivers, or flashes of hair bushes or tail that focus the attention of the viewer on the displayer's body size or weapons. Although weapons are often shown in these displays, they are not shown in position for use but are literally displayed to their best advantage, and usually are held laterally to the opponent. The displayer's motions strongly deviate from the normal and are either slow and stiff or fast and exaggerated. While in direct threat an opponent stares at the other; in a bravado display the performers normally look away from or past the opponent, as if not noticing his presence. Bravado displays also include demonstrations of feats and vigor against inanimate objects, such as violent thrashing of shrubs, branches, or grass bunches, as well as auditory signals, such as vocalizations in many deer or the gnu (Estes 1969), and olfactory signals such as deposition of glandular secretions, urine, and dung. The significance of olfactory marking has been particularly well studied in feral rabbits by Mykytowycz (1965, 1968). In general, bravado displays fill all channels available for communication. They are very common displays, seen most often when the animals are most active, as in the morning and evening, or when a stranger appears. One can consider bravado displays as signals which reinforce what the conspecific onlooker learned in interactions with dominants. Such signals should be adaptive to the actor because they would reduce the chances of combat and wounding, and consequently the loss of status and reproduction. Indeed, Walther (1965) has shown quantitatively for Grant's gazelles that bravado displays appear to save on combat and the same is strongly implied by Schaller's (1967) data for chital (*Axis axis*) and barasingha (*Cervus duvauceli*). It can be predicted that the animal prevented from displaying, or experimentally deprived of the effect of its display, is more subject to intraspecific combat and its consequences than the animal which is not.

It has been pointed out by Lorenz (1963) that animals with dangerous weapons rarely use them against conspecifics, in fact appear to be greatly inhibited from striking or seriously biting an opponent. However, the species used by Lorenz as examples had either no protection in the form of solid body armor and lacked organs to block and hold the opponent's weapons (e.g., some cichlids, wolves, baboons) or were poorly known to Lorenz such as the fallow deer (*Dama dama*). He described an instance in which one combatant failed to take advantage of an opponent's exposed flanks to gore him with his antlers. Lorenz mistook the antlers of this deer species as very dangerous. However, unlike their cousins the sika, red deer, or wapiti, large fallow bucks cannot execute a conspecific quickly. I witnessed in one zoological garden the constant persecution of a doe by a buck. Although the female was apparently gored daily it took the buck a week to kill her. This implies that a buck goring an opponent would be subject to instant retaliation and thus face a fight with an enraged opponent. Such a buck, quick and heedless to lunge into battle, is likely to deplete his strength quickly in many fights and lose out in breeding. This is just one consequence suffered by overt aggressors; others are discussed below.

Species that are dangerously armed but also possess excellent defenses, such as many deer, sheep, antelopes, and gazelles, can enter into fighting often and for a long time and suffer little for it. We have a parallel to this in medieval knights that engaged frequently in combat with rather deadly weapons but usually quit from exhaustion, not wounds, due to the protection of shield and armor.

In species devoid of good defenses, combat is rare because overt aggressors should be strongly selected against. The aggressive individual who readily attacks and inflicts painful slashes on his opponent is likely to trigger a desperate defense and emerge injured from his very first fight. Even if victorious he has already compromised his dominance rank, breeding success, health, and life because he is no match for opponents of equal or even smaller size in the many interactions that will follow every day. He is likely to sicken from his wounds, drop in rank, and lose out in the breeding and perhaps succumb to his injuries. I described this for mountain goats (Geist 1965). The only way in which uninhibited striking could evolve in a species devoid of armor or other morphological defenses would be for the aggressor either to *kill instantly* or in some other way *escape prompt and certain retaliation*. (To the human animal projecting rocks, spears, or bullets and hiding behind shield or concrete, such means are of course given.) Seen in this light, the reluctance of a dangerously armed dominant to engage with a subordinate is less a consequence of altruism than of self-preservation.

Intraspecific combat may be deprived of its potency in what might seem a peculiar manner. There are too few intensive studies on free-living ruminants to allow any generalization, but as has already been demonstrated in mountain sheep, and as my recent unpublished data on mule deer shows, most of the fighting is initiated by the subordinate and executed in a manner harmless to the dominant. In both species overt fighting is surprisingly common; in sheep more so than in deer. Subordinate rams mimic the behavior of an estrous female, and this happens to contain much overt aggression. He literally "parasitizes" the dominant's inhibition to blast females. There is no need to postulaté an evolutionary modification of the receiver's recognition system as Ewer (1968) did in order to account for the dominant's tolerance of the subordinate. The inhibition to strike females is there already, and the mimic takes advantage of it. It allows him to vent his aggression with impunity against the armored skull of the dominant. Thus the opponent with the heaviest horns, heaviest armor, and greatest capacity to deal out crushing blows is the recipient, not the donor, of most blows. It is likely that the subordinates habituate in directing their blows where they do no harm, namely at the larger's horns, for a painful blow on the dominant's body is likely to precipitate severe retaliation, a lesson not likely to be lost on a young ram. The same may explain in principle the observations of Walther (1966) on various African antelope that fighting partners strive to lock horns.

A common experience of anyone studying the behavior of animals is surprise at the clarity and distinctiveness of their social behavior patterns. The patterns are unambiguous. In fact, ambiguity of signals should be severely selected against, by reducing the reproductive success of the sender. How this would come about is probably best illustrated by visualizing a harem-guarding elk bull. He herds females back to his harem by assuming a low-stretched posture which happens to be a serious threat: a number of times I have seen bulls crash their antlers into females that were slow to heed this display. However, the bull must also court, and he assumes the exact antithesis of the low-stretched herding posture as well as the concomitant orientations and vocalizations (Geist 1966d). A bull who sloppily performs the herding behavior increases the chances of injuring or alienating the cows of his harem, which are the potential mothers of his offspring, and thus reducing his reproductive output. A bull who inexactly performs the courtship behavior is likely to frighten his females and hence lose them or chase them around much more than normal, thereby depleting his own energy stores and hence compromising his status as a harem bull as well as his life expectancy. Similarly, unambiguous signals of intent in agonistic situations are likely to reduce intraspecific combat to the minimum, greatly increase predictability within the social environment, and consequently reduce unnecessary excitement, energy loss, and chances of mortality of individuals.

It has been emphasized that to ruminants intraspecific combat tends to be dangerous, and one can ask if combat does aim at eliminating the opponent. A close observation of fighting ungulates indicates that their actions appear to have two aims: making the opponent withdraw by putting leverage on his body, distorting it, or piercing it, which are pain-evoking actions and quite likely aim at triggering the withdrawal reflexes; making the opponent lose control over his own body, which is not so much a painful as traumatic experience and would lead to flight from the source of the trauma. Fighting could not be selected to be more effective than the minimum required to satisfy these goals. However, defensive mechanisms would select for sharper or longer piercing organs as well as for actions that circumvent and defeat the species' specific defenses. Clearly, a blow into an unguarded flank with weapons that evolved to pierce heavy hides must have fatal consequences. There is, however, no compelling reason to postulate this as an evolutionary goal.

Above all, the study of social behavior teaches that its main function and selective advantage must lie in creating predictability in the social environment. Social behavior appears to be to the social environment what exploratory behavior is to the physical environment; both familiarize the individual with its environment and thus create and maintain order. Destroy predictability in the physical environment and the individuals suffer (see Metzgar 1967); destroy predictability in the social environment and the individuals suffer severely (see Bailey 1969). The contention advanced by Wynne-Edwards (1962) that social behavior evolved to satisfy the need for conserving each population's resources must also incorporate our present knowledge on the function of social behavior and be capable of being tested before it becomes acceptable. It still needs a convincing demonstration. That is not to say that ecological selection has no influence on social evolution. On the contrary, I attempted to demonstrate this in chapter 5 for sheep and moose and in chapter 10 for the social behavior of ewes. It is ecological selection that acts against single sheep. This forces on those that try to live in the company of other sheep adaptations which permit them to exist in the face of larger companions, namely, appeasement behavior and armored heads.

So far most attention has been paid to combat and threat behavior. However, a few concepts about principles and evolution of social behavior are in order, a subject little discussed in some recent texts of animal behavior, for instance, Hinde (1966) and Marler and Hamilton (1967). A scrutiny shows that much of social behavior aims at or takes advantage of preexisting responses and inhibitions. This is true not only for behavior that evolved within the social environment, as Wickler's pioneering work on intraspecific mimicry has shown (1962), but also those which evolved within the physical environment. Let me show this by example:

1. Threat behavior aims at or takes advantage of withdrawal from dangerous stimuli in the physical environment, for example, rapidly approaching large objects, loud and harsh noises, quick motions, "strange" objects, irritating secretions.

2. Combat behavior takes advantage of withdrawal from painful stimuli or from forces causing loss over voluntary actions. As in threat, withdrawal from such stimuli is essential to survive not only in the social environment but also in the habitat.

3. Appeasement behavior takes advantage of inhibitions to strike juveniles or females. Selection for such deception can occur only where animals recognize conspecifics less as individuals but more as "bundles of discrete releasers" as Ewer (1968) coined it. The appeasing individual hence mimics stimuli the dominant may disregard only at the pain of confusing females or

offspring as rivals and persecuting them, thereby decreasing his reproduction.

4. Courtship behavior may take advantage of maternal responses of the female. Ewer (1968) lists three species of rodents and some Canidae in which the males emit calls during courtship similar to the distress call of the young. To this list we can add the mule deer, whose juvenile mimicry in courtship, however, goes beyond emitting a slightly softer version of the distress call of the young. In carnivores the male may take advantage of the reflexlike relaxation and quiescence of the partner when grasped by the scruff of the neck. The young respond in this manner when carried about by the female, and this response appears to be carried over into adulthood. Ewer's (1968) observations that meercats (*Suricata*) picked up by humans by the scruff of the neck respond by relaxing and hanging motionless suggest that this response is not specific. It is there ready to be taken advantage of; little wonder that the male does.

More examples are available, but these suffice to make the point. For many social signals one need not postulate the evolution of a separate response mechanism. The advantage of attention-guiding adaptations and removal of threat-implying signals from appeasement and vice versa reduce ambiguity. How ambiguity would be selected against was illustrated by example earlier. The penalty for ambiguity as well as other maladaptive acts is not necessarily decreased individual survival, but reduced reproduction.

Since we can recognize primitive and advanced behavior, it is valid to ask why has evolution come to a halt in one species, but continued in another. This white elephant of evolutionary theory I shall tackle in chapter 11.

In explaining the evolution of social adaptations, I have in accordance with Williams's (1966) arguments evoked natural selection not as the first means but as the last. Moreover, an explanation based on natural selection should be testable by its predictions—in experiments and/or in the field. The evolutionary hypotheses I advanced all contain testable predictions, even though such predictions may not be spelled out as such because they are evident from the context.

8 Behavior of Ewes and Lambs

INTRODUCTION

The maternal behavior of mountain sheep is characterized by a minimum of care to a well-developed, independent young which readily parts company with its mother and leaves her a few weeks after weaning. The lambs are born in spring, about 175 days after conception. The lambing season varies in date and duration according to the severity of the climate. In the northern latitudes and high altitudes lambing seasons are short and come later in spring than in the warm uplands. In the hot deserts of the southern United States bighorns may lamb during any month of the year. About two weeks before lambing, pregnant ewes begin to withdraw from other sheep and disperse through rough, steep cliff terrain. Here they give birth in a sheltered location. The lambs weigh 6–11 lb at birth and are well developed. Their large size, the birth in a sheltered area, and the ewe's drying of the lamb appear to be adaptations aimed at preventing excessive cooling of the lamb, which is a serious cause of mortality among free-ranging domestic sheep. The ewe may also choose the rugged cliffs simply because she feels sick, and like any injured sheep she heads for terrain in which she is secure. In so doing she withdraws into terrain rarely visited by major sheep predators, and gives birth in a habitat more favorable to survival of the lamb than the open slopes.

When drying the lamb the female becomes "imprinted" on her offspring and rejects all other lambs thereafter. The ewe can distinguish her lamb visually, but she recognizes her offspring by the scent of its anal and tail gland, while it learns to recognize its mother visually within 3–4 days after birth. The female remains alone with the lamb 5–7 days after birth and then joins other lamb-leading females in a nursery band. These bands remain 3–4 weeks on the lambing area and depart thereafter to the summer ranges.

The appearance of the first newborn lamb causes excitement among barren ewes and juvenile sheep, and the ewe may butt these back. She protects the lamb against other sheep and minor predators only during the lamb's first two weeks of life and shows little concern for it thereafter, even if the lamb is injured. Lambs band into juvenile groups and only periodically search out their dam, particularly if the latter calls. The mother-young bond is weak; each keeps close to the other probably only because suckling relieves milk pressure in one and satisfies the appetite of the other. Ewes may leave their lambs in a juvenile band and move miles away to return hours later. Conversely, lambs may refuse to follow ewes temporarily and remain in a group on familiar ground. The lamb acts quite independently of its mother, but the mere presence of the ewe may protect the small lamb from trauma during stressful experiences.

Like most young ruminants, lambs play extensively. This activity appears to be adaptive not only because it insures proper skeletal development but also because it programs action and response patterns, and thereby preadapts the individual for adult life. Such programming must of necessity fall early into an individual's life, which play does.

At $2\frac{1}{2}$–4 months of age lambs shed their birth coat and assume adult coloration. They are now suckled less and less frequently and are weaned at 4–6 months of age. Thereafter the ewes appear to lose all interest in their lambs. The behavioral characteristics of lambs and ewes and the large size, agility, and independence of the lamb appear to be adaptations minimizing predation in a species in which the adult female cannot successfully ward off a major predator, but must run to escape getting killed.

LAMBING

The lambing seasons of North American sheep vary: where the climate is colder and the winter longer, they are shorter and later in spring (Sugden 1961). In the hot deserts of the southwestern United States, sheep may give birth during any month of the year (Hansen 1965), although most lambs are born between January and April, a span of about 12 weeks (Russo 1950). In warm southern British Columbia, California bighorn lamb between late April and June, a span of about 7 weeks (Sugden 1961; Blood 1963). In the Rocky Mountains of southern Canada and the northern United States, the lambing peak falls in the last week of May (Smith 1954), while in the cold, wet Cassiar Mountains where I studied Stone's sheep it occurred in the first week of June. Since here, as well as on the bighorn study area, ewes came into heat for a 3-week period, the lambing period is not likely to span more than 4–5 weeks. In Alaska, a Dall's sheep population lambed between May 6 and 27 (Jones 1963*b*). In the northern latitudes and high mountains, lambing is hence later and more closely synchronized than elsewhere. The lambing season might vary due to factors affecting the rutting season. Thus Preobrazhenskii (1961) describes that excellent feeding of reindeer advances the rutting season by 5–7 days, and consequently also the calving season. Since the rut is timed by the light regime in domestic sheep (Bissonnette 1941; Yeates 1949; Hafez 1952), it is theoretically possible that an unusually sunny summer advances the rut and an unusually cloudy one retards it.

Gestation period. The gestation period of bighorn sheep has been calculated by Frost (1942) and Smith (1954) by counting the days between the peaks of rutting activity and sightings of females with newborn lambs. Frost concluded that the gestation period was 181–89 days long, while Smith found it to be less than 180 days. I believe both overestimated the gestation period slightly by including in it all or part of the 5–7 days that ewes spend in seclusion after birth. For two Stone's ewes the periods between last day in estrus and birth of the lamb were 172 and 176 days respectively. However, for three ewes the periods between last day in estrus and first day on an open slope, away from the lambing cliffs and in company of other lamb-leading ewes, were 178, 183, and 184 days. Jones (1963*a*, 1963*b*) observed Dall's sheep in open terrain in Alaska. He found females to be in estrus from 27 November to 8 December, while the following lambing season lay between 6 and 27 May, which means that these sheep had a gestation period of less than 175 days. It can be concluded that American mountain sheep have gestation periods of about 175 days; perhaps a little less for the smaller races.

Domestic sheep have gestation periods of about 152 days (Krumbiegel 1954). For Asiatic sheep I found contradictory claims, but it may well be that they have shorter gestation periods than their American cousins. The large argalis from the Pamir and Tien-Shan Mountains apparently have gestation periods shorter than bighorn sheep (Heptner et al. 1961). American sheep have evolved a long gestation period just as ibex, which occupy a similar niche (see chap. 10).

Lambing habitat. The ewes begin to withdraw inconspicuously for lambing about 2–3 weeks prior to parturition. Their departure is indicated by an increase in the proportion of yearling lambs on the range (fig. 10) and in a drop in the number of adult ewes (figs. 8 and 9). Whereas at Gladys Lake Stone's ewes only withdrew into the high cliffs close to or above the wintering areas, the bighorn ewes from the Palliser Range and Grassy Mountain of Banff National Park went to separate lambing areas and deserted the winter ranges. Sheep observed by Blood (1963) and Jones (1963*b*) did like those of Gladys Lake; those observed by Wishart (1958) acted like those from Banff park.

The ewes selected primarily broken, rugged cliffs to lamb in as has been found by Spencer (1943), Murie (1944), Kennedy (1948), Smith (1954), McCann (1956), Jones (1963*b*), Blood (1963), Cherniavski (1962), and by myself. There are exceptions to this. Simmons et al. (1963) observed a female give birth in open terrain; a bighorn female lambed somewhere on a small, forested knoll just off Grassy Mountain. It may well be that in some areas patches of timber and scattered bushes substitute for cliffs as lambing habitat. The choice of cliffs as lambing areas may be due in part to the sheep's choice of such terrain when hunted, chased, scared, sick, injured, or dying. The last weeks of gestation, when the lamb may occasionally be seen kicking inside the ewe (Welles and Welles 1961), as well as parturition appear to be upsetting events. It follows that ewes would move to terrain where they are most secure. However, there may be another reason for the choice of such terrain as will be explained below.

We know little of the lambing habitats favored by Asiatic sheep. Walther (1961) noted that captive ibex and markhor preferred the shelter of rocks and huts for lambing, while argalis (*poli*) remained consistent in their dislike for rocks and boulders and lambed in open terrain. The urials he observed showed both types of behavior; the small lambs did go into rock piles and rest there, but birth occurred in the open away from the rubble. Heptner et al. (1961) make no mention of cliff terrain as lambing sites for Asiatic sheep but do mention that females prefer isolation and some shelter such as bushes.

A week prior to lambing the Stone's ewes at Gladys Lake stood alone widely dispersed through the cliffs and, occasionally, on mountains and cliffs not normally visited by sheep; these disappeared a few days after giving birth. Observations of individually recognizable ewes indicated that they remained in a rather restricted area where they grazed and rested, away from all other sheep. Domestic goats and sheep as well as various wild and captive caprids also withdraw prior to lambing from all conspecifics as has been noted by Haas (1958) for Barbary sheep,

Walther (1961) for various wild goats, urials, and argalis, Heptner et al. (1961) for Asiatic sheep, and Herscher et al. (1963) for domestic caprids.

Parturition. I did not observe a ewe give birth; however, good accounts have been published by Deming (1955) for captive Nelson's bighorns, Walther (1961) for captive urials, and Herscher et al. (1963) for domestic sheep and goats. Several days before lambing the ewe's udder enlarges and her genitalia appear swollen. The female becomes restless, her respiration rate increases, and her flanks appear sunken in front of her hips. Argali females pawed a bed before lying down to give birth in a prone position, a position assumed also by a urial ewe (Walther 1961) and bighorn ewes (Kennedy 1948). Simmons et al. (1963) noted that a bighorn ewe they observed shortly after parturition had scratched a bed, which is also done by domestic sheep (Herscher et al. 1963).

Birth begins with the rupture of the amnion, but several hours may pass before the lamb emerges. It normally appears with the head first and placed between extended front legs, while the ewe presses. The afterbirth which is not passed for several hours is eaten by the ewe. We know in only one instance how the umbilical cord broke. Walther (1961) noted that it broke when the lamb, unable to stand, crawled toward the head of the still resting mother.

Postpartum care of young. The lamb is dropped wet onto exposed ground in a cool surrounding with fluctuating air currents. As in domestic sheep, it probably leaves the birth canal at a temperature slightly higher than that of the ewe, and begins to cool rapidly (Alexander 1962b). Research on Australian range sheep by Alexander and his collaborators showed that lambs respond to cooling by increasing their metabolism to about five times basal (five times resting in infant caribou [Hart et al. 1961]). The energy for heat production comes primarily from the lamb's limited fat reserves, and the lamb must soon rise and suckle to replace the energy store lost, in order to sustain itself. Among lambs of domestic sheep, rapid cooling off right after birth is a major factor in their mortality (Alexander 1961a; Alexander et al. 1959; Alexander and Peterson 1961). It is hence most adaptive to reduce the heat loss of the lamb to a minimum and replenish its energy stores as soon as possible. Factors which favor the lamb's survival are to be born large, which gives a lower surface to mass ratio, to have a hairy rather than woolly coat, and to possess a large deposit of fat. Furthermore, the ewe should drop the lamb in a sheltered location, remove the moisture from its fur, massage its body to aid thorough circulation, and stimulate it into rising and suckling as soon as possible. The ewe's choice of cliffs as lambing habitat may be because here she finds shelter from winds.

Shortly after birth the ewe rises and begins to vigorously lick the lamb dry and remove amniotic fluid, mucus, and membranes from its body. She usually begins by cleansing the head (Herscher et al. 1963). Kirchshofer (1963) noted that it was the mother's licking which stirred antelope calves for the first time into life, while Herscher et al. (1963) noted that some domestic lambs not licked by the ewe died soon after birth without rising. Among the artiodactyla only the camelids (Krumbiegel 1954) and suids (Frädrich 1965, 1967) do not lick and dry the young right after birth. For suids it would hardly be necessary since the young are in no danger of freezing, as they are born either in dens or in large nests carefully built and roofed over by the sow. For camelids, particularly the vicuna in the cold, high Andes there is no satisfactory explanation how the young avoid cooling, born as they are when snow is still on the ground (Koford 1957).

The ewe's licking of her lamb fulfills another function. It appears to imprint her on her young, and all that is needed is 20–30 minutes of it to establish discrimination (Smith et al. 1966). Thereafter she accepts only her own lamb. The female recognizes its young by the odor of its anal and caudal glands as was demonstrated by Tschanz (1962) on mouflon lambs. His data also suggest that ewes recognize their lambs by their calls. Lindsay and Fletcher (1968) showed that ewes also could recognize their lambs by sight, while the lamb's call serves only to alert the ewe. The lamb learns to recognize its dam more slowly. It takes 3–4 days before it chooses correctly and selects its mother from among other sheep (Tschanz 1962). Caribou calves may have learned it by their second day of life (Lent 1966). Tschanz (1962) and Herscher et al. (1963) showed that lambs recognized their mothers primarily by sight; the lambs of domestic ewes which have just been shorn run about bewildered incapable of recognizing their dam. Grabowski's (1941) observations as well as my own indicated that lambs could also recognize their dam by her voice. The proof, however, is still outstanding.

Size of lamb.   Nelson's bighorn lambs stand at birth about 15 in high, while two newborn lambs weighed 8 lb and 8½ lb (3.6 and 3.9 kg) respectively (Hansen 1965). No other birth weights of North American sheep have been published to date; however, Mr. A. F. Oeming of the

Alberta Game Farm, Edmonton, kindly provided the following information: 9 bighorn lambs born at the farm weighed on the average 7.2 lb (6.2–8.2 lb) or 3.3 kg (2.8–3.7 kg), 5 Stone's lambs weighed 7.2 lb (6.5–8 lb) or 3.3 kg (2.9–3.6 kg), and 2 Dall's lambs weighed 6.9 and 7.8 lb (3.1 and 3.5 kg) respectively. Two newborn lambs of Siberian snow sheep caught by Cherniavski (1962*b*) weighed 7.7 and 8.2 lb. Since in domestic sheep birth weights and degree of development of lambs vary directly with the plane of nutrition (Wallace 1948; Schinkel and Short 1961) and the size of the female (Starke et al. 1958), and inversely with the severity of winter to which pregnant ewes are exposed (Robinson et al. 1961), the same will likely apply to mountain sheep. It is likely that 11–12 lb (5–5.5 kg) would be a maximum birth weight for bighorn sheep; they are probably born no smaller than argalis.

Seclusion period. The female remains in isolation close to the locality of birth for 5–7 days postpartum. Two Stone's ewes I observed stayed secluded for 6 or 7 days after birth, while Hansen (1965) found that desert bighorn females in captivity did not bring their lambs into the presence of man for 5–7 days after birth. At this time ewes tend to be quite shy as Murie (1944) noted, and the experimental work of Collias (1956), Liddell (1958, 1961), Alexander (1960), Tschanz (1962), and Herscher et al. (1963) indicates the significance of the ewe's shyness and her choice of seclusion and inaccessible terrain when the lamb is very small. If the female joined other sheep before its lamb had learned to recognize her, or if the female was separated from it shortly after birth for as little as one half hour, it is most likely that the lamb would suffer. It would fail to establish an exclusive bond with its mother, it would be butted by strange ewes more than normally, and it could become neglected and fail to achieve normal growth. Tschanz (1962) found that very young mouflon lambs followed any passing object, preferably the fastest one if there was a choice. The ewe's seclusion insures that when both move to join other sheep, the lamb has fully learned the mother's characteristics and is not likely to get lost. In domestic sheep "baby stealing" by ewes does happen, but the females are close together when lambing, which is an artificial situation (Alexander 1960; Herscher et al. 1963).

BEHAVIOR OF NEONATE AND EWE

During its first day, the lamb tends to be a little wobbly on its legs, but it is well developed; it jumps and frolics a little clumsily, but it can judge distance (see Gibson and Walker 1960). This was indicated when a 1-day-old Stone's lamb stopped in front of a crevice which its mother had just walked across, and after looking left and right walked around it. The lamb follows the ewe when the latter makes her minor excursions and does not hide as is typical of fawns (Dathe 1966) and the calves of various antelope and gazelles (Walther 1961, 1964, 1968). The true goats, however, may temporarily leave their young and retrieve them later, but the females are not far from their offspring and these apparently do not freeze, nor are they camouflaged like fawns (Collias 1956; Walther 1961). It appears to be typical for caprids and rupicaprids that their newborn usually follow and stay with their mothers (Walther 1961; Brandborg 1955; Holroyd 1967).

It is not known how soon lambs of American sheep rise after birth. In domestic sheep it is about 30 minutes, and half that time for kids of domestic goats (Liddell 1958); a urial lamb attempted to stand within 10 minutes after birth and succeeded after 25 (Walther 1961). Bubenik (1959) states that mouflon lambs walk 20 minutes after birth and run and jump 2–3 hours later. The lambs attempt to suckle as soon as possible, and their search for the udder is particularly intense during the first 2 hours after birth (Alexander and Williams 1966). These first attempts of the lambs are clumsy, poorly directed affairs. Walther (1961) observed newborns suckling on the mother's hair coat on the neck and front legs, and even on tree trunks before finally succeeding. There are no reports that the ewes guide and assist the young to the udder as Kirchshofer (1963) reported for some antelope females. The lamb during suckling pushes its snout vigorously into the ewe's udder and periodically quivers the tail while the ewe may arch her back slightly, spread the hind legs apart, and tense the belly. Rarely she lifts up the hind leg on the side from which the lamb suckles; this is the only aid to lamb I ever saw ewes give, and that only once in two lambing seasons.

Lambs suckle from the side and occasionally rear, but I never saw one suckle from the front while standing below the female and between her front legs, as I have seen mountain goat kids do. Older lambs may suckle while kneeling and occasionally when lying down. The ewe appears to signal her readiness to suckle by facing toward the lamb and calling, which is also done by domestic sheep (Scott 1945; Ewbank 1967) and ibex and markhor (Walther 1961). Lambs often run around the ewe's chest before diving under the udder as was also done by an argali lamb born in captivity (Walther 1961). This run-around is common to other ruminants also (Schloeth 1958) and is thought to be an action stopping the ewe. It occurred in bighorn sheep in 42% ($\text{N} = 72$) of the suckling intentions. Domestic lambs develop a preference for one side of the udder over the other (Ewbank 1964). While the lamb suckles the female nuzzles it quickly once or twice on the rump, but like argalis or urials, it does not lick the young extensively. Walther (1961) found that various goats were more prone to lick their young than sheep, but they did not do it as extensively as various deer and antelope (Walther 1964, 1968).

Contrary to antelope, gazelles, and deer, caprids apparently do not ingest the urine and feces of the newborn (Walther 1961). This would be essential in species in which the young are hidden from predators, since it would remove the evidence of the presence of the young. It would be part of the adaptations which make the young inconspicuous during its first weeks of life, such as hiding, remaining in a rigid position or "freezing" when danger approaches, a camouflage birth coat, a scent apparently unnoticeable to dogs (Johnson 1951) and presumably other carnivores, and rare visits by the mother. For sheep, such adaptations appear unnecessary. The lamb is born in rather inaccessible terrain from which the major predators such as wolves, bears, and coyotes are largely excluded. The lamb is born highly developed and capable of following its mother if need be within a day after birth; within a few days it becomes an incredibly agile, speedy little animal as Murie (1944) correctly and vividly described. The lamb is protected from its major predators by the terrain and its speed, and from minor predators, such as eagles, by its mother.

Suckling is very rarely terminated voluntarily by lambs in the wild. Like Smith (1954) and Blood (1963) I never saw a bighorn lamb quit suckling on its own, but I did record it in 8 of 84 suckling periods by Stone's lambs. It is most likely that lambs terminate suckling only when the ewes have an abundant milk supply. Usually the ewes terminate suckling (plate 71); in 76 instances ewes stepped over the lambs 45 times, turned away sharply on the spot 14 times, walked forward 13 times, and flexed the hind leg sharply 4 times. Domestic ewes act similarly (Ewbank 1967). Ewes discourage eager lambs from suckling in a similar manner, and lambs once rebuffed returned to their previous activity without persisting further in their attempts; Ewbank (1967) found that domestic lambs once discouraged would not attempt to suckle for up to an hour. I found that all attempts by lambs to suckle from resting ewes failed. One bighorn lamb whose dam lay ill with a broken leg, pawed the back and haunches of the ewe in its many attempts to get at her udder. This is also done by domestic lambs (Ewbank 1967). This big-horn lamb stole a few suckles from other ewes when these were nursing their lambs, but it was often butted away severely. Liddell (1961) made similar observations on a poorly mothered goat kid, which failed to grow properly and became a poor mother in turn. A major variable in the behavior of ewes and lambs appears to be the quality of the population; it seems to influence the frequency and duration of suckling and nuzzling. It appears to determine how often the lambs are rejected in their suckling attempts, how soon they are forced to feed on green forage, how aggressive the female is toward her offspring, how soon it is weaned, how lively the lamb, how well it grows, and how young it matures (see chap. 10).

The milk of bighorn sheep contains more fats and solids than that of domestic sheep (Chen et al. 1965; Baker et al. 1967), which would indicate that bighorns have the faster relative growth rate. However, proof is outstanding. The milk of bighorns appears to be similar to that of mouflons (see Bubenik 1959).

After the postpartum seclusion period, the ewe and her lamb leave the cliffs and move to the slopes where other sheep are found. The first appearance of a newborn lamb can cause great excitement among bar-ren ewes and subadults. This was well illustrated on the morning of 7 June 1962 when two Stone's ewes had come together for the first time after leaving their hideouts with their lambs. An old, barren ewe fol-lowed by a troupe of yearlings appeared on the slope. The old ewe stopped abruptly and stared at the lambs. She appeared tense and excited. Suddenly she crouched down and with her head and neck extended just above ground she crawled rapidly at a lamb. The little fellow hopped to its mother. The old ewe followed. Mother and lamb bolted. The old ewe followed at a run. The trio headed for the cliffs where they ran around, the old ewe still in her low-stretched posture. Finally the old ewe lay down and watched the lamb. A few moments later the lamb tried to suckle. At once the old ewe jumped to her legs and ran in a crouched posture toward the lamb. Again the lamb and its dam fled.

The yearlings showed their interest by crowding around the small lambs with their noses extended and following the ewe and lamb when these retreated. Even after the lamb has been in their company for a day or so, one yearling or another quits feeding and moves over to investigate it. I saw this among both Stone's and bighorn sheep. The ewes tend to be hostile to yearlings, particularly those that threatened or even butted a lamb, but the ewe's protection of the lamb wanes after a couple of weeks, and the ewe then ignores its lamb even when it is in trouble. However, when the lamb is small, the ewe offers some protection. Occasionally when an eagle appeared the ewe moved below a spruce tree with the lamb, and I have seen ewes jump and strike with their horns at diving eagles while the lambs stood below their mothers. Norman Tithrington, who kept a close watch on a band of sheep at Aylmer lookout in Banff National Park for seventeen summers, once saw a ewe hit an eagle. The raptor was hurled as a shapeless mass of feathers into the air and spun downhill, falling into a clump of alpine fir; it never rose. Walther (1961) noted that argali and urial ewes in captivity stood over their small lambs and stamped with a front leg when approached. So the ewe does attempt to protect the lamb when it is very small; however, most indications of concern soon disappear. The observations of Welles and Welles (1961) of a Nelson's ewe and her injured lamb illustrate how little the ewe is attached to her lamb. Domestic ewes exposed to severe climatic conditions may desert their lambs permanently (Spencer 1960, cited in Herscher et al. 1963). The behavior of female mountain goats differs drastically.

I have seen female mountain goats sprint from about 100 yards away to the aid of their young when the latter were threatened by subadults and chase the offenders away. Brandborg (1955) and Holroyd (1967) also noted how protective the female is of her young. This protection was still evident in females which were followed by yearlings. The behavior of the female mountain goat is, however, highly adaptive and necessary for the well-being of the young. Mountain goats carry short, very sharp horns which are highly dangerous weapons as autopsies of goats involved in fighting have shown (Geist 1965, 1967). One strike by a yearling could conceivably kill a kid; I have seen one kid with a round blood spot on its shoulder just like those which appear on goats punctured by a horn. Female mountain goats which protect their children obviously have a better chance of raising them than those which do not.

With sheep it is different. The horns of females and subadults are not lethal weapons, and the lambs are very agile and can easily escape. The female sheep is far too small to protect her lamb successfully from predators as can a cow moose, and it is evident that it is most adaptive for both to escape by running. The apparent lack of concern by the ewe for her sick or injured lamb may appear callous to us, but what can she do that would benefit the lamb? The best a ewe can do is supply milk abundantly so that the lamb can develop normally and just be close by, for her very presence appears to protect the lamb from trauma in dangerous situations unfamiliar to the young. This was well illustrated by the work of Liddell and Moore (see Liddell 1958, 1961) which showed that psychic trauma proved fatal to small lambs and kids when these were separated from their mother, but not if it occurred in her presence. Of course, one does observe often enough a ewe searching for her lamb and vice versa, running along, calling, and sniffing each appropriate sheep. A ewe whose little lamb was killed by a grizzly remained for three days close to where it died, and Walther (1961) noted that an argali ewe called and searched for its lamb for three days after its death. This behavior may indicate no more than painful milk pressure in the ewe's udder and her search for the appropriate subject to relieve it, while the searching lamb may be one which has not suckled for some time and is just plain hungry.

NURSERY BAND FORMATION AND DEPARTURE FROM THE LAMBING GROUNDS

Ewes with newborn young form nursery bands close to the lambing cliffs. In the Stone's sheep study area, such bands soon included the yearlings and barren ewes, while among bighorns in Banff National Park, females with small lambs formed and remained in separate bands. This same split has been reported for ibex by Nievergelt (1967) and Burckhardt (1961), while Walther (1961) noted that two argali ewes with lambs had a greater affinity for each other than for other sheep, as long as the lambs were small. For a short time after lambing one could observe two kinds of female bands among my bighorns, females with neonates and females with yearlings and 2-year-olds.

For about three weeks after lambing the nursery bands moved little. The bighorn ewes from Bare Mountain left the lambing ground for the first time when the lambs were about one month old. At Gladys Lake the Stone's ewes departed for the summer when the lambs were 3 weeks old. Blood (1963) observed that California bighorn ewes gave birth in early May and left the lambing grounds and wintering area in early June. It appears hence that after the 5–7-day seclusion period, the lambs remain for 3–4 weeks close to their birthplace in the company of ewes and lambs and then depart to the summer ranges. At this time the split in bighorn female bands into those with small lambs and those with older subadults disappeared.

The juvenile band. The nursery band consists of a cluster of lambs surrounded by widely dispersed grazing or resting ewes. The lambs soon form juvenile bands after entering nursery groups (plate 72), as is also typical of ibex and markhor (Walther 1961), cattle (Schloeth 1961a), elk (Altmann 1963), waterbuck (Kiley-Worthington 1965), and Uganda kob (Leuthold 1967). Smith (1954) noted correctly that lambs appear to have a greater affinity for each other than for their mothers. Hence the tendency of sheep to join others of equal body and horn size (Geist 1968a) begins early in life.

The lambs can act independently of the ewes. On a number of occasions a band of tame bighorn ewes came running to me in anticipation of salt, while the lambs remained behind as a group on the rocky slope. Eventually they joined the ewes. Hansen (1965) made similar observations on captive Nelson's bighorns; he wrote that young lambs tend to stay on familiar ground rather than follow their dam in some situations. The juvenile band roams about between the various ewes, associating with this and that female, or clumping about other elevated points such as logs, rock outcrops, or even myself when I stood behind the movie camera within a band. It appeared that the lambs made the choice with which adult they would associate. I found no evidence to support the view that females "baby-sit" lambs while others feed. If part of the ewe band left, the juveniles associated with the remainder; if all of the females left the lambs would hang back on familiar terrain and then gallop to join the band. Females did leave their lambs in the juvenile group and went off, sometimes a few miles away to a salt lick, to return hours later. On 30 June 1964 a band of bighorn ewes left for a salt lick, which was about two miles away, while their lambs remained behind on the mountain with two adult females and several yearlings. After $3\frac{1}{2}$ hours the ewes returned from the salt lick and, bleating, galloped toward their lambs. At other times these females visited the salt lick together with their lambs. It appears that ewe and lamb act rather independently of each other soon after the lamb's birth. The lamb associates with the ewe periodically to suckle, but otherwise it is much on its own. During the rut when the estrous ewe is chased about by eager rams, the lambs tend to remain with the nonestrous females; only rarely do they follow their dam.

The juvenile band is noticeable mainly when the female band is stationary and feeding. When all the ewes rest, the lambs tend to rest with their dam, usually close to her on the uphill side. When the female band is on the move, the lambs may follow as a group, or each behind a certain female. Scott (1945) found for domestic lambs that each lamb follows its mother, and the same is likely to be true for our native sheep. However, it appears that in domestic sheep the lamb sticks more closely to its dam than is the case among American sheep.

PLAY AND ITS EVOLUTIONARY SIGNIFICANCE

The lambs of American sheep are highly developed at birth and begin to play within a few hours afterward. The lamb may frolic around its mother or climb and jump on top of her. Small lambs have a great tendency to move about the ewe's head when she is feeding, which was also noted by Welles and Welles (1961). One small Stone's lamb accompanied its mother by hopping along with her in the cliffs. Suddenly it bounced on top of the walking ewe but fell off. Lambs in juvenile bands raced between rock outcrops on the slopes. On reaching the pinnacles they paused and suddenly, after a high leap into the air, dashed off again. This could be repeated over and over. Lambs sped to grazing ewes and subadults and proceeded to dart in zigzags between and beneath them. Some ewes and subadults attempted to butt passing lambs, a futile attempt, for the lambs raced past with incredible speed.

In social play, the lambs showed behavior patterns of overt aggression and sexual behavior but no displays or contact patterns (plate 73). They appeared to be born with such patterns as butting, mounting, clashing, and threat jumping, while other kinds of social behavior patterns are added gradually during ontogeny. The patterns mentioned are executed in a species-specific way at once by the youngest lamb. In 43 hours of observations of 3-week-old bighorn lambs, I saw them mount 20 times, butt and clash 23 times, and threat jump 11 times. The youngest lamb observed butting was 8 days old. It had associated with a second lamb a day prior to that. After the first butt, the lambs had an orgy of butting. The youngest lamb observed low-stretching was 6 months old. Haas (1958) found that butting and mounting predominates in the play of audad (*Ammotragus*) lambs.

Lambs could be persistent in performing one activity, apparently just after discovering it. This was evident after the lambs butted the first time, or in the case of the lamb which first began to paw the ground. It began pawing and interrupted this activity periodically to frolic. Lambs could also jump, kick, and frolic as a group on one spot as was also observed by Welles and Welles (1961). At other times lambs galloped back and forth along a strip cut in the soil, sliding downward with each jump while raising a cloud of dust.

Of what significance is play? We know that proper bone growth depends on the electric fields generated within bone, that these fields depend on the stress and torque put on bones (Bassett 1965), and these in turn on the activity of the animal. It follows that an optimally functioning skeleton is achieved only by animals which exercise frequently during their development. It may be that lambs which fail to play develop a weaker skeleton and suffer broken legs more frequently as adults than those that play extensively. However, no one knows. The surprisingly high frequency of broken legs among Banff bighorns, which is a low-quality population with somewhat listless lambs, is certainly suggestive.

Play has probably a more important role as a means of information gain—a developer of successful action and reaction programs to be stored in the individual's memory for later use. We can conceive of an individual sheep as a machine which in its useful lifetime must perform specific tasks lest it be discarded. Quite evidently such a machine is programmed before it goes into service, and it follows that programming (play) should be concentrated in the early life of the individual before it becomes an independent adult, and this is what one finds. In play the individual performs social and habitat behavior patterns, gains experience with conspecifics and the terrain, discards all actions which bring pain or trauma, and repeats what was found satisfying and successful. In case of emergency it is then preadapted to act in a manner which usually removes imminent danger; it acts quickly according to one of several programs stored in its central nervous system. Metzgar (1967) demonstrated with mice how much a set of stored action programs is worth to the survival of an individual. Deer mice were exposed to the predation of screech owls. Some of the mice were on familiar terrain, others on unfamiliar terrain during the experiment; the owl caught significantly more mice unfamiliar with the terrain. That sheep new to an area get lost in cliffs was described earlier (chap. 4).

Adult sheep play rarely. The huddles of rams had a playlike nature; in spring and early summer the rams occasionally bounced and frolicked over the hillsides and clashed with each other.[1] This could be observed particularly in the early morning, shortly after the rams rose. Stone's rams on the summer range that I observed in August 1961 performed exuberant running and jumping games in the cliffs each evening. Ewes play conspicuously less than rams. It can be seen now and

1. See film E 1333.

then how a band races and frolics across the slope for a short distance, then stops and feeds on as usual. Play was more common on cool than on hot days and most common in spring and rare in winter. The frequent aggressive interactions among rams appear necessary to maintain social predictability for the individual, be they performed as clashes in exuberant play or in short, terse interactions at the salt lick. As long as rams grow "brave" with age plenty of interactions with other rams must follow as a consequence. These in turn continue to "program" and "preadapt" the individual.

WEANING

Sometime between July and late September, depending on population quality, the lambs shed the light juvenile coats and now appear of similar color as adults. Birth coat shedding in domestic lambs is dependent on the degree of development of the lambs (Slee 1963). From their first week of life the lambs had nibbled on vegetation and this activity became more common with age. The lambs receive fewer and fewer suckles, but as yet we do not know how suckling duration and frequency decreases in mountain sheep in summer. In September, when the bighorn and Stone's lambs I observed were 3–4 months old, suckling was still common; in October it occurred occasionally; in November rarely. I observed the last suckling in December, although the lambs do attempt to reach the udder even in January but are warded off.

In spring 1964 I observed a female yearling in the Bare Mountain home range group attempt suckling successfully a number of times from one adult female. In June 1970 during a day's visit to the same poor-quality female group, I noted 5 out of 13 yearlings attempt suckling 11 times and succeeding once. It is not known if these yearlings each suckled from their mothers, or if they had been adopted by females that lost their lambs. In both springs there had been lambing failures, 7 lambs in 1964 and 3 lambs in 1970 being produced by about 30 and 38 females respectively. The small, poorly developed yearlings appeared to get some mothering in the absence of lambs during their second year of life. It appeared almost as if this poor-quality population channeled its limited resources for the benefit of its ill-developed juveniles in an attempt to conserve them. However, a simpler explanation does suffice, namely, that females bearing inviable lambs find willing recipients in the yearlings for their newly awakened maternal drive.

The weaning process is hence a gradual one. The ewe appears to lose all interest in the lamb thereafter and during severe winter weather may butt it away from some promising forage. The process of disassociation between mother and child probably begins now, but does not find expression till about March when the yearling lambs begin following sheep other than their mother. This process and what happens to the yearling lambs has already been described in chapter 4.

9 Habitat and Body Care Behavior

INTRODUCTION

One can conceive of mountain sheep as generalized mountaineers and specialized grazers, adapted to the boom and bust economy of the North. They grow, reproduce, and squander resources when these are superabundant in summer, but reduce energy waste when resources are scarce in winter. Large horns can probably evolve only where food is seasonally superabundant. Sheep differ little from mountain goats with which they share the same mountains. The goat is a more specialized rock climber with wider food habits than sheep and appears to be a little better adapted to handle deep snow. Sheep carry into winter a small, but apparently essential, fat or energy store; large, dominant rams may lose it during the rutting season. They avoid excessive heat loss in winter by moving to high elevations with warm air above thermoclines, by seeking shelter in caves at night where they may rest in groups, by reducing their surface area when resting, by being active in the warmest times of the day, probably by moving into sheltered localities when the wind is strong, and by searching out the sunlit areas of mountains just as ibex do. When feeding, sheep appear to maximize intake over energy expenditure. They work as little to get as much of the most digestible food as possible. Thus they do not paw to remove snow from forage as long as some stalks and seed heads are protruding; they do not paw in hard and crusty or wet and slushy snow but in soft snow, and they search out terrain cleared of snow by wind, avalanches, or sunshine. They feed selectively, plucking or pulling rather than biting off vegetation, apparently preferring seed heads to leaves or blades and these to stems. In so doing they obtain the more digestible parts of plants, which have a greater rate of passage than more fibrous plant matter, and of which they can consume more. The maximum food intake is controlled in ruminants by the passage of food through the digestive tract, and is hence directly related to forage digestibility. At the level of maximum food intake sheep cannot compensate for

256

energy loss by eating more forage but only by eating better forage. Rams tend to be more solitary in winter than in spring, summer, and fall; they reduce social activity, avoid movement through deep snow if possible, and in walking on hard crusts spread their legs and place hooves and dewclaws simultaneously on the surface to distribute their weight. Sheep wintering areas appear to be considerably warmer than are valley bottoms at lower elevations.

An organism, like a machine, must not only be fueled, but also maintained and cleaned if it is to function at peak efficiency. The comfort movements appear to be part of these adaptations. Sheep carry a coat of dense underhair and long, brittle guard hair which is largely rubbed off in spring during the major molt. Since the hair does not drop out easily, the comfort movements of sheep are characterized by much rubbing as the animals try to get rid of the coat; by contrast, mountain goats do not rub or only rarely. It appears that comfort movements evolve largely independent of habitat and social adaptations and are determined by the type of hair coat grown by the animal and the instruments at its disposal for cleaning the skin surface. One of the by-products of body care behavior, resting, and social activities of mountain sheep are large erosion sites on the hills which sheep perpetuate.

Habitat Behavior

As noted earlier, mountain sheep can be seen as rather generalized mountaineers who roam over all typical alpine terrain, who are capable of running at great speed over short distances, who jump rather than climb through cliffs in flight, who are specialized to live on abrasive, dry, often dusty plants, and who can economize their energy expenditure in winter. Their habitat behavior is best illustrated by contrasting it with that of the mountain goat which may share the same mountains with sheep. The goat is a muscular, apparently phlegmatic climber adapted to steep, snow- and ice-covered cliffs and it has rather wide food habits.

Locomotion

Mountain sheep and goats, like probably all mountain- and forest-living bovids, are normal cross-walkers; plains-dwelling ruminants such as gazelles, South American camelids, or giraffes are pacers as long as they are on unobstructed terrain (Walther 1966). During trotting or on broken terrain gazelles assume the common cross-walk again. Asiatic sheep, however, may pace on occasion, as I observed urials and mouflons do so in zoological gardens.

Unlike the mountain goat, sheep readily run, jump, and frolic. Mountain goats, in line with their adaptations as methodical climbers, rarely jump or run, and even when disturbed usually escape at a fast walk. The movements of the mountain goat are almost bearlike, since the legs are heavily muscled and terminate in short metatarsals and metacarpals and in broad, massive hooves. These are very flexible legs, which can be extended far or flexed till the brisket almost touches the ground on which the hooves are placed. Goats and sheep react quite differently to slipping in cliffs. Sheep which lost a foothold jumped away and landed on a foothold below. Two goats that I observed slip instantly spread their legs apart, flattened themselves against the rock, and clawed for footholds as they slid down. Goats appear capable of surviving some very bad falls in cliffs. Holroyd (1967) saw two newborn kids fall and roll 30 feet down a steep cliff but get up and walk away right after landing; I observed a shot, large male fall and bounce down a steep cliff for 150 feet and live after landing. The only mountain sheep which I knew fell for some distance was an old ram who lost his footing on a steep slope covered by hard snow. He slid 450–500 yards, broke his back and neck in the process, but was still alive one hour later.

There is no data demonstrating the jumping and running abilities of mountain sheep; however, their abilities to jump appear to be considerable. I have seen a large bighorn ram in captivity jump from the stance through a hole in the wall which was $7\frac{1}{2}$ feet (228 cm) above ground. Walther (1961) noted that captive argalis and urials were not very good climbers and jumpers compared with ibex and did not jump across fences which were 150 cm (60 in) high. The good climbing and jumping abilities of mountain sheep, as well as their flight into cliffs upon disturbance, correlates with their ibexlike body structure.

On crusted snow, mountain sheep spread their legs and place dewclaws and hooves simultaneously on the snow surface. They act a little like caribou by distributing their weight over a greater area of snow. After the first heavy snowfalls in October, I observed Stone's sheep bound through the deep snow, whereas mountain goats plowed steadily through it at a walk. Jumping through snow is not commonly resorted to by either sheep or mountain goats and occurs mainly when the animals are mired in deep snow. Sheep and goats avoid areas of deep snow and cross through cliffs or along rock outcroppings between areas of favorable terrain.

Resting

Before sheep lie down, they usually scratch in the bed with a foreleg. This removes rocks and pebbles which have rolled down the slope and come to lie on the resting site. Walther (1961) correctly pointed out that sheep show little insight when pawing, for they paw on any substrate prior to resting be it sheer rock, soft grass, or a concrete plate.

Sheep lie down similarly to deer by first going down in front and then in the rear. This subject has been treated comparatively by Zannier-Tanner (1965). During warm weather sheep often rest with legs extended, but during cold weather they draw their legs tight against the body. This is understandable for sheep have the poorest insulation on the inner side of the upper parts of the legs.

The prerequisite for bedding is a level area large enough to hold a sheep. The same beds are used over and over. In contrast to this, moose rarely use the same bed twice in winter. They appear to prefer deep, fluffy snow to rest in, apparently using the snow as an insulation to conserve body heat (Des Meules 1964). Moose slump into snow and partially bury themselves. Des Meules noted that moose left an area once the snow was trampled and searched out areas with fluffy, deep snow. I never saw sheep use snow in this manner.

Sheep tend to rest together. In late winter and spring they may rest high in the cliffs at night but on the lower slopes during the day. The repeated use of the beds and the frequent urinations and defecations by sheep and mountain goats on the bedding sites have an effect on the vegetation. Grass grows more vigorous below bedding sites and is darker in color than that on the slopes nearby. In early spring the first grass tends to sprout around the rim of sheep beds, and for a couple of weeks in the mountains about Gladys Lake the beds can be identified at long distance as green spots on the mountains.

Adaptations to Avalanches and Rockslides

The foremost danger in mountains comes from avalanches and rockslides, and the steep, rugged mountains on my Stone's sheep study area were particularly blessed with these hazards. All avalanches I saw were wet snow avalanches which came down during warm afternoons in April and May. They announced their coming by thunderous rumbling and in all cases followed along deep avalanche gorges. Rockslides also marked their descent with loud rumbling, but unlike avalanches, rockslides whirled across slopes and gorges and did not follow as predictable a route as avalanches.

Sheep reacted to the loud rumble by jumping to their feet and at once looking uphill. The moment a bouncing rock or an avalanche appeared they bolted across the slope and then stopped to watch the descent of the rockslide or avalanche. One small group of rams which I filmed, rigidly stood and watched an avalanche cascade past them a bare 30 paces away. It appeared on a number of occasions that sheep only ran as far as was necessary to avoid falling rock. As could be expected, sheep also jump out of the way of rocks trod loose by companions. In response to low-flying small aircraft Stone's sheep ran into cliffs (see plate 3).

Indirect evidence indicates that mountain goats react somewhat differently to avalanches and rockslides. In response to loud noises, such as rifle shots, goats were observed to run to cliffs, preferably with overhangs, and press their sides against the rock wall. They were observed to react in a similar manner to the loud drone of a bush plane rising from Gladys Lake. This indicates that mountain goats head for cover when they hear a loud rumbling which normally signals an avalanche. Though I did not see mountain sheep crouch against rock walls in the same manner, true goats will do it. In summer 1965, a hand-raised domestic goat demonstrated it convincingly. When a sudden hail shower descended, the animal jumped upon a verandah and pressed itself against the house wall. The animal appeared excited and urinated. I pulled the goat off the verandah, but the moment I let go, it jumped back up and again crouched against the house wall. Walther (1961) reports that ibex and markhor fled in response to low-flying aircraft into their shelters.

Mountain sheep showed no conspicuous reaction to strong winds, storms, or drifting snow. On one stormy day (7 January 1963) snow-devils formed and whirled across the slopes. Sheep approached by these whirling snow masses bolted for the cliffs. Soon they were engulfed, but emerged still galloping. They never left the cliffs that day.

Adaptations to Winter

Wintering mountain sheep typically reduce waste of energy by avoiding excessive heat loss and excessive energy expenditures in foraging and social life, while maximizing energy gain and retention for the lowest possible expenditure. In addition, circumstantial evidence indicates that fat stores accumulated in late summer and fall help sheep survive in winter, unless these stores are used up in active rut. Most of the evidence conforms to this hypothesis.

The sheep's major adaptation against cold appears to be its coat, for domestic sheep shorn of wool are as sensitive to temperature as a naked man (Armstrong et al. 1959). In addition to the coat, there are behavioral adaptations which appear to help sheep in heat conservation. In cold weather resting sheep bunch their legs underneath them, thereby reducing the body's surface area, or they seek shelter. The Sanctuary rams regularly frequented one of two caves at night during the winter of 1961/62 but did not do so in spring and early summer. Other sheep rested in crevices of cliffs when first seen on cold winter mornings. Nievergelt (1966a) demonstrated that ibex prefer in winter

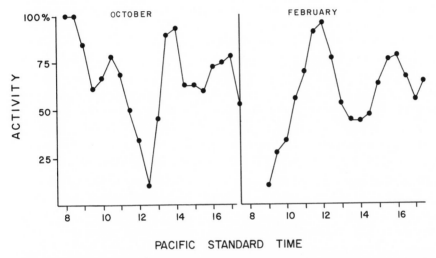

Fig. 31. Diurnal activity of Stone's rams in October and February. The October activity pattern reflects the normal pattern of four activity peaks, which was also observed in mountain goats. The February pattern may reflect the ram's avoidance of the cold morning hours.

the parts of the mountain exposed to sunlight and that ibex withdraw to sheltered areas as the wind velocity they are exposed to increases. It is very likely that mountain sheep act similarly. Furthermore, they appear to prefer the warmest elevations on the mountains, keeping in the warm air above the thermocline (see below), while concentrating their activity into the warmest part of the day.

Figure 31 illustrates the drastic change in the daily activity pattern of Stone's rams from October to February. In fall (as well as in summer) rams were out early in the morning and feeding low on the slopes. There were several successive feeding periods; the activity peaks indicate an average of four per day. In February (and January) the activity pattern is almost reversed. There was little feeding in the morning; the first major activity peak occurred at noon so most feeding was done after noon. In general, this was also true for Stone's ewes and mountain goats in December and January (fig. 32), and to a lesser extent for California bighorns, observed by Blood (1963) in southern British Columbia with its milder winters. Arnold (1962) studying domestic sheep in Australia also found that these reduced the number of feeding periods in winter with its short days and changed from a pattern of a major period at morning and night to one of reduced activity on winter mornings and increased activity on afternoons. Domestic sheep, Stone's rams and ewes, California bighorns and their distant relative the mountain goat hence tended to act similarly. Arnold's work showed that this shift in activity away from the morning in winter is not likely a response to cool morning temperatures. Nevertheless, such an activity pattern would place most of the activity of wintering sheep into the warmest part of the day. It remains to be demonstrated that sheep choose not only the warmest place but also the warmest hours.

A comparison of mountain goat and Stone's sheep activity (fig. 32) reveals a most peculiar difference between these species. Mountain goats search out and occupy a resting place in the cliffs before dusk; sheep generally do not. While sheep are active when night falls, the goats are resting by that time. The goats I observed moved away from the cliffs at noon to feed low on the slopes primarily on alpine fir (see fig. 35), and then retired to the cliffs before dusk. Here they could be located again on the following morning unless it had been a bright night. By contrast, sheep were still widely dispersed at nightfall, although they too could be found somewhere in the cliffs on the following morning. Arnold (1962) found that domestic sheep grazed extensively at night, and mountain sheep are likely to do the same.

These data suggest that mountain goats may be reluctant to move about at night, and maybe have worse vision at night than sheep. Mountain sheep do live north of the Arctic Circle, but not mountain goats; a cliff dweller must probably see where he steps. Goats did leave their bedding sites and wandered off during bright moonlight, and during most nights the individuals changed bedding sites.

The major changes in the activity of sheep from fall to winter appear to reflect the animals' preference for warmth, while the extended feeding periods may reflect the difficulties of sheep in obtaining sufficient forage in a short time. Other activity changes were minor. Social activities

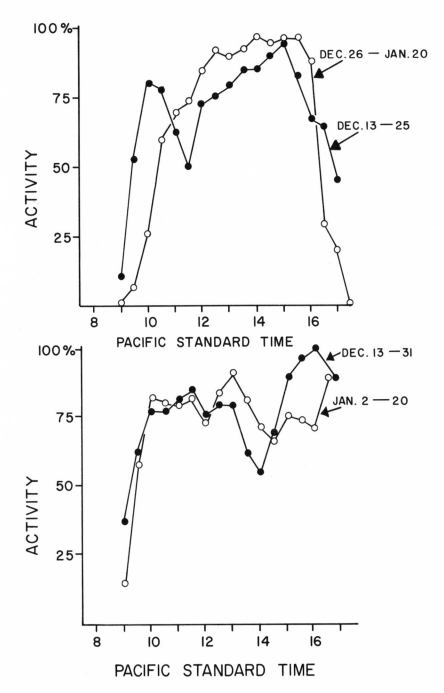

Fig. 32. Daily activity patterns of, *top*, mountain goats and, *bottom*, female Stone's sheep in December and January. In both species activity shifts away from the cold morning period.

are at the lowest ebb in winter, while the Stone's rams I observed entered a solitary existence (chap. 7).

Pruitt's investigations (1959, 1960) on the relationship of snow to caribou behavior stimulated me to do the same with sheep. The manner in which sheep respond to snow cover indicates that they avoid excessive energy expenditures. Snow covers the food supply and sheep must either remove it before they can feed or move to localities where no snow is present. Snow does not remain consistent in density throughout the winter. In fall and early winter it is generally fluffy; by midwinter it has increased in density and crusts form on areas exposed to sun; in late winter when temperatures begin to reach 32° F (0° C) in the day, snow melts and is frozen hard at night. Hence an impenetrable blanket of snow forms on most slopes. There is not only a hard crust on top, but often an ice pan on the bottom as well. This ice pan may well be formed by seepage of the first meltoff in the cliffs. The result is that in late winter most of the sheep's food supply is locked beneath a blanket of rock-hard snow and ice and is unattainable for the animals. It was noted earlier that sheep respond to this situation by dispersing into the cliffs where because of sun and wind most of the snow is removed early. In fall and early winter sheep tend to clip off feed which protrudes above the snow, and resort to snow removal only when the forage is entirely covered. If they have a choice they appear to prefer feeding on windswept ridges and on slopes cleared of snow by snowslides and avalanches, rather than pawing away snow. In general, they appear to dig for food only when they have no other choice.

Mountain sheep and mountain goats remove snow both by pushing it aside with their snouts and by pawing it away. Not all ruminants do this. Cattle do not scratch away snow but push it aside with the snout only. The same is true for the goral (Heptner et al. 1961). Asiatic mountain sheep paw snow away only rarely (Heptner et al. 1961) and this characteristic is apparently still present in domestic sheep of mouflon origin, for Grubb and Jewell (1966) report that these rarely paw snow aside.

Like caribou (Pruitt 1960), mountain sheep paw in a rather stereotyped manner compared with mountain goats. They assume a preparatory stance, oriented with their head uphill and the body across the slope. With a few powerful strokes they throw the snow downhill, forming a crater in front of their muzzle (plate 74). Mountain goats are more flexible; they push, pull, or throw snow with their hooves and even reach under snow crusts. Some goats placed a hoof beside the muzzle and kept it there enlarging the crater as required between a few mouthfuls of herbs. Intensely feeding sheep dig a crater every few feet, forming a distinctive feeding pattern which can be quickly identified at a distance or from an aircraft as a sign of sheep.

The pawing behavior of sheep changed in a peculiar manner with snow depth. To investigate how pawing rates changed with snow depth, an estimate of snow depth at the feeding site was essential. Such

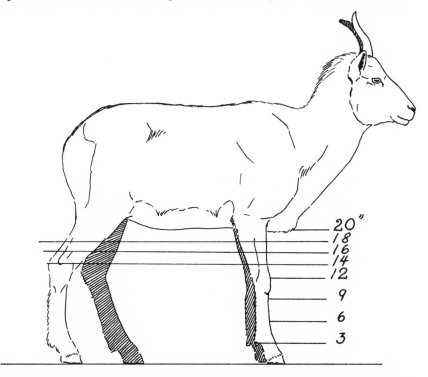

Fig. 33. An approximation of the depth of snow that a sheep is standing in can be obtained by using the sheep's anatomy. The approximate heights (in inches) of snow judged against the brisket and various joints of a Stone's ewe are shown here.

estimates were obtained by using the animals themselves as measuring sticks. Figure 33 illustrates the relationship of snow depth to the various joints on hind and front legs of a female Stone's sheep. By noting whether the snow blanket was above, below, or on a certain joint a reasonably accurate estimate of snow depth was obtained. The number of scratches in each series of scratches, or "bout," were counted, as well as the number of bouts; and the time spent feeding and not feeding was recorded. It was found that as snow depth increased so did the number of scratches within a series (fig. 34). The relationship is almost identical for female and male Stone's sheep and female mountain goats (only a little data was gathered for male mountain goats as few were seen on the study area). However, the rate of pawing did not show this relationship.

The data shown in figure 35 was obtained from the same animals from the same mountain, in the period between 27 and 31 December 1962. Deep snow prevailed, while temperatures ranged between

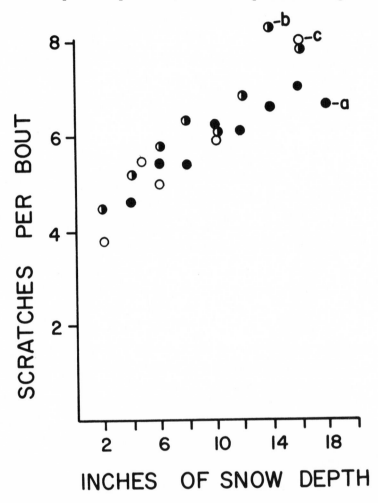

Fig. 34. The number of scratches in a series, or bout, increases with the snow depth in an almost identical manner for (a) Stone's ewes, (b) Stone's rams, and (c) female mountain goats.

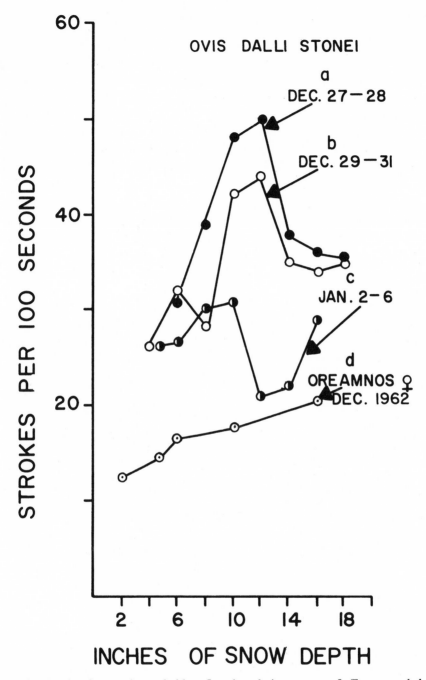

Fig. 35. Pawing frequencies probably reflect the relative amount of effort expended by female Stone's sheep and mountain goats when foraging. Most pawing by sheep was not done in very deep snow, but rather in snow 10–12 in deep. Goats on the same mountain as the ewes pawed considerably less at each snow depth compared. Graphs *a*, *b*, and *c* represent ewes; graph *d* represents goat females.

$-12°$ F to $-57°$ F. Then a thaw set in between 1 and 6 January 1963, and a maximum temperature of $38°$ F was recorded. It can be seen that during the cold days, the ewes observed pawed less in snow that was 2–6 and 14–18 in deep than in snow 10–12 in deep. The data for that period is consistent as shown by the two curves. Once the warm period came, pawing rates again changed. It is evident from this figure that the relationship of pawing rates to snow depth is complex, and as yet allows no firm conclusion. Mountain goats pawed consistently less than sheep. Since they used the same number of scratches per bout as sheep (fig. 34), mountain goats space their scratching in time more than mountain sheep. Similarly, in deep snow, sheep pawed extensively but spaced out their bouts of pawing more; they may have cleaned out the crater more thoroughly of forage before pawing again. Mountain goats pawed little more in deep snow than in thin snow (fig. 35).

Foraging

From the studies of Arnold (1960a, 1960b, 1962), we know that domestic sheep are very selective grazers, choosing not only specific plants but also preferring leaves and blades over stems. They hence prefer the more digestible parts of plants. Similar observations can be made on wild sheep. When grazing they do not bite off grass blades so much as pull them out. After the sheep plucks a mouthful of grass, not only can the green blades be seen protruding from its mouth, but also the soft, white, and, to us, sweetish-tasting lower parts of the blades. If sheep bit off rather than pulled out grass blades, they would presumably deprive themselves of its most nutritious part. If this is valid, then a pulling or plucking type of grazing increases the nutritional content of each mouthful. The consequences of this type of grazing remain to be investigated.

After the first severe frosts but before major snowfalls, Stone's sheep descended low in the valleys and often moved to gravel fans deposited by creeks where they fed extensively on the frozen leaves of various herbs and the seed heads of *Heracleum*. Occasionally mountain goats did the same and fed with sheep far away from the sheltering cliffs. Murie (1944), observing Dall's sheep in Alaska, reported much the same. The frost made available plants that sheep did not feed on when still green. Once deep snow covered the ground, sheep moved up to the grassy slopes and thereafter to the high country, as described earlier. In late fall they subsisted more on herbs and the leaves of shrubs, while in late winter they fed more on grasses and sedges, probably because they can obtain nothing else. Mountain sheep were very rarely observed feeding on conifers, except junipers, whereas mountain goats regularly did so (table 65). A detailed study of the food habits of sheep throughout the yearly cycle is still outstanding, although many range studies have been done. Cherniavski (1967) published a good report on the food habits of snow sheep in eastern Siberia.

The feeding mountain goat appears to fill the rumen at first rapidly and to become a more selective feeder thereafter. It can be seen in figure 36 that during the first half of the feeding period goats consume

TABLE 65
Feeding time of mountain goat spent on conifer browse

	Ghost Mt.	Sanctuary Mt.
Total feeding points	1,561	553
Conifer feeding points	367	162
% of feeding spent on conifer browse	21.6	29.4

NOTE: Ghost Mt. had few patches of alpine fir; Sanctuary had many.

primarily alpine fir and concentrate on other forage plants thereafter. The same principle is also reported for cattle by Hafez and Schein (1962) but has apparently not yet been reported for sheep.

Studies of the control of food intake and grazing behavior of domestic sheep have shown that grazing time decreases and food intake increases with pasture quality (Arnold 1960a, 1960b, 1962); the better the forage the more sheep eat and the less they graze. Blaxter et al. (1961) have shown that sheep appear to feed to a given distension of their digestive tract. The emptier the tract prior to feeding, the more sheep feed. However, the degree of fill depends on the rate of forage digestion and passage. Hence, food intake depends directly on the rate of passage of food, and it in turn is directly related to food quality. The higher the total digestible content of a food, the more rapidly it passes and the more sheep can feed on it. The maximum total bulk food intake of a sheep is directly related to the digestibility of that food. Therefore, the amount of energy a sheep can liberate for maintenance in severe cold or for reproduction and growth is directly related to the quality of forage available to it. Under extremely cold temperatures, for instance, sheep cannot compensate for energy loss by eating more of the same food, but only by eating better food. It can be predicted from the hypothesis of Blaxter et al. (1961) that mountain sheep in mid- and late winter will probably have a smaller food intake than in fall or early winter. Such a reduction in food intake in late winter when consuming poor-quality browse has been reported for moose (Heptner and Nasimovitsch 1968). It may well be caused by the slow passage rate of poor forage. Nevertheless there may be some additional factor, for captive mule deer (*Odocioleus hemionus*), fed ad lib on a high-plane

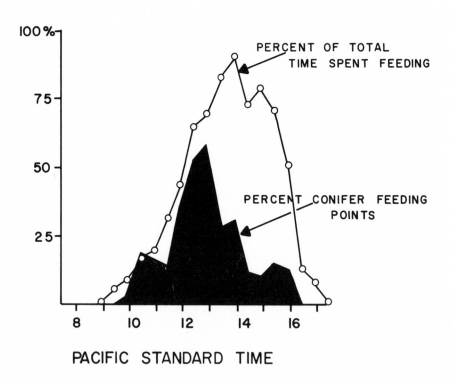

Fig. 36. Feeding activity of mountain goats in December and January. Feeding on conifers (alpine fir) takes place primarily in the beginning of the diurnal feeding period.

diet, lose weight or cease growing in winter (Wood et al. 1962) and reduce food intake (Cowan, personal communication). The same has been reported by French et al. (1960) for white-tailed deer and by Heptner and Nasimovitsch (1968) for moose. From the foregoing it follows that sheep can survive in the warm south on qualitatively much poorer forage than in the Arctic or in cold mountain ranges where sheep probably suffer a high heat loss in winter. Russian work cited by Cherniavski (1967) indeed indicates that forage consumed by snow sheep is exceedingly nutritious.

I did not study the utilization of salt licks by sheep, but it appeared that sheep were most eager to get at salt and visited salt licks primarily in late spring and early summer. This is made comprehensible by the following findings of Russian scientists on reindeer; it appears that during winter the skeleton is raided for its deposits of mineral salts which are scarce in the forage. The periosteum promotes dissolution in winter and deposition in summer when forage with an adequate mineral supply is consumed. Hence the skeletal elements become progressively lighter in winter and more porous, while the incidence of bone fracture reaches its peak in late spring (Nikolaevski 1961; Preobrazhenskii 1961). The skeleton hence appears to function as a reserve of mineral salts, and it appears reasonable that growing, molting, and lactating ungulates attempt to restore the lost deposits at the winter's end and also satisfy the now increased demands of the body.

A Comparison of Wintering Mountain Goats and Sheep

Compared to Stone's sheep at Gladys Lake, mountain goats preferred cliffs and did not venture far on open slopes. Whereas the Sanctuary Mountain rams were sighted in up to 52% of all instances on the open slopes below the cliffs (see chap. 10, table 69), I never saw one goat on that slope between January and March 1962. From 412 sheep in mid-winter 28% were in sheer cliffs, but from 147 goats it was 52%. These data are in line with the general adaptive syndrome of goats as specialized rock climbers.

Goats were more catholic in food habits, feeding extensively on alpine fir (*Abies lasiocarpa*) which was shunned by sheep. In 1,561 observations of feeding goats on Ghost Mountain, 21.6% fed on alpine fir; of 553 such observations from Sanctuary Mountain, 29.4% were on alpine fir. Although alpine fir obviously served as the major filler for goats descending to feed in the morning (fig. 36), it remained a favorite food even after chinooks cleared the ground of snow; goats would still dig down and uncover stands of low crawling fir, while sheep noticeably concentrated on cleared land. However, goats spent only one third of their feeding time or less on alpine fir and devoted the remaining time to foraging on other plants.

Goats pawed conspicuously less frequently than sheep, which is also reflected in the graphs of figure 35, by spacing their pawing bouts. They pawed less at comparable snow depths than sheep (fig. 35), which may indicate that deep snow is less a problem to them than to sheep. They were more phlegmatic than sheep and rested more during the day (table 66) but like sheep pushed their major activity period into the afternoon (fig. 36). They were less sessile than sheep and apparently could walk on softer snow crusts than sheep, which allowed them to disperse earlier in winter (plate 75).

TABLE 66
Time budget of Stone's ewes and female mountain goats, December and January

	Goats	Sheep
Total observation points	5,721	5,122
% of activity during daylight	63	72
% of day spent feeding	45	57
% of day spent resting	37	28

It does not appear that goats are a serious competitor for sheep as long as sheep get most of their forage from the open slopes and ridges. However, sheep could suffer if they depended exclusively on cliff terrain as a feeding ground in late winter and if the absence of alpine fir forced goats to feed extensively on grasses and herbs.

Winter Temperatures on a Bighorn Sheep Wintering Area

During many climbs into sheep country in mid- and late winter, it appeared to be noticeably warmer at higher elevations where sheep were found, than at the valley bottom. Together with the activity data, this observation indicated that sheep chose the warmest regions in the mountains. In Banff National Park it proved possible to test this view. With the kind help of Dr. J. M. Powell, three hygrothermographs were obtained on loan and erected along the valley and mountain slopes. Unfortunately a continuous temperature record was not obtained

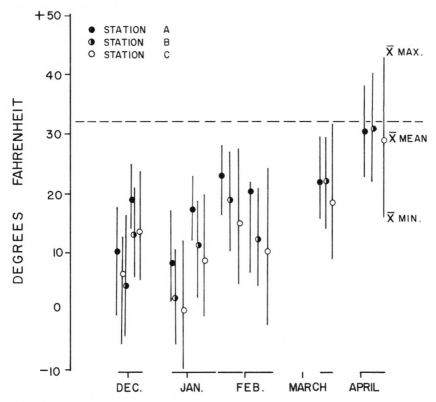

Fig. 37. Temperature characteristics at stations A, B, and C. On the winter range of sheep (A) temperatures averaged in midwinter higher than in the forest (B) and open valley (C), which were about 1,000 ft lower and one-half mile away. Temperature variations were greatest in the open valley, and least on the open slopes of the sheep range. In March the mean maximum temperatures of the day approach 32° F. This marks the beginning of rock-hard snow crusts on the mountain slopes.

since some of the hygrothermographs failed to function during very cold weather. For this reason figure 37 shows data only for those periods in which all three hygrothermographs were operating.

The first hygrothermograph (station A) was placed at 6,400 ft elevation, low on the open southwest-facing slope of the Palliser Range, just above Stoney Creek, facing the Cascade River. Station B lay at 5,600 ft elevation, about one half mile downhill from station A, in a stand of lodgepole pine. Station C, at 5,400 ft elevation, lay about 300 paces downhill from B in an open flat, about 100 paces from the Stoney Creek bridge. The instruments were housed in white, wooden shelters. Station C stood 4½ ft above ground, and in late winter about 1½ ft above the snow; B stood 1 ft above ground in deep shade. Although snow reached halfway up the box, the instruments remained in contact with the air above ground. Station A stood fully exposed 1 ft above the rocky slope. The instruments were serviced once a week, except during a two-week period in February when I was absent from the study area.

Figure 37 shows the average mean, minimum, and maximum temperatures averaged for each two-week period of recording from 24 November 1964 to 11 April 1965. Temperature variations during the 24-hour day are shown in figure 38, averaged for each of the three stations for the period 16–31 January 1965. From this data it is evident that from late November until March the average mean, minimum, and maximum temperatures were higher on the sheep range than lower down the valley. The daily minimum temperatures on the sheep range and at valley bottom differed from as little as 3.5° to 20° F, those on the sheep range being higher. However, during a cold snap the mini-

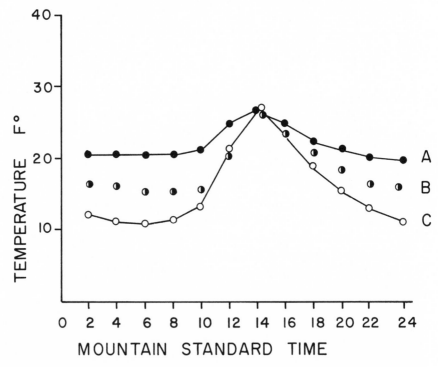

Fig. 38. Temperature fluctuations during the day on a bighorn sheep range (A), in the forest below (B), and in the open valley below (C). The stations differed primarily in the minimum temperatures. Early morning was the coldest part of the day. Data from 16–31 January 1965.

mum temperature at all three stations was alike, −31° F. The temperatures on the sheep range were more even; differences between minimum
and maximum daily temperatures ranged between 10° and 17° F,
but at the valley bottom between 20° and 27° F. During midwinter
it was considerably warmer 1,000 ft above the valley floor than in the
valley. It is evident then that moose in the Cascade Valley lived under
a harsher temperature regime than sheep on the slopes above.

Figure 37 also shows that maximum daily temperatures began to reach
the thawing point (32° F) in March. From this time on daily thawing
and nightly freezing often made the snow hard as rock.

Erosion Sites

The habitat behavior of sheep has some visible effects on the mountains
they inhabit. Foremost among these are erosion sites on the slopes,
bedding areas, and areas on ridges where rams congregate during social
interactions. The erosion sites are most likely started by grizzly bears
digging for ground squirrels, but they are perpetuated and enlarged by
sheep. Grizzly diggings create small, horizontal platforms of soft dirt
which are favored as resting places by sheep (plates 76 and 77). Since
sheep frequently paw the bedding place before lying down, they
enlarge the original erosion area. A small wall is usually formed on
the uphill side of the erosion site (plate 76). This is a favorite spot for
sheep to rub off their winter coat during late spring and summer (plate
78). Whole bands galloped and frolicked from as far as a quarter mile
to erosion sites and proceeded to vigorously rub their sides, shoulders,
and rears on the dirt walls. Such activities can only increase erosion.

During group interactions rams are found usually on small patches
of level ground—either erosion sites or ridgetops—where their frequent
activity leaves dusty patches of bare ground about 10 ft in diameter
which emit the strong odor of urine. Well-worn trails converge on these
arenas along which ram bands may race and frolic to clash and display
once the arena is reached.

BODY CARE BEHAVIOR

The peculiarities in the comfort movements of sheep appear to be
related to certain characteristics of their hair coat. Sheep have long,
brittle guard hairs underlain by an abundance of fine wool. In fall when
the coat is fully grown, it is at its darkest and the hairs often form waves
on the backs of sheep (plate 41). During the course of the winter the
coat grows lighter in color: a bighorn ram that is dark brown in fall

may be creamy yellow in spring. The coat may become so bleached that the white rump patch fails to stand out (plates 78 and 80). The hair is so brittle that a sheep walking through thick shrubbery may leave a spray of broken hairs in its wake.

Unlike mule deer, mountain sheep appear to have only one molt per year. Ryder (1960) found that mouflons had one conspicuous spring molt when the primaries (guard hairs) and the secondaries (wool) are shed and that a second peak of primary shedding appears in fall. The same may be true for American sheep; however, I have only noticed a spring molt despite the fact that I worked closely with tame sheep year round.

The molt in spring is a striking event. The hair comes off in matted bunches and may hang like towels about the sheep (plate 79). The first signs of molt, usually on the withers, appear in March, but the shedding is not complete until July. The molt seems to proceed bilaterally as in domestic sheep. During the molt, sheep occasionally show frantic comfort movements, which indicate that the loss of hair is associated with some discomfort.

The most common comfort movement in spring is body rubbing (plate 80). Sheep go to rock outcroppings, dead trees, small bushes, fields of coarse rubble, or erosion sites and proceed to rub hard against the rough surfaces. They polish their sides, shoulders, and rear ends back and forth against the obstacle. The hair is not always rubbed off, but sometimes broken off, resulting in strips and spots of old hair bases still firmly embedded in fields of newly growing ones (plate 56). I have never seen elk, deer, or moose act as sheep do, but neither do these cervids have a molt in which the matted guard hair and wool come off in strips and decorate the countryside wherever they go. From 650 comfort movements by rams in spring 1964, 263 (40.5%) were body rubbing.

The molt is greatly accelerated on the withers of small-horned sheep, probably because of the presence of the tick *Dermacentor andersoni*. Sheep scratch their withers with their horn tips and remove hair and scabs. The whole upper shoulder may be laid open and be covered by small scabs, round whitish marks where ticks apparently attached, broken brushes of guard hair, plus engorged or actively crawling ticks (plate 81). The ticks were surprisingly loose in the skin. Those which I plucked out came away with a scab. Wither scratching with a horn was the next common comfort movement and accounted for 151 of 650 comfort movements (24.0%). Rams with large horns were not very efficient removing hair from their withers, for unlike short-horned sheep, they could not reach their body with the horn tips.

A most common form of scratching is with a hind leg. Sheep scratch the brisket, upper parts of the front legs, neck, and head in this manner. It occurred 146 times (22.5%) in 650 comfort movements. Less frequently, sheep use the tongue and teeth for scratching or cleaning the fur. Such comfort movements occurred only 79 out of 650 times (12.2%), while shaking the body—a method of ordering the hair coat —occurred only 11 times. With their mouths sheep work over front and hind legs, the flanks, and occasionally the haunches.

Other comfort movements have nothing to do with grooming or care of the body surface. Sheep yawn, just as deer and moose do. They stretch after resting (fig. 39). I have rarely seen sheep hunch their backs during a stretch as moose, elk, or deer do occasionally (Geist 1966, fig. 1). When stretching the neck, sheep pull in the chin sharply.

The defecation posture in both sexes is inconspicuous and is just like the normal feeding or standing posture, except that the tail is raised. Sheep may defecate while standing, walking, feeding, or resting and do so particularly often after rising from a bed. Bedding sites are littered deep with droppings. Defecation has no apparent significance and does not appear to be part of social interactions as is true for gazelles (Walther 1965), cattle (Schloeth 1961), or South American camelids (Koford 1957; Pilters 1954).

The urination postures of ram and ewe differ greatly. Rams urinate from a nearly normal stance, except that the hind legs tend to be a little further back and the back is depressed slightly. Ewes squat and urinate backwards with a raised tail (see plate 41). This posture may have social significance, for rams often move to a ewe the moment she squats to lick her urine and lipcurl thereafter (see chap. 6). Again, unlike gazelles, mule deer, moose, and caribou, the ram's urination posture is not conspicuous. The deer of the species mentioned squat when urinating and may let the urine flow over the tarsi, impregnating themselves (Geist 1966c).

It appears that comfort movements have their own sphere of selection and evolve largely independent of social or habitat adaptations. For instance, mountain goats and sheep have rather similar habitat adaptations—although they emphasize the various adaptations differently— but differ greatly in the comfort movements and social behavior (Geist 1965). Mountain goats show comfort movements exceedingly rarely, and when they do, they appear clumsy and inept. Furthermore, their thick,

Fig. 39. Young Stone's ram stretching after rising from bed. (From photo.)

woolly coats would hardly allow efficient scratching, since it is incon-
ceivable how goats would reach the skin surface with either teeth or
hooves. However, goats sandbathe. They dig in dry sandy soil and
throw it over their flanks and haunches. Their thick underwool is
impregnated with sand. Sandbathing appears to have taken the role
played by the movements connected with body surface care (Eisenberg,
personal communication).

Unlike mountain sheep, moose or deer do not rub off their hair coats.
However, they possess comfort movements sheep do not have. When the
antlers are in velvet, deer and moose rub the antler tips under the
raised hind leg, thereby scratching the tender antler tips. The giraffe
has evolved comfort movements different from those of sheep, deer,
or mountain goat. It does not scratch itself with the hind legs or horns.
Its main method of cleaning its body surface is nibbling with the

incisors and licking or smacking the body surface with its tongue. In addition, giraffes rub on shrubs and trees, swat with the tail, and quiver the skin—presumably to dislodge insect pests (Backhaus 1961). To dislodge flies, sheep and caribou jerk their legs and flip the ears while caribou may gallop on large snow patches or partially submerge themselves in water.

It appears that comfort movements are primarily adjusted to the kind of body covering evolved by the animal, using the most accessible means, be it teeth, horns, hooves, or tongue to clean the fur or skin. In special cases, such as the mountain goat with its long, woolly fur, comfort movements atrophy but are replaced by specialized behavior. Ruminants evolving in common habitats will probably evolve similar body covers and comfort movements, though sheep and mountain goat demonstrate that this need not be so. Symbionts like tick-birds of Africa may contribute to cleaning (Backhaus 1961) and perhaps influence the evolution of comfort movements. A direct comparison of comfort movements between different species has little merit unless the biology of the species is known.

10 Population Dynamics and Population Quality

INTRODUCTION

If a mountain sheep survives to yearling age and thereafter becomes a social and reproductive failure, it can expect to reach a venerable old age. It may live many years, particularly if it is born in a static or declining population and like most individuals in that population is characterized by poor body and horn growth, late sexual maturation, and lethargic behavior. In mountain sheep the quality of individuals and their life expectancy appear to be inversely related. Large, vigorous individuals which reproduce well and reach high dominance rank enjoy few years of life. The quality of individuals and therefore of the population appears to be a function of the economic base of the population; hence, the vital statistics may reflect how well sheep live. The foregoing is of great importance to an understanding of the evolution not only of sheep but also of other large ungulates from periglacial regions.

Whereas Asiatic sheep appear to have a short life expectancy and a high reproductive potential, American sheep are characterized by a long life expectancy and a low reproductive potential. In this they resemble the northern ibex, with whom they share not only similar population dynamics and a long gestation period, but also similar habitat preference, body structure, and wintering behavior. It appears that life in cold, rugged mountains has favored similar adaptations in ibexes and American sheep.

The life expectancies of rams and ewes vary between populations. In declining or stable populations with a low recruitment of young adults, most adults die in excess of 10 years and may reach maximum ages of 20 years for rams and 20–24 years for ewes. Adult sheep born and raised in expanding populations which reproduce heavily reach on the average an age of 6–7 years. Within a population, it appears that rams of rapid body and horn growth die earlier than rams of poor growth, and hence the oldest rams in a population are characterized by small body and horn size.

280

Individual and population quality appears to be a function of how well individuals grow, which in turn is determined by the nutritional regime of the pregnant and lactating females. A high-quality population is typified by vigorous lambs, long suckling periods, large and early maturing yearlings, relatively early shedding of the milk dentition, vigorously interacting rams, short life expectancy of adults, high reproduction, and survival of young. This type of a population can be expected to arise when the population is expanding into new habitat, be it introduced by man or by natural means. The stable or declining population at carrying capacity appears to be characterized by individuals of low quality. The principles of ruminant reproduction and neonatal survival as elucidated by agricultural research and on which I base much of the following chapter appear to apply equally well to free-living sheep. A hypothesis predicting the sociology and social behavior characteristic of females also explains population control in sheep.

NATALITY

Number of Lambs Born

A single young is the rule for American sheep, including the Siberian snow sheep. Twinning is exceedingly rare, whether sheep are living in the field or under optimum conditions in captivity. In my field studies I found no twins and neither did Murie (1944), Smith (1954), Cherniavski (1962b), Welles and Welles (1961), or Woodgerd (1964). In the highlands of eastern Siberia, Cherniavski (1962b) autopsied 21 pregnant snow ewes and found no twins; he reported two second-hand observations of twinning. Averin (in Heptner et al. 1961) autopsied 19 snow ewes in Kamchatka and found no twins. Russo (1950) found only one fetus in a pregnant desert bighorn ewe. I autopsied a large, old Stone's ewe immediately after estrus and found only one ovulation. The data from zoological parks confirms the field data. In 63 births by American sheep recorded at the Alberta Game Farm, Okanagan Game Farm, San Diego Zoological Garden, New York Bronx Zoological Park, Chicago Zoological Park, and National Zoological Park in Washington, only two resulted in twins. However, Spalding's (1966) report on the autopsies of 11 California bighorn ewes killed by vehicles in southern British Columbia, is contrary to other observations. He found that 4 of 11 pregnant ewes carried twins.

Whereas multiple births are very rare among American sheep, they are exceedingly common among the large argalis, urials, and domestic sheep. Heptner et al. (1961) cite autopsies done by Antipin in his study of Tien Shan argalis; he found that from 66 pregnant ewes, 43 carried one lamb, 22 carried two, and 1 carried three. Heptner et al. also report reliable evidence for multiple births in urials and mouflons.

Size of Lamb Crop

Although every female mountain sheep exceeding 3 years of age could potentially lead a lamb in summer, this situation is only exceptionally attained, and the relative number of lambs which follow ewes in summer fluctuates greatly between years. In a home range group of bighorn ewes for which records were kept in 11 summers by a fire lookout operator, the number of lambs per 100 ewes fluctuated between 48.5 and 87.0. In the later summer and fall of 1964, the Palliser and Grassy Mountain bighorn ewes had a lamb crop of only 15.5 and 18 per 100 ewes ($N = 166$ and 161 ewes). Murie (1944) recorded 50 lambs per 100 ewes ($N = 261$ ewes) in fall 1939 among Dall's sheep in Mount McKinley Park, and in the following fall only 17 lambs per 100 ewes ($N = 208$). In an introduced, expanding bighorn sheep population from Wildhorse Island in Montana, the relative number of lambs fluctuated in 8 years between 67 and 100 lambs per 100 ewes (Woodgerd 1964). Further data are shown in chapter 2.

Factors Affecting Size of Lamb Crop

Density. It is a well-established observation that reproduction in ruminants decreases as the population density increases. Thanks to the detailed classified counts of a bighorn ewe group made during 11 summers by Norman Tithrington when he served as a fire lookout man on Aylmer Mountain in Banff National Park, this can now be shown for bighorn sheep. Tithrington's counts were summarized by the late E. J. Stenton, warden of Bankhead district, and are on file with the Banff Warden Service.

Figure 40 shows that the number of lambs seen during one summer is inversely related to the density of ewes in the preceding summer. The correlation is significant ($r = -0.75$, $t = 3.4$, $p < 0.01$), and the regression equation relating density to fecundity is $y = 78.5 - 2.78x$, $S_y = 4.4$ where y is the number of lambs per 100 females and x is the relative density of ewes, expressed as ewes seen per day. Unfortunately the absolute size of the female group in the various years is not known with certainty.

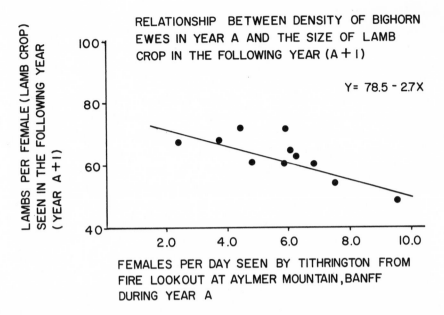

RELATIONSHIP BETWEEN DENSITY OF BIGHORN
EWES IN YEAR A AND THE SIZE OF LAMB
CROP IN THE FOLLOWING YEAR (A + I)

Y= 78.5 - 2.7X

LAMBS PER FEMALE (LAMB CROP) SEEN IN THE FOLLOWING YEAR (YEAR A + I)

FEMALES PER DAY SEEN BY TITHRINGTON FROM
FIRE LOOKOUT AT AYLMER MOUNTAIN, BANFF
DURING YEAR A

Fig. 40. There appears to be an inverse relationship between the density of ewes in a home range group and the number of lambs they lead in the following year.

Nievergelt (1966a) in his splendid review of the history of ibex introduced into Switzerland showed that fecundity dropped as the introduced populations reached their ultimate size and stabilized. The data for an introduced bighorn herd shows the same (Woodgerd 1964). Here, as in other examples, the birth rate must not be thought of as the absolute pregnancy rate, but rather the number of young which were viable enough to follow the female and be observed with her in summer.

Weather. Nievergelt (1966a) demonstrated for ibex that there was a close and significant correlation between precipitation during the gestation period and the crop of young seen thereafter. It is known from free-ranging domestic ewes that lambs are born smaller after hard winters than after mild ones and that many lambs are lost at birth if supplementary feed is not available (Robinson et al. 1961). This is also true for reindeer (Preobrazhenskii 1961), and probably for wild ruminants, although only Flerov (1952) mentions this for moose. Deep snow restricts sheep to small fractions of their habitat, thereby increasing the density of the population, reducing the resource base, and increasing competition while wind and cold drain heat energy from their bodies. Since the cost of survival goes up for the females, and the forage deteriorates in quality due to steady selection by sheep, less energy is available for the growth of the fetus.

Age of female. It has been demonstrated for domestic sheep and reindeer that the age of ewes has an effect on their reproduction performance (Turner and Dolling 1965; Preobrazhenskii 1961). As females grew older their performance became better, but began to drop after their eighth year. The peak in conception rate was reached by ewes 5–6 years old; the highest survival of lambs to weaning age came from ewes 6 years old; the highest number of lambs born per ewe came from 7-year-old ewes; the frequency of multiple births was greatest among ewes 7–8 years old. Nievergelt (1966*b*) analyzed the performance records of ibex females held in large enclosures and found that reproduction declined after the females had reached about 10 years of age. Young females lost most offspring. Alexander (1960) found that ewes which lambed for the first time and produced large lambs had longer labor than normal and tended to desert lambs. Some of these ewes failed to recognize the lamb and care for it, while others refused to stand and allow the lambs to suckle. Similar observations were made by Alexander et al. (1959), Alexander and Peterson (1961), and Watson and Elder (1961); the same principles are likely to apply to wild ruminants also.

SURVIVAL OF LAMBS

Early Postnatal Survival

If one considers that potentially each mountain sheep female 3 years of age and older could lead a lamb in summer, the low frequencies of lambs per 100 females observed and the great variability of these frequencies between years is surprising. Much the same has been observed in other ungulates (Pimlott 1959; Teer et al. 1965; Swank 1958; Dodds 1963). We are a little better informed about deer and moose and know that the pregnancy rates are very high, and the prenatal losses insignificant. In Siberian domestic reindeer resorption of fetuses can occur often if the females lose 17–24% of their body weight due to unfavorable winter forage conditions early in gestation (Preobrazhenskii 1961). There is a high mortality of young between parturition and a few days after birth, a condition which occurs even in domestic range sheep and has also been documented for ibex under the best care in large enclosures (Purser and Young 1959; Safford and Hoversland 1960; Nievergelt 1966b). What factors are responsible for this loss of young?

The superb work of agricultural scientists on the causes of early lamb mortality is of great theoretic significance, for not only does it point to an answer to the above question, but it suggests an explanation for why American sheep bear only one young, and a surprisingly small one at that, and why they have a much longer gestation period than the smaller domestic ewes which carry as much or more fetal mass. Although it cannot be discussed here, their work is vital to the understanding of birth number and size of young in ruminants as a whole, as well as their maternal adaptations.

The early survival of lambs in mountain sheep is probably just as much a factor of maternal nutrition and weather as it is in free-ranging domestic ewes lambing in open pastures, in reindeer from the Siberian tundra (Preobrazhenskii 1961), or in moose from the taiga (Heptner and Nasimovitsch 1968). Whereas the energy demands of adult ruminants are met primarily from volatile fatty acids, those of the fetus are met from glucose (Reid and Hinks 1962b; Alexander et al. 1962). The young's rapid growth places a heavy drain on the maternal glucose supply which is synthesized primarily from propryonic acid, a small fraction of the volatile fatty acid liberated in the rumen. Propryonic acid formation is favored by forage that has a high digestibility and hence is of high quality (Donefer et al. 1963). Poor forage, high in fiber and hence low digestibility, primarily favors acetic acid production that will maintain the pregnant female but not the growing fetus. Additional glucose could come from a breakdown of protein and its conversion to glucose (gluconeogenesis), but as McDonald (1962) points out, the fetus has also a high demand for amino acids and probably quickly removes the products of protein breakdown from the maternal blood supply, before these are converted. Since fetal growth comes in winter, it drains from the maternal resources when the energy cost of survival is already at its highest and forage conditions at their worst.

It appears from the work of Reid (1961) that a fat store could meet some of the energy demands of the fetus and compensate for food. Reid found that fat, well-fed pregnant ewes had only about half the forage intake of lean ewes which had been fed just a little above the level at which evidence of malnutrition can be observed. We do not know how much fat ewes carry over from fall into winter, nor how much of the fetal growth fat sustains. However, it is likely that in late winter the ewes must get most energy for maintenance and reproduction from forage.

In addition to the fetal demands the pregnant female must compensate for heat loss due to cold and wind, the increased mechanical energy expended in removing snow from forage and moving through snow, as well as escaping from predators and the energy loss due to a rise in metabolism when excited (Graham 1962). In extreme conditions of cold and snow, when ewes are restricted to small areas, when they even become antagonistic to their own lambs and chase them from available forage, the ewes are very likely to become stressed and increase their plasma cortisol and size of adrenal glands (Reid 1962). Psychological stress may produce here a far greater adrenocortical response than the climatic stressors (Reid and Miles 1962). This could be most unfortunate for the fetus. It is known that offspring from stressed female rats tend to be jittery and show abnormal behavior (Thompson 1957). It could be that the adrenal corticoids in abnormally high concentrations damage the fetal central nervous system. It was noted by Alexander et al. (1959), Alexander and Peterson (1961), and Watson and Elder (1961) that some lambs acted abnormally and were unresponsive to the ewes. This could have been due to stress experienced by their mothers (Alexander and Peterson 1961).

It is evident from the foregoing that a winter's severity will be reflected in the birth weights of lambs as indeed happens in domestic sheep (Robinson et al. 1961) or reindeer (Preobrazhenskii 1961), and is common knowledge among cattle ranchers. A severe long winter is likely to cause ewes to bear many relatively small lambs, while an exceptionally favorable winter will cause many large lambs to be born. However, both the very small and the very large lambs are faced with more hazards at birth than lambs of average size. This has been well demonstrated for domestic sheep.

Large lambs, particularly in fat ewes, pass the birth canal with difficulties. They are more likely to be stillborn, get stuck in the birth canal and cause difficult labor. Some ewes rest so long a time after heavy labor that the lambs do not get fed, are unsuccessful in their search for the teats, and finally die. Heavy labor is associated with increased lamb desertion, particularly by young ewes (Alexander et al. 1959; Purser and Young 1959; Alexander 1960; Alexander and Peterson 1961; Watson and Elder 1961; Gunn and Robinson 1963).

Lambs borne by ewes losing weight during gestation are at a severe disadvantage and are likely to die of hypothermy shortly after birth (Alexander 1961). They are of smaller than average size; their bodies are a little disproportionate containing relatively less muscle, skeleton, and particularly fat (Wallace 1948); the ossification of inter-vertebral disks and neural spines may be incomplete while their number of vertebrae may be reduced (Wallace 1948); their hair coat is thinner for they have fewer hair follicles (Schinkel and Short 1961), a condition they retain throughout life (Brown et al. 1966); their large surface to mass ratio accelerates heat loss, while their energy reserves to sustain this heat loss are perilously small. Females which have been losing weight in late pregnancy may not rise promptly and dry the lamb due to exhaustion by labor, in which case the lamb cools rapidly and may be inviable by the time the female becomes interested. Moreover, such ewes give less milk during summer than normally, if the lamb survives. Other weak females may desert the lamb even after a normal birth (Alexander and Peterson 1961). If adverse weather strikes at lambing time, smaller than average young are likely to succumb. That such small young suffer greater mortality primarily through cooling rapidly after birth was demonstrated by Alexander. Letting ewes lamb in warm shelters virtually obliterated early lamb mortality (Alexander and Peterson 1961) while advancing lambing time into a warmer season also drastically reduced lamb mortality (Watson and Elder 1961).

From the foregoing it follows that in ruminants with long adult life expectancy, which are adapted to exploit a stable, climax plant com-munity and are faced by severe energy cost of survival during preg-nancy, and in which the young are born in cool, exposed surroundings, selection will favor a single large young over two smaller and more poorly developed ones. The critical factor would probably be adequate glucose supply to meet fetal demands. It also follows that selection will favor a fetus that in reaching optimum size does not overburden the slim maternal resources; of necessity such a fetus would have a long gestation period and slow growth. The relatively small lamb borne by American sheep after a gestation period exceeding that of other sheep is probably an adaptation to life in periglacial regions and their long severe winters.

Survival during First Summer

If lambs survive their first few days of life, they have a very low mortality in the following summer, as is indicated by the data of several investi-gators. If one separates Tithrington's classified counts of a bighorn ewe group by months and lumps the data from the summers of 1956 to

1961, then there were 55 lambs per 100 ewes in July (N = 1,100 ♀), 60 in August (N = 1,410 ♀), and 60 in September (N = 654). Murie (1944) recorded in fall a lamb to ewe ratio which was a little higher than that in the preceding spring. Demarchi (1965) found a negligible change in the relative number of lambs between June and November. Cherniavski's (1962b) data from snow sheep are small, but may indeed reflect a severe summer mortality of lambs if the fall data was gathered from the same population.

Mortality figures are generally derived from classified counts, but these contain some biases and can reflect a variety of events, not only mortality. For instance, lamb to female counts taken in June can be nonrepresentative since (a) lamb-leading females may be in separate bands from barren females with juveniles and one is in danger of overcounting one type of band in favor of another, (b) females going to salt licks may have left their lambs behind elsewhere, and a good many of the yearlings as well, (c) late born lambs are likely to be missed. However, in July, August, and September, or later, all females and juveniles are in the same bands; so the lamb to female count is likely to be representative. Classified counts between early May and June do not reflect the mortality of yearling lambs, as much as the withdrawal of females to lambing areas (fig. 10). Sex ratios can be considered valid only if taken within two weeks prior to the ewes entering estrus; lamb to ewe ratios obtained at the height of the rut favor lambs since a good number of ewes are off in the cliffs being bred and their lambs associate with anestrous ewes. Migratory shifts can and do replace ewe groups on the same mountain, and each group may have had a different lambing success. Hence continuous census of one mountain often enough produces negative "mortality." Some ewe groups may pick up additional yearlings in summer. Therefore, classified counts obtained from a large population which moves seasonally are not likely to be an accurate reflection of population changes unless a large sample of sheep over a large area is sampled or a single home range group is censused continuously. Our best population dynamics data comes from small, isolated populations which the investigator knew intimately, such as the populations studied by Wishart (1958), Woodgerd (1964), or Blood (1963) and Demarchi (1965).

Survival during First Winter

The winter survival of lambs to yearling age varies greatly between populations, and within populations at various stages of population growth; it appears to be a function of population quality. Since lamb mortality can vary in winter between 0 and 75% or more, lambs between 6–12 months of age are clearly susceptible to high mortality. Their mortality appears to be inversely related to their quality and directly related to the severity of winter. By lambs of high quality one understands lambs of large size and dense coats, with a relatively small surface to mass ratio, such as are characteristic of expanding, low density populations. Lambs of poor quality are more likely found in stable populations. It is likely that single lambs which need not share the maternal milk supply are favored to survive the winter, for they are probably larger than twin lambs. Although domestic ewes which suckle twins increase their milk production, they do not double it, and twin lambs still remain at a disadvantage compared to singles (Alexander and Davis 1959).

Wishart (1958) studied a home range group of ewes which wintered in the foothills of southern Alberta along the Sheep River. Between May 1955 and January 1958 this band was stable in number, and there were 22–26 ewes present in various years. In the three consecutive summers beginning in 1955 the ewes produced 19, 17, and 21 lambs in summer. Of these 57 lambs which entered winter, 54 survived. The mortality was about 5.3%, virtually negligible. By comparison mortality of lambs in other herds often exceeds 60–70% (Demarchi 1965; Hansen 1967; Murie 1944).

Fortunately we know more characteristics of the Sheep River band. The ewes were exceedingly large. Twenty-four of them, weighed when they were older than 3 years of age, had a live weight between 144–82 lb and averaged 155 lb (Blood et al. 1970). The yearlings were large animals, indicating that they received optimum nutrition as lambs, while the high ewe to lamb ratio suggests that lambs were born large and well developed. These sheep showed every sign of being a high-quality population.

When a sheep population increases in density to carrying capacity, the available forage must deteriorate in quality during winter and less energy and nutrients in excess of maintenance are available for reproduction and growth. This should lead to smaller, inherently less viable young whose mortality should be higher than lambs raised when nutrients and energy are superabundant. Hence lamb mortality should be higher when a population is stable than when it is expanding. This is indeed found when examining the performance of bighorn sheep introduced on Wildhorse Island in Montana. Between 1951 and 1954, when the population was expanding, the difference in the number of lambs to ewes and the number of yearlings to ewes showed about an 11% decrease, indicating excellent lamb survival, while between 1959 and 1964 when the population stabilized, there was about 55% mortality of lambs (Woodgerd 1964, from table 3). On the whole one can expect in similar climates that populations characterized by high lamb to female ratios in summer will also show a better survival to yearling stage than populations showing the converse. This rule indeed appears to hold, but it must be insignificant in very warm and very cold climates.

A search of published information on the number of lambs seen in female company and their subsequent survival, using only data based on large samples and excluding desert sheep, showed that survival y (number of yearlings/number of lambs) is related to the lamb crop x (number of lambs/100 ewes) as $y = 0.74x + 7.0$ ($r = 0.66$, $t = 3.25$, $p < 0.01$). The relationship between lamb crop and survival, between *different* populations, is close and statistically significant. It indicates that the better the quality of the lambs, the better their survival (fig. 41).

This relationship must break down in very warm and very cold climates. In warm climates we expect warm weather at lambing time and a negligible loss of lambs due to hypothermy. Therefore we expect to see a relatively large number of lambs shortly after birth in summer which suffer heavy mortality before yearling age if the population is stable and of low quality. In such populations the points of lamb crop versus survival should fall below the regression line in figure 41. This is what one finds for desert sheep as can be calculated from the data published by Russo (1950) and Hansen (1967), and which is also supported by the small numerical data and general observations of Welles and Welles (1961).

Conversely, in cold climates we expect many weak lambs to die of hypothermy shortly after parturition. Hence many of the small, poor-quality lambs are already removed by the time we see the lambs in summer and the remaining lambs should have a good survival. It would appear that as the weaker lambs are removed shortly postpartum, the better a survival we can expect of the remainder. Hence, the points of lamb crop versus survival should fall above the regression line in figure 41. Scant data from my Stone's sheep and bighorn sheep study indicate that this is so; however, the case is still to be verified.

Expressed crudely, (*a*) if the points of lamb crop versus survival fall into the square formed by $x = 50–100$, $y = 0–0.5$, the population is one living in warm climates and is of low quality but stable, (*b*) if the points fall within $x = 0–50$, $y = 0.5–1.0$, the population is of poor quality, stable, and lives in a cold climate, (*c*) points falling within $x = 50–100$, $y = 0.5–1.0$ would indicate an expanding high-quality population and (*d*) points falling into the remaining square ($x = 0–50$, $y = 0–0.5$) would indicate the converse. The statements (*a*) and (*b*) are subject to the condition that the points fall above the line formed by $xy = 20$ for a low-quality and $xy = 40$ for a good-quality population (xy = number of yearlings/100 females); since low-quality populations have a lower turnover rate than high-quality populations, because individual life expectancies are longer in poor-quality populations (see below), there must be about 20 yearlings/100 females produced to maintain a poor quality, stable population, while for a population with high turnover rate the number of yearlings/100 females must be closer to 40.

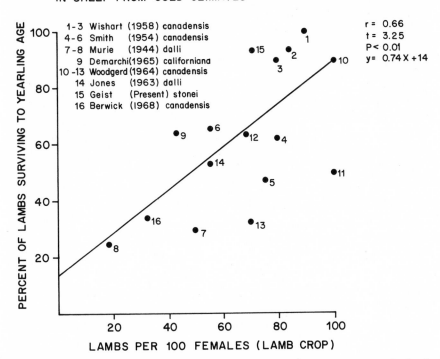

RELATIONSHIP BETWEEN LAMB CROP AND SURVIVAL OF LAMBS
IN SHEEP FROM COLD CLIMATES

Fig. 41. There is a significant direct relationship in cold climates between the lamb crop and their survival.

Sex Ratio and Differential Survival of Lambs

The available data do not contradict the view that at birth the sex ratio of mountain sheep is about 50:50. Woodgerd (1964) sexed 43 young lambs and found 22 males and 21 females. Of 21 lambs born to captive ewes at the Alberta Game Farm and the National Zoological Park, Washington, 11 were males and 10 were females. However, the sex ratio may begin to change rapidly soon after birth.

In the years 1959–62, when the introduced bighorn population on Wildhorse Island was stabilizing, the sex ratio of yearlings was about 100 ♀ to 163 ♂ (calculated from table 1, Woodgerd 1964). It appears that female lambs died off more rapidly than male lambs as was confirmed by the survivalship of 43 tagged lambs. However, prior to stabilization in the years 1951–65, the sex ratio of yearlings was less biased in favor of males, being about 100 ♀ to 120 ♂ (Woodgerd 1964, table 1). This suggests that in expanding or high-quality populations, female lambs survive as well as male lambs, a view supported by Wishart's (1958) data for the Sheep River herd and my data on Stone's and bighorn sheep.

Wishart (1958) found in four consecutive years a total of 27 ♀ and 25 ♂ approaching 2 years of age. My Stone's sheep study population which for various reasons was considered of high quality, produced in two years 19 ♀ yearlings and 11 ♂ yearlings. Conversely the poor-quality bighorn populations I studied produced far more males; the Palliser ewe group produced in three years about 27 ♂ yearlings and 15 ♀ yearlings (table 11), the Grassy ewes in four consecutive years 10 ♂ yearlings and 9 ♀ yearlings (table 10, exclude May 1964), and the Bare Mountain ewes in two years 6 ♂ yearlings and 5 ♀ yearlings. This adds up to about 43 ♂ yearlings versus 29 ♀ yearlings.

The better survival of male lambs in poor-quality populations may be due to better intrauterine growth of male lambs under conditions of adverse forage conditions as is known from domestic sheep (Robinson et al. 1961). After hard winters male lambs are born on the average heavier than female lambs, and gain in utero less weight than female lambs when the ewes are offered supplementary feed. This implies that female lambs are of smaller than average size, may suffer increased mortality due to hypothermy, and are somewhat less viable inherently than males. If this view is valid it will be found for mountain sheep that birth weight differences between male and female lambs are less in high-quality than in low-quality ewe populations.

SURVIVAL OF YEARLINGS

Once mountain sheep have survived to yearling age, they face a relatively long life expectancy. Their second winter finds them usually grown to near adult size, hence their surface to mass ratio has improved considerably and they can maintain themselves more economically than previously. At about 12 months of age they face a minor hazard, particularly in high-quality populations in which few barren females are found. As the females withdraw for lambing the yearlings are left on their own, and unless they can attach themselves permanently to a barren female, they may wander around aimlessly. It is possible that such a yearling band can wander off into strange terrain and get lost. Wishart (1958) did find a number of yearling remains, some of which were in localities not visited by sheep. On the whole getting lost and dying in the absence of leadership is probably only a minor hazard.

The survival of sheep through their second winter appears to be quite good. Wishart (1958) found that of 19 rams entering their second winter at least 17 survived, and of 26 ewes, 24 survived. However, these were offspring from a high-quality population and were probably large and well grown in turn. Woodgerd (1964) found that of 12 tagged yearling males 11 survived to 2 years of age, and 4 of 5 tagged yearling ewes. Of 6 known Stone's yearling females and 4 yearling lambs, all survived the winter of 1964/65. However, these observations come from sheep of high or good quality. Unfortunately the data for other populations are scant. However, since in the Banff bighorn populations the ratio of $2\frac{1}{2}$-year-old males per female is about the same as that for $1\frac{1}{2}$-year-old males per female (tables 10–12), it appears that yearling males have a very good survival. For females there are no data.

SURVIVAL OF ADULT SHEEP

Mortality data usually come from sheep found dead in the wild. In the case of rams, the age at death can be determined accurately by counting the number of horn segments; for ewes this aging method is less accurate and gives only a minimum estimate of age (Geist 1966c). Mortality data based on skeletal remains are subject to several biases; the assumption that each dead sheep has the same chance of being found by the investigator is invalid. First, since the skulls of female sheep and juveniles are light and far less sturdy than those of rams, they are more likely to be destroyed or carried off by predators. Hence one tends to find relatively more skulls of old males. However, for adult sheep, this bias does not appear to be serious. From Murie's data (1944, table 4) one can calculate the survival of rams and ewes between the ages of 2 and 6 years. Healthy rams have an apparent survival of 97% and healthy ewes of 94.6%. Clearly the bias could not be serious. Moreover, Murie found about the same number of dead ewes as rams, and the sex ratio in unmanaged populations of mountain sheep does appear to be close to one ram per female (chap. 2).

A second bias can arise if the ewe and ram wintering areas are unequally sampled. Skull samples collected from ewe wintering areas tend to be biased toward young rams and underestimate the average age of death among rams. This follows from the fact that mainly young rams associate with ewes in winter. Conversely, a sample of skulls from ram wintering areas tends to be biased in favor of old rams and overestimates the average age at death. In the field little can be done to overcome these biases except to search both ram and ewe winter ranges and to search not only close to the avalanche gorges and high cliffs but also away from these.

Since these biases cannot be evaluated directly, it is necessary to countercheck one's findings from skeletal remains against data from different sources. Alternative estimates of survival can be made from classified counts (see p. 40), while the formula predicting the return of rams to a given seasonal home range in successive years allows a second test of the mortality data derived from skeletal remains (see p. 81).

Mortality and Survival of Bighorn Rams

Table 67 gives the ram mortality data collected in the years 1963–68 on the Banff study area. The reason for including survivorship data in table 67 ("No. of cohorts alive") will become apparent later. The distribution of rams found dead by age approximates a normal distribution. Hence one can calculate not only a mean age at death, 10.12 years for this population, but also a standard deviation, 3.2 years for this population, and a standard error of the mean of 0.36 years. This is convenient for it allows one to calculate a minimum and maximum life expectancy. The minimum life expectancy is defined as the age at which 95% of the rams which survived to yearling age are still alive, while the maximum life expectancy is defined as the age at which 95% of them are dead. Hence mean age at death minus twice the standard deviation is the minimum life expectancy: $10.12 - 2(3.2) = 3.7$ years. Hence at about 4 years of age, close to 95% of the rams can be expected to be alive. Similarly the maximum life expectancy is the mean age at death

TABLE 67

Mortality and survival of bighorn rams from the Palliser Range

	Age at death (yrs)																	Σ
	1	2	3	4	5	6	7	8	9	10	11	12	13	14	15	16	17	
No. found	0	2	1	3	4	0	6	6	8	9	8	13	9	3	3	1	1	77
No. of cohorts alive	77	75	74	71	67	67	61	55	47	38	30	17	8	5	2	1	0	695
% survival	100	97	96	92	87	87	79	72	61	50	39	22	10	6.5	2.6	1.3	0	

plus twice the standard deviation: $10.12 + 2(3.2) = 16.5$ years. Hence at 16–17 years of age we can expect 95% of the rams to be dead. The slight deviation of the data from a normal distribution accounts for the small discrepancies between calculated and actual figures. The mean age at death or average life expectancy as well as minimum and maximum life expectancies are useful parameters for comparing different populations (see table 68).

It can be seen that there are two general phases in the survivalship curve of this and other ram populations.[1] There is a phase of low mortality between the ages of 2 and 8 years and a phase of accelerated mortality in the higher age categories. From table 67 the average annual mortality can be calculated as sum of number found dead over sum of number of cohort alive in previous year, times 100: $(77/695) \times 100 = 11\%$ mortality. The average mortality between the ages of 2 and 7 is $(16/431) \times 100 = 3.7\%$ and the average mortality of rams between the ages of 8 and 17 is $(61/264) \times 100 = 23.0\%$. The same pattern of mortality is found in rams from other sheep populations and is particularly striking in the Dall's sheep studied by Murie (1944).

Causes of Ram Mortality

The ages of low mortality in rams coincide with their low dominance status and near exclusion from breeding by larger-horned, older rams. Conversely, when rams reach near ultimate body and horn size and become dominant breeding rams during the rut, their mortality increases. This relationship between dominance and high mortality appears to be causal for the following reasons: large, dominant rams which breed most ewes virtually do not feed while guarding ewes and they fight extensively and do much running and chasing when following the estrous ewe and discouraging competitors. Unlike small rams, the large breeding males often return exhausted from the rut. They have

1. See also Bradley and Baker (1967).

probably lost most of their fat deposits whereas subordinate rams probably retain theirs. In the severe winter months following the rut, the rams that have lost their energy reserves probably succumb (see also Heptner et al. 1961 for other ruminants). Two predictions, as yet unverified, are that large rams should lose more weight during the rut than small-horned rams and that young rams will die off more rapidly if, due to circumstances, they are allowed to participate in breeding at the same level as older rams.

It also follows from the above hypothesis that in populations in which rams reach their ultimate proportions early because of vigorous growth, rams should have a relatively short life expectancy owing to advanced physiological age. In populations in which individuals grow and mature slowly, we expect rams to reach an older average age. Fast growth rates in individuals is expected in expanding, colonizing populations and slow growth rates in individuals in static or declining ones. Hence, in expanding sheep populations rams should have a shorter life expectancy than in stable or declining ones. This appears to be the case when Woodgerd's (1964) introduced bighorn population is compared with those studied by myself or Hansen (1967) (table 68). The above relationship between introduced versus stable populations and life expectancy has been demonstrated by Nievergelt (1966a) for a close relative of sheep, the European ibex. It was Brody (1945) who discovered the inverse relationship between growth rate and life expectancy.

The useful information available to date on the mortality characteristics of rams from four mountain sheep populations is summarized in table 68. There is considerable variation between the average, minimum, and maximum life expectancies. As indicated above, the short life

TABLE 68

Mortality of rams from four different populations of North American sheep

	Locality	Life expectancy (yrs)			Age of oldest ram found	Standard deviation	No. of skulls based on
		Mean	Min	Max			
O. c. canadensis	Banff	10.12 ± 0.36	3.7	16.5	17	3.2	77
O. c. canadensis	Montana	6.7 ± 0.58	2.0	11.5	11	2.4	17
O. c. nelsoni	Nevada	10.37 ± 0.25	5.2	15.5	16	2.5	120
O. d. dalli	Alaska	11.1 ± 0.13	10.0	12.2	14	1.1	65 [a]

SOURCES: Data for the first population were obtained during the present study; data for the other three are from Woodgerd 1964, Hansen 1967, and Murie 1944 (table 4).
[a] All rams that died 1937–41, excluding diseased ones.

expectancy of rams studied by Woodgerd (1964) conforms to the fact that they were grown in an expanding population. The desert bighorn rams studied by Hansen (1967) and the Rocky Mountain bighorns I studied in Banff National Park have the same average life expectancy; however, desert bighorn data have a smaller standard deviation. Hence the bighorn rams I studied have a higher maximum life expectancy. Both of these populations appear to be stable or declining populations. The Dall's sheep studied by Murie (1944) and widely cited in papers dealing with mortality patterns (e.g., Deevey 1947; Caughley 1966), had a turbulent population history and his data represent special cases only. The cohort of healthy rams whose skulls he found between 1937 and 1941 were born largely prior to 1932 and raised in a high-density population. They were young adults when the severe winter of 1932 caused the population to crash. Hence the rams which survived to die in the period 1937–41 were an especially hardy group of individuals of "low quality" rams. Their very high average life expectancy appears to reflect both their early background in a dense population as well as their hardiness to winter. The other data gathered by Murie, reflect the harsh winter of 1932 and are probably not typical of the high-density population prior to 1932. The data in table 68 fully support the view that mortality characteristics of rams are largely a function of population quality.

A recent paper by Neumann (1968) on the growth of red deer is of considerable importance to ruminant population dynamics. It demonstrated that stags reached a plateau in body and antler size at 4–5 years of age and remained there till 7–8 years of age. Thereafter the stags grew larger in body and antler size with each year, till at least 15 years of age. Why the resurgence in growth after 8 years of age? As in mountain sheep (table 50), in red deer the males aged 6–8 years are apparently the most active during the rut and interact socially most intensively (Gottschlich 1968). When older they are less active. From this it follows that stags and rams older than 7–8 years lose a little less fat during the rut than the 7–8-year-olds. Hence they are a little better off during winter, recuperate faster in spring, and gain proportionately more weight in the following summer. This would explain the increased body and antler growth. However, such older stags should also survive a little better than the 7–8-year-olds. It is hence probable that a stag's or ram's chances of mortality increase rapidly at the age when he first becomes a serious contender in the rut and declines somewhat thereafter.

The Death of Old B-Ram

The passing of a free-living animal is rarely witnessed, and the events preceding its death are usually unknown. The following is a short account of the end of one of my study animals. I first saw old B-ram in October 1961 on Sanctuary Mountain while he settled a few differences with the 6-year-old, three-quarter-curl Peter. B-ram was an exceptionally dark Stone's ram who lacked a white belly and carried a pair of wide flaring amber horns over a gray face and neck. He was old, but I did not discover how old till I found his remains on 12 March 1962, two days after last seeing him alive.

B-ram crossed to Ghost Mountain to rut and was successful that year. He was the largest-horned ram on Ghost Mountain and faced little challenge from the 1-year-older D-ram. When the rut drew to a close in the middle of December, it was noticeable that B-ram had some difficulty running fast after ewes and his eager rivals. It appeared occasionally that he limped.

At Christmastime the large rams began deserting the females on Ghost, Cliff, and Lupin mountains and appeared one after the other on Sanctuary. B-ram hung about the slopes of Ghost closest to Sanctuary Mountain. He was alone now, and like most rams after the rut he rested much of the time. It was not till 11 January 1962 that he crossed to Ghost. That day, he was already with the Sanctuary rams quite early in the morning. He was not only limping, now he was holding up his left hind leg. An injured or even broken leg is not a rarity among mountain sheep and how it affects the animal can be seen in plates 86 and 87.

B-ram confined his activity to the open grassy slope not far from the large cave used by Sanctuary rams as a resting area during winter nights. He did not follow the other rams but regularly joined them at night in the cave and hobbled down to the slope each morning.

In order to feed, a sheep must paw through snow. If one front leg is injured a sheep cannot paw and must rely on pushing snow with the snout, a method generally abandoned by sheep, ibex, and mountain goats. A sheep with a broken front leg can be expected to starve to death in winter. If the hind leg is broken, the sheep can barely balance when pawing and does this awkwardly. Quite likely it does not paw efficiently and does not feed as well as a healthy individual.

It was noticeable that old B-ram fed the whole day through and only rarely lay down for a rest as did his healthy companions. He also fed low on the slope where the others rarely ventured and where the grass and herbs grew tallest. For several days in early February old B-ram had trouble with the 6-year-old G-ram who followed him and clashed on the ram. I was to see this among bighorns later in which subordinates pestered and butted sick or injured dominants.

By February a change had come over the old ram. He looked gaunt; his backbone protruded as did his hips while the haunches grew thin. His thin body and slow tired movements contrasted with those of his healthy, fat, and spunky companions. He still climbed each evening to the cave, but he often paused and stood for a while before continuing on. Then, in late February, he abandoned the cave. He bedded down on the snow of the open slopes and braved the long, cold arctic nights. He bedded down where he last fed and moved very little.

The days passed slowly. A cold snap hit the mountains in late February. While the healthy rams rested in the cave, old B-ram lay exposed several hundred yards below. He moved a little lower each day. In the first week of March he had moved off the slope and fed on the tiny hills bordering the slopes where the wind had cleared some forage. Here I saw him last on 10 March. I walked on the ice of Gladys Lake and rounded a point to look for the old ram. He rested on a little hill in the rays of the setting sun. His head slowly turned toward me, as I stood on the snow-covered ice almost half a mile away.

That night a storm struck. It howled on the following day and visibility was almost nil in the blowing snow. On the 12th it cleared and I searched Sanctuary Mountain for rams. Old B-ram I could not find. Even when I moved to the lake and scanned the low hills, he was not to be found. For half a day I searched along the base of the mountain, till I saw a whiskey jack tug at something which protruded from below the snow behind a bush. It was old B-ram covered by snow.

Closer examination revealed a partially covered set of wolf tracks. B-ram had been killed as the toothmarks around his throat revealed. The wolf had not eaten him except for a sliver of flesh torn from the ribs. His left hind foot was swollen above the hoof and about half a cup of pus drained out when I cut open the swelling. When I articulated the hooves, there was a gritting in the joints between phalange and metatarsal. Old B-ram was void of fat, while his marrow in the long bones was red and jellylike. His skin was thin and could be torn easily. He had been a sick, emaciated old ram, almost 13 years old at death. For several days, old B-ram's carcass lay untouched. Then a wolverine found and dismembered it.

Survival of Female Mountain Sheep

The mortality data for females of American mountain sheep leaves much to be desired, and the conclusion that adult females have a shorter life expectancy than adult rams (Murie 1944; Sugden 1961; Woodgerd 1964; Hansen 1967) appears doubtful. This conclusion is based on the age distributions of ewes and rams found dead in the field. In all instances age was determined by counting the number of horn segments, a method which is reliable if used on rams but of doubtful reliability for females. Horn segment counts appear to underestimate the age of females, thus giving only a minimum age. Murie (1944) and Hansen (1967) collected large samples of female Dall's and Nelson's bighorn respectively. Since Nelson's ewes appear to grow relatively larger horns than Dall's ewes, it is probable that here the horn segment count is more reliable, but it is not known how reliable.

From Hansen's (1967) data for females one can calculate an apparent average life expectancy of 9.5 years ($N = 254$) with a standard deviation of about 2.54 years and a standard error of 0.25; the average mortality rate is about 11.7% per year. Since the calculated life expectancy underestimates the true life expectancy and the apparent average mortality overestimates the true value, quite evidently these females lived at least as long as the rams from the same population. The only other bighorn sheep population for which reliable data are available is the Sheep River population in southern Alberta studied by Wishart (1958). Over three years he found that from a total of 90 adult ewes which went into winter, 71 were alive the following spring. These ewes died at the rate of about 20% per year and showed an average age at death of about 6.1 years ($N = 17$, calculated from Wishart 1958, table 14). As was indicated earlier, this was a high-quality population with large individuals, a high reproductive rate and high survival of juveniles. The desert sheep studied by Hansen (1967) came from a declining population in which juveniles had very low survival. This suggests that for ewes as for rams the quality of a population and the average life expectancy are inversely related. This is also suggested by Nievergelt's (1966) figures for two groups of ibex females held in enclosures. In one the females matured later than in the others and produced fewer twins, but lived somewhat longer and reproduced later in life. It is probable that as in rams the reproductive load carried by the female influences her chances of survival: females which are barren or lose their young may have a better chance of survival than those that are pregnant or suckle young. This hypothesis needs to be verified.

Population Dynamics of Asiatic Sheep and Other Caprids

The similarity of American sheep to ibex extends itself not only to body build, jumping ability, and somewhat similar habitat preference, but also to their population dynamics. Like ibex, but contrary to their Asiatic cousins, American sheep are exceedingly long-lived. The oldest dead bighorn ram I found was 17 years old, while the oldest tagged ram alive on the Banff study area at my last visit in 1968 was 18 years old.[2] The oldest tagged bighorn ewe that I know of lived in the wild state and disappeared in her 20th year of life; Stenton recorded at Banff National Park one tagged bighorn female which last returned at 24 years of age. For other American sheep we have somewhat lower maximum ages, but these were arrived at by counting horn segments, a method which in females underestimates age. The oldest Nelson's ewe aged by Hansen (1967) was a minimum of 16 years old as was the oldest Stone's ewe I shot. The oldest Siberian snow ram found was aged at 18 years (Pfeffer 1967). These maximum ages are much the same as reported by Russian workers for ibex and tur (Heptner et al. 1961) and Nievergelt (1966a) for alpine ibex. The survivorship curves of ibex males published by Nievergelt are similar to those of poor quality American sheep. The mortality data published by Russian workers for ibex from populations exposed to apparently heavy wolf predation suggest a shorter life expectancy than that found for American sheep, but a considerably longer one than that reported for Asiatic sheep. Thus of 906 urials shot in Turkmenia only 2 reached the age of 8 years and none was older. Of another 187 sets of horns of urial rams taken in Turkmenia, 1% were of rams exceeding 7 years of age. Among urial rams found dead of natural causes, 4–6-year-old individuals predominated (Heptner et al. 1961). Mouflon rams appear to have a similar mortality pattern to urials (Pfeffer 1966). Argali rams appear to have a somewhat longer life expectancy, though none exceeding 12 years have been reported from the field by Russian workers. Heptner et al. (1961) cite data of *O. a. poli* rams from Egorov, which are shown in table 69.

These data show that with a mean age at death of 6–7 years these argali rams died considerably earlier on the average than bighorn or thinhorn rams from the few American populations for which data are available (see table 68). The life expectancy of these argali rams would appear to equal that of bighorn rams from an expanding high-quality population.

2. This ram was still alive in spring 1970 at 20 years of age.

TABLE 69

Survivorship and mortality of argali rams (O. a. karelini)

	Age (yrs)				
	2–3	4–5	6–7	8–9	10–12
% seen alive (N = 200)	14	40	26	17	3
% found dead (killed by wolves) (N = 61)	6.6	21.3	39.3	27.9	4.9

SOURCE: Data from Egorov (in Heptner et al. 1961).

Russian authors have suggested that the males of mountain sheep, ibex, saiga antelope, gazelles (*G. subgutterosa*), and red deer suffer a disproportionately high mortality in winter if they have been very active in the preceding rutting season (see Heptner et al. 1961). Apparently such males lose more weight than less active males and are the first to succumb to winter stresses and wolves. It follows that in populations heavily preyed on by wolves one should find a greater proportion of adult females.

If the gestation period of 5 months cited by Heptner et al. (1961) for *Ovis ammon* applies to the argalis as well as to the urials, then Asiatic sheep have considerably shorter gestation periods than American sheep or the ecotype of the latter, the Siberian ibex. Both the Siberian ibex and American sheep have a gestation period of 170–80 days, which would be at least 20 days longer than Asiatic sheep (or goats from southern Asia) of comparable body size.

American sheep differ from ibex in twinning exceedingly rarely. Although Siberian ibex do twin frequently in zoos, they do so rarely under natural conditions. Among the large, highly evolved goats such as Siberian ibex or tur (*C. caucascia* and *cylindricornis*), twins are born to about 4% of all females in the wilds. However, Siberian ibex and American sheep are alike and different from urials in bearing young weighing between 7.5 and 8.5 lb in weight, while urials from warm or hot climates bear young of about 5 lb in weight (Heptner et al. 1961).

From the foregoing it appears that relatively large young, long gestation periods, reduced twinning rates, and the long life expectancy of adults have been selected for by the cold, long alpine winters with their slim energy resources, a season which ibex and bighorn sheep must use for fetal growth.

For other caprids the population dynamics data are fragmentary and cannot as yet be satisfactorily explained. Caughley (1966) published excellent data on the mortality of female thar in New Zealand. These appear to have a survivalship similar to bighorn ewes from a poor-quality population and similar longevities. Thar twin rarely (Rammell and Caughley 1964). On the other hand *Ammotragus* bears twins and triplets commonly (Seitz 1957; Ogren 1965). Of the mortality in natural populations of *Ammotragus* nothing is known.

POPULATION QUALITY

In the preceding sections population quality was frequently alluded to, and since it is of some theoretical importance it is necessary to examine this concept in more detail. It is evident to any careful observer that sheep from different populations differ in size, age at maturation, yearling development, and reproductive characteristics. Klein (1964, 1965a) studied black-tailed deer in coastal Alaska and showed that differences in the characteristics mentioned were directly related to the resource base of each population. In sheep the differences are not only confined to external characteristics but also to behavior. When studying bighorn lambs in early summer of 1964 I was struck by the lethargic behavior of the lambs. These lambs used the same behavior patterns as the Stone's lambs I observed in 1962, but they played far less frequently. Although striking, there was no way to record the listlessness of the bighorn lambs.

At first glance the hypothesis that the bighorn lambs differed from the Stone's lambs on a genetic basis has merit. This view, however, is untenable. It was found that Stone's ewes suckled their lambs much longer at comparable ages than did the bighorn ewes from Bare Mountain. If Stone's ewes suckle their lambs inherently longer than do bighorns, then their respective suckling durations should cluster about two different means. However, this does not happen (see fig. 42). Most suckles of Stone's and bighorn lambs last only about 20 seconds. The longer average suckling duration for Stone's lambs was brought about by a series of long suckles. It is known that milk production is affected by the level of maternal nutrition in summer (Brody 1945) as well as by the size of the udder, which in turn is affected by the level of maternal nutrition during pregnancy (Wallace 1948). The fact that Stone's lambs were allowed to suckle longer suggested that they were better nourished and that observed differences in the vigor of lambs could well be due to differences in nutrition. This hypothesis proved fruitful.

Published reports indicate that a wide variation exists in suckling

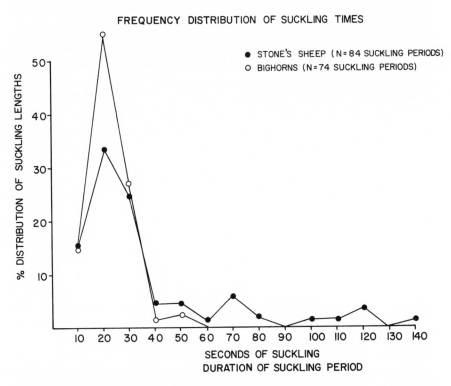

Fig. 42. The mean suckling duration of 20–30 seconds is the same for the Stone's and bighorn sheep population investigated; however, Stone's ewes occasionally allowed their lambs to suckle for rather long time periods.

durations between populations, even when one takes into account that the mean suckling duration decreases as the lamb grows older (Ewbank 1967). Spencer (1943) found that bighorn lambs suckled from 1.5 to 3 minutes in their first weeks of life. These values far surpass those I recorded for Stone's sheep (table 70). Welles and Welles (1961) recorded 26 suckling durations of a 4- and 5-week-old lamb: the mean suckling duration was 8 seconds, which is less than half the average suckling duration of the bighorn lambs from Bare Mountain at comparable age (table 70) or of domestic lambs (Ewbank 1967). If suckling durations are directly related to the milk production of ewes, then it appears that great differences exist in the amount of milk available to lambs in different populations. The Bare Mountain bighorn lambs looked more poorly nourished than the Stone's lambs, and the evidence is entirely in line with this view.

1. Bighorn lambs were refused suckling more frequently than Stone's lambs. Bighorn lambs in their second and third weeks of life were refused in 42% ($N_2 = 89$) and 36% ($N_3 = 58$) of their suckling attempts; Stone's lambs were refused 14% ($N_2 = 71$) and 21% ($N_3 = 37$) of their attempts respectively.
2. Bighorn lambs attempted to suckle more frequently than Stone's lambs. At 3 and 4 weeks of age they attempted suckling 4.3 and 4.5 times per hour of grazing by the ewe; Stone's lambs in their third week of life attempted suckling 3.5 times per

TABLE 70

Data on suckling by lambs

Age of lamb (wks)	No. of suckles timed	Duration of suckling (sec)			No. of suckles/ hr of ewe's activity	Seconds suckling/ hr of ewe's activity
		Av	Min	Max		
			Stone's			
1	8	56	4	105	4.1	226
2	54	29	1	120	3.2	94
3	31	36	4	135	1.9	72
			Bighorn			
2	52	18	4	45	1.80	33
3	37	19	7	46	2.06	40
5	7	18	14	25	1.30	24

hour. Ewbank (1967) found that twin lambs attempt to suckle more frequently than singles in their first 3 weeks of life. This finding also suggests that the less milk available per lamb the more frequently lambs will try to suckle.
3. I never saw a bighorn lamb quit suckling voluntarily; however, I observed Stone's lambs terminate suckling in 8 of 84 suckles.
4. The bighorn lambs spent more time feeding on vegetation than did the Stone's lambs (table 71).

It has been well demonstrated that the growth rate of lambs depends on their milk consumption (Wallace 1948; Schinkel and Short 1961; Slen et al. 1963; Ewbank 1967). It has also been shown that growth

TABLE 71

Activity data for ewes and lambs

Age of lamb (wks)	Observation points						% of activity feeding
	Feeding (a)	Standing (b)	Moving (c)	Resting (d)	Total (a + b + c + d)	Total activity (a + b + c)	
				Stone's ewes			
1	59	6	1	24	90	66	90
2	200	28	13	29	270	241	83
3	148	13	17	31	209	178	83
				Bighorn ewes			
2	336	19	14	203	571	369	91
3	171	32	11	108	322	214	80
5	161	27	55	93	336	243	66
				Stone's lambs			
1	15	16	9	36	76	40	37
2	26	79	50	111	257	146	18
3	27	67	32	82	208	126	21
				Bighorn lambs			
2	116	64	46	304	530	226	51
3	47	52	40	183	322	139	34
5	23	17	14	33	87	54	43

deficiencies in early life are not entirely compensated for in the later life of sheep (Schinkel and Short 1961) and that sexual maturation is advanced or retarded depending on how quickly or how slowly the animal grew (Watson et al. 1956). If the Bare Mountain lambs received considerably less milk than the Stone's lambs, then we expect them to be relatively smaller and to mature later than the Stone's lambs—which was found to be true.

When the Bare Mountain lambs returned in October, they had not yet shed their juvenile coats and had small barely visible horns (plate 82). The yearling rams from this population at 18 months of age tended to be much smaller than adult ewes: they carried small horns (plate 83), their testes were so small as to be barely visible, and they showed no interest in estrous ewes during the rut. Only in the Bare Mountain population did I ever see a 2½-year-old ram still sexually immature. The Stone's lambs, as well as bighorn lambs from the Mount Norquay population in Banff park, were at 18 months of age about as large as adult ewes and carried horns equal to or exceeding those of adult ewes (plates 25 and 84), and the Stone's yearling rams participated in the rut. Whereas the yearling Stone's rams dominated females, the bighorn yearlings from Bare Mountain were subordinate to ewes. It is important to note that the Mount Norquay bighorns were fed extensively by tourists prior to the lambing season. These sheep also exploited seeded road banks and well-fertilized lawns, as well as forest areas cleared off for skiing. This population was annually reduced, since some of these sheep were killed by cars on the Trans-Canada Highway.

Maturation by females at 18 months of age is known only from an introduced, expanding population of bighorn sheep (Woodgerd 1964) and from sheep raised in zoos, presumably under very good nutritional conditions (e.g., Chicago Zoological Park, Brookfield, G. R. Schreiber, personal communication). It appears that in sheep as well as in other ruminants, the nutritional state of the female is very important in determining maturation age (Preobrazhenskii 1961; Teer et al. 1965; Heptner and Nasimovitsch 1968).

Among the otherwise small, poorly grown bighorn yearlings from Bare Mountain, there was one female which was large and exceptionally well developed. This particular yearling still suckled off its dam as a yearling, a most unusual occurrence. This yearling, its dam, and the best-developed male yearling of the population are shown in plate 85. It appears that uncommonly good mothering was responsible for the large size and health of this yearling.

Conversely Liddell (1958, 1961) found that poor mothering was responsible for the poor growth and listlessness of a female goat. This female in turn bore and raised a poor-quality young despite ample food. When comparing a well-mothered kid with a poorly mothered kid, Liddell found that the former was able to withstand psychic stresses much better than the latter. Under conditions of psychic stress goats lost weight, while their new horn growth was soft and easily scraped away with a finger.

The circumstantial evidence suggests that in wild as in domestic sheep an individual's size and development depends on its mother's as well as its own nutritional regime, while the quality of mothering is probably also important in determining the quality of the young. Liddell's findings suggest that poor-quality females can be expected to raise poor-quality young, a viewpoint which has not been refuted during three years of observations of a poor-quality home range group of bighorn ewes from Bare Mountain in Banff park. In the falls of 1964, 1966, and

1968, the yearlings of this group as well as some 2½-year-olds were small, sexually immature individuals.

The adult rams raised from poor-quality populations appear to differ from those raised in high-quality populations in that they interact less intensely and less frequently with each other. At present the sole evidence for this view comes from experiences and data gathered from my three study areas, within which were found three different subspecies of sheep. Yet, the observed actions cannot be explained in terms of genetic differences; they are plausible only in terms of quality differences.

In comparison to the Stone's sheep about Gladys Lake, the bighorns on the Banff park study areas were less vigorous in their interactions, played less, interacted more in huddles, but appeared to clash more. The only quantitative data I have are on the intensity of social interactions of rams, which show that the Stone's rams interacted far more intensely (table 56). The Dall's sheep by contrast were quite lethargic and unlike the Stone's sheep not a high-quality population. Like the bighorns they interacted frequently in large huddles in a rather lethargic manner, but unlike bighorns they clashed very little. Since both the Dall's sheep and the bighorn sheep population I observed were rather low-quality sheep, it appears that increased intensity and rate of interactions of the Stone's rams is related to their better quality.

Jewell (1966) describes the reproductive performance of a poor-quality population of Soay sheep. He also found that rams fought very little, even at rutting time, which is in line with the evidence from American sheep.

In summary, it appears that sheep from a high-quality population are large, early maturing, vigorous individuals which grow large skulls and horns, replace milk teeth earlier (see p. 52), shed their hair coat relatively early, and interact socially frequently and intensely. The ewes of such a population bear a greater number of large, vigorous lambs and suckle them adequately; the rams fight more frequently than those in a low-quality population and die early. From the descriptions of Preobrazhenskii (1961) it appears that reindeer respond physiologically like sheep to forage conditions and that what has been hypothesized for sheep is probably also valid for the genus *Rangifer*, if not for all periglacial ruminants.

POPULATION CONTROL AND SHEEP SOCIETY

How are sheep populations controlled? The hypothesis answering this question explains also the social behavior of female sheep and shows how the means of control and this behavior are both adaptations to the habitat, in particular, to the long, cold winters.

The biological goal of a female sheep can be conceived as giving birth to a lamb of viable size and development. The forage ingested by a female sheep pays the energy cost of (1) maintenance, (2) work, social interactions, excitement, escape from predators, parasitism, illness, climatic stresses, and (3) reproduction and growth. The first two sets of requirements will have priority over the third and will be satisfied at its expense. It is evident that a female will be a reproductive failure and contribute no genes to future generations unless she consistently raises enough energy and nutrients above and beyond that required for maintenance, work, etc., to grow a fetus weighing a minimum of about 7.5–8 lb at birth. This is probably the weight needed to allow neonatal survival in northern sheep, as was discussed earlier. It is also likely that relatively few females in a population attain that goal.

Clearly, any increase in the cost of living to the female jeopardizes her reproductive success. It was suggested earlier that the relatively long gestation period, small young, and scarcity of twins were adaptations to the long, montane winter. This suggests that on the average females in stable populations at carrying capacity are hard put to obtain sufficient high-quality forage to support adequate fetal growth. If this concept is valid, then female sheep are under strong selection to reduce or eliminate all actions which increase the cost of living. Conversely, selection should favor actions which increase net energy available for reproduction. It follows from these considerations that:

1. Social interactions between females should be greatly reduced, compared with males, and there should be a minimum of aggression and little redundancy. This is found. Adult females interact rarely; when they do it is predominantly with overtly aggressive patterns, rarely with displays or contact patterns.

2. Anestrous females should avoid rams to reduce interactions since these increase excitement and chasing, and hence cost energy. This is found. Not only do anestrous females withdraw from rams, but they also use urination apparently as a distractant and respond passively to the courtships.

3. Females should avoid areas frequented by rams and thus avoid competition for high-quality forage. It is not known whether it is the females that avoid males or vice versa; however, the sexes are segregated spatially for most of the

year. From the foregoing it is evident that females choosing to stay with rams would select against their offspring.

4. Females should avoid meeting strange females since this leads to excitement, social interactions, and consequently an increased cost of living. Hence home range groups of females should not overlap, particularly during the critical late winter period. This is also the case (chaps. 3 and 4).

5. Females should be more gregarious than males, form larger groups, and be seen less often alone. It was shown by Reid and Miles (1962) that "loneliness" in sheep caused excitement, hence grouping would reduce this cost.

6. Females should roam less than rams and have smaller home ranges, which was found to be true (chap. 3).

7. Adult females should "play" less than adult rams. This has not been investigated closely, but the inescapable impression is that it is so. The only females I have seen engaging in play were several barren ewes and two-year-old females.

8. Females should fatten up in fall. It was shown by Reid (in McDonald 1962) for domestic ewes, and recently by Ozoga and Verme (1970) for female white-tailed deer, that prewinter fattening reduced dependency on forage in winter. It is not known to what extent this does take place in free-living sheep.

9. It is evident also that the kind of mother-young separation found in sheep has a secondary benefit. It does not drain energy from the pregnant female via excitation and aggressive interactions.

10. Females from long stable or declining populations that are not subject to periodic, random die-offs, should be less excitable than females from expanding populations. This remains to be tested.

11. There will be selection against females which are too small or too large to produce lambs of "survivable" size. For both extremes the cost of maintenance and work in hard winters may be too high, and may have to be satisfied at the expense of the energy and nutrients normally available to the growing fetus. Therefore, one can expect reproductive failures in very large and very small females following hard winters.

The above enumerations describe essentially the behavior and society of female mountain sheep, and list a number of predictions by which the above hypothesis may be tested. Furthermore, it is evident that the number of viable lambs declines as the female home range group increases in size and the average birth weight of the lambs declines toward the critical minimum. This would be achieved by increasing reduction of the quality of the available forage to a level where, on the average, insufficient long-chained fatty acids would be fermented in the rumen to be formed into glucose to supply the energy demands of the growing fetus. The number of viable lambs born would then be reduced to a level determined by the amount of resources freed to the pregnant females by the death of adult females and juveniles in winter. That is, birth rates would be causally determined primarily by the death rates of adult females. Conversely, an increase in the pregnant female's supply of energy and nutrients beyond the requirements of keeping her alive benefits the growing fetus and increases its chances of postnatal survival. This is achieved not only by the death of members of the female's home range group but also by a variety of other factors: mild temperatures and a reduced number of windy days and storms during winter; a winter with little and soft snow that reduces the work required for maintenance; an early snowfall that covers the ground and conserves green forage and prevents other forage from weathering and deteriorating in quality; an early and warm spring that causes an early growth of nutritious forage; a calm daily routine and less than average harassment by predators and particularly humans; a below average production of juveniles by the home range group in preceding years and hence less than average reduction of high-quality forage during winter. All events that increase or decrease the energy and nutrient supply of pregnant females can modify the effects of the annual death rate on the reproductive rate of the home range group. In this context it is meaningless to ask whether the food supply or the weather controls the population.

It follows that, given a population of high quality, in which the death rate of adult females is intrinsically high, there will also be a high rate of births and a high birth weight (the death rate of lambs in their first winter being negligible). Hence a high-quality population would tend to perpetuate itself, or change to a low-quality population only slowly. Conversely, a population of low-quality females with an intrinsically low death rate would cause a low birth rate and low birth weight, and would also lag or perpetuate itself in the face of improving forage conditions. Clearly, the same resource base could support sheep populations of different characteristics, composed of individuals of entirely different quality.

Sheep populations periodically reduced by catastrophic mortality, such as unpredictable avalanches, periodic heavy snowfalls, or frequent rockslides, should be composed of high-quality individuals, even when at great density. Such populations would be frequently thrown into the expanding phase, in which selection would favor females of large size and the bearing of large lambs due to the periodic superabundance of resources. Conversely, sheep populations not subject to periodic die-offs and free of predation, should be characterized by high relative density and individuals of calm disposition, slow growth, small average size, low intrinsic mortality, and low reproduction. Clearly, increased mortality of adult females would eventually result in a population characterized by high-quality individuals, and assuming no complication, severe cropping of adult females could increase reproduction and population growth explosively. For mountain sheep, however, this would probably be more than offset by alienation of females from the best feeding areas, if cropping were to be done by hunters.

11 The Effect of Glaciations on the Evolution of Behavior and Form of Mountain Sheep

INTRODUCTION

If one lets the mammals of Southeast Asia pass in review, one could justly conclude that south of the Himalayas evolution had fallen asleep. The row of primitive species, relics from past epochs, would be long indeed. Here we find the most primitive rupicaprid, the scrow (*Capricornis*), the most primitive caprid, the thar (*Hemitragus*), the most primitive of cattle, the anoa (*Anoa*), the most primitive bear, the sun bear (*Helarctos*), the most primitive badger (*Helictis*), and the most primitive lagamorph (*Pentalagus*). The small, hairy Sumatra rhino (*Dicerorhinus*) appears to be stuck at the same evolutionary level as the first members of this genus from the Oligocene. Almost every conceivable stage of cervine deer evolution would pass in review, beginning with *Tragulus*, little changed since Eocene times, and continuing with the Chinese water deer (*Hydropotes*), representing the Oligocene stage when long, curved canines not antlers were the fashion, then to *Muntjacus* and *Elaphodus* representing Miocene deer, to *Rusa* and *Axis* which illustrate Pliocene deer. The Indian elephant (*Elephas*) is also primitive in tooth and tusk structure compared to most of the great elephants which arose and vanished in the ice ages, while such creatures as the tree shrews appear to date clear back to the Cretaceous.

In contrast to these venerable species are the highly evolved forms from the glaciated North, most of which arose in the age of deteriorating climates and cold-warm oscillations, the Villafranchian, as well as in the following ice ages. Many of them are closely related to present-day primitives from southern Asia. The species arising in the glaciated North were often giants, particularly in Villafranchian times, while the ruminants, rhinos, and elephants were usually characterized by enormous horns, antlers, and tusks, the likes of which are all but unknown from previous epochs. There has been nothing unearthed from pre-Pleistocene times to rival the antlers of the Irish elk (*Megalocerus*) or Alaskan moose (*Alces alces gigas*), the "antlers" of *Sivatherium* among the

313

giraffes, the horns of *Bison latifrons*, *Syncaffer*, or the Siberian argali, the tusks of the Auvergne mastodon (*Anancus arvernensis*) or the woolly mammoth (*Mammutus primigenius*), or the horn of *Elasmotherium* among the rhinos. Huge hornlike organs are largely a Pleistocene phenomenon, although a few exceptions exist, for instance, *Arsinoitherium* from the Oligocene.

What caused evolution to go on a rampage during the Villafranchian? What is responsible for the evolutionary stagnation of many large mammals south of the Himalayas? Why the selection in the North for such enormous social organs—the antlers, horns, and tusks? Although many spectacular large Pleistocene mammals are now extinct, some forms no less spectacular have survived and may give us an answer. Among them are the large-horned sheep and goats. I believe that they can give us an insight into the causes of evolutionary advancement and stagnation in the large ungulates, and the theory presented in the following pages could well be applicable beyond mountain sheep.

THE ARGALI CLINE

Although mountain sheep evolved a bewildering diversity of forms and sizes, there is nevertheless order in the apparent chaos. Sheep do fall into two distinct groups, the Eurasian and the American sheep, and these in turn form several clines. Let us take the largest living sheep, the Altai or Siberian argali, and use it as the beginning of a lineup in which Asiatic sheep are arranged in order of resemblance. The sheep most similar to the Altai argali, the Tien-Shan argali (*O. a. karelini*) would then be second in line. Next to it would be the Pamir argali (*O. a. poli*), next closest in resemblance is the Kara-Tau argali (*O. a. nigrimontana*), then Severtzov's argali (*O. a. severtzovi*), followed by the northernmost urial from Turkestan (*O. a. arkal*), the Elburs urial (*O. o. orientalis*), the Armenian urial (*O. o. gemelini*), the Anatolian urial (*O. o. anatolica*), the Cyprus urial (*O. o. ophion*), and finally the most similar caprid is the Barbary sheep (*Ammotragus*) from North Africa. Most of this cline is shown in figure 43.

These sheep, arranged on the basis of external similarities also fall into a geographic cline, that is, the more alike they are the closer they live together, and the more unlike the further they live apart (fig. 44). The following changes occur along the cline from the Barbary sheep to the Altai argali:

> *Horns.* The horns of old rams change from heteronym to a homonym winding. The horns increase first in length and then in mass

Fig. 43. The *ammon* cline. A lineup of Asiatic sheep and *Ammotragus*, in order of resemblance. (1) *Ammotragus*, (2) *Ovis orientalis gemelini*, (3) *O. o. orientalis*, (4) *O. o. cycloceros*, (5) *O. ammon severtzovi*, (6) *O. a. poli*, (7) *O. a. karelini*, (8) *O. a. ammon*. Note the changes in horn shape and size, reduction of ventral neck ruff, and changes in ear length. In *karelini* the lateral horn edge shifts medianly.

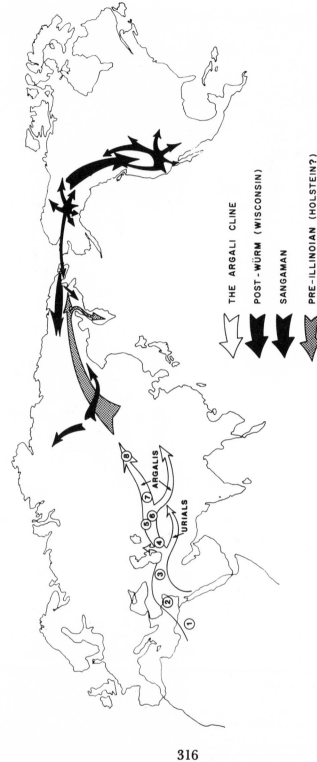

THE ARGALI CLINE

POST-WÜRM (WISCONSIN)

SANGAMAN

PRE-ILLINOIAN (HOLSTEIN?)

ARGALIS

URIALS

Fig. 44. The geographic location of the *ammon* cline, as well as the movements of mountain sheep into eastern Siberia and North America at the hypothesized geologic times and their post-Wisconsin dispersal. The circled numbers 1–8 correspond to the sheep illustrated in fig. 43. The Nelson's bighorn, at the very center of post-Wisconsin bighorn sheep radiation in southern California, is surrounded by advanced races.

(in *poli*, horns and skull weigh about 25 lb; in *ammon* 49 lb [Clark 1964]). The horns develop in the urials from the mainland a sharp lateral keel which fades away in the large argalis.

Ears. The ears become increasingly shorter and rounder.

Neck ruff. The cheek beard and ruff on the neck is progressively reduced and finally lost in the large argalis.

Rump patch. The Barbary sheep has only a somewhat lighter area on its rear and no rump patch to speak of; the males do have a light scrotum like all sheep. In the urials the area of light hair enlarges and forms a diffuse rump patch. In the argalis this diffuse area enlarges still and in *poli* covers the whole rear of the animal.

Skull. The pneumation of the skull increases relatively and absolutely. The bone-enclosed hollow spaces above the brain become larger and larger, reaching their greatest size in the Siberian argali while the horn cores increase relatively in length (see Zalkin 1951 in Pfeffer 1967, p. 196.) It is also likely that the relative size and weight of the skull increases.

This cline can be regarded either as the result of sheep adapting to some unknown geographical gradient or as an evolutionary cline in which one form gave rise to the next in line. The first alternative predicts that Siberian argalis transferred to Persia would soon evolve into uriallike forms, or if transported to North Africa, into *Ammotragus*-like forms. This appears ludicrous, but cannot be disproved at present. Nevertheless, I shall disregard the first alternative, for the second alternative predicts correctly.

For the present, let us assume that the cline from Barbary sheep to Siberian or Altai argali is an evolutionary cline. It must be determined in which direction sheep evolved, from *Ammotragus*-like forms to argalis or vice versa. Which end of the cline represents the primitive species? There are two ways in which to obtain an answer: First, we can compare the species to ancestral forms to determine which is the evolutionary older form. Second, we can relate the cline to the history of Pleistocene glaciations.

Rupicaprid Characteristics of *Ammotragus*

Paleontologists suggest that the caprids evolved from the short-horned rupicaprids (Thenius and Hofer 1960). If so, then the more primitive a caprid, the more rupicaprid characteristics it ought to show. In the case of the cline discussed, it is *Ammotragus* which shows by far the most rupicaprid characteristics and therefore represent the primitive end of the cline. This is evident from the following.

The caprid which is neither of the *Ovis* nor *Capra* lineage and which resembles *Ammotragus* is *Hemitragus*, the thar. It is a living connecting link between the caprids and rupicaprids. With the rupicaprids it shares the shortness and sharpness of its curved, backward pointing horns, the small occipital condyles, and four teats; with the caprids it shares the horn keel and only two functional teats (Rammell and Caughley 1964). It shares with *Oreamnos* the hair pants on hind and front legs, with *Capricornis* a neck ruff, and the narrow, pointed rupicaprid ear with both. Like *Oreamnos*, male thar have a thick hide, the tendency to drive their horns into an opponent's belly (they killed deer in Woburn Park by disemboweling them [Anderson and Henderson 1961]), the tendency to avoid fighting but display broadside, and the tendency to pair off during the rut with a female and guard her even when she is not in estrus (Anderson and Henderson 1961; Geist 1965, 1967). Advanced caprid both of the *Ovis* and *Capra* lineage guard estrous females only (Geist 1968a; Nievergelt 1967). The skull of a thar bull is considerably sturdier than that of mountain goats and has far more pneumation, although less than the skulls of other male caprids.

From the foregoing characteristics, coupled with the hypothesis that thar are intermediate in character between rupicaprids and caprids, one can predict the manner in which thar males will fight in serious combat. No such fight has been described to date; so the following prediction will serve as one test of the theory elaborated in this chapter.

Hemitragus males will use the most generalized combat techniques of all caprids and deliver damaging, bloody fights. Thar males will fight not unlike mountain goat males but will add a number of components. Combat will be initiated in a broadside display (fig. 45). Once blows are struck, the males will step into body contact and attempt to maintain it. This is a defensive behavior which decreases the effect of hooking with sharp horns, and thereby reduces wounding. The males will push each other with shoulders and hips; one may attempt to put his neck over the opponent's and wrestle him to the ground. They will butt, charge each other, and hook with the horns. Occasionally, one will catch the opponent's blows with the horns or will dive under the opponent's belly and hook him with the horns, attempting to throw him backward. They will emerge from battle lacerated and bleeding from small punctures, but only rarely will there be any serious wounds due to the protection afforded by their thick hide. The combat of thar

Fig. 45. The broadside display of *Hemitragus*. In contrast to the mountain goat, *Hemitragus* stretches the head and neck forward.

and mountain goat males will be comparable to the violent, un-ritualized brawls of mountain sheep males, and a distinction between violent and ritualized fights will probably not be possible.

In *Ammotragus* the rupicaprid ancestry is still apparent, but it does have features reminiscent both of true goats and sheep. Its molars are enlarged but not nearly as long as those of American sheep (Ogren 1965). Sexual dimorphism is not great, while the females are aggressive and can keep males at a distance (Ogren 1965; Haas 1958). The long, pointed ears and long face of *Ammotragus* are reminiscent of the thar. The horns of the Barbary sheep are sharp and it can inflict stab wounds with them (Haas 1958). Like the mountain goat, Barbary sheep may hook with their horns (Katz 1949). From this one can infer that the hide of old Barbary rams is likely to be thicker than that of true goats or sheep. The skull of old *Ammotragus* males is likely to be well pneumated and have thicker, more compact bone than that of the thar, but less so than that of true sheep. The occipital condyles of Barbary sheep are much larger than those of thar or mountain goat and equal or exceed in size even those of bighorn sheep. As in the thar, there is no distinct rump patch in *Ammotragus*, although there is some light hair on the rear and in males the scrotum is white—reminiscent of the urial condition. The tail of Barbary sheep is goatlike, naked on the underside, and rather long and hairy. The follicle arrangement of its hair coat is more similar to *Capra* than to *Ovis* (Ryder 1958). *Ammotragus* can be occasionally hybridized with domestic goats, but not with sheep, although not too much emphasis should be attached to that fact (see chap. 1).

In behavior *Ammotragus* is rather sheeplike. Males interact frequently. They butt and clash not unlike mouflons, withdrawing after each clash by walking backward and then running at each other again (Haas 1958). The males wrestle by hooking horns, shoving each other about with shoulders and hips, placing one horn over the opponent's neck, or placing the chin over the opponent's neck and pushing the opponent to the ground. These behavior patterns are still found in mouflons (Pfeffer 1967) but only in a most rudimentary form in American sheep. In general it appears that *Ammotragus* has more generalized combat techniques than either the true goats or sheep. As yet we do not know how these caprids act in serious combat; I have, however, seen captive males performing broadside displays in antagonistic interactions.

During the rut, *Ammotragus* rams guard one estrous female while several subordinate males surround the breeding pair (Ogren 1965). As in American sheep, subordinate males may mount each other. The males ejaculate spontaneously as do true goats and sheep, but resemble true goats in taking the penis into their mouths (Haas 1958). Unlike goats, but like sheep, *Ammotragus* males are not malodorous. As in sheep the low-stretch and twist appear to be present (Haas 1958; Katz 1949), but it is likely that neither display nor the contact behavior are nearly as well evolved as in sheep, for unlike sheep, *Ammotragus* males appear to be more solitary than their more advanced relatives (see Brehm 1916). Moreover, they lack the preorbital gland on which subordinates could impregnate themselves with the scent of the dominant as apparently occurs in sheep.

Ammotragus features a mixture of sheep and goat features, but in external appearance and behavior as well as in its serum proteins (Schmitt 1963) it is rather uriallike. The cheek beard, the ventral throat ruff, the short hair ridge running dorsally along the neck to the withers, and the horns with heteronym winding are features found almost only in urials. Even though *Ammotragus* stripped of its hair has a striking similarity to the Caucasian tur (*Capra cylindricornis*) as Petzsch (1957*b*) pointed out, and can be used as a link between the *Capra* and *Ovis* lineages, it is a near-perfect ancestral form for sheep and would have to be invented were it not alive.

The morphological changes from *Ammotragus* to *Ovis ammon ammon* in the cline have been enumerated. Concurrently there are a number of behavioral changes. Unfortunately we have only fragmentary information on the behavior of most caprids; nevertheless, there is a theme discernible which runs through sheep evolution. It appears that sheep became increasingly more specialized to deliver increasingly forceful clashes, with a concurrent reduction of other combat types. The vicious brawls, while still present, were reduced in favor of a specialized clash in which the force of collision was focused on one narrow horn keel. The relatively nondamaging fight arises from the actions of the attacker, which aim at increasing the clash force to the greatest possible extent, and the actions of the defending male, which are intended to catch the clash and render it harmless. In sheep the chief defense appears to be the heavy, pneumated skull, with which the blows are caught; in the thar there is both a thick hide and a pneumated skull. This indicates that in caprid evolution there was a change in the defense system from protecting oneself with a thick hide and evasive actions to catching the opponent's clash with an armored head. Concurrently, the body skin became thinner.

As horns enlarged and the long body hair was lost, the broadside display disappeared and was replaced by a horn display, while the horns became not only weapons and shield but also rank symbols (Geist 1966*b*).

The courtship behavior of caprids remained rather conservative, although where sexual dimorphism is less extreme, the females may be rather aggressive as in *Ammotragus* (Ogren 1965), a situation characteristic of the mountain goat (Geist 1965).

It also appears that during caprid evolution, the males changed from being rather solitary to gregarious and finally social forms. This was probably made possible first by the evolution of effective defensive mechanisms in fighting that reduced the chances of injury and the specialization of horns for clashing, which makes them ineffective in slashing wounds if used at short range. Second, conspicuous horn size differences allowed the prediction of fighting potential from horn size and allowed rams to live in a predictable social environment. However, these mechanisms, while permitting rams to live together, were not the

cause of socialization. Rather, this was achieved via increased neotenization (chap. 6). Let us now look at the behavior of mouflons, urials, and
argalis.

Mouflon observations have been taken from Pfeffer (1967) and have
been supplemented by observations of my own on a herd of captive
mouflons in the Hellabrun Zoological Park, Munich, in fall 1967.
I was fortunate in observing two severe fights between two large mouflon rams, fights which varied considerably from those of bighorns
but also had a few similarities. The two rams clashed rapidly, with
one clash falling every 3–5 seconds. They walked backward after each
clash for about five meters, then charged on all fours and jumped into
the clash. Like bighorns they slammed their horns forward and down.
During some clashes one or the other jumped up in the rear, riding the
clash home. When separating they kept the horns pointing at the
opponent. The slightly smaller, and subordinate, ram initiated all
clashes. During both fights the smaller made several charges at the
broadside of the larger ram but stopped short every time the larger
faced the charge. During the second fight the smaller, aggressive ram
gained the upper hand and began treating the other ram like a female
by twisting with a tongue flick, kicking him, and rubbing the preorbital
gland over the defeated ram's body.

Pfeffer's (1967) description of a dominance fight differs somewhat
from this, in that the rams spaced the clashes over longer periods,
grazed between clashes, and pawed the ground. Neither he nor I saw
a mouflon ram freeze after a clash and present in the manner of bighorn
or Stone's rams. The fights of mouflons, compared to bighorns, featured
rapid but less forceful clashes. That mouflons attempt to hit the
opponent with one horn edge remains to be seen. The manner of combat in urials is unknown, except for a few observations made by Walther
(1961) on one captive ram. It charged in a manner similar to mouflons.
Just prior to the clash it lifted the front legs off the ground as is apparently also done by mouflons. I have also seen a urial ram hook in the
manner of *Oreamnos* at an opponent.

Mouflons and urials can perform the twist and the low-stretch during
courtship and they do have the front kick (Walther 1961; Pfeffer 1967),
which is not reported to date in *Ammotragus*. Pfeffer (1967) described
presentlike frontal display in mouflon rams toward subordinate rams.
It is not clear to me from his writing if mouflon rams treat subordinates
like females, but it might be since Pfeffer does mention homosexual
behavior. The subordinate mouflon may act like a subordinate thinhorn

or bighorn ram by turning his rear on the opponent and feeding or moving away with lowered head, a posture assumed by courted mouflon ewes.

For argalis we have only the observations of Walther (1961) on a group of captive Pamir sheep, including one large ram. This ram behaved more similarly to bighorns than to mouflons. He charged bipedally, not on all fours like mouflons, and held his front legs, head, and body very much like an American sheep. This implies that the ram clashes with the lateral horn edge as American sheep do. This ram pawed exuberantly during social interactions, prior to rising on his hind legs to clash, which is done by mouflons and infrequently by American sheep. He used a low-stretch when running at the observer, and cocked his head at the observer when resting. This implies a well-developed horn display both from the low-stretch and the present. Hence the argalis not only resemble bighorns externally but also in behavior, and since they are of different lineages entirely, their similarities have apparently evolved convergently. I have here attempted to construct a consistent, testable model of sheep evolution, which in places is based on inadequate data. Nevertheless such a model is justified as it gives aim and direction to future research, even though its validity may not be established for some time.

THE GLACIATION HYPOTHESIS

The foregoing attempted to show that *Ammotragus* represents the primitive end of the sheep cline discussed, for it has more rupicaprid features than the other forms. There is a second concept which leads to the same conclusion. It can be seen that the cline runs from North Africa, across Persia into Turkestan, then into the Pamir Mountains, along the Tien-Shan to the Sair and finally Altai Mountains. This cline probably could not have existed during Pleistocene glaciations, for all the mountains inhabited by the argalis today were then probably under ice (Frenzel 1968). Since the glaciations in central Asia were restricted due to insufficient moisture, it appears that large cold deserts surrounded glaciated mountains, making it unlikely that sheep survived there. Asiatic sheep for all their plains adaptations are restricted to mountainous terrain and grasslands, not plains and deserts. This hypothesis implies that the sheep we find today in central Asia are of rather recent evolutionary origin, which surged from the unglaciated terrain into the mountain ranges after glacial withdrawal, and simultaneously changed in the manner indicated earlier the further they pushed into new living space. For Asiatic sheep this view cannot be verified or rejected at present, since our knowledge about glaciers and plant communities during the Pleistocene of Central Asia is as yet inadequate. However, the hypothesis can be tested on North American sheep.

The formal hypothesis is as follows: Mountain sheep evolved during postglacial dispersal into uninhabited, favorable terrain. They specialized increasingly toward delivering a more forceful clash and changed by growing relatively heavier horns, larger rump patches, acquiring more pneumation in the skull, increasing the length of horn cores, shortening and rounding the ears, and losing the cheek and neck manes. To test this hypothesis, only the horn, skull, and rump patch characteristics can be examined since American sheep lack manes and already have rather short ears.

How did sheep spread into and colonize North America? There are a number of competing views, namely, Sushkin (1925), Cowan (1940), McCann (1956), Stokes and Condie (1961), Cherniavski (1962a), and Flerov (1967). Of these, Cowan's view is the most acceptable since Flerov, Stokes and Condie, McCann, and Sushkin overlooked essential attributes of American sheep distribution and weighed superficial resemblances in skull size of northern bighorns and argalis to the exclusion of other features. Cowan's objections to the views of Sushkin are equally valid against those defended by Cherniavski (1962a), Flerov, Stokes,[1] and Condie.

Cowan (1940) proposed that sheep similar to those in Kamchatka spread to America from Siberia via the Bering-Chuckchi platform. They probably arrived sometime during the Illinoisan glaciation, maybe at the same time as the wapiti (*Cervus*) (Guthrie 1966). Thereafter they spread along the mountains of western North America, probably during the Sangamon interglacial. The Wisconsin glaciation divided American sheep populations, confining one to the Alaska-Yukon refugium and the other to the Southern refugium on the continent. After the last glacial withdrawal, sheep spread once more from their refugia into the mountains freed of glaciers.

If Cowan's original hypothesis and the hypothesis to be tested are valid, then the following should be found: (*a*) The most primitive American-type sheep should live in Siberia. They should have smaller rump patches, relatively smaller horns and less pneumated skulls

1. Stokes recently changed his mind and agrees with Cowan (*J. Mammal* 50 [1969]: 806).

than sheep from either the Alaska-Yukon refugium or from the Southern refugium. Sheep from the old Southern refugium should be most advanced and exceed the others in horn size, pneumation of skull, and rump patch size. (*b*) Since sheep moved from the refugia into formerly glaciated terrain, sheep from glaciated areas should have larger horns, a greater pneumation of the skull, and larger rump patches than sheep from the old refugia.

First test of hypothesis. Despite the scarcity of data, the first prediction can be verified. The Siberian snow sheep does have a smaller rump patch than the Stone's sheep and it in turn has a smaller rump patch than bighorn sheep. In snow sheep from Kamchatka the rump patch is narrow and does not extend beyond the root of the tail (Lydekker 1898; Clark 1964; Cherniavski 1962*a*). In Stone's sheep the rump patch extends beyond the root of the tail and is bisected middorsally by a wide strip of dark hair connecting the dark tail with the dark body hair. In bighorns the rump patch extends over the rear and the strip of dark hair connecting dark tail and body hair is very narrow, often interrupted and sometimes missing entirely (fig. 46).

At present we cannot compare the pneumation of the skull nor the length of horn cores between snow sheep and thinhorn sheep; however, it can be done for thinhorn and bighorn sheep. As demonstrated by the hypothesis, the horn cores of thinhorn sheep are shorter and smaller than those of bighorns (plate 12), while the pneumation of bighorn sheep is larger than that of thinhorn sheep. One can compare relative pneumation by comparing the maximum thickness of the pneumation to the maximum length of the brain. The maximum length of the brain was measured from a point just above the cribiform plate to the maximum posterior expansion of the cerebellum along the midline. For 5 Dall's rams in excess of 8 years of age the average brain length was 9.4 cm (9.0–10.0 cm) and the average maximum thickness of the pneumated bone layer above the brain was 5.3 cm (4.5–5.6 cm), the average pneumation index (pneumation/brain length) was 0.56 (0.48–0.62), that is, the thickness of pneumated bone was 0.56 times as great as the brain length. For 3 bighorn rams in excess of 8 years the average brain length was 9.8 cm (9.7–10.0 cm), the average pneumation thickness 6.1 cm (5.1–7.0 cm), and the average pneumation index was 0.63 (0.53–0.70). Snow sheep are likely to have less skull pneumation than Dall's sheep.

Cherniavski's (1962*a*) detailed skull measurements have shown that

Fig. 46. American-type mountain sheep. *Bottom*, the snow sheep (*O. nivicola*) sketched from descriptions of Kamchatka sheep; *middle*, the white Dall's and black Stone's sheep; *top right*, the Nelson's sheep; *top left*, the Rocky Mountain bighorn. The Kamchatka, Dall's, and Nelson's sheep live in glacial refugia; the Stone's sheep and Rocky Mountain bighorn, primarily in regions glaciated by the Wisconsin glaciation.

Dall's sheep are intermediate in skull characteristics between snow sheep and bighorn sheep.

As predicted by the hypothesis, snow sheep appear to have relatively and absolutely smaller horns than thinhorn sheep, while these in turn have smaller horns than the bighorns from the Southern refugium.

It appears that snow sheep are about as large as thinhorn sheep in body size. Heptner et al. (1961) list 3 snow rams, 6–8 years old, from Kamchatka as weighing 85–100 kg (187–220 lb); 5 females weighed 47–54 kg (103–19 lb). One exceptionally large male, shot in early fall, weighed 128.4 kg (281 lb). Cherniavski (1962b) lists the live weights of snow rams older than 6 years from the Koryak highlands of northeastern Siberia as weighing 70–6 kg (154–67 lb). For thinhorn sheep there are few weights available. Ulmer (1941) weighed 4 old Dall's rams shortly after they were shot; they weighed 79–85 kg (173–85 lb). A 6-year-old Dall's ram shot in early October in the Yukon weighed 103 kg (226 lb). A somewhat emaciated 7-year-old Stone's ram shot during the rut in late November weighed 170 lb (77 kg). This was the smallest of 4 mature Stone's rams shot by myself, and I estimate that the largest would have weighed about 240 lb (110 kg) live weight.

In horn size, snow sheep are clearly smaller than thinhorn sheep. The maximum dimensions listed by Heptner et al. (1961) and Cherniavski (1962a) are 111 cm (43 in) with a basal circumference of 36 cm ($14\frac{1}{2}$ in). Clark (1964) uncovered a good many horn measurements for *O. nivicola*. None exceeded 105 cm ($41\frac{1}{2}$ in) in length or 37 cm ($14\frac{1}{4}$ in) in basal circumference, while the heaviest set of dry horns and upper skull weighed 6.8 kg (15 lb). These dimensions are greatly exceeded by those from Dall's and Stone's sheep. The longest horns recorded for Dall's sheep measured 124 cm (49 in) and for Stone's sheep 130 cm (51 in); basal circumferences in excess of 38 cm (15 in) have been frequently reported (Baker 1964). The dry upper skull and horns of 5 Stone's rams 9–14 years of age weighed 7.5–9.6 kg (16–21 lb); yet much larger Stone's rams grow in northeastern British Columbia than in the northwest where I happened to have studied them. The differences in horn size between *O. dalli* and *O. nivicola* appear to be considerable and real despite spotty sampling.

Next we must compare sheep from the Alaska-Yukon and Southern refugia. One can compare either sheep living today within these refugia or sheep derived from populations formerly living in these refugia. In the first comparison the sheep from the Alaska-Yukon refugium is the Dall's sheep and the sheep from the Southern refugium will be the

Nelson's bighorn, the most primitive and *dalli*-like of all bighorns (Cowan 1940). In the second comparison the sheep derived from the Alaska-Yukon refugium will be the Stone's sheep and the one from the Southern refugium will be the Rocky Mountain bighorn; these races are the most advanced forms of *O. dalli* and *O. canadensis* respectively.

The hypothesis predicts that Nelson's sheep should have larger horns, longer horn cores, a heavier and more pneumated skull, and a larger rump patch. Since Dall's sheep are white, only the horn and skull characteristics can be compared, and at present there is only a small amount of horn size and skull dimension data available. These data show that Nelson's sheep have significantly larger horn bases than Dall's sheep (p. 48), while Cowan's (1940) skull measurements show that Nelson's sheep have longer and wider, that is, bigger skulls than Dall's sheep (their skull dimensions are quite similar to those of Stone's sheep). Yet Nelson's sheep are somewhat smaller than Dall's sheep in body size (p. 46). These limited data follow the predictions of the hypothesis.

There are a few more data available for a comparison of Stone's and bighorn sheep, and these follow entirely the predictions of the hypothesis. Stone's sheep have the relatively smaller horns (p. 48), smaller rump patch (fig. 46), shorter horn cores (plate 12), and a relatively narrower, hence less massive, skull than bighorns (Cowan 1940). A comparison of Stone's and bighorn sheep behavior is given later.

Second test of the hypothesis.   The prediction to be tested is that sheep living deep in glaciated terrain have relatively larger horns, skull pneumation, and rump patches than sheep living in the old refugia. The most thinhornlike sheep from the Southern refugium is the Nelson's bighorn. It has rather wide, flaring horns of small size *dalli*-like skull proportions (Cowan 1940), and a rather small rump patch bisected by a complete tail stripe. The Nelson's bighorn is surrounded by larger-horned, that is, advanced bighorn races. This suggests that bighorns were greatly restricted during the last glaciation to a small area in Nevada and California and radiated from there during postglacial dispersal (fig. 44). The most highly evolved forms should be the Rocky Mountain bighorn and the northern populations of the California bighorn. These races indeed appear to differ from Nelson's bighorn in the predicted direction (chap. 2); however, only future research making exacting measurements will demonstrate how great the differences are. It should also be found that Rocky Mountain and California bighorn populations located about midway between their northernmost populations and those of the Nelson's bighorns should be intermediate in characteristics between these. That is, California bighorns from California should have more flaring horns than those from British Columbia.

Among thinhorn sheep, Stone's sheep from British Columbia should be more highly evolved than those from the old refugium. Stone's sheep do indeed differ from Dall's sheep in the predicted direction as is indicated in maximum horn size (chap. 2) and skull measurements (Cowan 1940). However, this comparison is not strictly valid. It is valid to compare Stone's sheep from within and outside the Alaska refugium. Some relic populations of gray thinhorn sheep are found in the old refugium in the Yukon Territory. No data exists on these to date. The presence of these sheep suggests that dark as well as white sheep survived in Beringia during the last glaciation.

The foregoing comparisons demonstrate that the glaciation hypothesis predicts correctly for American sheep if combined with Cowan's theory of how sheep spread into America. It also indicates that Asiatic and American sheep evolved convergently. The hypothesis that sheep evolve predictably by increasing in horn size, rump patch size, and combat capability when spreading into uninhabited terrain appears equally applicable to other members of the caprid tribe.

Third test of the hypothesis. *Ammotragus* could serve not only as an exemplary ancestor of sheep, but also makes a passable ancestor for goats, at least of the round-horned forms. Stripped of its beard and mane, it is not dissimilar to the young tur male (*C. cylindricornis*) or the "blue sheep" (*Pseudois*). *Ammotragus* combined a number of goatlike characteristics and can be linked with intermediate forms not only to the argalis but also to ibex (fig. 47).

If *Ammotragus*-like ancestors gave rise to the round-horned goats, then these should show similar evolutionary tendencies as sheep when radiating from their ancestors. We can align *Ammotragus*, *Capra cylindricornis*, and *Pseudois* by similarity, and they do form a geographic cline. *Pseudois* is the furthest removed from *Ammotragus* and has changed the most toward a sheeplike habit. We find that: (1) *Pseudois* and *C. cylindricornis* have larger horns than *Ammotragus*; (2) *Pseudois* and *C. cylindricornis* have lost all of the cheek and neck mane; (3) these two species have evolved rump patches, that of *Pseudois* being the larger as demanded by the hypothesis, and in addition *Pseudois* has white margins on hind and front legs; (4) as in sheep, the sexual dimorphism

Fig. 47. *Ammotragus* (*bottom*) can be connected by intermediates to the most highly evolved of true goats, the Siberian ibex (*Capra ibex sibirica*) (*top*). Females are shown beside both. *Middle right*, the Caucasian tur (*Capra cylindricornis*) with female. *Middle left*, *Capra caucasica* from the western Caucasus.

of the two forms has increased over that found in *Ammotragus*. Moreover, *Pseudois* is sheeplike in that the males are highly social and there are either vestiges or the beginnings of preorbital and interdigital glands. *Pseudois* resembles a true sheep so greatly that its common name is "blue sheep" and taxonomists have quarreled over its phylogenetic position (see Thenius and Hofer 1960).

The round-horned goats differ from sheep in their evolution in that their horns although increasing in size retain the heteronym winding and their ears remain long and pointed. Evidently, homonym horn winding in sheep evolved for reasons other than increases in horn size.

Last, let us look at *Capra*. It is not my aim to tackle the phylogeny of this diverse genus of obscure origin. I only want to point out that the species with the longest and thickest horns, the least display hair on the body, neck, and face, and the largest body size are found deep in

Fig. 48. The rump patch of the Siberian ibex (*left*) is larger than that of the Alpine ibex (*center*) and apparently does not decrease in size with age. These two animals are 4 years old. *Right*, the rump patch of an old Alpine ibex. (From photos.)

formerly glaciated terrain. These are the ibexes. Of these, the one who has penetrated deepest along once glaciated mountain ranges into Central Asia and lives side by side with the giant argalis has apparently not only the largest horns, but also the largest rump patch—the Siberian ibex (*Capra ibex sibirica*) (fig. 48).

Furthermore, the true goats as well as the sheep have specialized their combat behavior toward dealing out harsher blows at the expense of wrestling and hooking. They differ in particular, not in principle, from sheep, and also rise on their hind legs to clash. *Pseudois* clashes like a goat, not like a sheep (Lydekker 1898).

At this point in my explanation of sheep evolution, it is necessary to: (1) identify and verify the selective forces which *simultaneously* produce in sheep increases in relative horn size, rump patch size, loss of neck manes, and specialization in combat behavior toward focusing the force of the clash on one horn edge; (2) show how evolution *stagnates* to produce the clines mentioned; and (3) test the evolutionary mechanisms postulated by their predictions.

THE NEOTENIZATION HYPOTHESIS

Increasing horn size is the first clue to sheep evolution. Larger horns are due to longer or more intense growth. Growth, however, is typical of juveniles, and we do know that rams continue to grow and enlarge for most of their life. Larger horn size can hence be achieved by making the rams more "juvenile" or neotenic, that is, by intensifying or enlarging the physiological mechanisms which keep the animal young. If sheep did become more neotenic, then relatively large horns are only one product of it, for the animals should also assume more juvenile features as they evolve. The adults of the advanced line should resemble the juveniles of the primitive forms, be it in external characteristics or behavior. A glance at fig. 43 shows that Asiatic sheep have lost beards in their evolution. Since the beard is typical of *old* males but not young males in the primitive sheep (Lydekker 1913), the advanced sheep are more juvenilelike or neotenic in lacking the beard. We need not postulate selection *against* the beard but only selection *for* neoteny; the beard would disappear with increasing neotenization.

The predictions of the neoteny hypothesis can be tested on American sheep. Rams from the more advanced races in evolution should be the more neotenic and should hence be more like lambs or juveniles in their behavior than adult rams of more primitive races. We noted a little earlier that the Rocky Mountain bighorn is the most advanced race of the most advanced species and the Stone's sheep is the most advanced race of the more primitive species. If the neoteny hypothesis is valid the following should be found: since it was shown that as they mature rams (1) display their horns more frequently, (2) kick subordinates more frequently with their front leg, (3) use fewer butts and (4) fewer mounts against subordinates, and (5) act more "bravely" by approaching equal-size opponents more frequently in horn display, thereby treating them as subordinates, it follows that the more neotenous a race and the more juvenile it acts, the greater the *proportion* of patterns typical of juveniles, and therefore the *less* it should display, kick with the front leg, and the *more* it should butt and mount. It also should act more "cowardly" than the adults of more primitive races. Hence bighorn rams should display less, kick less, be more aggressive and sexual as well as more "cowardly" than Stone's sheep. These predictions are fulfilled.

Table 72 shows that fully mature bighorn rams use a significantly greater proportion of overt aggressive behavior than equal-age Stone's rams, whereas young rams of both races act more alike as dictated by the hypothesis. Table 73 shows that bighorn rams use significantly fewer front kicks than Stone's rams do toward equal-size opponents.

TABLE 72

Aggressive patterns (butting, clashing, rushing) performed by dominant bighorn' and Stone's rams on subordinates

	Bighorn				Stone's			
	IV	III	II	♂y	IV	III	II	♂y
Class IV rams								
Aggressive patterns	12	6	9	4	6	7	12	1
Other patterns	86	64	53	36	227	258	196	61
Total	98	70	62	40	233	265	208	62
Classes III and II rams								
Aggressive patterns		7	6	3		7	16	1
Other patterns		45	109	130		190	315	91
Total		52	115	133		197	331	92

NOTES: Class IV bighorn rams use significantly more aggressive patterns than Stone's rams of the same class ($\chi^2 = 25.6$, $v = 4$, $p < 0.001$). Younger bighorn rams use slightly, but not significantly, more aggressive patterns than Stone's rams of equal age ($\chi^2 = 7.0$, $v = 3$, N.S.).

TABLE 73

Frequency of front kicks and other behavior patterns performed by bighorn and Stone's rams on opponents of equal size

	Bighorn			Stone's		
	IV	III	II	IV	III	II
Front kicks	33	25	13	124	112	84
Other patterns	109	52	87	170	139	211
Total	142	77	100	294	251	295

NOTE: Stone's rams performed significantly more front kicks than bighorn rams ($\chi^2 = 26.2$, $v = 3$, $p < 0.001$).

Not only here, but also during courtship this difference in frequencies persists, although it was not statistically significant with the sample size used and these data have been omitted.

Table 74 shows that bighorn rams mount nonestrous ewes significantly more frequently than do Stone's rams of comparable age. The greater "sexuality" of bighorn rams is demonstrated by their relatively more frequent licking and sniffing of the caudal end of young males and females (table 75 and fig. 49). Table 76 shows that bighorn rams display horns significantly less frequently than Stone's rams during courtship, as is demanded by the hypothesis. Table 77 shows that mature bighorn

TABLE 74

Frequency of mounting and other behavior patterns performed by bighorn and Stone's rams on nonestrous females

	Bighorn				Stone's			
	IV	III	II	♂y	IV	III	II	♂y
Mounts	6	6	6	35	10	7	50	34
Other patterns	302	198	267	73	784	510	1,073	326
Total	308	204	273	108	794	517	1,123	360

NOTE: Bighorn rams performed significantly more mounts than Stone's rams ($\chi^2 = 45.5$, $v = 4$, $p < 0.001$).

TABLE 75

Frequency with which bighorn and Stone's rams sniffed the rears of young males and females

	Bighorn		Stone's	
	II & ♂y	♀ & ♀y	II & ♂y	♀ & ♀y
Sniffings	22	168	8	350
Other patterns	409	623	685	1,984
Total	431	791	693	2,334

NOTE: Bighorn rams perform significantly more sniffings than Stone's rams ($\chi^2 = 31.9$, $v = 2$, $p < 0.001$).

rams are less likely to approach opponents of equal size in a horn display when initiating a social interaction than Stone's rams; bighorns hence act less "bravely." These data indicate that the neoteny hypothesis is valid. It predicts that the argalis will be more neotenous than urials, but this prediction has not been tested as yet.

Selection for Neoteny

By itself, the neoteny hypothesis does not fully explain sheep evolution. It fails to tell us why there was selection for larger horns, more pneumated skulls, and larger rump patches in advanced sheep. It can be

TABLE 76

Frequency of horn displays by bighorn and Stone's rams during courtship of nonestrous females

	Bighorn				Stone's			
	IV	III	II	♂y	IV	III	II	♂y
Horn displays	108	77	97	20	283	202	484	89
Other patterns	196	125	175	70	286	169	338	131
Total	304	202	272	90	569	371	822	220

NOTE: Stone's rams of all classes display significantly more than bighorn rams of comparable age and horn size ($\chi^2 = 66.5$, $v = 4$, $p < 0.001$).

understood as a by-product of selection for larger horns, so that many characters were reduced or enlarged due to a dominant selection for just one trait, namely larger horns. We know that large horns allow rams to reach high dominance rank and that horn size and breeding success are related (chap. 7). What gives larger-horned rams the advantage?

It is evident that all things being equal, the larger the horns, the heavier they are and the more forceful a blow a ram can strike. If the skulls of rams act as shields, clearly the larger the horns of a race, the heavier and sturdier must be the shield to withstand the blows. There-

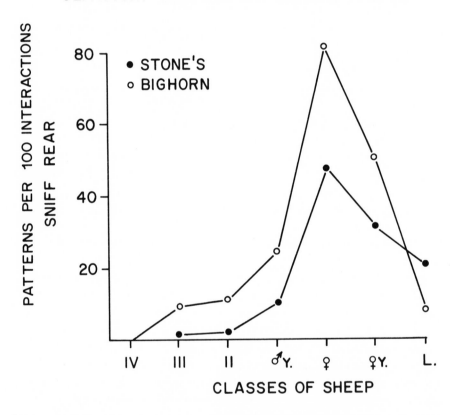

Fig. 49. Relative frequencies with which Stone's and bighorn rams sniffed the rears of sheep of various sex-age classes. The more sheep resembled an adult ewe, the more they were sniffed by rams. Bighorn rams sniffed the rears of sheep significantly more frequently than did Stone's rams (see also table 74).

TABLE 77

Frequency with which bighorn and Stone's rams initiated engagements on opponents of equal size with a horn display

	Bighorn			Stone's		
	IV	III	II	IV	III	II
Initiations with display	37	23	33	54	13	23
Initiations without display	9	9	40	37	9	24
Total	46	32	73	91	22	47

NOTES: Bighorns approach others less frequently in a display than Stone's rams, but the difference is not significant except for class IV rams ($\chi^2 = 6$, $p < 0.05$).

fore, pneumation should enlarge with increased horn size, and we saw that it does in American and Asiatic sheep.

Selection for large horns hence indicates selection for more efficient combat. But if it is so, then we can expect all sorts of behavioral and morphological adaptations which will not only increase the effects of the clash, but also adaptations which will neutralize the blows. Indeed the differences in the behavior of primitive and advanced sheep can be explained by this view. The primitive combat type in which many forms of combat are used is gradually replaced by a simplified combat type in which the efficiency of the clash increases. The clashes become fewer but more forceful as rams grow heavier horns, concentrate the clash on one horn keel, grow larger, move further back to clash, rise on their hind legs, and use gravity to increase the force of their blows (plate 88).[2] Simultaneously skulls grow heavier to absorb the increased impact of the blows. It was discussed earlier how rams use every means to increase clash force, and it appears to me not unlikely that the deliberate feeding or snow pawing prior to clashing, or the nonchalant walking away of the aggressor prior to attack, are deceptive acts which aim at throwing the opponent off guard and occasionally give the aggressor a split-second advantage over the opponent. If the aggressor is able to surprise his opponent and crash into him before the latter is ready to neutralize the blow, the attacker is more likely to throw the defender off balance.

If the rump patch is an appeasement signal which motivates the

2. Film E 1334.

dominant ram sexually, then it appears plausible that it should increase in size the more aggressive the race. Since overt aggressiveness is a juvenile characteristic, the more neotenous races of sheep should be the more aggressive ones and should have the greater need for a large rump patch. At present the evidence demonstrating the proposed function of the rump patch is still outstanding.

Three questions are to be answered yet. Why did the horns of Asiatic rams change from the heteronym to the homonym winding, spiral out, and then become shorter but thicker? Under what conditions was there a selection for large, heavy horns? Why did the various races stagnate at different stages of horn growth and neoteny? Let us turn to the first question.

Evolution of Horn Form in Asiatic Sheep

At present there is no plausible explanation why urial horn initially began to grow in one plane forming a sicklelike horn, primarily because we know so little of the behavior of these sheep. However, once the change in horn form began, it had to go on. Note that the circular horns of the urial rams point directly at the neck (plate 89). If such sheep were subject to selection for longer horns, rams would grow the horn tips into their neck, hence selection would favor rams whose horn tips miss the neck. This would result in the familiar homonym winding as we see it in the northern cycloceros forms (fig. 43).

The urials evolved a sharp angle on the lateral side of the horns. This indicates that in clashing, rams cock the head slightly and—like American sheep—hit first with one horn, thereby concentrating the clash force on one horn keel.

The trend for long, thin, angular horns continued as we move via *severtzovi* and *nigrimontana* to *poli*. Here, in the Pamir argali, it reached its maximum expression, for *poli* grows the longest horns of all sheep (up to 75 in). However, horns much longer than those of *poli* are not possible—at least not with the manner in which *poli* clashes. These rams clash similarly to bighorns by racing bipedally at the opponent, inclining the head slightly away and down, hence bringing one lateral horn edge forward for clashing. If two *poli* rams with large horns were to clash in this fashion, they almost inevitably would hit their horn ends first. This would lead to breakage of the rather light though long horns. This happens in bighorns. Clark (1964), in his interesting account of *poli* in the Russian Pamir reported the following: horn breakage among large *poli* rams was frequent. Unlike bighorns, *poli* rams do not broom their horns but break them off usually at the end of the horn cores or even closer to the skull. Although *poli* horns tend to be nearly twice as long as those of bighorns and have similar circumferences at the base (55–75 inches long, 14–16 inches in circumference), they weigh no more than the horns of bighorns and often less. Clark (1964) reports the weight of the upper skull and horns of a large *poli* ram at 25 lb (11.4 kg). I weighed the heads of 8 heavily broomed bighorn rams, ages 8–16 years, and obtained a range of 20–32 lb (9–14.5 kg), average 25.3 lb (11.5 kg) (skull and horns thoroughly dry). This indicates that *poli* horns are rather lightly constructed. Horn fractures appear to me to be serious injuries, irrespective of what consequences the broken horn has on the ram's social success. If the horn cores are injured or frozen during winter, the door is open for bacterial attack of the membrane inside the horn sinuses. It seems to me that selection would set against *poli* rams with very long horns. Clearly, if horns were to evolve further some change had to appear.

The change came in the next member of the cline to the northeast of the Pamir, in the Littedale's sheep from the Tien-Shan (fig. 43). The angle of the horn shifts away from the eye toward the median line of the skull. This can be seen partially in figure 43. It is best seen in Clark when comparing the *poli* ram with *karelini* and *littedalei* (1964, pp. 59, 89, 95). This results in a ridge which appears to run down the center of the anterior horn face (see also Lydekker 1913, fig. 30). The implication is evident. Rams with a more frontally located edge would probably clash more frontally. This would swing the horn tips away and reduce the chances of horn breakage during the clash. In the Littedale's sheep the horns have also increased in diameter and mass.

As we move further northeast, the horn mass of argalis increases steadily. The skull and horns of a good *poli* weigh about 25 lb but those of a good *ammon* weighed 49 lb (Clark 1964). While the weight of skull and horns almost doubles, the body weight increases only from about 300–350 lb to 400–450 lb (after Clark 1964; Heptner et al. 1961). Furthermore, the horn angle, so prominent in *nigrimontana* or *poli*, becomes lost as horns increase in diameter in *ammon* and *darwini*. A similar relationship exists also in the American sheep. The horns of *stonei* rams had prominent lateral horn angles; the upper skull and horns of 4 rams, ages 8–16 years, weighed 16–22 lb, average 18 lb while live weight of old rams would have been about 200–220 lb. Northern *canadensis* rams, weighing about 250 lb, live weight, had horns and skull weights of about 26 lb, but occasionally reaching more than 30 lb. Similar to *ammon, canadensis* rams have more rounded horns and though the horn keel is present, it is not as prominent as in thinhorn sheep. On the basis of neoteny, it can be expected that thick-horned Siberian argalis will clash more frequently than the thin-horned *poli*—just as it is found in American sheep.

Selection for Large Horns and the Stagnation of Such Selection

The very factors which advance sheep evolution by selecting for large horns and effective combat, will stagnate sheep evolution if reversed. The size of horns and degree of neoteny achieved by each race depends on how often or how long it experienced selection for large horns; the races furthest along a cline have experienced such selection longest and accumulated neotenizing genes. Since sheep evolution is linked with the distance they penetrated into uninhabited terrain, selection for large horns is associated with dispersal.

This is not surprising. When invading new habitat in the wake of glacial withdrawal, colonizing sheep would live in expanding, high-quality populations due to superabundance of forage. In such populations rams grow large in body and horn size, interact intensely and frequently, but have a short life expectancy. In high-quality populations reproduction is heavy. The ranks of the rams are filled by males which have grown to the limit allowed by their genotype. Hence there are many vigorous rams about, and the strife for dominance must of necessity be severe. In such a situation the rams with a heavier weapon (horns), more robust defenses (skull), and more skillful combat techniques are in the advantage and can be expected to do most of the breeding. Rams with genetically determined small horn size are relegated to lower dominance, and though their life expectancy may be greater than that of their large-horned rivals, they are faced by a new set of large-horned rams each year. Small-horned rams cannot make good their social disadvantage by breeding ewes during more rutting seasons, for in the expanding population *high reproduction assures rapid replacement of dead large rams by equals.*

Small-horned rams with their long life expectancy will begin siring more offspring than large-horned rams only when rams fail to grow close to their potential genetic maximum. This should happen in the stagnant or declining population that exists on a slim resource base. Each colonizing population must reach that stage despite a tendency for a high-quality population to perpetuate itself as suggested in the discussion of population control (chap. 10). Then large horns may be advantageous within each year, but less advantageous than somewhat smaller horns which allow their bearer to live a few more rutting seasons. As sheep populations disperse into vacant mountain ranges, each colonizing population goes through the phases of high quality and selection for large horns, then saturates its habitat, and declines in quality, which brings further selection for neoteny to a halt. This population in turn gives rise to the next population in line. That new population again experiences selection for neoteny during the expansion phase and becomes a little more evolved than the parent population. So each population in a cline is a little advanced over the one behind and a little more primitive than the one ahead. The main evolution of sheep can hence be explained by a different selection in the expanding high-quality population versus the declining or stable low-quality one.

What is the evidence for this view? When the ice of the last glaciation (Würm III—Wisconsin) retreated, it was followed by a dry steppe with some willows and birch in the moist sites (Heusser 1965; Bonatti 1966). There is evidence for a warm, dry climate following glacial retreat, which must have greatly favored the spread of grasslands. In early postglacial times we would probably find in the interior of continents sheep habitat similar to the one found today on the outskirts of the St. Elias Range in the Yukon. Here Dall's sheep live in the face of huge, retreating glaciers.

When sheep crossed to an uninhabited range, they would find a superabundance of forage, even during the critical late winter months. The budding population would respond to this forage regime in a predictable fashion. Reproduction can be expected to be high (see Klein 1965a; Woodgerd 1964), the lambs would be born large (Wallace 1948; Schinkel and Short 1961) and very vigorous (chap. 10); neonatal mortality would be low (Gunn and Robinson 1963; Alexander and Peterson 1961; Purser and Young 1959); there would be an abundant milk supply for the lambs (Slen et al. 1963); the lambs would grow rapidly and probably survive well during the winter (p. 289); the yearlings would mature earlier, as was shown for domestic sheep (Watson et al. 1956), and they would be of large body size. The lambs born to sheep living on a superabundance of forage would be expected to become large adults (Schinkel and Short 1961; Klein 1965a). Therefore, in the expanding, colonizing population we can expect sheep to reach their maximum body size, while phenotypic size variation would be reduced. Such sheep should be vigorous, high-quality animals with a short average life expectancy (p. 296).

The very existence of a large number of large, vigorous rams would have as a consequence many minor group battles and severe dominance fights or vicious fights during the intense competition for the estrous female. It was noted earlier that the 6–7-year-old rams interacted much more intensely (table 57) and had relatively more dominance fights than did older or younger rams. In Woodgerd's (1964) colonizing bighorn population rams died at about 6–7 years of age on the average (table 68). This correlation between age of maximum social activity (6–8 years of age) in a stagnant population and mean age at death in an expanding one is suggestive. The inverse relationship between horn size and life expectancy (fig. 26) lends further support to the view that rams which interact extensively, and soon reach a high dominance rank, die early.

Once the population has expanded to fill the habitat to capacity, competition and trampling of soil would reduce quality and quantity of forage. Less energy and nutrients are then available for reproduction and growth. The population can now be expected to deteriorate in quality. Reproduction and survival of young decline, growth rates decrease, maturation is delayed, the rams act listless and fighting is reduced, parasitism may become burdensome, and the life expectancy of the individual adults increases. Phenotypic size variation increases for two reasons: mild winters allow females to bear and raise periodically lambs of better than average quality; and some females happen to occupy better home ranges than others during the crucial late winter months when the fetus grows most and the udder becomes developed. When stagnation does take place, each population has accumulated more neotenizing genes than its parent population and is slightly more neotenic than the latter.

In the stagnant population, large-horned and vigorous rams are as likely to be a social and reproductive success within any rutting season as ever; however, such rams are uncommon and their life expectancy is likely to be short. They cannot be expected to make as large a contribution as somewhat smaller-horned rams with a long life expectancy. The breeding rams in such a population may have achieved their relatively large size due to phenotypic as well as genotypic factors, while subordinate small-horned rams with their long life expectancy may outbreed the larger rams. Selection for large horns is hence reduced or stagnated.

The foregoing is a simplified conceptual model of the factors that must follow when sheep colonize new terrain in the wake of withdrawing glaciers. The model is constructed from verified concepts and facts but remains to be tested as a whole. Much could be added to it but this would only obscure the concept, and I prefer to leave it in the present purposely oversimplified version, with only a few essential thoughts added.

This model requires that the gene flow between the parent and colonizing population be soon broken or greatly reduced. At present there is little point in discussing why and how this could occur with fluctuating timberlines. However, there are two factors arising from the model itself which would restrict gene flow. First, high-quality rams moving from the colonizing to the parent population would be selected against due to their short life expectancy. Conversely, rams crossing from the parent population to the colonizing one would be selected against because such rams would be of relatively smaller horn and body size and would breed at a much lower rate than the colonizing rams. When sheep move between mountain ranges across a height of land, the zone of possible contact between parent and colonizing populations is small and of short duration while the populations are large; little gene flow can take place here. In total, short duration of small zones of contact between populations and selection against dispersing rams would maintain the characteristic gene pool of each population. Rising timberlines would soon isolate populations of sheep to individual mountain ranges.

From the foregoing it follows that mountain sheep live in tiny, isolated relict populations between major glaciations. Indeed, this is apparently what one finds in the mountains of northern British Columbia and the central Yukon. How do such populations prevent inbreeding? It is likely that this is achieved by selection for heterosis. It was demonstrated by Craig and Baruth (1965) that in domestic fowl dominance rank is directly related to heterosis. If this relationship is valid for mountain sheep, then clearly this would counteract the tendency for inbreeding in small populations. In addition, the reproductive advantage gained by dispersing rams during the breeding season would also increase heterosis in the population.

DISCUSSION AND PREDICTIONS

The foregoing theory of sheep evolution has a number of consequences. First, it is evident that big, large-horned sheep must have evolved repeatedly with every major glaciation of the Pleistocene. Since there has been convergence in several caprid lineages toward larger horns and robust skulls, the end products of diverse sheep lineages are likely to appear similar, and similarity of skulls among large sheep is no indication of close relation. The argalis, contrary to the thoughts expressed by Sushkin (1925), Cherniavski (1962a), Flerov (1967), and Stokes and Condie (1961), are not likely the close relatives of bighorns, but resemble American sheep due to convergent evolution. In serological, as well as in their DNA and RNA characteristics, they will probably resemble urials and mouflons closely, just as they do in reproductive characteristics and in population dynamics. In my view, argalis are neotenous urials. The fact that large sheep were found in the late Pleistocene of southwestern North America (Stokes and Condie 1961) no more indicates that argalis were the bighorn's ancestor than the findings of large Pleistocene bears (*Ursus arctos*) in Europe (Kurten 1968) implicate the Alaskan Kodiak bear as their direct ancestor. We know that Pleistocene mammals varied greatly in size with glacial and interglacial periods (Kurten 1968), and from the foregoing theory we can expect that colonizing sheep are large animals. The earliest sheep found in America hence should be large individuals.

The hypothesis advanced allows a number of predictions about the behavior and evolutionary status of American sheep found in Siberia. The most primitive of all American sheep appears to be the Kamchatka variety. Kamchatka was probably a refugium for sheep during maximum glaciations. Sheep could well have lived along the coastal terraces as they do now, a view supported by the fact that sheep are found on Atlasowa Island off the southern tip of Kamchatka. According to Lydekker (1898) these sheep have the smallest rump patch. It should be found that these sheep are the least neotenous in their behavior. Compared to thinhorn sheep from the old Alaska-Yukon refugium, Kamchatka sheep should therefore (1) use relatively fewer aggressive behavior patterns and fight more rarely, (2) display horns more frequently and use the front kick more often, (3) approach equal-size rivals in horn display more frequently, and (4) mount nonestrous females and subordinate rams less frequently. I would expect also that rams rarely back up as far as bighorns when clashing in serious fights. It should also be found that Kamchatka sheep rarely break their horn tips (because of the infrequency of fighting).

Since the glaciation patterns of Siberia are complex and as yet hedged with much uncertainty (Giterma and Golubeva 1967; Kind 1967), it is not possible to state with certainty where sheep became extinct during maximum glaciations and where not. There are some exceptions. Kamchatka was probably one refugium for sheep. A second one lay almost certainly north of Lake Baikal, on the left shore of the present-day Lenna River. From here sheep must have moved north along the height of land toward the Central Siberian Plateau and Putorana Mountains as the glacier that covered central Siberia and the Taimyr lowlands retreated northward. A relict population, deep in formerly glaciated terrain, lives today on the Putorana Mountains (Norilsk Highlands). If the view is correct, then sheep from the Putorana Mountains should resemble those from the Stanovoi Mountains more than those from the Verkhoyansk Mountains. I do not believe that sheep crossed the lower Lenna River, which during meltoff must have been a still larger torrent than it is today. The Siberian mountain ranges, such as the Stanovoi, Verkhoyansk, Dzugzur, or Kilyma Ranges carried valley glaciers of varying sizes and were probably largely uninhabitable for sheep. Yet sheep can and do live in the sight of glaciers and they could well have survived glacial maxima low on the Dzugzur Range, at the sea of Okhotsk, or along the foothills of the Kilyma Ranges in addition to the possible refugia mentioned. It is hence difficult to decide a priori how sheep dispersed after the last, the Sartan, glaciation. Moreover, some Alaskan sheep could have moved sometime during or shortly after the Zerianka and Sartan glaciations into Siberia. Little can be said at present beyond the following: Neotenous sheep can be expected to live in the major Siberian mountain ranges, which are advanced further in horn size, rump patch size, and behavioral characteristics than Kamchatka sheep. At present there are no published data to verify or reject this hypothesis.

It appears that neotenization of sheep leads to a simplification and reduction of "ritual" in mountain sheep. The mature individual resembles behaviorally the juvenile of the original parent population and not the adult. It appears then that neotenization produces a more "immature" behavior, although the individuals are more highly evolved. Thus the dominance fights of bighorn rams are rather rough and unpolished still.

It appears that after an initial size increase during colonization, the individuals of a species decline in size, but may fluctuate in size thereafter with glacial and interglacial periods (and locally with environmental conditions). There are ample paleontological data for this, compiled by Kurten (1968). The first lions to reach Europe during the Villafranchian were giants and were never surpassed in size; so were the first leopards, cheetahs, hunting dogs (*Lycaon*), and hyenas. As the saber-tooth cats (*Smilodon*) invaded America, they grew into giants as they advanced south. The first auerochs (*Bos*) to appear in Europe during mid-Pleistocene times were far larger than their later followers (Zeuner 1967). On the whole, the large mammals which flooded into Europe and Asia during the Villafranchian grew to immense sizes before either disappearing or surviving as smaller individuals. This is valid not only for the examples above but also for gorals (*Naemorhaedus*), the thar, the first sheep (*Megalovis*), and true goats (*Soergelia*), and it is probably true for the first Australopithecines also since the giant among them, *Gigantopithecus*, appears to be of Villafranchian origin from China (Wen-chung 1957; Thenius and Hofer 1960).

It is hence probable that sheep also declined in size after the initial colonization. The Siberian snow sheep, rather small in body size but highly evolved, are probably the offspring of larger sheep that first invaded Siberia, while the southern desert bighorns are offspring of larger sheep which first came to southwestern North America probably in the Sangamon interglacial. The reduction in size could be due to selection for longevity in qualitatively poor populations and, consequently, the evolution of slower growing, small individuals. If this speculation is valid, the giants of a species among large northern mammals should be shorter lived than the dwarfs.

The theory of sheep evolution shows that evolutionary changes can be adaptations not to the physical habitat but to changes in the social environment. The differences in external appearance between the various races of northern ungulates are primarily due to altered hornlike organs, display hair, and color; our classification of these mammals is largely based on their morphological social adaptations. It is likely that social selection in the expanding colonizing populations of various large northern mammals has been similar to that experienced by mountain sheep. Deer of the genus *Cervus* in going from southern Europe and North Africa to North America change by growing larger rump patches, losing the white spots in the adult coat, and by and large increasing relative antler size. Similarly, moose grow larger and more palmate antlers and larger bells in going from Europe across Siberia to North America (Heptner and Nasimovitsch 1968). Finally one must point out that man himself neotenized when moving across Asia into North America, probably in the wake of expanding game herds after glacial withdrawal. He neotenized by decreasing sexual dimorphism in body build, reducing or losing beard and body hair as well as reducing frontal baldness and gray hair with age. It appears that these changes can be related to selection in the expanding colonizing populations of successful hunters.

12 Conclusions

This study departs somewhat from classical ethological studies in that it attempts to explain behavior less in terms of proximal causation and ontogeny or evolutionary origin than in terms of its adaptive value. There appear to be three largely independent realms of selection: the social environment, the habitat, and the body care requirements of the species. Although the question by what physiological and onto-genetical process did a behavior pattern arise is interesting, the wilder-ness is not the best place for its perusal. Nor have I found much of the framework of classical ethology to be relevant. As far as natural selection is concerned it is quite inconsequential to an individual's reproductive success by what means a species-specific act is formed or transmitted. It is only important that the act be there when required. The precious time in the field can be more usefully spent investigating the poorly known relationship between social and ecological selection. It was John F. Eisenberg who stimulated me to think along this line during our personal contacts and by his studies of rodent and mammalian societies (Eisenberg 1966). Is there a consistent relationship between the ecological niche of a species and its social adaptations? For instance, certain "life forms" such as the "mouse," "duiker," or "rhino" have been repeatedly filled by mammals of unrelated lineages. There are placental as well as marsupial mice, while among the former insectivores and rodents both appear in the form of mice. Similar life forms appear to fill similar niches. Can the same be said of behavior? Can we predict the social adaptations of a species from its ecological niche, and are there consistently repeated "behavioral forms" whose total one can predict from a few of its parts? In the foregoing study I attempted to form a comprehensive theory of mountain sheep evolution and used behavior as a tool to study the species, rather than the species as a tool to study behavior. It is an attempt to discover the major selective forces which formed and maintain the characteristics of mountain sheep. However, the findings will probably apply to other ice age ungulates as well.

Sheep arose during the Villafranchian of Eurasia together with a large number of other ungulates, many of which were characterized by large hornlike organs. Sheep appear to be descendants of rupicaprid ancestors, which innovated a new, effective defense against horn blows in combat. They caught and neutralized such blows with the head. It cannot be explained at present how this innovation arose (it was apparently innovated independently in a number of ungulate lineages [Geist 1966a]), but it had far-reaching consequences.

Selection for such defense mechanisms favors heavy, pneumated skulls to absorb concussion, sturdy horn bases to resist fracture, a set of broad occipital condyles, a massive atlas to counteract lateral torque, and a thick hide over the nasal and frontal bones for added protection of the skull. Concurrently, ancestral defense mechanisms lose their adaptive functions and are no longer maintained by selection. These are a thick, heavy hide covering the body, a variety of evasive tactics, and an inhibition to enter into combat. Since horn blows are neutralized by catching them against an armored skull, males can interact aggressively with little injury to each other (this is not possible with the ancestral rupicaprid defenses against combat). Therefore, there followed a reduction in selection against overt fighting among males, as well as against extreme cautiousness in courtship of the now harmless female. The effective defense permits males to live in groups, although it does not select by itself for gregariousness. Selection for socialization came from two different sources, one being ecological selection, the other selection for neoteny or "juvenileness," the consequences of which produced more gregarious adults. We may now consider the ecological selection.

Since sheep as grazers exploit patches of stable grasslands and alpine vegetation in the mountains and all such patches are exploited by sheep under pristine conditions, there is selection against dispersing juveniles. Automatically this selects for gregarious juveniles which follow adults closely and against females which chase away their offspring after weaning. Consequently, juveniles inherit home ranges from adults and in turn pass them on as a living tradition to the next generation. The above ecological conditions favor strong fidelity of adults to their home ranges and this is found to be the case. Geographical range extension apparently occurs only when sheep habitat becomes extensive and is probably performed by bands of roaming rams in spring. A second consequence of selection against dispersing juveniles is the loose mother-young relationship of sheep. The female appears to lose interest in her offspring shortly after weaning and the young lamb gradually begins to follow not only its dam but other sheep as well and becomes independent of its mother. Were it not so, the female would have to chase the yearling away during the next lambing season. This would probably increase the chances of the yearling leaving the band and getting lost in the expanse of unsuitable terrain surrounding the pockets of sheep habitat. A third consequence is that sheep, which are aggressive animals, are thrown by selection into groups. This necessitates adaptations which allow young, subordinate animals to maintain themselves in the presence of large and potentially dangerous companions.

An increase in the gregariousness of individuals was brought about by selection for neoteny during colonization of uninhabited mountain ranges. Neoteny increases juvenile characteristics in adults, one of these being the tendency to follow larger sheep. One effect of neoteny is a postpuberal maturation period of 5 to 6 years for rams in which they increase in body and horn size and mature in social behavior. In consequence one finds age-dependent horn-size differences among rams, which can be used by the animals to predict dominance rank of strangers. In other words, horns function as rank symbols. Females are paedogenic in that they are frozen in their development at the level of a juvenile male and retain this appearance throughout life. Selection for neoteny increases such juvenile characteristics in rams as overt aggressiveness and the tendency to mount others. It also leads to a loss of the neck ruff typical of primitive sheep.

Since the adult females and juvenile, but sexually mature, rams strongly resemble each other, there is no distinct "female" form. In correlation one finds that males court not only females but also subordinate males. The closer a subordinate male resembles a female, the more sexual patterns are directed his way by larger males. Conversely, subordinate males respond to the courtship of the dominant in female fashion. The evolution of female mimicry appears to be a consequence of selection against independent, straying young rams, and hence for sociality.

Since the estrous female acts quite aggressively toward the breeding ram during her courtship and subordinate males appear to mimic estrous females, it is not surprising that the subordinate rams act quite aggressively toward the dominant. Overt aggression is largely the prerogative of the subordinate ram. The dominant is in no way endangered by this, since he can neutralize the blows with an armored head. The dominant ram's prerogative is to act sexually toward the subordinate. Female mimicry appears to help rams maintain themselves in the midst of larger, dangerous rams until they have established their home ranges at 4–5 years of age.

Segregation of sexes is in part achieved by a peculiar mechanism. For approximately 363 days of the year adult females act in the manner of sexually immature juveniles. They withdraw if kicked or mounted by rams; they use primarily overt aggressive patterns and threats, but not contact patterns, in social interactions; and they follow older females rather than large rams. With estrus, the female's behavior changes drastically into the converse state. It appears hormones control the female's "male behavior." Once estrus is past, the females make poor social partners for the rams, since unlike dominant males, they cannot be fought with, and unlike subordinate males, they will not stand for courtship. The selection for neoteny hence precipitates a considerable number of secondary and tertiary consequences.

What selects for neoteny? This is postulated to be the indirect result of selection for large horns. Originally an increase in horn size was probably only a response to an increase in horn-core thickness. Thin cores were probably subject to fracture during fighting, hence a selection for larger horn bases. This could be achieved by prolonging the growth of the head. Since horn growth is greatest when the body growth is greatest, and since growth is a characteristic of juveniles, prolonged horn and body growth can be achieved by enlarging and prolonging the action of the "physiological machinery" which typifies juvenile animals. This hypothesis was tested and found to be valid.

It was shown that sheep evolution can be linked with dispersal into uninhabited terrain and that it is stimulated by glacial withdrawal. The further sheep move into previously glaciated terrain, the larger their horns and rump patches become and the more they specialize in delivering a forceful clash. If large horns are the product of increased juvenileness or neoteny, then advanced sheep should also be more juvenilelike in their behavior. It is hence expected that they act more lamb-like, that is, they should use aggressive and sexual patterns relatively frequently, use fewer displays, and act less "bravely." These expected differences were found in a comparison of Stone's sheep with the larger-horned bighorn sheep.

Since increase in horn size is correlated with distance penetrated into new terrain, selection for large horns and colonizing appear to be related. It is postulated that this occurs in the expanding, colonizing population as follows: during colonization of newly available habitat, the population experiences a superabundance of high-quality forage. This results in a high-quality population which is characterized by a high reproductive rate and large, vigorous, early maturing individuals, their growth rate approaching their genetic potential. Such sheep appear to have a short life expectancy. In such populations males appear to interact often and intensely, which should lead to intense competition for the estrous female. Under these conditions the chances that rams with poor horn growth breed are small, despite the fact that such have a longer life expectancy and are active in more rutting seasons than larger-horned individuals. Each rutting season these small-horned rams are faced with a fresh group of large-horned rams produced by the high reproductive rates and high survival of juveniles in the population.

In the expanding, vigorous population there must be a premium not only on large horns but also on an armored head and improved defensive techniques and on methods which increase the clash force. Rams display their horns immediately following a clash. In this way individuals can associate the force of the clash experienced with the size of the horns responsible for it. Therefore, this would allow rams to judge the fighting potential of strangers and assume at once a correct rank position in relation to them. It is this ability to predict rank from horn size without combat that allows rams to live in an open society.

The social behavior of sheep appears to be an adaptation to create and maintain a predictable social environment, and can hence be considered analogous to exploratory behavior in the habitat. That is, both create to the individual a familiar, predictable surrounding and allow it to function with a minimum of energy waste and exposures to danger. Thus rams do not fight for females but for dominance or, conversely, for a reduction of uncertainty in social status. Their actions allow them to experience the rival and act adaptively when meeting him next. One factor which may well reduce uncertainty of identity is the secretion of the preorbital gland. When the subordinate ram rubs himself on the dominant's face, he must impregnate himself with the scent of the dominant. Such an impregnation should be to the advantage of the subordinate, particularly when meeting the dominant at night. The latter can recognize him at once as a subordinate and treat him accordingly. The face-horning would appear responsible for the selection of the short, pliable hair found on the face of sheep, which —unlike body hair—is resistant to breakage. The consequence or effect of a predictable social environment is the dominance hierarchy.

The selection for large horns, and hence neoteny, must come to a halt in the stable or declining population which exists on a slim, unfavorable resource base, created by intraspecific competition and the population's impact on soil and vegetation. In this situation, individuals fail to reach their potential maximum size, reproduction and juvenile survival is low, the adults can act listless, the social interactions are relatively short and infrequent, while the life expectancy of adults is high. In the stable or declining population, long-lived, small-horned rams may leave more offspring than large-horned, short-lived individuals. Hence further evolution toward neoteny would cease. The external appearance of the female appears to passively follow changes in the male.

In the colonizing population the gene pool would experience an increase in genes favoring neoteny. As the colonizing population becomes stable, it would retain whatever genes in favor of neoteny had been accumulated. If this population gives rise to the next, that population during colonizing will accumulate more genes favoring neoteny before stagnating and so on. This concept explains the geographic clines in external appearance of sheep along mountain ranges of continents. Retention of neotenizing genes is favored since large-horned rams can be expected almost always to leave offspring.

In general, sheep evolution was rapid and revolved about the perfection of a new combat type and the problems this precipitated. Superimposed on this essentially social evolution were adaptations to the habitat. The latter is characterized by a boom and bust economy, of feasts in summer and famine in winter. The evolution of large horns, so typical of northern Pleistocene ungulates, may well have been permitted by the superabundance of food in summer. The fattening of males prior to rut and the squandering of these energy stores during the rut appear to be typical of almost all northern ruminants, regardless of family (excepting the roe deer and maybe buffalo, both of which rut in summer). In Asia sheep appear to have been influenced by competition from a close relative. Except in eastern Siberia, sheep are generally found together with true goats. Goats occupy the broken, rocky terrain while sheep keep to the open, rolling mountain uplands. In eastern Siberia and in North America, sheep occupy the rocky broken terrain and appear to evolve convergently with northern ibex. This concept explains the close resemblance between American sheep and the ibex in body structure, habitat preference, jumping ability, a long gestation period, long life expectancy, and high birth weight. These similarities can be explained as adaptations to the long, cold winters and scarcity of forage found in the northern mountains; these characteristics evolve when populations live close to carrying capacity on stable plant communities. The behavior of wintering sheep appears to be such as to maximize energy conservation. The female's social behavior can be understood as adaptations to conserve energy and nutrients in order to grow a fetus large enough to escape hypothermy at birth. This view also suggests that sheep populations are controlled in number by the number of viable lambs born, which in turn is determined by the amount of high-quality forage freed to pregnant ewes by the death of sheep in the home range group. Hence, death rate (dependent on population quality) should control birth rate. This hypothesis is testable by its predictions.

References

Aldous, M. C.; Craighead, F. C.; and Devan, G. A. 1958. Some weights and measurements of desert bighorn sheep (*Ovis canadensis nelsoni*). *J. Wildl. Mgmt.* 22:444–45.

Alexander, G. 1960. Maternal behavior in the merino-ewe. *Proc. Aust. Soc. Anim. Prod.* 3:105–14.

———. 1961a. Energy expenditure and mortality in new-born lambs. *Proc. 4th Internatl. Cong. Anim. Reprod.* 3:630–37.

———. 1961b. Temperature regulation in the new-born lamb, III. Effect of environmental temperature on metabolic rate, body temperatures, and respiratory quotient. *Aust. J. Agric. Res.* 12:1152–74.

———. 1962a. Temperature regulation in the new-born lamb, IV. The effect of wind and evaporation of water from the coat on metabolic rate and body temperature. *Aust. J. Agric. Res.* 13:82–99.

———. 1962b. Temperature regulation in the new-born lamb, V. Summit metabolism. *Aust. J. Agric. Res.* 13:100–21.

———, and Davis, H. L. 1959. Relationship of milk production to number of lambs born or suckled. *Aust. J. Agric. Res.* 10:720–24.

———, and Peterson, J. E. 1961. Neonatal mortality of lambs. *Aust. Vet. J.* 37:371–81.

———; Peterson, J. E.; and Watson, R. H. 1959. Neonatal mortality in lambs. *Aust. Vet. J.* 35:433–41.

———, and Williams, D. 1966. Teat-seeking activity in lambs during the first hours of life. *Anim. Behav.* 14:166–76.

———; Reid, R. L.; Schinkel, P. G.; and Ferguson, K. A. 1962. Nutrition of the pregnant ewe. *Proc. 8th Internatl. Cong. Anim. Prod.* 3:269–73.

Allred, G. L.; Baker, L. R.; and Bradley, W. G. 1966. Additional studies of anomalies of the skull in desert bighorn sheep. Transactions California-Nevada Section Wildlife Society, 1966, pp. 40–47. Mimeographed.

Altmann, Margarete. 1952. Social behaviour of elk (*Cervus canadensis nelsoni*) in the Jackson Hole area of Wyoming. *Behaviour* 4:116–43.

———. 1963. Naturalistic studies of maternal care in moose and elk. In *Maternal behavior of mammals*, ed. L. H. Rheingold, pp. 233–54. New York: Wiley.

Altmann, S. A. 1962. A field study of the sociobiology of rhesus monkeys (*Macaca mulatta*). *Ann. N.Y. Acad. Sci.* 102:338–435.

Anderson, J. A., and Henderson, J. B. 1961. *Himalayan thar in New Zealand.* N. Z. Deerstalkers Association, Special Publication no. 2.

Armstrong, D. G.; Blaxter, K. L.; Graham, N. McC.; and Wainman, F. W. 1959. The effect of environmental conditions on food utilisation by sheep. *Anim. Prod.* 1:1–12.

Arnold, G. W. 1960*a*. Selective grazing by sheep of two forage species at different stages of growth. *Aust. J. Agric. Res.* 11:1062–133.

———. 1960*b*. The effect of the quantity and quality of pasture available to sheep and their grazing behaviour. *Aust. J. Agric. Res.* 11:1034–43.

———. 1962. The influence of several factors in determining the grazing behaviour of border Leicester × merino sheep. *J. Brit. Grassland Soc.* 17:41–51.

Ausser, C. 1946. *Der Alpensteinbock*. Vienna: Universum.

Backhaus, D. 1959*a*. Experimentelle Untersuchungen über die Sehschärfe und das Farbsehen einiger Huftiere. *Zs. Tierpsychol.* 16:445–67.

———. 1959*b*. Beobachtungen über das Freileben von Lelwel-Kuhantilopen (*Alcelaphus buselaphus*, Heuglin 1877) und Gelegenheitsbeobachtungen an Sennar-Pferdeantilopen (*Hippo tragus equinus bakeri*, Heuglin 1863). *Zs. Säugetierkde.* 24:1–34.

———. 1961. Beobachtungen an Giraffen in zoologischen Gärten und freier Wildbahn. Inst. Pares. Nat. Congo et Ruanda-Urundi, Brussels.

———. 1964. Zum Verhalten des nördlichen Breitmaulnashornes (*Diceros simus cottoni*, Lydekker 1908). *Zool. Garten* (n.s.) 29:93–107.

Bailey, E. D. 1969. Immigration and emigration as contributory regulators of populations through social disruption. *Can. J. Zool.* 47:1213–16.

Baillie-Grohman, W. A. 1900. *Fifteen years sport and life in the hunting grounds of Western America and British Columbia*. London: Horace Cox.

Baker, B. E.; Blood, D. A.; and Chen, E. C. H. 1967. Rocky Mountain bighorn sheep, II. Electrophoretic analysis of proteins and carbohydrate content of casein. *Can. J. Zool.* 45:369–75.

Baker, L. R., and Bradley, W. G. 1966. Growth of the skull in desert bighorn sheep. Transaction Desert Bighorn Council 1966, pp. 48–109. Mimeographed.

Baker, M., ed. 1964. *Records of North American big game*. New York: Holt, Rinehart & Winston.

Banfield, A. W. F. 1958. The mammals of Banff National Park, Alberta. *National Museum of Canada Bull.*, no. 159. Ottawa.

Banks, E. M. Some aspects of sexual behaviour in domestic sheep (*Ovis aires*). *Behaviour* 23:249–79.

Bannikov, A. G.; Zhirnov, L. V.; Lebedeva, L. S.; and Fandeev, A. A. 1961. *Biology of the saiga*. English translation. Springfield, Va.: U.S. Dept. of Commerce.

Barnett, S. A. 1967. *Instinct and intelligence*. London: Macgibbon & Kee.

Bassett, C. A. J. 1965. Electrical effects in bone. *Sci. Am.* 213:18–25.

Beilharz, R. G., and Mylrea, P. J. 1963. Social position and movement orders of dairy heifers. *Anim. Behav.* 11:529–33.

Beninde, J. 1937. *Naturgeschichte des Rothirsches*. Monographie Wildsäugetiere, IV. Leipzig: P. Schöps.

Berwick, S. H. 1968. Observations on the decline of the Rock Creek,

Montana, population of bighorn sheep. Master's thesis, University of Montana, Missoula.

Bissonnette, T. H. 1941. Experimental modification of breeding cycles in goats. *Physiol. Zool.* 18:299.

Blaxter, K. L. 1962. The fasting metabolism of adult wether sheep. *Brit. J. Nutr.* 16:615–26.

———; Wainman, F. M.; and Wilson, R. S. 1961. The regulation of food intake by sheep. *Anim. Prod.* 3:51–61.

Blood, D. A. 1963. Some aspects of behaviour of a bighorn herd. *Can. Field-Nat.* 77:79–94.

———. 1967. Food habits of the Ashnola bighorn sheep herd. *Can. Field-Nat.* 81:23–29.

———; Wishart, D. W.; and Flook, D. R. 1970. Weights and growth of Rocky Mountain bighorn sheep in western Alberta. *J. Wildl. Mgmt.* 34:451–55.

Bonatti, E. 1966. North Mediterranean climate during the last Würm glaciation. *Nature* 209:984–85.

Boyd, M.; Doney, J. M.; Gunn, R. G.; and Jewell, P. A. 1964. The Soay sheep of the Island of Hirta, St. Kilda. A study of a feral population. *Proc. Zool. Soc. London* 142:129–63.

Bradley, W. G. 1964. The vegetation of the Desert Game Range with special reference to the desert bighorn. Transaction Desert Bighorn Council 1964, pp. 43–67. Mimeographed.

———. 1967. Boon and Crockett scores from the Desert Game Range and their significance to management. Transaction Desert Bighorn Council 1967, pp. 99–112. Mimeographed.

———, and Allred, L. G. 1966. A comparative study of dental anomalies in desert bighorn sheep. Transaction Desert Bighorn Council 1966, pp. 78–85. Mimeographed.

———, and Baker, L. R. 1967. Range of variation in Nelson bighorn sheep from the Desert Game Range and its taxonomic significance. Transaction Desert Bighorn Council 1967, pp. 114–40. Mimeographed.

———, and Baker, D. P. 1967. Life tables for Nelson bighorn sheep on the Desert Game Range. Transaction Desert Bighorn Council 1967, pp. 142–70. Mimeographed.

Brandborg, S. M. 1955. Life history and management of the mountain goat in Idaho. *Idaho Dept. of Fish & Game Wildl. Bull.*, no. 2. Boise.

Brehm, A. 1916. *Brehms Tierleben.* Säugetiere 4.

Briedermann, L. 1968. Die Westvorstösse des Elchwildes (*Alces alces* L.) in Mitteleuropa in ihrer populationsdynamischen Bedeutung. *Zool. Garten* 35:224–29.

Brody, S. 1945. *Bioenergetics and growth.* Reprint, 1964. New York: Hafner.

Brown, G. H.; Turner, Helen N.; Young, S. S. Y.; and Dolling, C. H. S. 1966. Vital statistics for an experimental flock of merino sheep, III. Factors affecting wool and body characteristics, including the effect of age of ewe and its possible interaction with method of selection. *Aust. J. Agric. Res.* 17:557–81.

Bruce, J.; Goodall, E. D.; Kay, R. N. S.; Phillipson, A. T.; and Vowles, L. E. 1966. The flow of organic and inorganic materials through the alimentary tract of the sheep. *Proc. Royal Soc. B.* 166:46–62.

Bruhin, H. 1952. Zur Biologie der Stirnaufsätze bei Huftieren, I & II. *Physiol. Comp. et Oecol.* 3:61–127.

Bubenik, A. 1959. *Grundlagen der Wildernährung.* Berlin: Deutscher Bauernverlag.

Buechner, H. K. 1960. The bighorn sheep in the United States, its past, present and future. *Wildl. Monog.*, no. 4.

––––––. 1963. Territoriality as a behavioural adaptation to environment in the kob. *Proc. XVI Internatl. Cong. Zool.* 3:59–63.

––––––, and Schloeth, R. 1965. Ceremonial mating behaviour in Uganda kob (*Adenota kob thomasi*, Neumann). *Zs. Tierpsychol.* 22:209–25.

Burckhardt, D. 1958. Kindliches Verhalten als Ausdrucksbewegung im Fortpflanzungszeremoniell einiger Wiederkäuer. *Rev. Suisse de Zool.* 65:311–16.

––––––. 1961. Aus dem Leben des Steinbockes. *Schweitzer Naturschutz* 27:10–14.

Byrne, A. R. 1968. Man and landscape change in the Banff National Park area before 1911. In *Studies in land use, history and landscape change.* National Park Series, no. 1. Calgary: University of Calgary.

Calhoun, J. B. 1963. The social use of space. In *Physiological mammalogy,* ed. W. V. Mayer and R. G. van Gelder, pp. 2–187. New York: Academic Press.

Caughley, G. 1966. Mortality patterns in mammals. *Ecology* 47:906–18.

Chen, E. C. H.; Blood, D. A.; and Baker, B. E. 1965. Rocky Mountain bighorn sheep (*Ovis canadensis canadensis*) milk. *Can. J. Zool.* 43:885–88.

Cherniavski, F. B. 1962a. On the systematic relationships and history of the snow sheep of the Old and New World. (Translation, Boreal Institute, The University of Alberta, Edmonton.) *Bull. Moscow Soc. Nat. Biol. Sect.* 68:17–26.

––––––. 1962b. On the reproduction and growth of the snow sheep (*Ovis nivicola* Esch). (Translation, Canadian Wildlife Service, Ottawa.) *Zoologisheskii Zhurnal* 41:1556–66.

––––––. 1967. Ecology of bighorn sheep and their value as a game animal on the Koryak uplands. (Translation, National Research Council, Ottawa.) *Problemy Severa* 11:128–41.

Christie, A. H. C., and Andrews, J. R. H. 1964. Introduced ungulates in New Zealand. Himalayan thar. *Tuatara* 12:67–77.

Clark, J. L. 1964. *The great arc of the wild sheep.* Norman: Univ. of Oklahoma Press.

Collias, N. E. 1956. The analysis of socialization in sheep and goats. *Ecology* 37:228–39.

Cowan, I. McT. 1940. Distribution and variation in the native sheep of North America. *Am. Midl. Nat.* 24:505–80.

Craig, J. V. and Baruth, R. A. 1965. Inbreeding and social dominance ability in chickens. *Anim. Behav.* 13:109–13.

Crofton, M. D. 1958. Nematode parasite populations in sheep on lowland farms, IV. Sheep behaviour and nematode infections. *Parasitology* 48:251–60.

Dalton, D. C.; Pearson, M. E.; and Sheard, M. 1967. The behaviour of dairy bulls kept in groups. *Anim. Prod.* 9:1–5.

Darling, F. F. 1937. *A herd of red deer.* London: Oxford Univ. Press.

Dasmann, R. F., and Taber, R. D. 1956. Behavior of Columbia black-tailed deer with reference to population ecology. *J. Mammal.* 37:143–64.

Dathe, H. 1966. Zum Mutter-Kind-Verhältnis bei Cerviden. *Beiträge zur Jagd und Wildforschung* 5:83–93. Deutsche Akademie der Landwirtschaftswissenschaften, Berlin.

Deevey, E. S. 1947. Life tables for natural populations of animals. *Quart. Rev. Biol.* 22:283–314.

Demarchi, R. A. 1965. An ecological study of the Ashnola bighorn winter ranges. Master's thesis, The University of British Columbia, Vancouver.

Deming, O. V. 1952. Tooth development of the Nelson bighorn sheep. *Calif. Fish & Game* 38:523–29.

———. 1955. Rearing bighorn lambs in captivity. *Calif. Fish & Game* 41:131–43.

Denniston, H. R. 1956. Ecology, behavior and population dynamics of the Wyoming or Rocky Mountain moose (*Alces alces shirasi*). *Zoologica* 41:105–18.

Denton, G. H., and Stuiver, M. 1967. Late Pleistocene glacial stratigraphy and chronology, Northeastern St. Elias Mountains, Yukon Territory, Canada. *Geol. Soc. Am. Bull.* 78:485–510.

Des Meules, P. 1964. The influence of snow on the behaviour of moose. Master's thesis, Ontario Agricultural College, Guelph.

De Vos, A. 1958. Summer observations on moose behavior in Ontario. *J. Mammal.* 39:128–39.

———. 1964. Range changes of mammals in the Great Lakes region. *Am. Midl. Nat.* 71:210–31.

———. 1967. Rubbing of conifers by white-tailed deer in successive years. *J. Mammal.* 48:146–47.

Dodds, D. G. 1963. The white-tail deer in Nova Scotia. Nova Scotia Dept. Lands & Forests, Halifax.

Donefer, E.; Lloyd, L. E.; and Crampton, E. N. 1963. Effect of varying alfalfa:barley ratios on energy intake and volatile fatty acid production by sheep. *J. Anim. Sci.* 22:425–28.

Edwards, R. Y. 1954. Fire and the decline of a mountain caribou herd. *J. Wildl. Mgmt.* 18:521–26.

Eibl-Eibesfeld, J. 1963. Angeborenes und Erworbenes im Verhalten einiger Säuger. *Zs. Tierpsychol.* 20:705–54.

———. 1966. *Grundrisse der vergleichenden Verhaltensforschung.* Munich: R. Pieper & Co.

Eisenberg, J. F. 1966. The social organization of mammals. *Handbuch der Zoologie,* vol. 8, pt. 10, no. 26, pp. 1–92. Berlin: De Gruyter.

Estes, R. D. 1966. Behaviour and life history of the wildebeest. *Nature* 212:999–1000.

———. 1967. The comparative behavior of Grant's and Thomson's gazelles. *J. Mammal.* 48:189–209.

Ewbank, R. 1964. Observations on the suckling habits of twin lambs. *Anim. Behav.* 12:34–37.

———. 1967. Nursing and suckling behaviour amongst clun forest ewes and lambs. *Anim. Behav.* 15:251–58.

Ewer, R. F. 1968. *Ethology of Mammals*. London: Logos Press.

Flerov, C. C. 1952. Musk deer and deer. *Fauna U.S.S.R. Mammals*. Vol. 1, no. 2. Acad. Sci. U.S.S.R., Moscow. English translation, Washington, D.C.: U.S. Dept. Commerce.

———. 1967. On the origin of the mammalian fauna of Canada. In *The Bering Land Bridge*, ed. D. M. Hopkins, pp. 271–80. Stanford: Stanford Univ. Press.

Flook, D. R. 1964. Range relationships of some ungulates native to Banff and Jasper National parks, Alberta. In *Grazing in Terrestrial and Marine Environments*, pp. 119–28. Dorking, G.B.: Blackwell's Sci. Pub., Adlard & Sons.

———. 1967. A study of the apparent unequal sex ratio of wapiti. Doctoral dissertation. The University of Alberta, Edmonton.

Foote, R. H., and Trimberger, G. W. 1968. Artificial insemination. In *Reproduction in farm animals*, ed. E. S. E. Hafez, pp. 135–53. Philadelphia: Lea & Febiger.

Frädrich, H. 1965. Zur Biologie und Ethologie des Warzenschweines (*Phacochoerus aethiopicus* Pallas) unter Berücksichtigung des Verhaltens anderer Suiden. *Zs. Tierpsychol.* 22:328–93.

———. 1967. Das Verhalten der Schweine (Suidae, Tayassuidae) und Flusspferde (Hippopotamidae). *Handbuch der Zoologie*, vol. 8, pt. 10, no. 26, pp. 1–44. Berlin: De Gruyter.

French, C. E.; McEwen, L. C.; Margruder, N. D.; Rader, T.; Long, T. A.; and Swift, R. W. 1960. Responses of white-tailed bucks to added artificial light. *J. Mammal.* 41:23–29.

Frenzel, B. 1968. The Pleistocene vegetation of northern Eurasia. *Science* 161:637–48.

Frost, N. M. 1942. Gestation period of bighorn sheep (*Ovis canadensis*). *J. Mammal.* 23:215–16.

Geist, V. 1960. Feral goats in British Columbia. *Murrelet* 41:1–7.

———. 1963. On the behaviour of the North American moose (*Alces alces andersoni* Peterson 1950) in British Columbia. *Behaviour* 20:377–416.

———. 1965. On the rutting behavior of the mountain goat. *J. Mammal.* 45:551–68.

———. 1966a. The evolution of horn-like organs. *Behaviour* 27:175–214.

———. 1966b. The evolutionary significance of mountain sheep horns. *Evolution* 20:558–66.

———. 1966c. Validity of horn segment counts in aging bighorn sheep. *J. Wildl. Mgmt.* 30:634–46.

Geist, V. 1966d. Ethological observations on some North American cervids. *Zool. Beiträge* (n.s.) 12:219–50.

————. 1967. On fighting injuries and dermal shields of mountain goats. *J. Wildl. Mgmt.* 31:192–94.

————. 1968a. On the interrelation of external appearance, social behaviour and social structure of mountain sheep. *Zs. Tierpsychol.* 25:199–215.

————. 1968b. On delayed social and physical maturation in mountain sheep. *Can. J. Zool.* 46:899–904.

————, and Cowan, I. McT. 1968. Film E 1333. *Ovis canadensis* (Bovidae): Social behaviour of males. Enc. Cin. Göttingen.

————. 1968. Film E 1334. *Ovis canadensis* (Bovidae): Fighting between males. Enc. Cin. Göttingen.

————. 1968. Film E 1335. *Ovis canadensis* (Bovidae): Rutting behaviour. Enc. Cin. Göttingen.

————. 1968. Film E 1336. *Ovis canadensis* (Bovidae): Sociology of young. Enc. Cin. Göttingen.

————. 1968. Film E 1337. *Ovis canadensis* (Bovidae): Foraging behaviour. Enc. Cin. Göttingen.

————. 1968. Film E 1338. *Ovis dalli* (Bovidae): Courtship of males. Enc. Cin. Göttingen.

————. 1968. Film E 1339. *Ovis dalli* (Bovidae): Social behaviour in female groups. Enc. Cin. Göttingen.

Gibson, E. J., and Walker, R. D. 1960. The visual cliff. *Sci. Am.* 202:64–71.

Gilbert, B. K., and Hailman, J. P. 1966. Uncertainty of leadership-rank in fellow deer. *Nature* 209:1041–42.

Giterma, R. E., and Golubeva, L. V. 1967. Vegetation of eastern Siberia during the anthropogene period. In *The Bering Land Bridge*, ed. D. M. Hopkins, pp. 232–44. Stanford: Stanford Univ. Press.

Goldthwait, R. P. 1966. Evidence from Alaska glaciers of major climatic changes. In *World climate from 8000 to 0 B.C.*, ed. J. S. Sawyer, pp. 40–51. London: Royal Meteorological Soc.

Gottschlich, H. J. 1968. Brunftkämpfe beim Rotwild. *Unsere Jagd.* Berlin: VEB Deutscher Landwirtschaftsverlag.

Grabowski, V. 1941. Prägung eines Jungschafs auf den Mensch. *Zs. Tierpsychol.* 4:326–29.

Graham, N. Mc C. 1962. Measurement of the heat production of sheep: The influence of training and of tranquilizing drugs. *Proc. Aust. Soc. Anim. Prod.* 4:138–44.

Gray, A. 1954. *Mammalian hybrids.* Tec. Comm. no. 10, Commonwealth Agric. Bureau, Edinburgh.

Grubb, P., and Jewell, P. A. 1966. Social grouping and home range in feral Soay sheep. *Symp. Zool. Soc. London*, no. 18, pp. 170–210.

Gundlach, H. 1961. Beobachtungen bei Versuchen zur Wildschadenverhütung am Rotwild des Georg von Opel-Freigeheges. G. von Opel-Freigehege, Kronberg Ts., Germany.

Gunn, R. D., and Robinson, J. F. 1963. Lamb mortality in Scottish hill flocks. *Anim. Prod.* 5:67–76.

Guthrie, R. D. 1966. The extinct wapiti of Alaska and Yukon Territory *Can. J. Zool.* 44:47–57.

Haas, G. 1958. Untersuchungen über angeborene Verhaltensweisen bei Mähnenspringern (*Ammotragus lervia* Pallas). *Zs. Tierpsychol.* 16:218–42.

Hafez, E. S. E. 1952. Studies on the breeding season and reproduction of the ewe, I–V. *J. Agric. Sci.* 42:189–265.

Haltenorth, Th. 1961. Fruchtbare Rückkreuzung eines weiblichen Mähnenschaf-Hausziegenbastards mit einem Steinbock. *Säugetierkdl. Mitt.* 9:105–9.

———. 1963. Die Klassifikation der Säugetiere: Artiodactyla. *Handbuch der Zoologie*, vol. 8, no. 32. Berlin: De Gruyter.

Hansen, G. 1965. Growth and development of desert bighorn sheep. *J. Wildl. Mgmt.* 29:387–91.

———. 1967. Bighorn sheep populations of the Desert Game Range. *J. Wildl. Mgmt.* 31:693–706.

Harper, J. A.; Harn, J. H.; Bentley, W. C.; and Yocom, C. F. 1967. The status and ecology of the Roosevelt elk in California. *Wildl. Monog.*, no. 16.

Hart, J. S.; Heroux, O.; Cottle, W. H.; and Mills, C. A. 1961. The influence of climate on metabolism and thermal response of infant caribou. *Can. J. Zool.* 39:845–56.

Hatter, Y. 1950. The moose of central British Columbia. Doctoral dissertation, Washington State College, Pullman.

Hemming, J. E. 1967. Mandibular dentition and horn development as criteria of age in the Dall's sheep, *Ovis dalli* Nelson. Master's thesis, University of Montana.

Hendrichs, H. 1963. Wiederkauen bei Klippschliefern und Känguruhs. *Naturwissenschaften* 50:454–55.

Heptner, W. G.; Nasimovitsch, A. A.; and Bannikov, A. G. 1961. *Mammals of the Soviet Union*. German translation. Jena: VEB Gustav Fischer-Verlag.

———, and Nasimovitsch, A. A. 1968. *Der Elch*. Die Neue Brehm Bücherei, no. 386. Wittenberg-Lutherstadt: A. Ziemsen Verlag.

Herre, W., and Kesper, K. D. 1953. Zur Verbreitung von *Ovis ammon* in Europa. *Zool. Anzeiger* 1953:204.

———, and Röhrs, M. 1955. Über die Formenmannigfaltigkeit des Gehörns der *Caprini* Simpson 1945. *Zool. Garten* 22:85–110.

Herscher, L.; Richmond, J. B.; and Moore, A. V. 1963. Maternal behavior in sheep and goats. In *Maternal behavior in mammals*, ed. H. L. Rheingold, pp. 203–32. New York: Wiley.

Heusser, C. J. 1965. A Pleistocene phytographic sketch of the Pacific Northwest and Alaska. In *The Quaternary of the United States*, ed. E. H. Wright and D. G. Frey. Princeton: Princeton Univ. Press.

Hinde, R. A. 1966. *Animal behavior*. New York: McGraw-Hill.

Holroyd, J. C. 1967. Observations of Rocky Mountain goats on Mount Wardle, Kootenay National Park, B.C. *Can. Field-Nat.* 81:1–22.

Hornocker, M. G. 1967. An ecological study of the mountain lion. Doctoral dissertation, The University of British Columbia.

Houston, D. B. 1968. *The Shiras moose in Jackson Hole, Wyoming*. National Parks Service, Dept. Interior, Technical Bull. no. 1.

Hulet, C. V.; Blackwell, R. L.; Ereanback, S. K.; Price, D. A.; and Wilson, L. O. 1962. Mating behaviour of the ewe. *J. Anim. Sci.* 21:870–74.

Hunter, R. F. 1962. Hill sheep and their pasture: A study of sheep grazing in southeast Scotland. *J. Ecol.* 50:651–80.

———. 1964. Home range behaviour in hill sheep. In *Grazing in terrestrial and marine environments,* ed. D. J. Crisp, *Symp. Brit. Ecol. Soc.,* no. 4, pp. 155–71.

———, and Davis, G. E. 1963. The effect of method of rearing on the social behaviour of Scottish blackface hoggets. *Anim. Prod.* 5:183–94.

———, and Milner, C. 1963. The behaviour of individual, related groups of south country Cheviot Hill sheep. *Anim. Behav.* 11:507–13.

Jewell, P. A. 1966. Breeding season and recruitment in some British mammals confined on small islands. In *Comparative biology of reproduction in mammals,* ed. J. W. Rowlands, *Symp. Zool. Soc. London,* no. 15, pp. 89–116.

Johnson, E. D. 1951. Biology of the elk calf (*Cervus canadensis nelsoni*). *J. Wildl. Mgmt.* 15:396–410.

Jones, F. F. 1963a. Sheep and goat investigations: Ecology and behavior. Unpublished report on project W-6-R-3, E, 2b. Alaska Dept. of Fish & Game, Juneau.

———. 1963b. Sheep investigations. Unpublished report. Alaska Dept. of Fish & Game, Juneau.

Jones, F. L. 1950. A survey of Sierra Nevada bighorn. *Sierra Club Bull.* 35:29–76.

Jonkel, C. F. 1967. Black bear population studies. State of Montana. Big Game Research. Job completion report, Federal Aid Project, W-98-R-1,2,3,4,5,6.

Jordan, P. A.; Shelton, P. C.; and Allen, D. 1967. Number turnover and social structure of the Isle Royale wolf population. *Am. Zool.* 7:233–52.

Joyce, J. P., and Blaxter, K. L. 1964. The effect of air movement, air temperature and infrared radiation on the energy requirements of sheep. *Brit. J. Nutr.* 18:5–27.

———; Blaxter, K. L.; and Park, C. 1966. The effect of natural outdoor environments on the energy requirements of sheep. *Res. Vet. Sci.* 7:342–59.

Katz, J. 1949. Behavioral interactions in a herd of Barbary sheep. *Zoologica* 34:9–18.

Kaufmann, J. H. 1967. Social relations of adult males in a free-ranging band of rhesus monkeys. In *Social communication among primates,* ed. S. A. Altmann, pp. 73–98. Chicago: Univ. of Chicago Press.

Kelsall, J. P. 1968. *The Caribou.* Ottawa: The Queen's printer.

Kennedy, C. A. 1948. Golden eagle kills bighorn lamb. *J. Mammal.* 29:68.

Kiley-Worthington, M. 1965. The waterbuck (*Kobus defassa* Ruppel 1935 and *K. ellipsiprimus* Ogilby 1833) in East Africa: Spatial distribution. A study of sexual behaviour. *Mammalia* 29:177–204.

Kind, N. V. 1967. Radiocarbon chronology in Siberia. In *The Bering Land Bridge,* ed. D. M. Hopkins, pp. 172–92. Stanford: Stanford Univ. Press.

Kirchshofer, R. 1963. Das Verhalten der Giraffengazelle, Elenantilope und des Flachland-Tapirs bei der Geburt. *Zs. Tierpsychol.* 20:143–59.

Klein, D. R. 1964. Range-related differences in growth of deer reflected in skeletal ratios. *J. Mammal.* 45:226–35.

———. 1965*a*. Ecology of deer range in Alaska. *Ecol. Monog.* 35:259–84.

———. 1965*b*. Postglacial distribution patterns of mammals in south coastal regions of Alaska. *Arctic* 18:7–20.

Klingel, H. 1967. Soziale Organisation und Verhalten freilebender Steppenzebras. *Zs. Tierpsychol.* 24:580–624.

Knappe, H. 1964. Zur Funktion des Jacobsonschen Organs (*Organon vomeronasale Jacobsoni*). *Zool. Garten* 28:188–94.

Knaus, W. 1960. *Das Gamswild*. Berlin: P. Parey-Verlag.

Koford, K. B. 1957. The vicuna and the puna. *Ecol. Monog.* 27:153–219.

Krämer, A. 1969. Soziale Organisation und Sozialverhalten einer Gemspopulation (*Rupricapra rupricapra* L.) der Alpen. *Zs. Tierpsychol.* 26:889–964.

Krumbiegel. J. 1954. *Biologie der Säugetiere*. Krefeld: AGIS Verlag.

Kühme, W. 1965. Freilandstudien zur Soziologie des Hyänenhundes (*Lycaon pictus lupinus* Thomas 1902). *Zs. Tierpsychol.* 22:495–541.

Kurt, F. 1963. Zur Carnivorie bei *Cephalophus dorsalis*. *Zs. Säugetierkde.* 28:309–13.

Kurten, B. 1968 Pleistocene mammals of Europe. In *The world naturalist*, ed. R. Carrington. London: Weidenfeld & Nicolson.

Lent, P. C. 1965. Rutting behaviour in a barren-ground caribou population. *Anim. Behav.* 13:259–64.

———. 1966. Calving and related social behaviour in the barren ground caribou. *Zs. Tierpsychol.* 23:701–56.

Leuthold, W. 1966. Variations in territorial behaviour of Uganda kob (*Adenota kob thomasi*, Neumann 1896). *Behaviour* 27:214–51.

———. 1967. Beobachtungen zum Jugendverhalten von Kob-Antilopen. *Zs. Säugetierkde.* 32:59–63.

Levine, S. 1966. Sex differences in the brain. *Sci. Am.* 214:84–90.

Liddell, H. S. 1958. A biological basis for psychopathology. In *Problems of addiction and habituation*, ed. P. H. Hook and J. Zubin, pp. 120–33. New York: Grune & Stratton.

———. 1961. Contributions of conditioning in the sheep and goat to an understanding of stress, anxiety and illness. *Lectures on experimental psychiatry*, pp. 227–55. Pittsburgh: Univ. of Pittsburgh Press.

Lindsay, D. R. 1965. The importance of olfactory stimuli in the mating behaviour of the ram. *Anim. Behav.* 13:75–78.

———. 1966. Mating behaviour of ewes and its effect on mating efficiency. *Anim. Behav.* 14:419–24.

———, and Ellsmore, J. 1968. Effect of breed, season, and competition on mating behaviour of rams. *Aust. J. Exp. Agric. & Anim. Husb.* 8:649–52.

———, and Fletcher, J. C. 1968. Sensory involvement in the recognition of lambs by their dams. *Anim. Behav.* 16:415–17.

Lindsdale, J. M., and Tomich, P. A. 1953. *A herd of mule deer*. Berkeley: Univ. of Calif. Press.

Lorenz, K. 1963. *Das sogenannte Böse*. Vienna: Dr. G. Borotha-Schoeler-Verlag.

Lutz, H. L. 1960. *Early occurrence of moose on the Kenai Peninsula*. Misc. pub. no. 1. Forest Service, U.S. Dept. Agric., Juneau.

Lydekker, R. 1898. *Wild oxen, sheep and goats of all lands*. London: Rowland Ward.

———. 1913. *Catalogue of the ungulate mammals*. Vol. 1, Artiodactyla. British Museum, London.

McCann, J. L. 1956. Ecology of the mountain sheep. *Am. Midl. Nat.* 56:297–325.

McCullough, D. R., and Schneegas, E. R. 1966. Winter observations on the Sierra Nevada bighorn sheep. *Calif. Fish & Game* 52:68–84.

McDonald, J. W. 1962. Ewe fertility and neonatal lamb mortality. *New Zealand Vet. J.* 10:45–52.

McHugh, T. 1958. Social behavior of the American buffalo (*Bison bison bison*). *Zoologica* 43:1–40.

McMahan, C. A. 1964. Comparative food habits of deer and three classes of livestock. *J. Wildl. Mgmt.* 28:798–808.

MacNeish, R. S. 1964. Investigations in southwest Yukon. Archeological excavation, comparison and speculations. Papers, Robert S. Peabody Foundation. *Archeology* 6, 2, 201.

Marler, P., and Hamilton, W. J. 1967. *Mechanisms of animal behaviour*. New York: Wiley.

Martin, P. S., and Wright, E. H., eds. 1967. *Pleistocene extinctions. The search for a cause*. Vol. 6. Proc. VII Cong. Internatl. Assoc. Quaternary Res. New Haven: Yale Univ. Press.

Mech, D. 1966. *The wolves of Isle Royale*. Fauna Series, no. 7. Washington, D.C.: U.S. Fauna National Parks.

Metzgar, L. H. 1967. An experimental comparison of screech owl predation on resident and transient white-footed mice (*Peromyscus leucopus*). *J. Mammal.* 48:387–91.

Michael, E. D. 1965. Movements of white-tailed deer on the Welder wildlife refuge. *J. Wildl. Mgmt.* 29:44–52.

Mills, H. B. 1937. A preliminary study of the bighorn of Yellowstone National Park. *J. Mammal.* 18:205–12.

Modha, M. L. 1967. The ecology of the Nile crocodile (*Crocodylus niloticus* Laurenti) on Central Island, Lake Rudolf. *E. A. Wildl. J.* 5:74–95.

Mohr, E. 1960. *Wilde Schweine*. Die Neue Brehm Bücherei, no. 247. Wittenberg-Lutherstadt: A. Ziemsen Verlag.

Munro, J. 1962. The use of natural shelter by hill sheep. *Anim. Prod.* 4:343–49.

Murie, A. 1944. *The wolves of Mount McKinley*. Fauna Series, no. 5. Washington, D.C.: U.S. Fauna National Parks.

Mykytowycz, R. 1965. Further observations on the territorial function and histology of the submandibular cutaneous (chin) glands in the rabbit (*Oryctolagus cuniculus* L.) *Anim. Behav.* 13:400–412.

———. 1966*a*, *b*, and *c*. Observations on odoriferous and other glands in the Australian wild rabbit, *Oryctolagus cuniculus* (L.) and the hare, *Lepus* *europaes* (P.). I, The anal glands. II, The inguinal glands. III, The submandibular glands. *C.S.I.R.O. Wildl. Res.* 11:11–29, 49–64, 65–90.

———. 1968. Territorial marking by rabbits. *Sci. Am.* 218:116–26.

Neumann, A. 1968. Rotwildpopulation Hohenbucko. *Beiträge zur Jagd und Wildforschung* VI, pp. 93–101. Berlin: Deutsche Akademie der Landwirtschaftswissenschaften.

Nievergelt, B. 1966a. Der Alpensteinbock. *Mammalia Depicta*. Berlin: P. Parey-Verlag.

———. 1966b. Unterschiede in der Setzzeit beim Alpensteinbock. *Rev. Suisse de Zool.* 73 Fasc. 3:446–54.

———. 1967. Die Zusammensetzung der Gruppen beim Alpensteinbock. *Zs. Säugetierkde.* 82:129–44.

Nikolaevski, L. D. 1961. Diseases of reindeer. In *Reindeer husbandry*, ed. P. S. Zhingunov, pp. 230–93. English translation. Springfield, Va.: U.S. Dept. of Commerce.

Ogren, H. A. 1965. Barbary sheep. *New Mexico Dept. Game & Fish. Bull.*, no. 13.

Ozoga, J. J., and Verme, L. J. 1970. Winter feeding patterns of penned white-tailed deer. *J. Wildl. Mgmt.* 34:431–39.

Peterson, R. L. 1955. *North American moose*. Toronto: Univ. of Toronto Press.

Petzsch, H. 1957a. Lebender ♀-Bastard aus *Ammotragus lervia* Pall. × ♂ *Capra hircus* L. im Berg-Zoo Halle-S. geboren. *Zool. Anzeiger* 159:285–90.

———. 1957b. Reflexionen zur Phylogenie der Capridae im allgemeinen und der Hausziege im besonderen. *Wiss. Zeit. der M. Luther Univ.*, Halle-Wittenberg 6:995–1019.

Pfeffer, P. 1967. Le Mouflon de Corse (*Ovis ammon musimon*, Schreber 1782). Position systématique, écologie et éthologie comparées. *Mammalia* 31, supplement.

Pielowski, Z. 1969. Die Wiedereinbürgerung des Elches *Alces alces* (L.) im Kampinos-Nationalpark in Polen. *Zs. Jagdwissenschaft* 15:6–17.

Pilters, H. 1954. Untersuchungen über angeborene Verhaltensweisen bei Tylpoden, unter besonderer Berücksichtigung der neuweltlichen Formen. *Zs. Tierpsychol.* 11:213–303.

Pimlott, D. H. 1959. Reproduction and productivity of Newfoundland moose. *J. Wildl. Mgmt.* 23:381–401.

Preobrazhenskii, B. V. 1961. Management and breeding of reindeer. In *Reindeer husbandry*, ed. P. S. Zhigunov, English translation. Springfield, Va.: U.S. Dept. of Commerce.

Pruitt, W. O. J. 1959. Snow as a factor in the winter ecology of the barren ground caribou. *Arctic* 12:158–79.

———. 1960. Behavior of the barren ground caribou. Biol. papers, University of Alaska, no. 3.

Purser, A. F., and Young, G. B. 1959. Lamb survival in two hill flocks. *Anim. Prod.* 1:85–91.

Radford, H. M., and Watson, R. H. 1957. The influence of rams on ovarian activity and oestrus in merino ewes in spring and early summer. *Aust. J. Agric. Res.* 8:460–70.

Radulesco, C., and Samson, P. 1962. Sur un centre de domestication du mouton dans le Mesolithique de la grotte "La Adam" en Dobrogea. In *Zur Domestikation und Frühgeschichte der Haustiere. Symp. Zs. Tierzüchtung und Züchtungsbiologie* 76:282–320.

Rammell, C. G., and Caughley, G. 1964. Composition of thar's milk. *New Zealand, J. Sci.* 7:667–70.

Rausch, R. A. 1967. Some aspects of population ecology of wolves in Alaska. *Am. Zool.* 7:253–66.

Reid, R. L. 1961. *Digestive physiology and nutrition of ruminants.* London: Butterworth.

———. 1962. Studies on the carbohydrate metabolism of sheep, XV. The adrenal response to climatic stress of cold wind and rain. *Aust. J. Agric. Res.* 13:296–306.

———, and Hinks, N. T. 1962. Studies on the carbohydrate metabolism of sheep, XVII. Feed requirements and voluntary feed intake in late pregnancy, with particular reference to prevention of hypoglycaemia and hyperketoneaemia. *Aust. J. Agric. Res.* 13:1092–111.

———, and Miles, S. C. 1962. Studies on the carbohydrate metabolism of sheep. The adrenal response to psychological stress. *Aust. J. Agric. Res.* 13:282–95.

Robinette, W. L. 1966. Mule deer home range and dispersal in Utah. *J. Wildl. Mgmt.* 30:335–48.

Robinson, C. S., and Cronemiller, F. P. 1954. Notes on the habitat of the desert bighorn in the San Gabriel Mountains of California. *Calif. Fish & Game* 40:267–71.

Robinson, J. F.; Currie, D. C.; and Peart, J. N. 1961. Feeding hill ewes. *Transaction Royal Highland Agric. Soc. Scotland*, pp. 1–16.

Robinson, R. M.; Thomas, J. W.; and Marburger, R. G. 1965. The reproductive cycle of male white-tailed deer in central Texas. *J. Wildl. Mgmt.* 29:53–58.

Russo, J. P. 1950. The desert bighorn sheep in Arizona. *Arizona Dept. Game & Fish. Wildl. Bull.*, no. 1. Phoenix.

Ryder, M. L. 1958. Follicle arrangement in skin from wild sheep, primitive domestic sheep and in parchment. *Nature* 182:781–83.

———. 1960. A study of the coat of the mouflon (*Ovis musimon*) with special reference to season change. *Proc. Zool. Soc. London* 135:387–400.

Safford, J. W., and Hoversland, A. S. 1960. A study of lamb mortality in a western range flock, I. Autopsy findings on 1051 lambs. *J. Anim. Sci.* 19:256–73.

Schaffer, W. H. 1968. Intraspecific combat and the evolution of the caprini. *Evolution* 22:817–25.

Schaller, G. B. 1963. *The mountain gorilla.* Chicago: Univ. of Chicago Press.

———. 1967. *The deer and the tiger.* Chicago: Univ. of Chicago Press.

———. 1969. Life with the king of beasts. *Nat. Geogr.* 135:494–519.

Schenkel, R. 1966a. Zum Problem der Territorialität und des Markierens bei Säugern—am Beispiel des schwarzen Nashorns und des Löwens. *Zs. Tierpsychol.* 23:593–626.

———. 1966b. Play, exploration and territoriality in the wild lion. *Symp. Zool. Soc. London* 18:11–22.

———. 1967. Submission: Its features and function in the wolf and dog. *Am. Zool.* 7:319–30.

Schinkel, P. G., and Short, B. F. 1961. The influence of nutritional level during pre-natal and early post-natal life on adult fleece and body characteristics. *Aust. J. Agric. Res.* 12:176–202.

Schloeth, R. 1958. Über die Mutter-Kind-Beziehungen beim halbwilden Camargue-Rind. *Säugetierkdl. Mitt.* 6:145–50.

———. 1961a. Das Sozialleben des Camargue-Rindes. *Zs. Tierpsychol.* 18:574–627.

———. 1961b. Einige Verhaltensweisen im Hirschrudel. *Rev. Suisse de Zool.* 68:242–47.

———. 1966. Verwandschaftliche Beziehungen und Rudelbildung beim Rothirsch (*Cervus elaphus*). *Mitt. Schweiz. Zool. Gesellschaft, 1966*, pp. 434–40.

Schloeth, R., and Burckhardt, D. 1961. Die Wanderungen des Rotwildes *Cervus elaphus* L. im Gebiet des Schweizerischen Nationalparkes. *Rev. Suisse de Zool.* 68:146–55.

Schmitt, J. 1963. *Ammotragus lervia* Pallas, Mähnenschaf oder Mähnenziege? *Zs. Säugetierkde.* 28:7–12.

Schultze-Westrum, T. 1963. Die Wildziegen der ägäischen Inseln. *Säugetierkdl. Mitt.* 11:145–82.

Scott, J. P. 1945. Social behaviour, organization and leadership in a small flock of domestic sheep. *Comp. Psychol. Monog.* 18:1–29.

Scotter, G. W. 1964. Effects of forest fires on the winter range of barren-ground caribou in northern Saskatchewan. *Can. Wildl. Serv. Wildl. Mgmt. Bull.* ser. 1., no. 18.

Seitz, A. 1951. Untersuchungen über das Formsehen und optische Grössenunterscheidung bei der Skudde (ostpreussisches Landschaf). *Zs. Tierpsychol.* 8:424–41.

———. 1957. Tragzeit, Fruchtbarkeit, Todesursachen beim Mähnenschaf (*Ammotragus lervia* Pallas). *Zool. Garten* (N.F.) 23:54–57.

Servinghaus, C., and Cheatum, E. 1956. Life and times of the white-tailed deer. In *The deer of North America*, ed. W. Taylor. Washington, D.C.: Stackpole Co.

Simmons, N. M.; Levy, S.; and Levy, J. 1963. Observation of desert bighorn sheep lambing, Kofu Game Range, Arizona. *J. Mammal.* 44:433.

Simpson, G. G. 1961. *Principles of animal taxonomy*. New York: Columbia Univ. Press.

Slee, J. 1963. Birth coat shedding in Wiltshire horn lambs. *Anim. Prod.* 5:301–16.

Slen, S. D.; Clark, R. D.; and Hironaka, R. 1963. A comparison of milk production and its relation to lamb growth in five breeds of sheep. *Can. J. Anim. Sci.* 43:16–21.

Smith, D. R. 1954. The bighorn sheep in Idaho. *Idaho Dept. Fish & Game Wildl. Bull.*, no. 1. Boise.

Smith, F. V.; Van-Toller, C.; and Boyes, T. 1966. The "critical period" in the attachment of lambs and ewes. *Anim. Behav.* 14:120–25.

Spalding, D. J. 1966. Twinning in bighorn sheep. *J. Wildl. Mgmt.* 30:207–8.

Spencer, C. C. 1943. Notes on the life history of Rocky Mountain bighorn sheep in the Taryall Mountains of Colorado. *J. Mammal.* 24:1–11.

Spencer, D. L., and Hakalu, Q. B. 1964. Moose and fire on the Kenai. *Proc. Tall Timbers Fire Ecol. Conf.* 3:11–33. Tallahassee.

Starke, J. S.; Smith, J. B.; and Joubert, D. M. 1958. The birth weight of lambs. *Union of S. Africa Dept. Agric. Sci. Bull.*, no. 382.

Steinhauf, D. 1959. Beobachtungen zum Brunftverhalten des Steinwildes (*Capra ibex*). *Säugetierkdl. Mitt.* 7:5–9.

Stewart, J. C., and Scott, J. P. 1947. Lack of correlation between leadership and dominance relationships in a herd of goats. *J. Comp. Physiol. Psychol.* 40:255–64.

Stokes, W. M. L., and Condie, K. C. 1961. Pleistocene bighorn sheep from the Great Basin. *J. Paleontology* 35:598–609.

Struhsaker, T. T. 1967. Behaviour of elk (*Cervus canadensis*) during the rut. *Zs. Tierpsychol.* 24:80–114.

Sugden, L. G. 1961. *The California bighorn in British Columbia.* B.C. Dept. of Recreation & Conservation, Victoria.

Sushkin, P. P. 1925. Wild sheep of the world and their distribution. *J. Mammal.* 6:145–57.

Swank, W. G. 1958. The mule deer in Arizona chaparral. *Arizona Dept. Game & Fish. Wildl. Bull.*, no. 3. Phoenix.

Taylor, C. R. 1966. The vascularity and possible thermoregulatory function of the horns in goats. *Physiol. Zool.* 39:127–39.

Taylor, R. A. 1962. Characteristics of horn growth in bighorn rams. Master's thesis, Montana State University.

Teer, J. G.; Thomas, J. W.; and Walker, E. A. 1965. Ecology and management of white-tailed deer in the Llano Basin of Texas. *Wildl. Monog.*, no. 15.

Thenius, E., and Hofer, H. 1960. *Stammesgeschichte der Säugetiere.* Berlin: Springer Verlag.

Thompson, W. R. 1957. Influence of prenatal maternal anxiety on emotionality in young rats. *Science* 125:698–99.

Tinbergen, N. 1969. On war and peace in animals and man. *Science* 160:1411–18.

Tschanz, B. 1962. Über die Beziehungen zwischen Muttertier und Jungen beim Mufflon (*Ovis aires musimon* Pall.). *Experientia* 18:187–90.

Türck, F., and Schmincke, S. 1965. *Das Muffelwild.* Berlin: P. Parey-Verlag.

Turner, Helen N., and Dolling, C. H. S. 1965. Vital statistics for an experimental flock of merino sheep, II. The influence of age on reproductive performance. *Aust. J. Agric. Res.* 16:699–712.

Ullrey, D. E.; Yovatt, W. G.; Johnson, H. E.; Ku, P. K.; and Fay, L. D. 1964. Digestibility of cedar and aspen browse for the white-tailed deer. *J. Wildl. Mgmt.* 28:791–97.

Ulmer, F. 1941. On the weights of Dall's sheep. *J. Mammal.* 22:448–49.

Uloth, W. 1966. Die Taxonomie der recenten Wildschafe im Blickpunkt der Verkreuzung. *Säugetierkdl. Mitt.* 14:273–78.

Viereck, L. A. 1963. Sheep and goat investigations: Range survey. Unpublished report on project W-6-R-3, E, 2-a. Alaska Dept. of Fish & Game, Juneau.

———. 1966. Plant succession and soil development on gravel outwash of the Muldrow Glacier, Alaska. *Ecol. Monog.* 36:161–99.

Wallace, R. L. 1948. The growth of lambs before and after birth in relation to the level of nutrition. *J. Agric. Sci.* 38:93–153, 243–302, 367–401.

Walther, F. 1958. Zum Kampf- und Paarungsverhalten einiger Antilopen. *Zs. Tierpsychol.* 15:340–80.

———. 1960. Antilopenhafte Verhaltensweisen im Paarungszeremoniell des Okapi (*Okapi jonstoni* Scatter 1901). *Zs. Tierpsychol.* 17:188–210.

———. 1961. Einige Verhaltensbeobachtungen am Bergwild des Georg von Opel-Freigeheges. *Jahrbuch,* vols. 60–61.

———. 1964. Einige Verhaltensbeobachtungen an Thomsongazellen (*Gazella thomsoni* Günther, 1884) im Ngorongoro-Krater. *Zs. Tierpsychol.* 21:871–90.

———. 1965. Verhaltensstudien an der Grantgazelle (*Gazella granti* Brooke, 1872) im Ngorongoro-Krater. *Zs. Tierpsychol.* 22:167–208.

———. 1966. *Mit Huf und Horn.* Berlin: P. Parey-Verlag.

———. 1968. *Verhalten der Gazellen.* Die Neue Brehm Bücherei, no. 373. Wittenberg-Lutherstadt: A. Ziemsen Verlag.

Watson, R. H., and Elder, E. M. 1961. Neonatal mortality in lambs. *Aust. Vet. J.* 37:283–90.

———, and Radford, H. M. 1960. The influence of rams on onset of oestrus in merino ewes in the spring. *Aust. J. Agric. Sci.* 2:67–71.

Welles, R. E., and Welles, F. B. 1961. *The bighorn of Death Valley.* Fauna Series, no. 6. Washington, D.C.: U.S. Fauna National Parks.

Wen-chung, P. 1957. Giant ape's jaw bone discovered in China. *Am. Anthropologist* 59:834–38.

Wickler, W. 1962. Ei-Attrappen und Maulbrüten bei afrikanischen Cichliden. *Zs. Tierpsychol.* 18:129–64.

Williams, G. C. 1966. *Adaptation and natural selection.* New York: Princeton Univ. Press.

Wishart, W. D. 1958. The bighorn sheep of the Bighorn Sheep River valley. Master's thesis, The University of Alberta, Edmonton.

Wood, A. J.; Cowan, J. McT.; and Nordan, H. C. 1962. Periodicity of growth in ungulates as shown by deer of the genus *Odocoileus. Can. J. Zool.* 40:593–603.

Woodgerd, W. 1964. Population dynamics of bighorn sheep on Wildhorse Island. *J. Wildl. Mgmt.* 28:381–91.

Wynne-Edwards, V. C. 1962. *Animal dispersion in relation to social behaviour.* London: Oliver & Boyd.

Yeates, N. T. M. 1949. The breeding season of the sheep with particular reference to its modification by artificial means using light. *J. Agric. Sci.* 39:1–43.

Young, S. P., and Manville, R. H. 1960. Records of bighorn hybrids. *J. Mammal.* 41:523–25.

Zalunardo, R. A. 1965. The seasonal distribution of a migratory mule deer herd. *J. Wildl. Mgmt.* 29:345–51.

Zannier-Tanner, E. 1965. Vergleichende Verhaltensuntersuchungen über das Hinlegen und Aufstehen bei Huftieren. *Zs. Tierpsychol.* 22:696–723.

Zeuner, F. E. 1967. *Geschichte der Haustiere.* Revised by J. Boessneck & Th. Haltenorth. München: Bayerischer Landwirtschafts Verlag.

Index

GLASSBORO STATE COLLEGE